Treasure Hunt Volume I
Romans Thru Galatians

By Marianne Manley

Treasure Hunt Volume I

All scripture references are taken from the King James Bible. The King James Bible is our final authority in all matters of faith and practice. Permission is granted to copy all contents of this book. Timeline on page 259.

Acknowledgments

To God be the glory for helping me write this book! I am grateful for the support of my dear husband Chuck and my children during this time. I would like to thank some of the many grace pastors and teachers who have helped me understand God's word rightly divided: Les Feldick, Richard Jordan, Tom Bruscha, Rick Jordan, Henry Meneses, David Reid, and David O'Steen. I was particularly helped by Shawn Brasseaux's informative articles on Forwhatsaithscriptures.org. I would like to thank LeighAnn Mycko, Aaron Howay, and others for their memes. I am thankful to Maureen Parker, Patty Carlson, and Aaron Howay for proofreading. In preparing these books, I primarily read and study the word of God over and over again until the Holy Spirit helps me to understand His word better, but I also listen to sermons, read articles, and many other books on the Bible.

Treasure Hunt Volume I covers all the chapters in Romans through Galatians. God's word is given in bold and the commentary is given within brackets. The purpose of the book is to edify the Church, the body of Christ by increasing our understanding of His word, and to exalt our Lord Jesus.

How to use this book: read it using a ruler and a pen, when you find a great cross reference or comment you can mark it in your Bible, circle important words (color some of them), make notes, so that you have them next time you read that passage. I recommend the Scofield Study Bible III in the King James Version. It is wise to get a leather cover for it that holds a pen and zips. I recommend reading *God's Secret A Primer with Pictures for How to Rightly Divide the Word of Truth* before this book. It is an overview of the Bible in 100 pages and covers the basics of right division (available on Amazon).

Romans: A Concise Commentary **and** ***First Corinthians: A Commentary and Second Corinthians: A Commentary and Galatians: A Commentary*** **are also available on Amazon. These books all have an explanation introducing each chapter and other interesting facts, while Treasure Hunt is purely a commentary.** ***Through the Book of Books*** **by Lori Verstegen is also helpful.**

Table of Contents

Introduction

By reading and studying His word we can learn more about the Lord Jesus Christ. Paul wrote, "That I may know him . . ." (Philippians 3:10).

We can go on a treasure hunt in the Bible, to not only know more about our Lord Jesus Christ, but also God's plan and purpose for the body of Christ. We will find that when we understand the word of God rightly divided we can function properly, by His life working in and through us. "But we have this treasure in earthen vessels, that the <u>excellency of the power</u> may be of God, and not of us" (2 Corinthians 4:7). There is a supernatural interaction that takes place between the word of God and His Spirit in us when we believe it.

Before starting on our treasure hunt <u>be sure that you are saved by believing the gospel</u>: "how that <u>Christ died for our sins</u> according to the scriptures; And that <u>he was buried</u>, and that <u>he rose again</u> the third day according to the scriptures" (1 Cor. 15:3, 4).

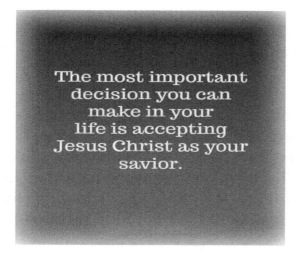

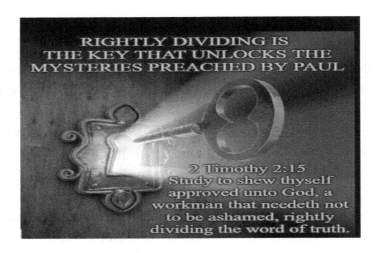

The Key Verse in the Bible:

The only verse in the Bible that tells us how to study the Bible is <u>2 Tim. 2:15</u>: "<u>Study</u> to shew thyself approved unto God, a workman that needeth not to be ashamed, <u>**RIGHTLY DIVIDING THE WORD OF TRUTH**</u>."

Mandate: Study.

Motive: to shew thyself approved to God, a workman that needeth not to be ashamed (at the Judgment Seat of Christ).

Method: Rightly dividing the word of truth (making the divisions that God makes in His word).

Second Timothy which contains this instruction was the last book of the Bible to be written (Col. 1:25, 26).

Four divisions in Romans:
1-5 Justification
6-8 Sanctification
9-11 What about Israel?
12-16 Practical application

1-5 Justification – How God solved the sin problem
6-8 Sanctification – God has provided a way that we can live above sin now
9-11 What about Israel? The nation of Israel has been temporarily blinded until the Gentile opportunity to be saved ends. After that, God will be done forming the body of Christ to live in heaven and will again focus on Israel.
12-16 Practical application – How to offer our bodies a living sacrifice for Christ to live through and manifest Himself to the world.

PROPHECY (Acts 3:17-24)	MYSTERY (Rom. 16:25-26)
Concerns a KINGDOM; a political ORGANIZATION (Dan. 2:44)	Concerns a BODY; a spiritual ORGANISM (Eph. 1:22, 23, 4:15, 16)
The kingdom is to be established forever ON EARTH (Jer. 23:5, 6; Matt. 6:10)	The Body of Christ is to live eternally in the HEAVENLY places (2 Cor. 5:1; Eph. 2:6, 7)
The kingdom was PROPHESIED since the world began (Luke 1:67-75)	The Body was chosen in Christ before the world began, but kept SECRET since the world began (Eph. 1:4, 3:9)
Israel to be given SUPREMACY over the nations (Isa. 61:6)	Jew and Gentile baptized into ONE body (1Cor. 12:12-13; Gal. 3:27, 28)
The Gentiles blessed through Israel's RISE AND INSTRUMENTALITY (Isa. 60:1-3; Zech. 8:13, 23)	The Gentiles blessed through Israel's FALL AND DIMINISHING (Rom. 11:11-12, 15)
God deals with His NATION Israel and other NATIONS (Isa. 2:4)	God builds the body one INDIVIDUAL (2 Cor. 5:17) at a time
Blessings are both MATERIAL and spiritual, on EARTH (Isa. 11:1-10)	All SPIRITUAL blessings in HEAVENLY places (Eph. 1:3)
Christ the King comes to His people, Israel, ON EARTH (Rev. 1:7)	Christ the Head meets His body, the Church, IN THE AIR (1 Thess. 4:17)
Justification is by a man's faith, but he proves his faith by his WORKS (James 2:23, 24)	Justification is by the believer's faith in the faith of Christ (Gal. 2:16) WITHOUT WORKS (Rom. 3:28; 4:5)
12 apostles (Matt. 19:28; Acts 1:6-8)	One apostle, PAUL (Col. 1:23-29)

The Two Ministries of Christ

By Paul M. Sadler

Earthly Ministry (Four Gospels and Early Acts)	Heavenly Ministry (Paul's Epistles and Mid-Acts)
King of Israel—John 1:49	Head of the Body—Col. 1:18
Declaration: The Law and the Prophets (coming wrath) —Matt. 5:17,18	Declaration: Grace and Peace —Phil. 1:2
Gave Himself a ransom for the sins of His people —Matt. 20:28; Luke 1:68,77	Gave Himself a ransom for the sins of the world —I Tim. 2:5,6
Seated at the right hand of the Father until His enemies are made His footstool —Acts 2:34-36	Seated at the right hand of the Father in a position of exaltation over all things to the Church —Eph. 1:20-23
Called 12 Apostles on the earth—Matt. 4:18-22; 10:1-5	Called one Apostle (Paul) from heaven—Acts 9:1-4; 26:13,19
Christ commands the 12 Apostles to confine their ministry to Israel —Matt. 10:5,6	Christ appoints Paul the Apostle of the Gentiles —Rom. 11:13
Instructs the 12 to carry out the Great Commission —Mark 16:14-18	Instructs us to carry out the Commission of Reconciliation —II Cor. 5:18,19
Gospel of the Kingdom proclaimed—Mark 1:14,15	Gospel of the grace of God proclaimed—Acts 20:24
Terms of salvation: Repent, believe on His name, submit to water baptism—Mark 1:15; 16:16; John 3:16; 20:31	Terms of salvation: Believe Christ died for your sins, was buried, and rose again —Acts 16:31; I Cor. 15:1-4
Earthly hope and calling —Matt. 5:5	Heavenly hope and calling —Col. 1:5
Christ's visible return to the earth —Matt. 24:29,30; Acts 1:10-12	Christ's invisible return in heaven —I Thes. 4:13-18
Eternal reign from the New Jerusalem on the New Earth —Rev. 21	Eternal reign with Christ from the New Heavens —Eph. 1:10; 2:6,7

As members of the Body of Christ we are responsible to proclaim, defend, and stand for the heavenly ministry of Christ.

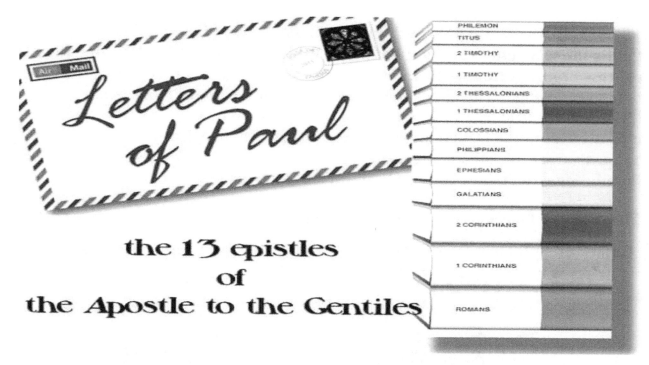

the 13 epistles
of
the Apostle to the Gentiles

*Please notice that the order of the books begins at the bottom with Romans.

13 Letters Written by Apostle Paul (order, structure, and purpose)

Philemon a letter of appeal to a friend – demonstration (intercession)
1 & 2 Timothy and Titus letters to individual church leaders – utilization (exhorts)
1 & 2 Thessalonians letters to a questioning church – expectation (encourages)
Colossians a letter to a wavering church – culmination (admonishes)
Philippians a letter to a giving church – subordination (servanthood)
Ephesians a letter to a stable church – exaltation (identification)
Galatians a letter to a legalistic church – liberation (correction)
1 & 2 Corinthians letters to a carnal church – sanctification (reproof)
Romans a letter to stabilize a church far away – justification (explained)
(The above is written with help of Dr. W. Edward Bedore of Berean Bible
Institute, P.O. Box 587, Slinger, WI 53086.)

Each of Paul's letters builds on the other and is designed to edify our inner man. So
that we go from being spiritual babies to mature useful sons of God. "That the man
of God may be perfect, throughly furnished unto all good works" (2 Tim. 3:17).

The 13 letters of Paul follow the order given in 2 Tim. 3:16: All scripture is
given by inspiration of God, and is profitable for DOCTRINE, for REPROOF, for
CORRECTION, for INSTRUCTION IN RIGHTEOUSNESS: "That the man of
God may be perfect, throughly furnished unto all good works" (2 Tim. 3:17).

The pre-prison letters were written during Acts, the transition period.

Paul's thirteen letters are laid out in the Bible according to God's edification process. Romans (foundational doctrine), 1 & 2 Corinthian (reproof for not living according to the doctrine in Romans), and Galatians (correction for leaving grace declared in Romans and living under the law). Paul was put on house arrest in the last chapter of Acts, Acts 28. These epistles were written before Paul received the full revelation of the mystery. **They focus on foundational doctrines and are best understood when read together.**

The order of Paul's Acts epistles including when and where they were written:

Galatians	1 Thess.	2 Thess.	1 Cor.	2 Cor.	Romans
Acts 15:35	Acts 18:5	Acts 18:11	Acts 19	Acts 20:1	Acts 20:3
Antioch	Corinth	Corinth	Ephesus	Macedonia	Corinth

Christ's ministry from heaven:

New Apostle (Paul)
New Gospel (of Christ)
New Dispensation (of grace)
New Agency (the Church, the body of Christ)
New Audience (all people)
New Operating System (Grace, not Law)
New Des tiny (Heaven)

Romans Commentary
Romans Chapter 1 Gentiles under sin
1:1-7 Salutation
1:8-17 Purpose for writing the letter
1:18-32 Righteousness needed

Romans 1:1 Paul, [All his 13 letters begin with his name, Paul, c/w James 1:1. Notice that the period does not come until after verse 7 and that a new paragraph begins then, every word and comma is important in the KJV.] **a servant of Jesus Christ, called to be an apostle,** [Gal. 1:1, 11, 12; Eph. 3:1-6 How did Paul get his message? Did the 12 or anyone else know about the mystery before Paul?] **separated unto the gospel of God,** [Paul was separated in Acts 9, Gal. 1:15. The gospel of God is the general gospel of the promised coming Redeemer (Gen. 3:15), a far reaching gospel that relates to all mankind.] **2 (Which he had promised afore by his prophets in the holy scriptures,)** [The coming Redeemer was prophesied elsewhere Psa. 22, 89:20-37; Isa. 9:6, 7, 53).] **3 Concerning his Son Jesus Christ our Lord, which was made of the <u>seed of David</u> according to the flesh;** [He is Man and the Son of God (Isa. 7:14; Matt. 1:23) and would be a Jewish man of the seed of David (1 Chron. 17:11-14; Matt. 1:1, notice the Davidic and Abrahamic covenants). Because Jesus was the Son of David according to the flesh, He was the God-Man who could Redeem us by dying in our place. His royal lineage also entitles Him to rule Israel's earthly kingdom (<u>Luke 1:31-33</u>). <u>Paul the due time testifier will explain the significance of all that Christ accomplished for mankind at Calvary</u>. This is one of the reasons Romans is such an important book]; **4 And declared to be the Son of God** [The Father declared the Lord Jesus Christ to be the Son of God when He resurrected Him because He had the power over death. "This day have I begotten thee" (Acts 13:33; Psa. 2:7; Heb. 1:5, 5:5, Eph. 1:20)] **with power, according to the spirit of holiness,** [Christ lived a perfect life so the justice of God's holiness demanded that He could not stay dead; death could not hold Him (see Psa. 16:10; 69:15; Acts 2:24)] **by the resurrection from the dead:** [His resurrection proved His power to overcome sin, Satan, and death, that His blood payment for our sins was accepted, 1 Cor. 15:20] **5 By whom we have received grace and apostleship,** [God showed grace to Paul, a blasphemer, making him His minister, 15:16] **for obedience to the faith among all nations,** [That all nations would believe. Was this true in Mark 10:24? c/w 1 Tim. 2:6.] **for his name:** [the Lord Jesus Christ] **6 Among whom are ye also the called of Jesus Christ:** [called by His gospel, 2 Thess. 2:14] **7 To all that be in Rome, beloved of God,** [God calls us the same as He did His Son in Matt. 3:17] **called *to be* saints:** [After believing we are no longer called sinners but saints, not because of anything we did, but only because of what Christ did for us. We are now set apart for God's possession and service.] **Grace to you and peace from God our Father, and the Lord Jesus Christ.** [God offers grace and peace today because Christ has <u>PAID IN FULL</u> for all sins so God is not imputing sins today. "To wit, that God was in Christ, reconciling the world unto himself, not imputing their trespasses unto them; and hath committed unto us the word of reconciliation" (2 Cor. 5:19). Furthermore, God is holding back His wrath (Jacob's trouble) until after the rapture. At this time, He is dispensing grace and offering salvation to anyone who will believe what Christ has done for him. God is offering grace and peace to believers (5:1).]

8 ¶ First, I thank my God through Jesus Christ for you all, that your faith is spoken of throughout the whole world. [When Paul prays he thanks God for the fame of their faith. He wants what God wants, for the body of Christ to thrive and succeed.] **9 For God is my witness, whom I serve with my spirit in the gospel of his Son,** [Our spirit is in our mind (Eph. 4:23).] **that without ceasing I make mention of you always in my prayers;** [God knows Paul prays for them] **10 Making request, if by any means now at length I might have a prosperous journey by the will of God to come unto you.** [Paul asked God to allow him to come and see them.] **11 For I long to see you, that I may impart unto you some spiritual gift, to the end ye may be established;** [You can hear the excitement in Paul's words that he can't wait to share what Christ has revealed to him so that they can be solid in the faith. <u>Paul's purpose is to "impart unto you some spiritual gift, to the end that ye may be established," see Rom. 16:25.</u>] **12 That is, that I may be comforted together with you by the mutual faith both of you and me.** [Paul wants the Romans to understand everything he understood (all the revelation given to him) so they could have this mutual faith together.] **13 Now I would not have you ignorant, brethren, that oftentimes I purposed to come unto you, (but was let hitherto,)** [Paul was hindered, not by Satan but because he was so busy with ministry opportunities that there may be some fruit among the Gentiles, 15:19-23.] **that I might have some <u>fruit</u>** [That they may win some souls and help the weaker believers just like Paul was.] **among you also, even as among other Gentiles. 14 I am debtor both to the Greeks, and to the Barbarians; both to the wise, and to the unwise.** [Paul owes a debt to all unsaved people to have a chance to hear the gospel so that they may be saved. Likewise, we should do what we can to share the gospel.] **15 So, as much as in me is, I am ready to preach the gospel to you that are at Rome also.** [Paul shares all that he has learned and is willing to share with those at Rome. Next Paul will follow a logical sequence of explanation. Notice how Paul makes use of the word "for" (which explains why the previous statement is correct) while "because" is similar indicating the cause and its effect.] **16 For I am not ashamed of the gospel of Christ: for it is the power of God unto salvation to every one that believeth;** [Paul knows that hearing and believing the gospel of what Christ has done has the power for God to translate them out of Adam and into Christ (Col. 1:13). See 1 Cor. 1:18 about God's power. Every time a person is saved, God does a miracle. The Gospel of Christ works and Paul knew that.] **to the <u>Jew first</u>, and <u>also to the Greek.</u>** [In the past, Jesus was sent to Israel only (15:22-24), but Gentiles could be blessed at that time by blessings Israel (Gen. 12:3). After Jesus ascended to heaven, salvation was still sent only to the Jews (Acts 2:5, 10, 14, 3:12, 25, **26**, 11:19) not until Jesus saved Paul did salvation go to the Gentiles (Acts 26:16-18; Rom. 10:12, 13). Paul went to the Jew first and then to the Greek until the end of Acts, then preached only to Gentiles after that. God wanted the Jews that lived outside of Israel to hear that He had changed the program from Peter to Paul so that they would be without excuse and have a chance to be saved. <u>Salvation is an encompassing word that includes</u>: <u>justification, imputation, propitiation, redemption, forgiveness, sanctification, grace, and glorification. Salvation is in three tenses. One, the Christian has been saved from the PENALTY of SIN. Second, he is being saved from the POWER of SIN. Third, he will be saved from the PRESENCE of SIN at the Rapture. A person who studies the Bible rightly divided is also saved from false doctrine.</u>] **17 For therein is the righteousness of God revealed from faith to faith:** [God's righteousness is revealed from Christ's faith to our faith. <u>Two faiths are necessary for God's righteousness to come upon man. We place our faith in CHRIST'S faith.</u>] **as it is written, The just shall live by <u>faith.</u>** [This is a quote from Hab. 2:4, which actually says "the just shall live by <u>his</u> faith." We are "justified by the faith of Christ" (Gal. 2:16). There is only one cloak for our sin, His faith. We live (walk) by His perfect faith, as He lives in us. "I am crucified with Christ: nevertheless I live; yet not I, but Christ liveth in me: and the life which I now live in the flesh I live by the faith **of** the Son of God, who loved me, and gave himself for me" (Gal.2:20).].

18 ¶ For the <u>wrath of God is revealed from heaven against all ungodliness and unrighteousness of men</u>, who hold the truth in unrighteousness; [Did not believe. Just like God's righteousness is revealed so is His wrath revealed on all those who reject truth which God has showed them. God's righteousness demands His justice. Man knew the truth but rejected it. Paul will now explain how Gentiles ended up "without God in the world" (Eph. 2:11, 12). God's righteousness was offended at the Tower of Babel (Gen. 11) so God gave the Gentiles up and men are in need of God's righteousness. The ungodly and unrighteous acts mentioned at the Tower of Babel still continue in the unbelievers of today. <u>It is not evolution, but devolution because man has become like a beast. Paul warns the Gentiles (and then the Jews in chapter 2) about the wrath of God so they can do something about it. Like a brilliant prosecuting attorney Paul unfolds the predicament mankind is in so</u>

that they will listen to him when he delivers God's remedy to them with "But now . . . (Rom. 3:21).] **19 Because that which may be known of God is manifest in them;** [The knowledge of God is "inside" the Gentiles] **for God hath shewed it unto them** [God showed them who He is by two means, creation and conscience (external and internal evidence of God).] **20 For the invisible things of him from the creation** [In the beginning God created the heaven and the earth (Gen. 1:1)] **of the world are clearly seen** [all around us]**, being understood by the things that are made,** [His creatures know that God made these things.] **even his eternal power** [God's eternal character and His infinite everlasting power (Almightiness) is everywhere in the DNA, blood, the sun, water, plants, our eyes and so forth.] **and Godhead;** [Trinity.] **so that they are without excuse:** [People are without excuse because: "The heavens declare the glory of God; and the firmament sheweth his handiwork" (Psalm 19:1, Psa. 97:6).] **21 Because that, when they knew God,** [They knew who God was.] **they glorified him not as God, neither were thankful;** [They did not give God the credit, the glory He deserved, and they were not grateful for all that He did.] **but became vain in their imaginations,** [Not only man's Greek and Roman philosophy, but intellectual thoughts, and theories are "vain" which means empty or useless. Man believes that because he can imagine things in his mind that he can create, and is god. The theory of evolution, that something can evolve out of nothing with a big bang is an example of this. Sadly, "scientists" like Carl Sagan and Richard Dawkins know better now.] **and their foolish heart was darkened.** [Their hearts have no light, Eph. 4:17-19.] **22 Professing themselves to be wise, they became fools,** [Pride is man's problem and it leads him to be a fool, Psa. 10:4, 14:1. Previously the Gentiles were ignorant but now they are warned and should change their minds (repent) and believe God, Acts 17:29-31.] **23 And changed the glory of the uncorruptible God into an image made like to corruptible** [mortal] **man, and to birds, and fourfooted beasts, and creeping things.** [They idolized man and other created things like beasts. Notice the de-evolution from man to creeping things.] **24 Wherefore <u>God also gave them up to uncleanness</u> through the lusts of their own hearts, to dishonour their own bodies between themselves:** [Jer. 17:9. Notice the downward spiral of idolatry. <u>An idol is a man-made god</u>. Man creates a god in his mind that he can feel comfortable with so he can feel superior. Paul is describing a man-made religious system. They should be worshipping the true and living God who made them. At the Tower of Babel, the people disobeyed God's word. They made an evil one world religion and government apart from faith in God, and said they were able to reach heaven, that they were gods. <u>Idolatry is spiritual adultery.</u> <u>Therefore, God gave them over to physical sexual adultery.</u>]

25 Who changed the truth of God into a lie, [Satan's lie program worshipped man 'ye shall be as gods, knowing good and evil" (Gen. 3:5). The same lie that Satan believed that he could be "like the most High" (Isa. 14:14) as God, "possessor of heaven and earth" (Gen. 14:22).] **and worshipped and served the creature** [Changing this truth results in idolatry.] **more than the Creator, who is blessed or ever. Amen. 26 For this cause God gave them up unto vile affections:** [Emotions of the soul.] **for even their women did change the natural use into that which is against nature:** [Notice that homosexuality is against nature.] **27 And likewise also the men, leaving the natural use of the woman, burned in their lust one toward another; men with men working that which is unseemly,** [homosexuality] **and receiving in themselves that recompence of their error which was meet.** [They got their just reward.] **28 And even as they did not like to retain God in their knowledge,** [Today also, many do not want to read the Bible and know God.] **God gave them over to a reprobate mind,** [The mind is the spirit of man (Eph. 4:23). So God gave them up body-soul- and spirit The opposite order which is true for saved people, see 1 Thess. 5:23. Their hearts and minds were hardened. "Reprobate" means not passing the test, discredited. No one without God's imputed righteousness can pass the test to stand before Holy God. God let the Gentiles go at the Tower of Babel hoping to save them later through the nation He would create through Abraham. Unbelievers today are also the enemies of God.] **to do those things which are not convenient;** [They did and still do disgusting vile things. Paul gives a list of some of them here.] **29 Being filled with all unrighteousness, fornication, wickedness, covetousness, maliciousness; full of envy, murder, debate, deceit, malignity; whisperers, 30 Backbiters, haters of God, despiteful,** [Insolent.] **proud,** [Satan had pride.] **boasters, inventors of evil things, disobedient to parents,** [Hating those that love and care for them most.] **31 Without understanding, covenantbreakers,** [They broke their contracts and promises.] **without natural affection,** [No real care for others.] **implacable,** [relentless] **unmerciful: 32 Who knowing the judgment of God,** [Job. 32:8. They know that God is going to judge but they disregard that truth. God has given man free will and does not force them to believe.] **that they which commit such things are worthy of death, not only do the same, but have pleasure in them that do them.** [These reprobates are the mobs of the past and unbelievers of the present.]

Romans Chapter 2 Jews under sin
2:1-29 Paul says the Jews are under sin naming them in 2:17.

Romans 2:1 Therefore thou art inexcusable, O man, whosoever thou art that judgest: for wherein thou judgest another, thou condemnest thyself; for thou that judgest doest the same things. [Paul addresses those who think they will be accepted by God because of their human good. Paul says that the things that the self-righteous people judge others about are the things that they themselves do.] **2 But we are sure that the judgment of God is according to truth** [God will judge fairly knowing all things.] **against them which commit such things. 3 And thinkest thou this, O man, that judgest them which do such things, and doest the same, that thou shalt escape the judgment of God?** [Adam found out that the wages of even one sin is death (Gen. 2:17; Rom. 6:23; James 2:10).] **4 Or despisest thou the riches of his goodness** [God's grace, Him giving what is not deserved] **and forbearance** [God restraining Himself by holding back His judgment] **and longsuffering;** [Patient enduring 2 Peter 3:9, 15] **not knowing that the goodness of God leadeth thee to repentance?** [Repentance simply means to change our mind. It does not mean to be sorry for what we have done or to stop sinning. That is impossible, because a sinner is unable to stop sinning. That is why we come to God by faith in His gospel just as the imperfect sinners that we are. We cannot clean ourselves up until after we are saved and have Christ in us. God doesn't force people to have faith but wants them to] **5 But after thy hardness** [stubborn] **and impenitent** [not feeling shame or guilt for actions, unwilling to believe] **heart treasurest up** [storing and adding up, accumulating] **unto thyself wrath against the day of wrath** [2 Thess. 1:9, 2:12; Rev. 20:9] **and revelation of the righteous judgment of God;** [at the Great White Throne Judgment (GWT) (Rev. 20:11-15).] **6 Who will render to every man according to his deeds:** [all people will be judged by God according to what they have done] **7 To them who by patient continuance in well doing seek for glory and honour and immortality, eternal life:** [Those who seek and find God and put their faith in what He says. The problem is that only Christ lived a perfect life we cannot because we are born with the sin nature (Jer. 13:23; Rom. 8:3a, b).] **8 But unto them that are contentious, and do not obey the truth, but obey unrighteousness, indignation and wrath,** [unbelievers will get wrath] **9 Tribulation and anguish, upon every soul of man that doeth evil, of the Jew first, and also of the Gentile;** [Paul warns against unbelief. The Jews will be judged in the tribulation, and then the Gentiles at His Second coming] **10 But glory, honour, and peace, to every man that worketh good, to the Jew first, and also to the Gentile:** [With Christ's righteousness believers can do good works.] **11 For there is no respect of persons with God.** [God will judge everyone by the same standard.] **12 For as many as have sinned without law shall also perish without law: and as many as have sinned in the law shall be judged by the law;** [According to the light or truth available to a person, for example if he did not have the law he will not be judged by it (Luke 12:47, 48 and Matt. 11:21-24). Sin has the same effect on a person with or without the law. Sin produces death (Rom. 5:12-14). Next is a parenthesis from v. 13-15.] **13 (For not the hearers of the law are just before God, but the doers of the law shall be justified.** [Just knowing right from wrong does not justify anyone.] **14 For when the Gentiles, which have not the law, do by nature the things contained in the law, these, having not the law, are a law unto themselves: 15 Which shew the work of the law written in their hearts, their conscience also bearing witness, and their thoughts the mean while accusing or else excusing one another;)** [Everyone has a conscience, God's law written on their hearts, that is why 1:18-20 is about the guilt of the whole world. God's wrath against the ungodly and unrighteous who deny God's power and deity that God has revealed both "in them" (1:19) and in His "creation" (1:20).] **16 In the day when God shall judge the secrets of men by Jesus Christ according to my gospel.** [At the GWT, God will judge the secrets of men's hearts (their motives) not just their actions. God sees and knows everything even our thoughts. God will judge by Jesus Christ "by Jesus Christ." "For the Father judgeth no man, but hath committed all judgment unto the Son: That all men should honour the Son, even as they honour the Father . . . And shall come forth; they that have done good, unto the resurrection of life; and they that have done evil, unto the resurrection of damnation" (John 5:22, 23a, 29). The first time Jesus came to earth, He came to save the world, but the next time He will come to <u>judge</u>. The Lord Jesus will judge "<u>according to my gospel</u>" Paul's gospel.]

17 ¶ Behold, thou art called a Jew, ["Called" does not necessarily mean that they are true Jews in their heart.] **and restest in the law,** [The Jew's religion set Israel apart from all other nations (Deut. 4:5-8). They thought that their religious works could save them. They should not think that just because they were given the law that that makes them any better. They became self-righteous thinking they could keep the law (9:31, 32). <u>Similarly, today, many "Christians" depend on their religion to save them, but have no knowledge of or faith in the word of God.</u>] **and makest thy boast of God,** [The Jews were proud and puffed up because God had given them His law.] **18 And knowest his will,** [But having the law made the Jews more accountable to God because they knew His will.] **and approvest the things that are more excellent, being instructed out of the law;** [The Jews had the benefit of God's excellent law but many did not believe God. <u>Thanks to the revelation of the Lord Jesus Christ given to Paul the members of the body of Christ now have their own word of God and can "approve things that are excellent" (Phil.</u>

1:9).] **19 And art confident that thou thyself art a guide of the blind, a light of them which are in darkness,** [God's purpose for Israel was that they were to be His nation of priests (Ex. 19:5, 6) to teach His word to the other nations (Isa. 2:1-4). The nation will fulfil its purpose in the future and be a light to the Gentiles (Isa. 60:1-3 *Notice this will be at Israel rise, not their fall (Rom. 11:11; Isa. 62:1, 2; Matt. 5:14).] **20 An instructor of the foolish, a teacher of babes, which hast the form of knowledge and of the truth in the law.** [Heb. 4:2, Rom. 8:3a, b, the Jews didn't know that without God's Spirit in them by faith and the understanding of His times they were not qualified to teach yet. They will be qualified after they have received their glorified bodies and the New Covenant in the 1,000-year Kingdom of Christ. At that time, they will have the right heart to serve the Lord out of gratitude and care for others.] **21 Thou therefore which teachest another, teachest thou not thyself? thou that preachest a man should not steal, dost thou steal?** [Because they do not have Christ's Spirit yet they still have the sin nature with its evil thoughts and intents.] **22 Thou that sayest a man should not commit adultery, dost thou commit adultery? thou that abhorrest idols, dost thou commit sacrilege?** [Sadly the Jews were notorious for idolatry (Isa. 65:2, 3).] **23 Thou that makest thy boast of the law, through breaking the law dishonourest thou God? 24 For the name of God is blasphemed [spoken badly of] among the Gentiles through you, as it is written.** [Ezek. 36:21, 22] **25 For circumcision verily profiteth, if thou keep the law:** [God gave circumcision to the nation of Israel as a token of the covenant He made with Abraham after Abraham had a son by his own effort in the flesh (Gen. 17:11), not the son of promise which was a miracle since at that time both Abraham and Sarah were unable to conceive. Things done in the flesh are not approved by God, but the things done by faith are. Circumcision means death to the flesh, and alive unto God] **but if thou be a breaker of the law, thy circumcision is made uncircumcision.** [Worthless] **26 Therefore if the uncircumcision keep the righteousness of the law, shall not his uncircumcision be counted for circumcision?** [God values and approves of righteousness (Psa. 33:4, 5) and therefore the Gentile who does them is approved to God] **27 And shall not uncircumcision which is by nature,** [who naturally do what is right because the law on their hearts.] **if it fulfil the law, judge thee, who by the letter and circumcision dost transgress the law?** [Those Gentiles are righteous in God's sight] **28 For he is not a Jew, which is one outwardly; neither is that circumcision, which is outward in the flesh:** [notice Paul's modest, concise, and clear language.] **29 But he is a Jew, which is one inwardly; and circumcision is that of the heart, in the spirit,** [Circumcision represents the heart and spirit that God desires in them (Deut. 10:12-14, 30:5,6; Ezek. 36:26-28).] **and not in the letter;** [His law and Spirit will be in their hearts and they will not need to follow what is written because they will know it] **whose praise is not of men, but of God.** [God considers unbelieving Israel spiritually uncircumcised like Gentiles.]

The Four Sections of Romans by LeighAnn Mycko

1. JUSTIFICATION. In Romans chapters 1-5 Paul delivers to us Jesus Christ's teaching on our JUSTIFICATION during this present dispensation of grace: (A) INTRODUCTION: The Author (1:1-5), The Audience (1:6-10), The Purpose (1:11-14); (B) THE GOSPEL OF CHRIST: The Power of God (1:15-17), The Wrath of God (1:18-32), The Guilt of Man (2:1-3:19), The Provision of Grace (3:20-26), The Law of Faith (3:27-31), The Testimony of Faith (4:1-25), The Eternal Result of JUSTIFICATION (5:1-21).

2. IDENTIFICATION. In Romans chapters 6-8 Paul delivers to us Jesus Christ's teaching on our IDENTIFICATION once we are IN Christ during this present dispensation of grace: (A) WE ARE DEAD TO SIN: Declaration (6:1-2), Description (6:3-10), Application (6:11-23); (B) WE ARE DEAD TO THE LAW: Declaration (7:1-4); Description (7:5-12); Application (7:13-25); (C) WE ARE DEAD TO THE FLESH: Declaration (8:1-4), Description (8:5-8), Application (8:9-13); (D) WE ARE SONS OF GOD: Declaration (8:14), Description (8:15-17), Application (8:18-39).

3. DISPENSATION. In Romans chapters 9-11 Paul delivers to us Jesus Christ's teaching on the DISPENSATION change: (A) ISRAEL'S PROGRAM SUSPENDED: Israel's Purpose (9:1-5), Israel's Suspension Explained (9:6-33); (B) ISRAEL'S SPIRITUAL STUMBLING: Israel's Stumbling Explained (10:1-13), Israel Without Excuse (10:14-21); (C) ISRAEL'S PRESENT STATE & FUTURE HOPE - DELAYED: Israel's Present Fall and Blindness (11:1-25), Israel's Future Hope (11:26-29), God's Present Purpose (11:30-36).

4. APPLICATION (or WALK AS A SON). In Romans chapters 12-16 Paul delivers to us Jesus Christ's teaching on how we are to walk as a Son of God IN Christ, today, because of what he taught us in Romans chapters 1-11. (A) OUR SERVICE TO GOD (12:1-2); (B) OUR SERVICE TO THE BODY (12:3-16); (C) OUR SERVICE TO THE UNSAVED (12:17-21); (D) OUR SERVICE UNDER HUMAN GOVERNMENT (13:1-7); (E) OUR SERVICE IN THE WORLD (13:8-14); (F) OUR SERVICE TO THE WEAKER BRETHREN (14:1-15:7); (G) CONCLUDING INFORMATION: Christ's Past Age Ministry (15:8-12), Paul's Present Age Ministry (15:13-33), Paul's Love (16:1-16), Paul's Warning (16:17-20), Paul's Salutations (16:21-24), Paul's Commendation (16:25-27).

Romans Chapter 3 Justification explained
3:1-20 The Bad News (which really began in 1:18): The whole world is under sin and worthy of God's wrath. No human has kept His law perfectly.

Romans 3:1 What advantage then hath the Jew? or what profit is there of circumcision? [What good was it to be a Jew if they are under sin just like the Gentiles] **2 Much every way: chiefly, because that unto them were committed the oracles of God.** [Israel had God's written word (Deut. 4:5-8; Psa. 147:19) as well as their conscience, while Gentiles only had the conscience. Therefore, the Jews had an extra way to know that they were sinners in need of a Saviour.] **3 For what if some did not believe? shall their unbelief make the faith of God without effect? 4 God forbid: yea, let God be true, but every man a liar;** [[God is true and just even if people do not believe. If every man disagrees with God's word, then who is a <u>liar</u>? The only way man can have eternal life is if God is true to His word to save his soul and give him that life. Next Paul shows some foolish arguments mortals (liars) have against God.] **as it is written, That thou mightest be justified in thy sayings, and mightest overcome when thou art judged.** [In <u>Psa. 51:4</u> David confesses his adultery with Bathsheba and murder of her husband. David admits his guilt and puts up no defense so that God may be just in His judgment. David says that his sin is only against God and that God is not unjust in forgiving him. David put his faith in God as the only one who could save Him. God is justified in saying David is forgiven and will overcome the argument that He is not just. <u>Acknowledging our guilt before God shows that we realize our need for a Saviour.</u>] **5 But if our unrighteousness commend the righteousness of God, what shall we say? Is God unrighteous who taketh vengeance? (I speak as a man)** [Here is some men's crazy arguments: since my sin reveals God's righteousness should He not be grateful and not punish me for it?] **6 God forbid: for then how shall God judge the world?** [God's justice demands that He judge the wrong things people do.] **7 For if the <u>truth</u> of God hath more abounded through my lie unto his glory; why yet am I also judged as a sinner?** [If God's truth is increased by our lying, should we sin more to make God greater? The end does not justify the means; sin is not excusable if God can use it for His good. God would not be just if He excused sin and did not judge it.]. **8 And not rather, (as we be slanderously reported, and as some affirm that we say,) Let us do evil, that good may come? whose damnation is just.** [Paul says, this foolish thinking is justly damned. He mentions this slander experience in order to warn the saints that they most likely will encounter it also.]

9 ¶ What then? are we [Jews] better than they? No, in no wise: for we have before proved both Jews and Gentiles, that they are <u>all under sin</u>; [Paul now lists several OT verses to show man's total sinfulness.] **10 As it is written, There is none righteous, no, not one:** [Psa. 14:1] **11 There is none that understandeth, there is none that seeketh after God. [Psa. 14:2] 12 They are all gone out of the way, they are together become unprofitable; there is none that doeth good, no, not one.** [Psa. 14:3, says "filthy" [with sin] instead of unprofitable.] **13 Their throat is an open sepulcher** [Psa. 5:9] **with their tongues they have used deceit;** [Psa. 140:3] **the poison of asps is under their lips:** [Psa. 140:3. Deceit, concealing or misrepresenting the truth, begins in the heart (Jer. 17:9). Without Christ people are selfish, self-centered, and evil. "For from within, out of the heart of men, proceed evil thoughts" (Mark 7:21).] **14 Whose mouth is full of cursing and bitterness:** [Psa. 10:7] **15 Their feet are swift to shed blood:** [Prov. 1:16] **16 Destruction and misery are in their ways:** [Isa. 59:7, they are the evil children of disobedience like we used to be "Wherein in time past [before we were saved] ye walked according to the course of this world, according to the prince of the power of the air [Satan], the spirit that now worketh in the children of disobedience" (Eph. 2:2).] **17 And the way of peace have they not known:** [Isa. 59:8] **18 There is no fear of God before their eyes.** [Psa. 36:1. People do not fear God's judgment. So unsaved people are helpless to improve themselves because they lack any respect or knowledge of God. If God did not use the gospel in His word to seek us, we would be helplessly lost and no one would be saved.]

19 ¶ Now we know that what things soever the law saith, it saith to them who are under the law: [Who were under the law? Yes, the Jews. But so are the Gentiles because they have the law written in their hearts (2:15). The only ones that are not under the law are the believers (6:14). God is not imputing sin in this age of grace. But the law is still in effect for unbelievers to bring them to Christ. "Wherefore the law was our schoolmaster to bring us unto Christ, that we might be justified by faith" (Gal. 3:24). "Knowing this, that the law is not made for a righteous man, but for the lawless and disobedient . . ." (1 Tim. 1:9)] **that every mouth may be stopped, and all the world may become guilty before God:** [Paul has put the closing remark on his case proving mankind's total sinful depravity. The final verdict – the whole world is GUILTY before God.] **20 Therefore by the deeds** [Works] **of the law there shall no flesh be justified in his sight:** [Even if someone could keep the law it could not save anyone.] **for by the law is the knowledge of sin.** [Paul just stated the purpose of the law. The legitimate use of the law today in this age of grace is to show a person their sin and need for a Saviour. God cannot ignore sin. Every sin will be paid for, either by the sinner or by Christ.]

21 ¶ But now the righteousness of God without the law is manifested, [But now God has revealed to mankind through Paul how God can be righteous in declaring a sinner just apart from the law (through the sacrificial system).] **being witnessed by the law and the prophets;** [The law verified that Christ's blood legally paid the price for our sin as the law demanded (Lev. 5:6) and the prophets predicted (Isa. 53:11).] **22 Even the <u>righteousness of God</u> *which is* <u>by faith of Jesus Christ</u> <u>unto all</u> and <u>upon all</u> them <u>that believe</u>: for there is <u>no difference</u>.** [All them that believe are saved. There is <u>no difference</u> in salvation. Adam was created sinless but disobeyed and sinned. Christ was born of a virgin and did not inherit the sin nature. Having perfect faith was still difficult. He was tempted by Satan but overcame in the wilderness. In the garden of Gethsemane, the temptation not to go to the cross was very strong Jesus prayed: "Saying, Father, if thou be willing, remove this cup from me: nevertheless not my will, but thine, be done . . . being in an agony he prayed more earnestly: and his sweat was as it were great drops of blood falling down to the ground" (Luke 22:42-44). But unlike Adam the faith of Jesus was perfect. He yielded His will and trusted the Father's plan of redemption and obeyed. "And being found in fashion as a man, he humbled himself, and became obedient unto death, even the death of the cross" (Phil. 2:8). It took <u>Jesus Christ's faith</u> to manifest God's righteousness to man. <u>Paul just gave everyone the solution to our sin problem – faith in what Christ has done by His faith</u>. We are "justified by the faith of Christ" (Gal. 2:16). It is by the faith "of" Jesus Christ (Phil. 3:9). The modern Bibles replace "of" with "in" putting the emphasis on the believer instead of on Christ. God's righteousness is offered "unto all and upon all" that believe in time past and in the present. So how do we get the righteousness of God? By believing in Jesus! Christ "gave himself a ransom for all" (1 Tim. 2:6) and "he tasted death for every man" (Heb. 2:9). <u>God substituted Himself and died in every man's place</u>! (2 Cor. 5:21). God's will is "to save them that believe" (1 Cor. 1:21). He is the "Saviour of all men, specially of those that believe" (1 Tim. 4:10). Notice that today during Christ's ministry to us from heaven through Paul salvation does not require going through Israel. Is this the same gospel mankind had to believe during Christ's earthly ministry? No! Our gospel is not in John 3:16-18, 20:31; nor Matt. 16:15, 16 because if you read those verses you see that it is talking about believing that Jesus is the name of Israel's Messiah the Son of God. Notice how the disciples did not understand about His death, burial, and resurrection for our sins in Luke 18:31-34. But what about Peter after Jesus rose what did he preach in Acts 2:22, 23, 36? Did Peter preach the good news of Christ death as payment for our sins and resurrection for our justification? No! He preached the cross as bad news, and repent and be baptized just like John the Baptist and Jesus had done. <u>The gospel of our salvation is not revealed until Paul</u> (Acts 9). Whenever Paul says "but now" it usually signals that God has changed His dealings with men, Eph. 2:11-16 is a good example of another "but now."] **23 For all have sinned, and come short of the glory of God;** [There is <u>no difference</u>

in sin; all have come short of God's standard (Eccl. 7:20).] **24 Being justified freely by his grace through the redemption that is in Christ Jesus:** [God freely and graciously provided His Son and His Son's righteousness.] **25 Whom God hath set forth to be a propitiation** [Perfectly satisfying sacrifice.] **through faith in his blood,** [Christ's perfect blood paid for all sins of all time, even of the past. In the past the blood of animals atoned (covered) for sins but never took sins away, never paid for them completely (Heb. 9:15, 22, 10:1-4; Lev. 17:11).] **to declare his righteousness for the remission of sins that are past,** [Forgiveness for all the sins of those in paradise or "Abraham's Bosom" (Luke 16:22). Christ went to paradise after paying for all sins and declared His payment and righteousness to them. Remember Jesus Christ told the thief on the cross that He would be with him in paradise that day Luke 23:43? God had passed over those sins in anticipation of the cross. They could not come into His presence without Christ's payment or righteousness because they would have incurred His wrath, but now they can.] **through the forbearance of God;** [God's patient self-restraint and withholding of His wrath knowing that Christ would pay for their sins.] **26 To declare, I say, at this time his righteousness: that he might be just and the justifier of him which believeth in Jesus.** [Paul was the one to declare the full impact of the cross. God at this time (in the dispensation of grace) offers His righteousness to anyone who will believe. God can remain just and justify a sinner which believes in Jesus. When we agree with God to trust His sacrifice (provision) for our sin He imputes to our account the righteousness of Christ. Salvation is by faith ALONE in what He did. He paid our sin debt and rose. Many people who think they are saved may not be saved if they add anything of their own work to what Christ has done, which is an insult to God! If they think they also played a part in their salvation by saying a prayer, confessing their sin, asking forgiveness, being water baptized, walking the isle, dedicating their lives, or any other work on their part they have insulted God! It is critical to know precisely how to be justified by God. So you can be sure you are saved and can accurately help others to be saved.] **27 Where is boasting then? It is excluded. By what law? of works? Nay: but by the law of faith.** [Boasting is excluded by the "law of faith" because faith is not a work. Christ finished work on the cross saved us. He gets all the glory and we have nothing to boast about.] **28 Therefore we conclude that a man is justified by faith without the deeds** [Works] **of the law.** [We are declared righteous or justified apart from doing any deeds or works of the law of any kind. Salvation is a free gift (Eph. 2:8, 9). Man's pride is our biggest problem so God set things up so that "no flesh should glory in his presence" (1 Cor. 1:18, 29; Jer. 9:23, 24). Any worthwhile thing that we think or do is because "Christ liveth in me" (Gal. 2:20) so boasting is excluded. The only thing we can glory in is "the cross of our Lord Jesus Christ" (Gal. 6:14). People in Israel's program are saved by faith but they are required to do works that are motivated by their faith (Matt. 7:21, 19:16-21; Mark 16:16; James 2:14-26). God hates works that are not motivated by faith (Amos 5:21-26; Isa. 1:10-14; Psa. 51:17-19).] **29 Is he the God of the Jews only? is he not also of the Gentiles? Yes, of the Gentiles also:** [In time past Gentiles were "without Christ, . . . having no hope, and without God in the world (Eph. 2:11-14). But now, Israel has been concluded in unbelief like the Gentiles, so God can offer mercy to all equally (11:32). In the future, God will still keep His special promises to Israel of ruling together with their King in His Kingdom on earth forever. But God has temporarily interrupted Israel's program (11:11-15, 25-30) ever since they fell in Acts 7:51-53 when the nation rejected the renewed offer of the King and His kingdom by stoning the Holy Ghost filled Stephen. God has begun a new program revealed through the apostle Paul (Eph. 3:1-6) so that He can call out a special people (the body of Christ) to rule with Him in the heavenly places.] **30 Seeing it is one God, which shall justify the circumcision by faith, and uncircumcision through faith.** [Paul reveals that both Jews and Gentiles are justified by faith. Gentiles are the uncircumcision. Since Israel has fallen to our level they are also considered Gentiles today. Gentiles are saved by believing Christ's sacrifice and doing nothing (3:28; Rom. 4:5). Gal. 2:7 shows that the gospel of the uncircumcision was committed and limited to the apostle Paul. While the gospel of the circumcision was committed to Peter. Do you see the difference between the two gospels in Gal. 2:7-9? Peter and His group died out because of God put Israel's believing remnant on hold and began the dispensation of grace. Today there is only one gospel that saves and that is Paul's. In the body of Christ circumcision is unimportant: "For in Jesus Christ neither circumcision availeth any thing, nor uncircumcision; but faith which worketh by love" (Gal. 5:6).] **31 Do we then make void the law through faith? God forbid: yea, we establish the law.** [Does faith make the law unnecessary? No, it establishes the law. The purpose of the law is to prove guilt so that people will seek forgiveness for their sins through a blood sacrifice, not to give eternal life. Faith in God's ultimate sacrifice establishes the law, it does not void it. "I do not frustrate the grace of God: for if righteousness come by the law, then Christ is dead in vain" (Gal. 2:21). Faith comes "by hearing, and hearing by the word of God" (10:17). "Is the law then against the promises of God? God forbid: for if there had been a law given which could have given life, verily righteousness should have been by the law. But the scripture hath concluded all under sin, that the promise by faith of Jesus Christ might be given to them that believe. But before faith came, we were kept under the law, shut up unto the faith which should afterwards be revealed. Wherefore the law was our schoolmaster to bring us unto Christ, that we might be justified by faith. But after that faith is come, we are no longer under a schoolmaster. For ye are all the children of God by faith in Christ Jesus" (Gal. 3:21-26). When we trust the Lord Jesus Christ and receive His righteousness it is as if we kept the law perfectly. <u>His performance is credited to our account.</u> <u>Salvation is 100% what God has done, and 0% what man has done!</u> See Romans 5:8]

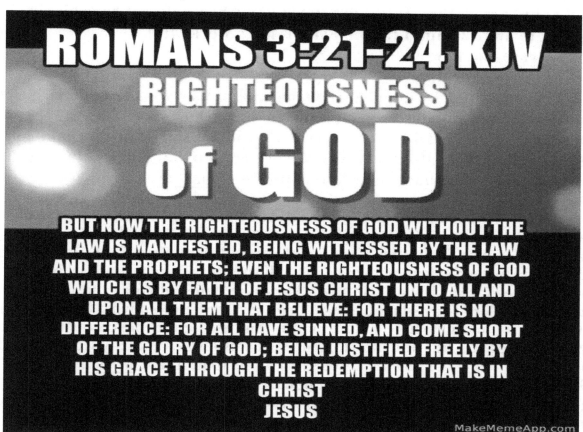

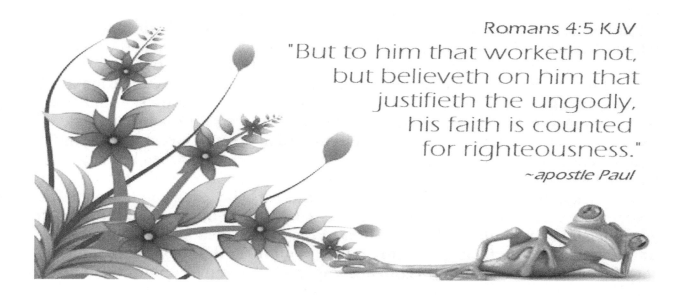

Romans Chapter 4 Imputation. The case of Abraham
How to be totally forgiven and free of the fear of death.
Blessings of Abraham, not Israel. A series of contrasts
4:1-8 Faith, not works – When did David know he would not have his sin imputed to him? 2 Sam. 12:9, 13. Faith is not a work (4:5).
4:9-12 Grace, not law
4:13-17 Life, not death
4:18-25 Justification by imputed righteousness of Christ – born of a virgin (no inherited sin nature), lived a perfect life, no blemish or sin (2 Cor. 5:21; 1 Peter 1:18, 19, 2:22; Heb. 4:15), because He had not sinned death could not hold Him (Rom. 6:23; Psalm 16:10). We are saved by faith in what Christ has done. The most important verse in the Bible is <u>Gen. 15:6</u>.

Romans 4:1 What shall we say then that Abraham our father, as pertaining to the flesh, hath found? [How was Abraham justified?] **2 For if Abraham were justified by works, he hath whereof to glory; but not before God.** [If Abraham had earned His own salvation then he could boast, but no man can boast before God.] **3 For what saith the scripture? Abraham <u>believed God</u>, and it was counted unto him for righteousness.** [Gen. 15:6, he believed what God told him, so God made him righteous.] **4 Now to him that worketh is the reward not reckoned of grace, but of debt.** [If someone earns his salvation by working for it God owes it to him and it is not a free gift.] **5 But to him that <u>worketh not</u>, but believeth on him that justifieth the ungodly, <u>his faith is counted for righteousness.</u>** [The person who simply trusts what God has told him and believes God, his faith is counted for righteousness in God's sight but anyone who adds their own work to what Christ has done insults God. David received the same by faith.] **6 Even as David also describeth the blessedness of the man, unto whom God imputeth righteousness without works, 7 Saying, Blessed are they whose iniquities are forgiven, and whose sins are covered. 8 Blessed is the man to whom the Lord will not impute sin** [Psa. 32:1, 2. When did David know that he would not have his sins imputed to him? 2 Sam. 12:9,13.] **9 Cometh this blessedness then upon the circumcision only, or upon the uncircumcision also?** [Does God impute righteousness only to the Jews? Gal. 3:6.] **for we say that faith was reckoned to Abraham for righteousness. 10 How was it then reckoned? when he was in circumcision, or in uncircumcision? Not in circumcision, but in uncircumcision.** [God did not reckon Abraham as righteous when he obeyed God and left Ur because that would have been a work that made him righteous, but God waited to pronounce Abraham righteous after he believed that God would give him descendants before he was circumcised.] **11 And he received the sign of circumcision, a seal of the righteousness of the faith which he had yet being uncircumcised: that he might be the father of <u>all</u> them that <u>believe</u>, though they be not circumcised; that righteousness might be imputed unto them also:** [In His foreknowledge, God made provision for us, the uncircumcision.] **12 And**

the father of circumcision to them who are not of the circumcision only, but who also walk in the steps of that faith of our father Abraham, which he had being yet uncircumcised. 13 For the promise, that he should be the heir of the world, was not to Abraham, or to his seed, through the law, but through the righteousness of faith. [Everyone is saved by faith like father Abraham, Heb. 11:6.] 14 For if they which are of the law be heirs, faith is made void, and the promise made of none effect: [If keeping the law can save someone then faith in God to save would not be necessary. Similarly, if we add our own doings to what Christ has done, such as believing that saying a prayer or being water baptized contributed to our salvation we void our salvation or make it of none effect.] 15 Because the law worketh wrath: for where no law is, there is no transgression. [The purpose of the law is to reveal our transgression and need for a Redeemer.]

16 Therefore it is of faith, that it might be by grace; [Imputed righteousness, v.11, is of faith by grace, God imparts the gift of His righteousness.] to the end the promise might be sure to all the seed [all believers are Abraham's seed (Gen. 22:17)]; not to that only which is of the law, [The written law was given to the Jews.] but to that also which is of the faith of Abraham; who is the father of us all, 17 (As it is written, I have made thee a father of many nations,) before him whom he believed, even God, who quickeneth the dead, and calleth those things which be not as though they were. [Only God gives spiritual life to the spiritually dead. In His foreknowledge God knew Abraham would be the father of all who believe, both earthly and heavenly people (Gen. 17:5).] 18 Who against hope believed in hope, [Hope of the promised seed (child), descendants.] that he might become the father of many nations; according to that which was spoken, So shall thy seed be [God would make His nation the seed-line to His Son.] 19 And being not weak in faith, he considered not his own body now dead, when he was about an hundred years old, neither yet the deadness of Sara's womb: [God waited till he was too old to have children and had proved that his wife Sarah was barren before life miraculously sprang from them (Isaac) who were reproductively dead.] 20 He staggered not at the promise of God through unbelief; but was strong in faith, giving glory to God; 21 And being fully persuaded that, what he had promised, he was able also to perform. [Abraham had faith that God could and would do what He said]. 22 And therefore it was imputed to him for righteousness [The righteousness of God was imputed to Abraham.] 23 Now it was not written for his sake alone, that it was imputed to him; 24 But for us also, to whom it shall be imputed, if we believe on him that raised up Jesus our Lord from the dead; [It was written that God imputed His righteousness to Abraham in Gen 15:6, so that all believers would know that they would receive God's righteousness if they believed Him.] 25 Who was delivered for our offences, and was raised again for our justification. [We need to believe that God delivered Christ to die for our offences and raised Him for our justification. When a person believes this they receive Christ's imputed righteousness and can stand before holy God.]

Romans Chapter 5 Result of justification
5:1-5 Result of justification.
5:6-11 God's immense love for us.
5:12-21 Justification compared with condemnation.

Romans 5:1 Therefore being <u>justified by faith,</u> [Having Christ's imputed righteousness by faith.] <u>**we have peace with God through our Lord Jesus Christ**</u>: **2 By whom also we have access by faith into this grace wherein we stand,** [Our position or standing in Christ] **and rejoice in hope of the glory of God.** [Rejoice in our hope to be with God eternally.] **3 And not only so, but we glory in tribulations also:** [External and internal tribulations - circumstances, bad decisions, the enemy, stress and fears give us a chance to live by faith.] **knowing that tribulation worketh patience; 4 And patience, experience;** [Skill in grace living and control over our sinful bodies 1 Cor. 9:27. We let Christ live through us Gal. 2:20 which gives God the glory because it was Him in us, not us, 2 Cor. 4:7. <u>God leaves us in the flesh so that He can perform a work in us Phil 1:6 and conform us to Christ,</u> and we do not think we are something when we are not.] **and experience, hope:** [Confident expectation awaiting our glorified bodies.] **5 And hope maketh not ashamed; because the love of God is shed abroad in our hearts by the Holy Ghost which is given unto us.** [We have "hope of the glory of God" (8:2). God's love for us which is spread in our hearts by the Holy Ghost.] **6 For when we were yet without strength,** [When we were helpless and could do nothing to save ourselves.] **in due time Christ died for the ungodly.** [At the right time God died for the ungodly (us).] **7 For scarcely for a righteous man will one die: yet peradventure for a good man** [a great leader] **some would even dare to die. 8 But God commendeth** [Approved] **his love toward us, in that, while we were yet sinners,** [when there was nothing good in us] <u>**Christ died for us.**</u> [<u>HE TOOK OUR PLACE! Paul, as a prosecuting attorney, tells us that the Judge died for the accused! What a love story! God substituted Himself in our place and then He gave us His righteousness! What love! Greater love has no man! What a great and loving God He is! Thank You, LORD!</u>] **9 Much more then, being now justified by his blood,** [The price of redemption cost God enormously.] **we shall be saved from wrath through him.** [Christ saved us from eternal death and the Tribulation.] **10 For if, when we were enemies,** [no one but God dies for His enemies] **we were reconciled to God by the death of his Son,** [God the Father spared not His own Son, 8:32.] **much more, being reconciled, we shall be saved by his life.** [We not only received His imputed righteousness but His life in us as we live now.] **11 And not only so, but we also joy in God through our Lord Jesus Christ, by whom we have <u>now</u> received the <u>atonement</u>.** [We have been made one with Christ, are reconciled to the Father and Christ's atonement now.]

12 ¶ **Wherefore, as by one man sin entered into the world, and death by sin; and so death passed upon all men,** [All inherited the sin nature.] **for that all have sinned:** [We have much more in Christ, than what we lost in Adam. Both men were born <u>without</u> the sin nature. The word "one" occurs "eleven times" in this chapter. Adam is the federal head of lost mankind, while Christ is the federal head of saved mankind. When God looks out over mankind He sees us in one or the other of these two men. We are either spiritually dead or spiritually alive. The next section is parenthetical] **13 (For until the law sin was in the world: but sin is not imputed when there is no law. 14 Nevertheless <u>death reigned from Adam to Moses,</u>** [People died because the "wages of sin is death."] **even over them that had not sinned after the similitude of <u>Adam's transgression,</u>** [Those who have not knowingly violated a specific command as Adam did.] **who is the figure of him that was to come.** [The last Adam, Christ 1 Cor. 15:45.] **15 But not as the offence,** [Adam choosing to sin.] **so also is the free gift.** [The imputed righteousness of Christ.] **For if through the offence of one many be dead, much more the grace of God, and the gift by grace, which is by one man, Jesus Christ, hath <u>abounded</u> unto many. 16 And not as it was by one that sinned, so is the gift: for the judgment was by one to condemnation,** [Condemned to eternal spiritual death (separation from God)] **but the free gift is of many offences unto justification.** [Declared righteous and given Christ's life by God.] **17 For if by one man's offence death reigned by one; much more they which receive abundance of grace and of the <u>gift of righteousness</u> shall reign in life by one, Jesus Christ.)** [By His abundant grace we received the gift of righteousness and eternal life now.] **18 Therefore as by the offence of one judgment came upon all men to condemnation; even so by the righteousness of one the free gift came upon all men unto justification of life.** [We gained so much more in Christ than we lost in Adam; we gained <u>Christ's imputed righteousness and life</u> (5:10) when we believe.] **19 For as by one man's disobedience many were made sinners, so by the obedience of one shall many be made righteous.** [Those who believe.] **20 Moreover the law entered, that the offence might abound.** ["by the law is the knowledge of sin," 3:20.] **But where sin abounded, grace did much more abound:** [Christ's righteousness "abounds" does not only cancel out Adam's sin <u>but is stronger than it.]</u> **21 That as sin hath reigned unto death, even so might grace reign through righteousness unto eternal life by Jesus Christ our Lord.**

Romans Chapter 6 Our new position in Christ
6:1-13 Our <u>identity</u> in Christ (baptized into His death, dead to sin, raised in newness of life)
6:14-23 Free from sin, servants of righteousness and gift of eternal life.

Romans 6:1 What shall we say then? Shall we <u>continue in sin</u>, that grace may abound? [Paul anticipates questions, and answers them.] **2 God forbid. How shall we, that <u>ARE dead to sin</u>, live any longer therein?** [Sin has no power over a dead man.] **3 Know ye not, that so many of us as were <u>baptized into Jesus Christ</u> were baptized <u>into his death</u>?** [Identified with His death.] **4 Therefore we are buried with him by baptism into death: that like as Christ was raised up from the dead by the glory of the Father, even so we also should <u>walk in newness of life</u>.** [His resurrection life in us.] **5 For if we have been <u>planted together</u> in the likeness of his <u>death</u>, we shall be also in <u>the likeness of his resurrection</u>:** [Our new identity in Christ.] **6 Knowing this, that our old man is crucified with him, <u>that the body of sin</u> might be <u>destroyed</u>,** [Gal. 2:20, Christ broke the power of sin. <u>Our "old man" is who we were in Adam before we were saved</u>.] **that henceforth we should not serve sin. 7 For he that is dead is <u>freed from sin</u>.** [A corps does not sin.] **8 Now if <u>we</u> be <u>dead with Christ</u>, we believe that we shall also live with him:** [Our eternal life began at salvation.] **9 Knowing that Christ being raised from the dead dieth no more; death hath no more dominion over him. 10 For in that he died, he died <u>unto sin ONCE</u>:** [Once is all that it took for Jesus Christ to finish paying for our sin on the cross.] **but in that he liveth, he liveth unto God.** [Christ lives unto God and so shall we.] **11 <u>Likewise reckon</u> [count on it] <u>ye also yourselves to be dead indeed unto sin, but ALIVE unto God through Jesus Christ our Lord</u>. 12 Let not sin <u>therefore reign</u> in your <u>mortal body</u>, that ye should obey it in the lusts thereof. 13 Neither <u>yield</u> ye your <u>members</u>** [Hands, feet, voice, skills, talents, bodies (Rom. 12:1, 2; 1 Tim. 2:4).] **as instruments of unrighteousness <u>unto sin</u>: but <u>yield</u> yourselves <u>unto God</u>, as those that are <u>alive</u> <u>from the dead</u>, and your <u>members as instruments of righteousness unto God</u>. 14 For <u>sin shall not have dominion</u> over you: for <u>ye are not under the law, but under grace</u>.** [We have resurrection life now! Serve God since you are free to do so.] **15 What then? shall we sin, because we are not under the law, but under grace? God forbid. 16 Know ye not, that <u>to whom ye yield yourselves servants to obey, his servants ye are</u> to whom ye obey; whether of sin unto death, or of obedience unto righteousness?** [Don't serve sin, live right.] **17 But God be thanked, that ye were the servants of sin, but ye have obeyed from the heart that form of doctrine which was delivered you. 18 <u>Being then made free from sin, ye became the servants of righteousness</u>.** [You believed Paul's good news and doctrine and are free from bondage to the law.] **19 I**

speak after the manner of men because of the infirmity of your flesh: for as ye have yielded your members servants to uncleanness and to iniquity unto iniquity; even so now yield your members servants to righteousness unto holiness. [New life serve God.] 20 For when ye were the servants of sin, ye were free from righteousness. 21 What fruit had ye then in those things whereof ye are now ashamed? [We are now ashamed of those things we did 1 Cor. 6:9-11; Gal. 5:19-21.] for the end of those things is death. 22 But now being made free from sin, [Because Christ destroyed the power of sin, it no longer has power over us.] and become servants to God, ye have your fruit unto holiness, [Fruit that is acceptable to God and will stand the test of fire at the Judgment Seat of Christ (1 Cor. 3:12-15).] and the end everlasting life. 23 For the wages of sin is death; but the gift of God is eternal life through Jesus Christ our Lord. [The result of unbelief is death. We have Christ's life in us now for all eternity.]

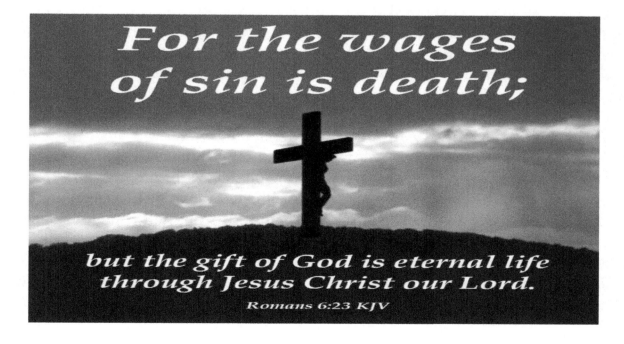

31

Romans Chapter 7 Our new problem in the flesh
7:1-6 Dead to the law
7:7-14 The law condemns
7:15-25 The sin nature is still in our flesh, so in it we can do nothing good

Romans 7:1 <u>Know ye not</u>, **brethren, (for I speak to them that know the law,) how that the law hath dominion over a man <u>as long as he liveth</u>?** [But we are dead to the law.] **2 For the woman which hath an husband is bound by the law to** *her* **husband so long as he liveth; but if the husband be dead, she is loosed from the law of** *her* **husband. 3 So then if, while** *her* **husband liveth, she be married to another man, she shall be called an adulteress: but if her husband be dead, she is free from that law; so that she is no adulteress, though she be married to another man. 4 Wherefore, my brethren, ye also are become <u>dead to the law</u> by the body of Christ; that ye should be <u>married to another</u>,** *even* **to him who is raised from the dead, that <u>we</u> should bring forth fruit unto God.** [Paul includes himself, Gal. 3:12-14] **5 For when we were** [Past tense.] **in the flesh, the motions of sins,** [Evil working in us.] **which were by the law, did work in our members to bring forth fruit unto death. 6 <u>But now we are delivered from the law</u>, that being dead wherein we were held; that we should <u>serve in newness of spirit</u>,** [Delivered from the bondage of sin, to serve God in newness of life.] **and not** *in* **the oldness of the letter.** [the Law]

7 ¶ What shall we say then? *<u>Is the law sin? God forbid.</u>* **Nay, I had not known sin, but by the law:** [Gal. 3:24-28] **for I had not known lust, except the law had said, <u>Thou shalt not covet</u>. 8 But sin, taking occasion by the commandment,** [Law] **wrought in me all manner of concupiscence** [lust for what is forbidden]. **For without the law sin** *was* **dead. 9 For I was alive without the law once:** [He was alive under grace, Rom. 6] **but when the commandment came,** [when he placed himself back under the law, sin came alive again and he died unto God, 6:11] **sin revived, and I died. 10 And the commandment, which** *was ordained* **to life, I found** *to be* **unto death.** [Life was not in the law, it reveals our sins, our failures.] **11 For sin, taking occasion by the commandment, deceived me,** [tricked] **and by it slew** *me*. [Not operating as God intends.] **12 Wherefore the law** *is* **holy, and the commandment holy, and just, and good. 13 Was then that which is good made death unto me? God forbid. But <u>sin</u>, that it might appear sin, working death in me by that which is good; that sin by the commandment might become exceeding sinful.** [The law magnified sin in us.] **14 For we know that <u>the law is spiritual</u>: but I am carnal, sold under sin** [tainted by sin]. **15 For that which I do I allow not: for what I would, that do I not; but what I hate,**

that do I. 16 If then I do that which I would not, I consent unto the law that *it is* good. 17 Now then it is no more I that do it, but sin that dwelleth in me. 18 For I know that in me (that is, in my flesh,) dwelleth no good thing: for to will is present with me; but *how* to perform that which is good I find not. [Man's good is not good.] 19 For the good that I would I do not: but the evil which I would not, that I do. 20 Now if I do that I would not, it is no more I that do it, but sin that dwelleth in me. 21 I find then a law, that, when I would do good, evil is present with me. 22 For I delight in the law of God [The perfect standard of God in the Law given through Moses.] after the inward man: [Our spirit and soul.] 23 But I see another law in my members, warring [The war between the flesh and the Spirit in the believer.] against the law of my mind, [Desire to live perfectly unto God.] and bringing me into captivity to the law of sin which is in my members. [True fact that sin dwells in me.] 24 O wretched man that I am! who shall deliver me from the body of this death? [The self-condemnation that comes because of sin in our flesh being magnified by the law.] 25 I thank God through Jesus Christ our Lord. [With Christ working in us we can win this war.] So then with the mind I myself serve the law of God; [Our minds desire to serve God perfectly.] but with the flesh the law of sin. [Our flesh only produces sin, wrong motives and deeds so we cannot do what is "good" or pleasing to God.]

"For the law of the Spirit of life
IN Christ Jesus
hath made me free
from the law of sin and death."

~PAUL, Romans 8:2 KJV

Romans Chapter 8 Our new power in the Spirit
8:1-39 Life in the Spirit; or Living the Victorious Grace Life

Romans 8:1 *There is* therefore now <u>no condemnation</u> to them which are <u>in Christ Jesus, who walk not after the flesh, but after the Spirit</u>. **2 For the <u>law of the Spirit of life in Christ Jesus</u>** [We are not condemned by the law when we live remembering that our old man was crucified with Christ and have received the gift of Christ's imputed righteousness. We walk by faith after the Spirit (trusting Paul's "my gospel," justification by faith).] **hath made me <u>free</u> from the <u>law of sin and death</u>.** [We are unshackled from the power of sin that results in death.] **3 For what the <u>law could not do</u>, in that <u>it was weak through the flesh</u>,** [No one could keep it, except Christ.] **God sending <u>his own Son in the likeness of sinful flesh, and for sin, condemned sin in the flesh</u>:** [Christ destroyed sin, 6:6.] **4 That the <u>righteousness of the law might be fulfilled in us</u>,** [Now we can live right if it is His Spirit working in us using His word rightly divided.] **who <u>walk not after the flesh, but after the Spirit</u>. 5 For they that <u>are after the flesh do mind the things of the flesh</u>;** [Selfish pride, having wrong motives, thoughts, and deeds.] **but they that <u>are after the Spirit the things of the Spirit</u>.** [Pleasing God.] **6 For to be <u>carnally minded</u>** [in the flesh] *is* **death; but to be <u>spiritually minded</u> *is* life and peace.** [Confidence in Him.] **7 Because the <u>carnal mind</u> *is* <u>enmity against God</u>:** [The enemy of God.] **<u>for it is not subject to the law of God</u>,** [Does not want to obey God.] **<u>neither indeed can be</u>.** [Totally incapable.] **8 So then <u>they that are in the flesh cannot please God</u>.** [Functionally useless to God.] **9 But <u>ye are not in the flesh, but in the Spirit, if so be that the Spirit of God dwell in you</u>. Now <u>if any man have not the Spirit of Christ</u>,** [The Spirit here is clearly the Spirit of Christ.] **<u>he is none of his</u>. 10 And <u>if Christ *be* in you, the body *is* dead because of sin</u>;** [the flesh, the body of sin, our old self, has been crucified with Christ, Gal. 2:20. The soul was redeemed, but not the flesh, the spirit was made alive.] **but the Spirit *is* life because of righteousness.** [The Spirit of Christ works righteousness in and through us.] **11 But if <u>the Spirit of him that raised up Jesus from the dead dwell in you</u>,** [All three members of the Godhead: the Father, Son, and Holy Ghost, raised Christ from the dead, Gal. 1:1, John 10:18, Rom. 8:11 all three live in us.] **he that raised up Christ from the dead <u>shall also quicken your mortal bodies by his Spirit that dwelleth in you</u>.** [In the future, believers will receive a glorified body like Jesus has because of the down payment of the Spirit, 2 Cor. 1:22.] **12 Therefore, brethren, we are <u>debtors, not to the flesh</u>, to live after the flesh.** [We are not under obligation to the flesh.] **13 For if <u>ye live after the flesh, ye shall die</u>:** [Functional death, not bear fruit that pleases God.] **but if ye through the Spirit do <u>mortify the deeds of the body</u>,** [Put the deeds of the flesh to death, Gal. 6:8.] **<u>ye shall live</u>** [Bear God fruit and please God.] **14 For as many as are**

led by the Spirit of God, [Gal. 5:18] **they are the sons of God.** [We believers ARE sons of God now. It is interesting that God calls the good angels sons of God in Job 38:7, also the believing remnant in John 1:12. We function as adult sons now. Sons want to please their fathers and labor with them out of love when no one is looking. Not as hired people who serve because they have to, but because they want to.] **15 For ye have not received the spirit of bondage again to fear;** [We are not under sin or the law that condemns us, 6:14.] **but ye have received the Spirit of adoption,** [Son-ship, the Spirit in us is the guarantee or down payment of the redemption of the future redemption of the body Eph. 1:13, 14 when the sons of God will be revealed, 8:19.] **whereby we cry, Abba, Father.** [We can call Father God "Daddy" like Christ did Mark 14:36, "Abba" is also mentioned for the third and last time in Gal. 4:6.] **16 The Spirit itself beareth witness with our spirit, that we are the children of God:** [The Holy Spirit confirms with our spirit that we are God's children, since we are in His Son Jesus Christ.] **17 And if children, then heirs; heirs of God, and joint-heirs with Christ;** [Being in Him we share in Christ's inheritance, everything Christ has is ours and everything we have belongs to Him.] **if so be that we suffer with *him*, that we may be also glorified together.** [We suffer because we live in a sinful world (Gal. 1:4) and because we understand the mystery Christ gave to Paul. We are persecuted by the unsaved and by wrong dividers. We "are partakers of the afflictions of the gospel" (2 Tim. 1:8). We "suffer with him" (2 Tim. 2:12) as we try to share the gospel and right division with others (1 Tim. 2:4)]

18 ¶ For I reckon that the sufferings of this present time *are* not worthy *to be compared* with the glory which shall be revealed in us. [We suffer because we live in a sin cursed world (Gen. 3 and Gal. 1:4) but God has a wonderful future glory plan for those who love Him.] **19 For the earnest expectation of the creature** [All living things, creation.] **waiteth for the manifestation of the sons of God.** [To see who will be revealed to be the true sons of God, in the body of Christ at the Rapture and in the kingdom at that resurrection Ezek. 37:12.] **20 For the creature was made subject to vanity, not willingly,** [God cursed creation when Adam sinned, Gen. 3:17.] **but by reason of him who hath subjected *the same* in hope,** [God has promised to redeem creation, Isa. 11:6-10; Acts 3:21.] **21 Because the creature itself also shall be delivered from the bondage of corruption into the glorious liberty of the children of God.** [When Christ restores all.] **22 For we know that the whole creation groaneth and travaileth in pain together until now.** [In the meantime, all creation suffers because it is not as God intended it to be. Satan and his host have not been cast out of the Second heaven yet.] **23 And not only *they*, but ourselves also, which have the firstfruits of the Spirit,** [We have His Spirit and life now (4:25, 8:2).] **even we ourselves**

groan within ourselves, [We and all creation are not as we were meant to be.] **waiting for the adoption, *to wit*, the redemption of our body. 24 For we are saved by hope:** [The confident expectation of being redeemed from the presence of sin at the Rapture.] **but hope that is seen is not hope: for what a man seeth, why doth he yet hope for? 25 But if we hope for that we see not, *then* do we with <u>patience wait for *it*. 26 Likewise the Spirit also helpeth our infirmities: for we know not what we should pray for as we ought: but the Spirit itself maketh intercession for us with groanings which cannot be uttered.</u>** [Prayer is us talking with God. Our infirmities are "the sufferings of this present time" (8:18); living in a fallen world in a mortal fallen body. The Holy Spirit intercedes for us when we pray to the Father.] **27 And he that searcheth the hearts knoweth what *is* the mind of the Spirit, because he maketh intercession for the saints according to *the will of* God.** [The "he" is the Father that relates with the Spirit, God said His will in His word. The mind of the Spirit is the mind of Christ the Word. The Holy Spirit helps us understand His word and to pray.]

28 And we know that <u>all things work together for good to them that love God,</u> [The "all things" are the "sufferings of this present time" (8:11) in a sin cursed world. God uses everything that happens to us to mature us and make us choose the right thing as we follow our "pattern" Paul to follow Christ (1 Cor. 11:1). We learn to beseech others instead of commanding them, to be content in all circumstances, to forgive as God in Christ Jesus has forgiven us. I am still not sure if I would sing at midnight after being tortured, or have enough love in my heart to stop a jailer from committing suicide. The Spirit helps us to say no to the flesh and yes to God. To not grumble or complain. To not be talebearers, to study to be quiet and mind our own business. To be kind and say uplifting things. "Being confident of this very thing, that he which hath begun a good work in you will perform *it* until the day of Jesus Christ" (Phil. 1:6). "For our light affliction, which is but for a moment, worketh for us a far more exceeding *and* eternal weight of glory" (2 Cor. 4:17).] **<u>to them who are the called according to *his* purpose.</u>** [God's purpose is to conform us to Christ.] **29 For <u>whom he did foreknow,</u>** [God, the Creator of the Heaven and the Earth is outside of time and foreknew who would believe but still gave us free will.] **<u>he also did predestinate</u>** [predetermined] ***<u>to be</u>* <u>conformed to the image of his Son,</u>** [God is working in us to conform us to His Son, "holy and without blemish" (Eph. 5:27).] **<u>that he might be the firstborn among many brethren.</u>** [Christ was the first to be in a glorified body prepared for Him, Heb. 10:5.] **30 Moreover <u>whom he did predestinate, them he also called:</u>** [How does God call us? See 2 Thes. 2:14.] **and whom he called, them he also <u>justified</u>: and whom he justified, them he also <u>glorified.</u>** [Past tense our eternal life is a done deal, Rom. 4:17.] **31 <u>What shall we then say to these things?</u>** [What shall we say to all these glorious things?] **If God *be* for us, who *can be* against us?** [Five questions and answers.] **32 He that spared not his own Son, but delivered him up for us all, how shall he not with him also freely give us all things?** [Abraham was a father willing to sacrifice his son, but his son Isaac was also willing to be offered up. God stopped Abraham from slaying his son, Isaac. But God spared not His own Son. Also our Lord Jesus Christ was "obedient unto death, even the death of the cross" (Phil. 2:8). This great love of the Father and the Son is more precious and wondrous than our hearts and minds can comprehend. If God gave us His beloved Son what else shall He not freely give us? Abraham proved that he loved God more than his son. Christ proved that he loved the Father more than Himself. Christ trusted in His Father plan of redemption. He knew that His friends Abraham and Moses and all of us who love Him could not be redeemed any other way.] **33 Who shall lay any thing to the charge of God's elect?** [Christ is God's elect Isa. 42:1 and we, the body of Christ are in Christ and are called "the elect of God" (Col. 3:12).] ***It is* God that justifieth.** [God decided to justify us based upon our faith His Son's perfect sacrifice and imputed righteousness.] **34 Who *is* he that condemneth?** ***It is* Christ that died, yea rather, that is risen again, who is even at the right hand of God, who also maketh intercession for us.** [Satan cannot condemn us, nor the dead flesh. Christ won the victory. His blood atonement satisfied the Father, He rose, and now He is seated at His right hand of power as proof that it is finished. He paid the sin debt mankind owed in full.] **35 Who shall separate us from the love of Christ?** [It is interesting that Paul says who instead of what, then mentions 7 circumstances that Paul himself endured including his beheading.] ***shall* tribulation, or distress, or persecution, or famine, or nakedness, or peril, or sword** [government]**? 36 As it is written, For thy sake we are killed all the day long; we are accounted as sheep for the slaughter**. [This is how Satan sees us.] **37 Nay, in all these things we are more than conquerors through him that loved us.** [Christ is the One who is the Conqueror. Through Him who loved us we are more than conquerors in our circumstances. This is how the Father sees us now, in Christ.] **38 For I am persuaded, that neither death, nor life, nor angels, nor principalities,** [Evil or good.] **nor powers, nor things present,** [In the dispensation of grace.] **nor things to come,** [In the future.] **39 Nor height, nor depth, nor any other creature,** [Not Satan or even ourselves.] **shall be able to separate us from the love of God which is in Christ Jesus our Lord.**

***Note v. 31 the power of God is "for us," v. 32 the grace of God is "for us," vs. 33, 34 the justice of God is for us, and vs. 35-39 the love of God is "for us."]

Romans Chapter 9 Election and rejection of Israel
9:1-5 Paul had a strong burden for Israel's salvation and security.
9:6, 7 They had all the privileges of God yet they are <u>not all</u> "seed of Abraham" who is "the father of all them that believe" (4:11). The children of the flesh are not the children of God, but the children of faith are. Paul under the inspiration of the Holy Spirit says that in the past God elected the nation of Israel to come through Isaac the child of promise that God provided miraculously. The seed-line continued through Isaac. Also, before Rebecca's twins were born, God said that His nation would come through Jacob, not Esau (the elder who would serve the younger). To fulfill His purpose, God as the potter made Israel (a lump of clay in His hands) a vessel of honour. <u>God's purpose to bring in His Son depended on God's decisions and His purposes</u> (election for service, not salvation).
9:8-21 God decides who He will have compassion and mercy on. So then, just as God had hardened Pharaoh's heart, now God has hardened unbelieving nation Israel's heart. **The "thing formed" (Israel) cannot blame their Creator for making them first a "vessel unto honour" and now deciding to make them a "vessel of dishonor." God has decided to show mercy to the Gentiles.**
9:22, 23 God was willing to postpone His wrath. God has endured with much longsuffering the "vessels of wrath fitted for destruction" (unbelieving Gentiles and Jews) so He can "make known the riches of his glory" on the vessels of mercy (little flock and the body of Christ) which were "afore prepared unto glory."
9:24 "Even us [body of Christ believers], **whom he hath called, not of the Jews only, but also of the Gentiles" so that God could show His power.**
9:27 <u>God always had a remnant of believers in the nation of Israel</u>.
9:29 God always "left them a seed" of believers otherwise the nation would have been destroyed like Sodom and Gomorrah.
9:30 The Gentiles "attained the righteousness of God . . . which is of faith."
9:32 The nation of Israel did not follow after righteousness by faith, but thought they could be righteous "by works of the law."
9:33 The nation of Israel stumbled at the stumblingstone because they did not believe in Him, the Lord Jesus Christ. Believers in him will not be ashamed.

Romans 9:1 I say the truth in Christ, I lie not, my conscience also bearing me witness in the Holy Ghost, [Paul had a strong burden for his Jewish kinsmen to be saved into the body of Christ and have the eternal security that he just spoke of in 8:30-39.] **2 That I have <u>great heaviness</u> and continual sorrow in my heart. 3 For I could wish that myself were <u>accursed from Christ</u>** [Paul could wish that God had not saved him so Israel would still have all their privileges.] **for my brethren, <u>my kinsmen according to the flesh</u>:** [He was willing to trade places with the unbelieving Israelites.] **4 Who are Israelites; to whom *pertaineth* the**

adoption, and the <u>glory</u>, and the <u>covenants</u>, and the <u>giving of the law</u>, and the <u>service</u> *of God*, and the <u>promises</u>; **5 Whose** *are* **the father,** [Abraham, Isaac, Jacob] **and <u>of whom</u> as concerning the flesh <u>Christ</u>** *came*, [Jesus was a Jew born under the law, Gal. 4:4] **who** [Christ] **is over all, God blessed for ever. Amen.**

6 ¶ Not as though the <u>word of God</u> hath taken <u>none effect</u>. [Some have been saved, a remnant.] **For they** *are* **<u>not all Israel, which are of Israel</u>:** [Rom. 2:28, true Israel are those that believe God.] **7 <u>Neither, because they are the seed of Abraham,</u>** *are they* **<u>all children: but, In Isaac shall thy seed be called</u>.** [God promised Abraham a son when he was old, and Sarah was barren so that He could fulfill His purpose. God sovereignly decreed by whom the nation's the seed-line would come because He knew they would be believers. The seed-line led to Christ (Gal. 3:16), the promised Redeemer of Gen. 3:15.] **8 That is, They which are the children of the <u>flesh</u>,** [Ishmael, Abraham's son begotten in the flesh by self-effort.] **these** *are* **not the children of God: but the children of the promise are counted for the seed.** [Begotten by faith.] **9 For this** *is* **the word of promise, At this time will I come, and Sara shall have a son. 10 And not only** *this*; **but when Rebecca also had conceived by one,** *even* **by our father Isaac; 11 (<u>For</u>** *the children* **<u>being not yet born, neither having done any good or evil, that the purpose of God according to election might stand</u>, not of works, but of him that calleth;) 12 It was said unto her, <u>The elder shall serve the younger</u>.** [Not only the nation of Edom but all nations will serve Israel in the kingdom.] **13 As it is written, <u>Jacob have I loved, but Esau have I hated</u>.** [God knew Jacob would believe and made him a nation of honor, from Esau came Edom the nation of dishonor, Mal. 1:1-4]

14 ¶ What shall we say then? *Is there* **<u>unrighteousness</u> with God? God forbid.** [No, God is not unrighteous because He has a new agency, the body of Christ. He will yet accomplish His purpose and promise to Israel.] **15 For he saith to Moses, I will have <u>mercy</u> on whom I will have mercy, and I will have compassion on whom I will have compassion.** [God can dispense grace and mercy as He chooses. Paul uses Moses (Ex. 33:19) and Pharaoh (Ex. 9:16) to show that God can do as He wants in showing His grace and mercy. <u>Nobody deserves God's mercy, and no one can condemn God for His choice of forming Israel and not choosing another nation. Nor can anyone condemn God for deciding to show mercy to the Gentiles.</u>] **16 So then** *it is* **<u>not</u> of him that willeth, nor of him that runneth, <u>but of God</u> that sheweth mercy.** [God decides to show mercy to those He chooses. This verse is not talking about individual salvation, but nations.] **17 For the scripture saith unto Pharaoh, Even for this same <u>purpose</u> have I raised thee up, that I might <u>shew my power</u> in thee, and that my name might be declared throughout all the earth.** [God put Pharaoh (representing Egypt) in power knowing he would not let Israel go right away so that God could show His power, Ex. 9:16.] **18 Therefore hath he mercy on whom he will *have mercy*, and whom he will he hardeneth.** [Currently, Israel is temporarily hardened, with a vail over their heart 2 Cor. 3:13, 14; 2 Peter 3, 4, 9, 10, 15, 16.] **19 Thou wilt say then unto me, Why doth he yet find fault? For who hath resisted his will?** [Some will say it is God's fault if someone is not saved since He is in control.] **20 Nay but, O man, who art thou that repliest against God? Shall the thing formed say to him that formed *it*, Why hast thou made me thus?** [Shall someone blame God because he is an unbeliever instead of a believer?] **21 Hath not the potter power over the clay, of the same lump to make one vessel unto honour,** [Peter's group.] **and another unto dishonor?** [unbelieving apostate Israel.] **22 *What* if God, willing to shew *his* wrath, and to make his power known, endured with much longsuffering the vessels of wrath fitted to destruction:**[Unbelieving Jews and Gentiles.] **23 And that he might make known the riches of his glory on the vessels of mercy,** [the "little flock" and the body of Christ are the vessels of mercy.] **which he had afore prepared unto glory,** [Peter's group (1 Peter 2:9). Since before the foundation of the world the body of Christ was prepared for His glory Eph. 1:4, 2:7; 1 Cor. 2:6-8; Col. 1:25-27.] **24 Even us,** [body of Christ believers.] **whom he hath called, not of the Jews only, but also of the Gentiles?** [A believing remnant, Peter's group had been saved into the kingdom on earth (Matt. 19:28), but since the Jerusalem Council only Paul's group is accepting new converts into the body of Christ (Acts 15; Gal. 1:6-9, 2:7-9) by God's mercy.] **25 As he saith also in Osee, I will call them my people, which were not my people;** [These verses are speaking about Peter's group being called "my people" before, during, and after the Tribulation. Osee is Greek for Hosea be sure to read Hosea 1:8-10, 2:23, 1 Peter 2:9, 10.] **and her beloved, which was not beloved.** [God will reform Israel to be a vessel of honor again.] **26 And it shall come to pass, *that* in the place where it was said unto them, Ye *are* not my people; there shall they be called the children of the living God. 27 Esaias** [Greek for Isaiah.] **also crieth concerning Israel, Though the number of the children of Israel be as the sand of the sea, a remnant shall be saved:** [God has always had a remnant of believers even in Elijah's day. Peter's group is His believing remnant, "the little flock" (Luke 12:32).] **28 For he will finish the work, and cut *it* short in righteousness: because a short work will the Lord make upon the earth.** [I believe the short work is twofold, referring to both Daniel's 70th week (the Tribulation) and God's work calling believers on earth. God is calling out two groups of people to populate the Heaven and the Earth in a mere 7,000 years. Why will He cut the work short? Because "except those days should be shortened, there should no flesh be saved" (Matt. 24:22). After Antichrist signs the covenant with apostate Israel mentioned in Dan. 9:26 there will be a seven-year Tribulation with much destruction.] **29 And as Esaias** said before, **Except the Lord of <u>Sabaoth</u>** [Lord of the armies.] **had left us <u>a seed</u>, we had been as <u>Sodoma</u>, and been made like unto <u>Gomorrha</u>.** [Unless God left Israel a remnant they would have been <u>completely destroyed</u>, Isa. 1:4-9, 4:2-4; 10:21-23, God will bring forth "a seed out of Jacob" 65:8, 9; Zech. 13:8, 9. God will never totally destroy Israel. God will finish regaining back the earth from Satan and to rule it in righteousness.] **30 What shall we say then? That the <u>Gentiles</u>, which followed not after righteousness, have attained to righteousness, even the righteousness which is of <u>faith</u>.** [The Gentiles, who <u>previously had nothing to do with God (Eph. 2:11, 12), can now have God's righteousness by faith in Christ</u> (Eph. 2:13). They believed Paul's gospel Rom. 3:22-26, 4:5, were saved and became members of the body of Christ because they had faith to believe what Christ had done for them.] **31 <u>But Israel</u>, which followed after the law of righteousness, hath <u>not</u> attained to the law of righteousness. 32 Wherefore? Because *they sought it* <u>not by faith</u>, but as it were <u>by the works</u> of the law.** [Unbelieving apostate Israel did not seek righteousness by faith in Christ, but tried to be righteous in themselves by trying to keep the law.] **For they stumbled at that <u>stumblingstone</u>;** [Christ is the stumbling stone (Gen. 49:24, Isa. 8:13-16; 28:16 1 Peter 2:4-10; Matt. 21:42-44, and Israel's Rock 1 Cor. 1:23, 10:4; Deut. 32:18, 30, 31). Israel did not receive and believe their Redeemer. They were looking for a Messiah who would set them free from their Roman captors. They did not realize that they had to be redeemed from bondage to sin and Satan. Instead, in their ignorance, Israel demanded His crucifixion.] **33 As it is written, Behold, I lay in <u>Sion</u>** [capital of Israel, where Christ was crucified] **a stumblingstone and <u>rock of offence</u>: and <u>whosoever believeth on him</u> shall <u>not</u> be ashamed.** [Not ashamed at the GWTJ. Isa. 45:17-25. The builders of the temple were the religious Jewish leaders, who left out the corner stone. <u>Jesus was an offence to Israel's corrupt religious system</u>, Matt. 23, but those who trust that He was Israel's Christ are not ashamed. At Christ's Second Coming Israel will say that He is their potter, their Creator. "But <u>we are all as an unclean thing, and all our righteousnesses are as filthy rags</u>; [The believing remnant of Israel will <u>confess their sins</u> in the Tribulation and believe God.] and we all do fade as a leaf; and our iniquities, like the wind, have taken us away . . . <u>But now, O LORD, thou art our father; we are the clay, and thou our potter; and we all are the work of thy hand</u>" (Isa. 64:6-8). That is so wonderfully amazing!]

SO THEN FAITH COMETH BY HEARING, AND HEARING BY THE WORD OF GOD.

ROMANS 10:17

Romans Chapter 10 Present salvation opportunity for individual Jews
10:1-13 The nation stumbled, but individual Jews can believe Christ is the end of the law for righteousness as proved by the Father raising Him from the dead; and have Christ's righteousness by faith, not by keeping the law.
10:14-21 God is saving a Jewish remnant through Paul during Acts using "no people," the Gentiles and "a foolish nation" little flock (Deut. 32:21; Isa. 65:1).

Romans 10:1 Brethren, <u>my heart's desire and prayer</u> to God for <u>Israel</u> is, that <u>they might be saved</u>. [During the Acts period, Paul prayed and traveled to synagogues everywhere preaching so that a remnant of Israel might be saved.] **2 For I bear them record that they have <u>a zeal</u> of God, but not according to <u>knowledge</u>.** [Like Paul when he persecuted the "little flock" and was "zealous toward God" they didn't know that <u>Jesus of Nazareth</u> (Acts 22:8) really was their Messiah.] **3 For they being <u>ignorant of God's righteousness</u>, and going about to establish their own righteousness, have not submitted themselves unto the righteousness of God. 4 For <u>Christ _is_ the end of the law for righteousness to every one that believeth</u>.** [They are ignorant the God is willing to impute His Son's righteousness by faith to them. They were seeking their own righteousness by trying to keep the law.] **5 For Moses describeth the righteousness which is of the <u>law</u>, That the man which <u>doeth</u> those things shall <u>live by them</u>.** [Lev. 18:5; James 2:10. The law must be kept perfectly which is something only Jesus Christ could do.] **6 But the righteousness which is of faith speaketh on this wise, Say not in thine heart, Who shall ascend into heaven? (that is, to bring Christ down _from above_:) 7 Or, Who shall descend into the deep? (that is, to bring up Christ again from the dead.) 8 But what saith it? <u>The word is nigh thee</u>, _even_ in thy <u>mouth</u>, and in thy <u>heart</u>: that is, the <u>word of faith</u>, <u>which we preach</u>;** [Paul said you do not have to go anywhere, Christ is found in God's word, to have His righteousness <u>just believe the gospel</u> "we preach" (Deut. 30:11-14).] **9 That if thou shalt confess <u>with thy mouth the Lord Jesus</u>, and shalt <u>believe in thine heart</u>** [The soul] **that God hath raised him from the dead, thou shalt be <u>saved</u>.** [If they believe in their heart that Jesus Christ, the Son of God finished the work of the cross as evidence by God raising Him from the dead they will be saved. It is faith in His work ALONE that saves.] **10 For with the <u>heart man believeth unto righteousness</u>; and with the mouth confession is made unto salvation.** [For with the heart man believes and receives righteousness and with the mouth of the soul <u>declaration to God is made that he believes that Jesus Christ really is the Son of God who died for his sins and that God really did raise Him from the dead.</u>] **11 For the scripture saith, Whosoever <u>believeth</u> on him shall not be <u>ashamed</u>.** [Anyone that believes will not be ashamed when God judges (Isa. 28:16).] **12 For there is <u>no difference between the Jew and the Greek</u>: for the same Lord over**

all is <u>rich</u> unto all that call upon him. [Both individual Jews and Gentiles are saved by believing the gospel and having the imputed righteousness of Christ.] **13 For <u>whosoever</u> shall <u>call</u> upon the name of the Lord shall be saved.** [Israel must realize that Jesus of Nazareth is the Messiah, and be saved by trusting in Paul's gospel. All Jews and Gentiles can be saved into the body of Christ by believing Rom. 3:21-26).] **14 <u>How</u> then shall they <u>call</u> on him in whom they have not believed? and how shall they believe in him of whom they have not heard? and how shall they hear without a preacher? 15 And how shall they preach, except they be sent? as it is written, How beautiful are the feet of them that preach the <u>gospel of peace</u>, and bring <u>glad tidings of good things</u>!** [Israel has heard the preaching of Jesus Christ by the believing remnant (Peter's group), but Israel did not all obey (believe) the gospel. How beautiful are the feet of those who preach the gospel of peace!] **16 But they have not all <u>obeyed</u>** [Believed] **<u>the gospel</u>. For Esaias saith, Lord, who hath <u>believed our report</u>?** [Isa. 53:1, just like in Isaiah's day Israel is resistant to believing the little flock.] **17 <u>So then faith *cometh* by hearing, and hearing by the word of God</u>.** [The sinner cannot be saved some mystical way apart from hearing the word of God, so tell them the word. The power is in His word!] **18 But I say, Have they not heard?** [Psa. 19:4; Col. 1:23] **<u>Yes</u> verily, their sound went into <u>all the earth</u>, and their words unto the ends of the world.** [Israel heard the gospel.] **19 But I say, Did not Israel know? First Moses saith, I will provoke you** [unbelieving Israel] **to <u>jealousy</u> by *them that are* no people,** [The little flock, Deut. 32:21] ***and* by a foolish nation.** ["A" singular is the remnant, the "little flock."] **I will anger you** [unbelieving Israel.] **20 But Esaias is very bold, and saith, <u>I was found of them that sought me not</u>; I was made manifest unto them that <u>asked not after me</u>.** [The believing remnant is again referred to as the ones who found Messiah, Isa. 65:1.] **21 <u>But to Israel</u>** [the unbelieving nation] **he saith, All day long I have stretched forth my hands unto a disobedient and gainsaying people.** [But apostate, disobedient, arguing Israel would not come into His open arms. They have resisted and opposed His many offers while others have believed.]

ROMANS 11: 13 KJB

13 FOR I SPEAK TO YOU GENTILES, INASMUCH AS I AM THE APOSTLE OF THE GENTILES, I MAGNIFY MINE OFFICE:

Romans Chapter 11 Has God Cast Away His People?
11:1-6 Peter's group was elected serve God by His grace.
11:7-10 Election (Peter's group was saved) and the rest were blinded.
11:11, 12, 15, 25 The nation of Israel has temporarily been blinded, postponed
11:13 Paul is the apostle of the Gentiles.
11:17 <u>Gentiles are graft into the olive tree and have access to God.</u>
11:25 Israel is blinded in part so that God can give the Gentiles a salvation opportunity until the "fulness of the Gentiles" (Rapture).
11:26 After that, God will resume His prophesied dealings with Israel.
11:31-36 Paul is jubilant because by joining in the Gentiles' mercy, individual Jews may also be saved in this age. God has declared all people to be in unbelief so that He can show mercy to anyone that does believe (Gal. 3:22).

Romans 11: 1 I say then, <u>Hath God cast away his people</u>? God forbid. For I also am an Israelite, of the seed of Abraham, of the tribe of Benjamin. [The fact that individual Jews (like Paul) can still be saved from the penalty of their sin, proves that God has not cast off His people Israel. Rather, He has given them another opportunity to be His people and have eternal life, along with Gentiles, in the body of Christ.] **2 God hath not cast away his people which he <u>foreknew</u>.** [Before God formed Israel, He had a plan for them to be His holy nation of priests, ruling on earth (Ex 19:6; Isa. 2:1-4, 60:1-3, 12). God is giving them another chance to be in the body of Christ.] **Wot** [Know.] **ye not what the scripture saith of <u>Elias</u>? how he maketh intercession to God against <u>Israel</u>, saying, 3 Lord, they have killed thy prophets, and digged down thine altars; and I am left alone, and they seek my life. 4 But what saith the answer of God unto him? I have reserved to myself <u>seven thousand men</u>, who have not bowed the <u>knee *to the image*</u> of Baal. 5 Even so then <u>at this present time</u> also there is a <u>remnant</u> according to the <u>election of grace</u>. 6 And if by <u>grace</u>, then is it no more of <u>works: otherwise grace is no more grace</u>. But if it be of works, then is it <u>no more grace</u>: otherwise work is no more work.** [This verse is not talking about salvation, but about God electing or choosing Peter's group for His service. As in Elias' day when God had a remnant of seven thousand, there is a remnant (Peter's group) according to election of God grace, not works. They were <u>elected to serve by God and were still alive when Paul wrote this letter</u>. Just like in Elias' day when it seemed that all of Israel was against God (1 Kings 19), God knew those that were His, even if they were not standing with Elias. God has not cast away His people, for He saved a remnant of Jews, the "<u>little flock</u>" (Luke 12:32). They will be His nation of priests to evangelize the Gentiles in the millennial kingdom (Ex. 19:5, 6; 1 Peter 2:9). In the Tribulation, more will be added to this believing remnant, Peter's group.]

7 ¶ What then? Israel [The nation.] **hath not obtained that which he seeketh for;** [*Notice not called she, because that Israel is not His Bride at this time. They were seeking for eternal life with God.] **but the election** [Peter's group and the remnant of Jews saved by Paul into the body of Christ during Acts.] **hath obtained it, and the rest were blinded** [The apostate nation of Israel.] **8 (According as it is written, God hath given them the spirit of slumber, eyes that they should not see, and ears that they should not hear;) unto this day.** [Isa. 6:9, 10; Jer. 5:21, 6:10; Ezek. 12:2; Matt. 13:14; Jn. 12:40; Acts 28:26. The prophets, Jesus Christ and Paul all said that they are not be able to see or hear because their hearts are uncircumcised. Paul's first apostolic miracle was a picture of Israel's national blindness. The blinding of the Jewish sorcerer who tried to prevent a Gentile from being saved "for a season" Acts 13:11.] **9 And David saith, Let their table be made a snare,** [God's provisions became a snare because of the pride of Israel.] **and a trap, and a stumblingblock, and a recompence unto them:** [Let them get what they deserve.] **10 Let their eyes be darkened, that they may not see, and bow down their back always.** ["Loins to continually shake" (Psalm 69:23) under the burden of their sin.] **11 I say then, Have they stumbled** [They stumbled over Christ, their rock of offence at the cross Rom. 9:31-33; Isa. 8:13-15; 28:16.] **that they should fall?** [Christ prayed on the cross that "Father forgive them" (Luke 23:34). Even after Christ's resurrection, and during the renewed offer of the kingdom in Acts 1-7 God was still speaking only to Israel (for example Acts 2:5, 14, 22, 36, 3:12, 25, 5:30, 31).] **God forbid: but rather through their fall salvation is come unto the Gentiles,** [So they did fall after she stumbled at the cross they fell at the stoning of Stephen in Acts 7. The Holy Ghost had come down in Acts 2 and empowered the believing remnant. Stephen summarized Israel's rebellion when he called them "uncircumcised" (Acts 7:51). This meant that they had broken God's covenant, and were no better than the Gentiles (Gen. 17:10-14; Rom. 2:25-27). Israel fell when the religious leaders (who represented the nation) demonstrated that they refused to believe that Jesus was their Messiah by stoning Stephen to death.] **for to provoke them to jealousy.** [God's favor to the Gentiles in mystery causes the Jews to be jealous so that they may be saved in this new dispensation.] **12 Now if the fall of them be the riches of the world, and the diminishing of them the riches of the Gentiles;** [The riches of the world is direct access to God without having to go through Israel. Israel fell from being God's preferred nation and diminished during Acts. They rejected Peter and the Holy Ghost filled remnant of believers that had trusted that Jesus was their Messiah when He was on earth committing the unforgivable blasphemy of the Holy Ghost, Matt. (12:31, 32). And then they rejected the Holy Spirit filled Paul (Acts 13:46, 18:6, 28:28). Paul's frequent visits to the synagogues were to notify the lost Jews that they now needed to be saved through his ministry.] **how much more their**

fulness? [Israel has fallen temporarily, but God will resume His dealing with them. How much more glorious will her rise be when the nation is saved at His return?]

13 ¶ For I speak to you Gentiles, inasmuch as I am the apostle of the Gentiles, I magnify mine office: [Paul's motive for magnifying his office is to win his kinsmen. *Notice the mini-timeline: stumbled at the cross, fell at the stoning of Stephen, then Paul saved on the road to Damascus. His office as apostle of the Gentiles was given to him by Christ after his unique salvation on the road to Damascus in Acts 9. Paul is the only one to write to the body of Christ about the dispensation of grace . . . that was kept secret (Eph. 3:1-6; Rom. 16:25, 26.] **14 If by any means I may provoke to emulation them which are my flesh, and might save some of them** [Paul had a distinct ministry and hoped to save his kinsmen.] **15 For if the casting away of them** [Those in the apostate nation who did not believe were cast away.] **be the reconciling of the world,** [The world's people have an opportunity to be saved directly by believing the gospel of grace in the dispensation of grace, apart from the prophetic program of Israel (blessing Israel), apart from keeping their laws (water baptism and circumcision, and so on).] **what shall the receiving of them be, but life from the dead?** [Israel will have their national sins atoned at the Second Coming (our sins are atoned now, 5:11), and will have His Spirit and eternal life in eternal bodies. God will resurrect them in the kingdom and there will be a great Gentile revival on earth.] **16 For if the firstfruit be holy,** [The remnant (Peter's group) also a holy beginning of the nation through Abraham and his seed through Isaac, Jacob, and the 12.] **the lump is also holy:** [Jer. 18:4-6] **and if the root be holy, so are the branches. 17 And if some of the branches be broken off, and thou,** ["Thou" is the Gentiles.] **being a wild olive tree, wert graffed in among them, and with them partakest of the root** [Jesus the "root of Jesse" (Rom. 15:12).] **and fatness of the olive tree;** [The blessing of a chance for eternal life (Psa. 52:8; Gal. 3:14-16).] **18 Boast not against the branches.** [Unbelieving Israel, broken branches Jer. 11:16.] **But if thou boast, thou bearest not the root, but the root thee.** [Don't boast you have a temporary opportunity by God's grace.] **19 Thou wilt say then, The branches were broken off, that I might be graffed in. 20 Well; because of unbelief they were broken off, and thou standest by faith.** [This opportunity to believe Christ is because of Israel's unbelief.] **Be not highminded, but fear: 21 For if God spared not the natural branches,** [Israel.] **take heed lest he also spare not thee** [the body of Christ]. **22 Behold therefore the goodness and severity of God: on them which fell, severity;** [Israel has been postponed for nearly 2,000 years.] **but toward thee, goodness, if thou continue in his goodness: otherwise thou also shalt be cut off.** [Those not saved into the body of Christ will be "cut off" at the Rapture.] **23 And they also, if they abide not still in unbelief, shall be graffed**

in: for God is able to graff them in again. [When they believe in the future, God will graft them in and give them access to Him.] **24 For if thou wert cut out of the olive tree which is wild by nature, and wert graffed contrary to nature into a good olive tree:** [A graft is usually a better branch cut in from a good olive tree, NOT a wild inferior one. God had put the Gentiles aside in Gen. 11, but now He shows mercy.] **how much more shall these, which be the natural branches, be graffed into their own olive tree?** [Israel is the natural branch of the olive tree.]

25 ¶ For I would not, brethren, that ye should be ignorant of this mystery, lest ye should be wise in your own conceits; that blindness in part is happened to Israel, until the fulness of the Gentiles be come in. [The "fulness of the Gentiles" is the Rapture. Israel is partially (not totally) blinded in two ways: first Paul communicated to the leaders of the little flock that God had begun a new dispensation and was forming the body of Christ through his ministry in Acts 15 and in Galatians, they "saw" and "perceived" (Gal. 2:7-9) so they were not blind. Second, since individual Jews can be saved today the nation is blinded, but not the individual. However, a vail is over their hearts which is taken away when they believe (2 Cor. 3:13-16).] **26 And so all Israel shall be saved: as it is written, There shall come out of Sion the Deliverer [Christ], and shall turn away ungodliness from Jacob:** [All believing remnant that survive the Tribulation will be saved at His Second Coming Isa. 59:20, 21.] **27 For this is my covenant unto them,** [This is a covenant that God has promised to Israel that He will not be angry with them forever. God will make them His people again. Then at that time He will implement His New Covenant, (Jer. 31:31-34, Heb. 8:8-12, Isa. 59:20, 21, and Ezek. 36:24-28) God will supernaturally cause Israel to keep the law by writing it in their heart and minds, so they will keep the law and stop sinning with His Spirit in them. God can then give them all physical blessings and promises for obedience, instead of curses (Ex. 23:25-27; Deut. 7:12-16; 28:1-28.] **when I shall take away their sins.** [God will take away Israel's sins at Christ's Second Coming. No one is sin free currently so we are not under the New Covenant now. But the body of Christ believers have already been forgiven all trespasses at salvation (Col. 2:13, Eph. 4:32) because they have His righteousness.] **28 As concerning the gospel, they are enemies for your sakes:** [Jews generally do not want to believe that Jesus of Nazareth is the Christ who died for their sins, was buried and rose again the third day according to the scriptures.] **but as touching the election, they are beloved for the fathers' sakes.** [God will keep His promises to their fathers (Deut. 4:37, 7:6-8, 10:15). Believing Israel is part of God future plan for Israel to be a kingdom of priests to evangelize Gentiles in prophecy (Ex. 19:6; 1 Peter 2:9).] **29 For the gifts and calling of God are without repentance.** [God will not change His mind about giving them the gift of eternal life in Him.] **30 For as ye in times**

past have not believed God, [Rom. 1:18-32; Eph. 2:11-13] **yet have now obtained mercy through their unbelief:** [Israel was to be a blessing, but now Gentiles have mercy.] **31 Even so have these also now not believed, that through your mercy they also may obtain mercy**. [While God is dispensing grace and mercy on the Gentiles the individual Jews can be saved also, especially if the Gentiles share the gospel with them. This is the <u>opposite</u> of Israel's program. Paul committed the <u>blasphemy of the Holy Ghost</u> which would not be forgiven (Matt. 12:31, 32) yet because God has interrupted Prophecy and inserted the Mystery, Paul was forgiven and became the first member of the body of Christ, our pattern (1 Tim. 1:12-17).] **32 For <u>God hath concluded them all in unbelief, that he might have mercy upon all.</u>** [God has concluded all in unbelief so all can be saved by faith in Christ's work on Calvary. His substitutionary death for our sins and give them His imputed righteousness (2 Cor. 5:21).]

33 ¶ <u>O the depth of the riches both of the wisdom and knowledge of God! how unsearchable</u> are his judgments, and <u>his ways past finding out!</u> [Paul marvels at the wisdom of God. His great plan was so unsearchable that no one knew it, not even Satan, "for had they know it, they would not have crucified the Lord of glory" (1 Cor. 2:8). If Satan would have known that God would not only reclaim the earth, but also the heavenly places, and give the Israelites another chance in a new dispensation then Satan would not have crucified our Saviour. Paul is ecstatic because he is so thrilled that God has introduced a new dispensation so that not only he (who was a former blasphemer, see 1 Tim. 1:11-17) can be saved but also his kinsmen, and anyone who would believe the gospel of grace (Acts 13:38, 39, 20:24.] **34 For <u>who hath known the mind of the Lord? or who hath been his counsellor?</u>** [No one knew "the things that God hath prepared for them who love him. But God has revealed them unto us by his Spirit" through His word (1 Cor. 2:9, 10). "Wherein he hath abounded toward us in all wisdom and prudence" (Eph. 1:8). God is a giver. He had no counsellor. No one was in on God's plan, it was a complete secret until He revealed it to us through Paul (Eph. 3:1-9.)] **35 Or <u>who hath first given to him, and it shall be recompensed unto him again?</u>** [God came up with His plan on His own, so He does not owe anything to anyone.] **36 <u>For of him, and through him, and to him, are all things: to whom be glory for ever. Amen.</u>** [Paul brakes out in a jubilant praise of God's magnificent wisdom. It is God, who "worketh all things after the counsel of his own will" (Eph. 1:11). <u>Paul is so happy because he has realized that God has made a way to save both Jews and Gentiles in this age of amnesty in which we live (2 Cor. 5:19). In the future Millennial Kingdom, Gentiles will have a 1,000-year opportunity to be saved.</u>) All things are of God, through Him, and to Him. To Him be all glory forever!]

The Wild Olive Branch Explained

Paul is speaking to Gentiles (11:13). The "thou" (11:17) is the "Gentiles" NOT the Body of Christ. The Gentile opportunity to stand by faith ends at their fullness.

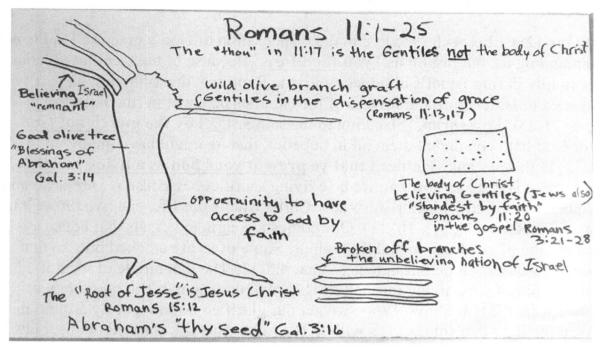

The Trees of Israel (Judges 9:7-15)
Olive Tree – represents the spiritual life of Israel (access and communication with God). The body of Christ has spiritual advantages (imputation, justification, forgiveness, sanctification, etc.), not physical promises about a land and a nation (Gen.12:2, 13:15; Psa. 52:8; Jer. 11:16) and spiritual promises (resurrection and eternal life). The root is Abraham's "thy seed" (Gal. 3:14-16) which is Christ "the root of Jesse" (Romans 15:12), the fatness is blessings through Christ.

Vine – represents Israel's national life (Psa. 80:8-16; Isa. 5:1-7; John 15:1-5).

Fig – Israel's legal-religious system (faith) (Luke13:6-9).

Bramble – represents Israel when in rebellion against God.

It is significant that Paul uses the olive tree (access opportunity to God) in his illustration in Romans 11. It is the **only** one of the four trees that can apply to us since Abraham was a Gentile when he trusted that God would give him an heir (a son) and received the imputed righteousness of God by faith (Gen. 15:6). We receive the righteousness of Christ, there is no salvation apart from being in Christ.

49

Romans Chapter 12 How do we live a life of service to God?
12:1-8 How to live a life of Christian service for the **glory of God**.
12:9-16 How to serve all men especially those in the faith.
12:17-21 How to treat those outside the body of Christ and our enemies.

Romans 12:1 I beseech [We live in the dispensation of God's grace so Paul is not commanding us, but urging us.] **you therefore,** [Because of the Gentile salvation opportunity during Israel's blindness until the Rapture, "that blindness in part Is happened to Israel, until the fulness of the Gentiles be come in [the Rapture]" (Rom. 11:25).] **brethren,** [Speaking to the saints, 1:7.] **by the mercies of God,** ["For God hath concluded them all in unbelief, that he might have <u>mercy</u> upon all" (11:32) both Jews and Gentiles.] **that ye <u>present your bodies a living sacrifice,</u>** [A sacrifice is dead so how can we be a living sacrifice? Because we are dead and have been crucified with Christ, so now Christ who is our life, can live through us (Gal. 2:20, Rom. 6:4, 8:2, 10, 11). <u>Our bodies are earthen vessels that house a treasure, the life of Jesus in and through us.</u> Some of us are cracked pots so that more of Jesus can shine through us (2 Cor. 4:7-11) The magnitude of what it means to have Christ living through us is hard to understand. But by faith, we believe what the Bible says. When we get our glorified bodies and fly around in heaven the light that shines in us will be His light. <u>This life is not about us, but about Christ and what He has done and serving Him and His people.</u>] **holy,** [Christ in us is holy.] **acceptable unto God,** [We are accepted because of him (Eph. 1:6).] **which is your reasonable service.** [Since God has done all this for us, it is only reasonable that we should want to serve Him (1 Cor. 6:19, 20; 2 Cor. 5:14, 15).] **2 And be <u>not conformed to this world:</u>** [Satan is the "god of this world" (2 Cor. 4:4), and the "prince of the power of the air" (Eph. 2:2) we need to make sure that we are not sucked into watching TV (the airwaves) or wasting our time on social media or on other pursuits that have no eternal value. We are to be conformed to "the image of his Son" (Rom. 8:29). We conform to Christ by reading, studying and meditating on His word (Col. 3:16, 17).] **but be ye transformed by the renewing of your mind,** [We are renewing (ongoing) our minds by reading the Bible (Eph. 4:22-24; Col. 3:6-13) so we can have the "mind of Christ" (1 Cor. 2:16) and make the right decisions because we think like Christ. We need to control our minds moment by moment (2 Cor. 10:5). We need to reprogram our minds with the truth of His word rightly divided.] **that ye may prove what is that good, and acceptable, and perfect, will of God.** [We need to join into what He is doing, and promote His good, and acceptable, and perfect will (1 Tim. 2:4; Phil. 1:9-11; Eph. 1:9, 10; Col. 1:9, 10, 25 28). We need to walk by faith and be led by the Spirit (2 Cor. 5:7; Gal. 5:16) God's word is complete now, so we do not expect

God to speak to us in any other way (2 Tim. 3:16, 17). Remember Christ is in us; He is our resource (Col. 1:27).]

3 ¶ For I say, through the grace given unto <u>me</u>, [Christ made Paul our apostle.] **to every man that is among you, not to think of himself more highly than he ought to think;** [God is showing the Gentiles mercy because of Israel's unbelief. Gentiles have an opportunity to be eternally saved from the penalty of our sin, justified by the faith of Jesus, having received His imputed righteousness, we will spend eternity with Him in glory – all because of what our Lord Jesus Christ did for us. We have no goodness or merit apart from Him (Rom. 3:10-12). We have what we have because we have received it of Him (1 Cor. 4:3, 7).] **but to <u>think soberly</u>,** [Cautiously.] **according as God hath dealt to every man the <u>measure of faith</u>.** [We all had faith to believe, now by studying God's word our faith grows (10:17).] **4 For as we have many members in <u>one body</u>, and all members have not the same office:** [A body is made up of different parts, fingers, toes, eyes, and ears that function differently but together, controlled by the brain. Likewise, each believer has a different function in the <u>body of Christ</u> in their service for God.] **5 So we, being many, are <u>one body in Christ</u>, and every one members one of another.** [We are one organism, agency, or team; the one new man (Eph. 2:15).]

6 Having then <u>gifts differing according to the grace that is given to us, whether prophecy, let us</u> *prophesy* <u>according to the proportion of faith</u>; [Sign gifts were still in effect when <u>Romans was written in Acts 20 and did not end until Acts 28</u>. There is so much confusion today about sign gifts. <u>Let us distinguish between talents, spiritual (sign) gifts, and the life of Christ in us as our resource</u>. We learn from each other because everyone is valuable but have different strengths, capabilities, and functions. Talents are skills in things like music, art, sports, and so on, they are a result of heredity, environment, and hard work. Talents are not spiritual gifts and even unsaved people who are dead to God have talents. Some spiritual gifts were promised to Israel as a sign of their impending kingdom on earth (Isa. 35:5, 6; Mark 16:17, 18; Luke 9:1, 2). When God postponed the kingdom these gifts were briefly carried over into our time period to verify to the Jews that Paul's ministry was from God (Acts 15:12, 19:11, 12, 28:9). Other gifts were given to inform and edify the <u>new</u> body of Christ when there was little or no scripture written for it yet (1 Cor. 12:7-11, 28, 14:26; Eph. 4:8, 11-14). All these sign gifts <u>ceased</u> when the full revelation for the body of Christ was made known to Paul and written (1 Cor. 13:8-12). Now that the scripture is complete and fulfilled (Col. 1:25), it is everything we need to be edified and made "perfect, throughly furnished unto all good works" (2 Tim. 3:16, 17). Today we still have pastors, evangelists, and teachers (2 Tim. 2:2; 4:5) but they are <u>not supernaturally</u>

filled with knowledge. Today they have to desire the office (I Tim. 3:1) and study the scriptures to be approved unto God (2 Tim. 2:15). Remember that Romans is one of Paul's early letters still written during the Acts period when he was still going to the Jews in the synagogues first and then to the Gentiles. By the end of Acts Paul stops going to the Jew first and just goes to the Gentiles (Acts 28:28) and the sign gifts stopped. Remember from chapter 8 that all three Persons of the Godhead are Spirit. We have all three in us. Therefore, "Holy Spirit" can refer to any One of the Godhead, while Holy Ghost refers to the third member of the Godhead. The context will help us determine which Spirit is being referred to. The Holy Spirit uses His word to teach us and to work effectually in us (1 Thess. 2:13). There is power in His blood and there is power in His word. Knowledge is power. God wants us to use the power in His word, with His motivation, to edify His body, to help the body of Christ to grow and thrive (Eph. 4:11-16 * There are no apostles or prophets today. There are evangelists, pastors, and teachers but they are not supernaturally gifted.) We are to study and teach the things that we have learned from Paul's letters (2 Tim. 2:2; 1 Cor. 4:16, 17, 11:1, 14:37). Therefore, the power of Christ living in us is far superior to having spiritual gifts. We must allow Him to live out His life through us, this is how He manifests Himself to the world today (1 Tim. 3:16). We do not need spiritual gifts because we have His word and Christ living through us.] **7 Or ministry, let us wait on our ministering: or he that teacheth, on teaching;** [The gifts in verses 7 and 8 apply to us today (but we are not supernatural endowed). Ministry (serving) and teaching are things that can be done by every one of us today because they depend on knowledge of the word of God, not on having a supernatural gift.] **8 Or he that exhorteth, on exhortation:** [We encourage and comfort others with our blessed hope (2 Cor. 1:4, 4:16, 17; 1 Thess. 4:13-18).] **he that giveth, let him do it with simplicity;** [Let us give so others may be saved and know the truth. Whether it is time, treasure, talents, or whatever giving is meant for God to see and not men (2 Cor. 8:1-7, 9:7).] **he that ruleth, with diligence;** [This may refer to the "overseers" of the church (Acts 20:28), also called bishops and elders (1 Tim. 3:1-7; Titus 1:5-9). This could also be the ruling of the home, or over people.] **he that sheweth mercy, with cheerfulness.** [Cheerfully not giving someone what they deserve, but forgiving them (Eph. 4:32)].

9 ¶ Let love be without dissimulation. [Without hypocrisy, not false or with an ulterior motive.] **Abhor that which is evil;** [Hate evil, like God does. I must admit that I hate the modern bible versions. I, myself, was deceived by one of the counterfeit bibles, the NKJV which are devoid of the Holy Spirit for more than 15 years, until I learned better.] **cleave to that which is good.** [I trust the King James Bible.] **10 Be kindly affectioned** ["Walk in love as Christ also hath loved us" (Eph. 5:2)] **one to another with brotherly love;** [Show genuine love and care for

52

each other like in a family.] **in honour preferring one another;** [Esteem others better than yourselves.] **11 Not slothful** [lazy] **in business; fervent** [enthusiastic] **in spirit; serving the Lord;** ["And whatsoever ye do, do it heartily, as to the Lord, and not unto men" (Col. 3:23).] **12 Rejoicing in hope;** [Of the Rapture.] **patient in tribulation** [Present sufferings.] **continuing instant in prayer;** [Pray (talk) to God often.] **13 Distributing to the necessity of saints;** [Share, including financially to a worthwhile cause, person, or ministry.] **given to hospitality.** [Welcome, invite and care for people in your home or restaurant, etc.]. **14 Bless them which persecute you:** [Speak well of.] **bless, and curse not** [Speak badly of.] **15 Rejoice with them that do rejoice,** [Joy with those who rejoice (1 Cor. 12:25-27).] **and weep with them that weep.** [Show empathy with those who are sad.] **16 Be of the same mind one toward another.** [We in the body of Christ should be thinking the same thing. There is a seven-fold unity in the body (Eph. 4:3-6) our common purpose is to exalt the Lord Jesus Christ.] **Mind not high things, but condescend to men of low estate.** [Treat people kindly regardless of social standing.] **Be not wise in your own conceits.** [Be humble. Don't think you are something (Pro. 26:12).] **17 Recompense to no man evil for evil,** [1 Thess. 5:15, 22]. **Provide things honest in the sight of all men. 18 If it be possible, as much as lieth in you, live peaceably with all men. 19 Dearly beloved, avenge not yourselves, but rather give place** [Make room for and trust that God will judge rightly.] **unto wrath: for it is written, Vengeance is mine; I will repay, saith the Lord. 20 Therefore if thine enemy hunger, feed him; if he thirst, give him drink: for in so doing thou shalt heap coals of fire on his head.** [This is a quote from Prov. 25:21, 22. When we do good to someone their sinfulness is pointed out to them, and they get a small reminder of the Lake of Fire that awaits them. So they have a chance now to do something about it before the Great White Judgment when it will be too late. This is why doing good is better for our enemy and more powerful than doing evil, because only more evil can come from evil] **21 Be not overcome of evil, but overcome evil with good.** [If we return evil for evil we have been overcome by evil. But if we do not seek revenge, but do good to all men (Gal. 6:10) including our enemies, then we have overcome evil with good. Then evil has failed to affect your inner peace (Gal. 5:22, 23) and to distract us from God's purposes (2 Cor. 4:5, 6, 6:4-10).]

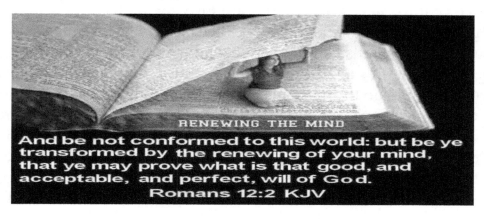

RENEWING THE MIND

And be not conformed to this world: but be ye transformed by the renewing of your mind, that ye may prove what is that good, and acceptable, and perfect, will of God.
Romans 12:2 KJV

Romans Chapter 13 Living with government
13:1-7 God has set up governmental structures in heaven and earth to maintain law and order for the believers good. Christians are to be good citizens. **13:8-14 How to show love to our neighbor. Love is seeking the other person's highest good.** We should love our neighbor as ourselves. Our motive should be to edify others. When we love others we automatically fulfill the law.

Romans 13:1 Let every soul be subject unto the <u>higher powers</u>. [Governmental powers Titus 3:1, 2; 1 Peter 2:13-15.] **For there is no power but of God: the powers that be are <u>ordained of God</u>.** [God has set up governmental structures in heaven and on earth (Col. 1:16; Eph. 1:21). It is the office of government that God has ordained, not the men that fill those offices. We are free to vote for who we want. Some men (like Hitler and Stalin) misuse the office of government to do awful things.], even Christ while on earth as a man was subject to the brutal Roman government Matt. 22:17.] **2 Whosoever therefore resisteth the power, resisteth the <u>ordinance of God</u>:** [Governmental structure arranged by God.] **and they that resist shall receive to themselves <u>damnation</u>.** [Punishment from government for doing wrong, not going to hell.] **3 For <u>rulers</u> are not a terror to <u>good</u> works, but to the <u>evil</u>. Wilt thou then not be afraid of the power? do that which is <u>good</u>, and thou shalt have <u>praise of the same</u>:** [If we do good, we are not likely to get in trouble with our government (1 Peter 3:13; Prov. 16:7).] **4 For he is the <u>minister of God</u> to thee <u>for good</u>. <u>But if thou do that which is evil, be afraid; for he beareth not the sword in vain</u>: for he is the minister of God, a revenger to <u>execute wrath</u> upon him that doeth evil.** [God created government for our good, to protect us. Evil is deterred and restrained by strong rules that are reinforced with punishments. Therefore, Theodore Roosevelt said, "Talk softly, but carry a big stick." The stick is the "wrath" or punishment that fits the crime. We are to pray for our governmental officials (1 Tim. 2:1-3). The right to bare arms, the Second Amendment is a deterrent to evil government.]

5 Wherefore ye must <u>needs be subject, not only for wrath</u>, but also for <u>conscience sake</u>. [We should not only obey because the government says so, but because our conscience tells us what is right and wrong.] **6 For for this cause <u>pay ye tribute</u>:** [Tax] **for they are <u>God's ministers</u>, attending continually upon this very thing.** [Our taxes go to attendants who keep law and order.] **7 Render therefore to all their dues: <u>tribute</u> to whom tribute is due; <u>custom</u>** [import and export fees] **to whom custom; <u>fear</u>** [respect] **to whom fear; <u>honour</u>** [our leaders who do their best to rule righteously] **to whom honour.** [God is the highest authority, therefore there are exceptions when government disobeys God we should obey God rather than men, Acts 4:19, 5:29; Daniel's friends decided not to worship the statue (Dan: 3:10-18), and also Daniel chose to pray (Dan. 6:5-10).] **8 Owe no man any thing,** [Pay your bills, your monthly payment if you take a loan] **but to love one another:** [Love is seeking the other persons highest good. Notice how Paul opens and closes with love in verses 8-10, 1 Tim. 6:11; Phil. 1:9. When we love others we keep the law. God considers us as adult sons who can do what is right without having to follow a list of rules. More people are won to God by love than arguments. Christians who walk with the love of Christ in them have something that others recognize and want. They are the best citizens and the best witnesses] **for he that loveth another hath fulfilled the law. 9 For this, Thou shalt not commit adultery, Thou shalt not kill, Thou shalt not steal, Thou shalt not bear false witness, Thou shalt not covet; and if there be any other commandment,** [Paul mentions the last 5 commandments here because they are the ones that deal with our relationship to others. He mentions all except keeping the Sabbath in his writings.] **it is briefly comprehended** [We follow the basic principle, not a list of do's and don'ts.] **in this saying, namely, Thou shalt love thy neighbour as thyself. 10 Love worketh no ill to his neighbor:** [Gal. 5:13-16; 1 Thess. 2:7, 8; 1 Cor. 13:6-8a] **therefore love is the fulfilling of the law.** [God's law was given to show us our sin, Rom. 3:19, 20; Deut. 31:26. Human nature is self-centered Rom. 7:18, so the only way we can ever keep God's law is for Christ's Spirit to live through us Rom. 8:2, 7-10.] **11 And that, knowing the time,** [This present time of suffering in which we now live (8:18). God has interrupted and postponed Israel's prophetic program and inserted the dispensation of grace which He began with Paul (2 Cor. 5:15-19).] **that now it is high time to awake out of sleep:** [Notice the urgency, time is running out! (1 Cor. 7:29-31). We have a short life on earth (Psa. 90:10, 12; James 4:14) wake up and share the gospel with unbelievers and "knowledge of the truth" (1 Tim. 2:4) with wrongly dividing believers so they can join the body of Christ believers and not be left behind when the Rapture happens and know the truth (Thess. 4:13-18, 2 Tim. 4:1, 8). It has been the last days in the dispensation of grace for a long time, nearly 2,000 years (2 Tim. 3:1-5). Paul expected Christ return to come at any time. So now nearly 2,000 years later we are nearer than before.] **for now is our salvation nearer than when we believed.** [We are looking for our Saviour Jesus Christ to catch us up in the air to Himself (Titus 2:13).]

12 The night is far spent, the day is at hand: [Our time period is not forever, it is short, limited, "the night is far spent" the dispensation of grace has continued beyond the expected time, and could soon end. We are living in this "present evil world" (Gal. 1:4), Satan's domain serving our Lord in heaven as His ambassadors waiting to be called home. "The day" of Christ, when we are with Him, will soon be here.] **let us therefore cast off the works of darkness** [Let us stop doing things

that have no profit (1 Thess. 5:4-10; Col. 1:13, 14).] **and let us put on the armour of light.** [Put on Christ, He is the light (Col 3:12-17; Eph. 4:22-24), Christ is the "new man."] **13 Let us walk honestly,** [We should be honest, not wasting our time in unfruitful works of darkness.] **as in the day;** [As we would if Christ was physically with us.] **not in rioting** [reveling] **and drunkenness, not in chambering** [Sexual indulgence, lewdness.] **and wantonness,** [Unrestrained, reckless.] **not in strife and envying.** [Fighting against people, and wanting what they have.] **14 But put ye on the Lord Jesus Christ, and make not provision for the flesh, to fulfil the lusts thereof.** [Let Christ's Spirit live in us and through us (Rom. 12:1, 2; Gal. 2:20). Paul reminds us to keep the flesh in subjection and not let it have a chance to lust (1 Cor. 9:24-27; Gal. 5:16, 25; Rom. 8:1, 4; Gal. 3:27). Decide to walk in the Spirit because the law energizes the sinful flesh (6:14; 7:13, 8:1, 4). We are to say "No" to our flesh with its' sinful lusts. We are in Him and He is in us (Col. 1:27; 2:10). Christ is the light and truth (John 1:9, 8:12, 14:6).] **The armour of light is really the sound doctrine given to us through Paul and Christ living through us.** The whole armour in **Eph. 6** has to do with the Person of our Lord Jesus Christ, His word rightly divided, and prayer to Him:
be strong in the Lord, and in the power of **his** might (10).
Put on the whole armour of God . . . stand against the wiles of the devil (11).
having your loins girt about with truth (14) [Jesus is the truth, John 14:6]
breastplate of righteousness (14) [His imputed righteousness]
feet shod with the preparation of the gospel of peace (15) [with God, Rom. 5:1]
shield of faith (16) [faith of Christ and our faith in Him, Gal. 2:16]
helmet of salvation (17) [the battle is for the mind, our spirit, Eph. 4:23]
the sword of the Spirit, which is the word of God (17) [Heb. 4:12]
Praying always with all prayer and supplication in the Spirit (18) [part of the armour is being able to pray to God with help of the Spirit anytime, anywhere].

I say then, Have they stumbled that they should fall? God forbid: but rather through their fall salvation is come unto the Gentiles, for to provoke them to jealousy. Now if the fall of them be the riches of the world, and the diminishing of them the riches of the Gentiles; how much more their fulness? For I speak to you Gentiles, inasmuch as I am the apostle of the Gentiles, I magnify mine office: For if the casting away of them be the reconciling of the world, what shall the receiving of them be, but life from the dead?

Romans thru PHILEMON
Romans 11:11-13, 15
Jesus sent Paul

56

Romans Chapter 14 Consideration for the weaker brother
14:1-15:7 How to deal "with him that is weak in the faith: (14:1) who does NOT know sound doctrine and is not rightly dividing the word of truth" (2 Tim. 2:15).

Romans 14:1 Him that is weak in the faith [saints who are NOT strong in Pauline doctrine] **receive ye, but not to doubtful disputations.** [We are not to argue about minor issues.] **2 For one believeth that he may eat all things: another, who is weak, eateth herbs.** [Someone may be fine eating food offered to idols, others may abstain, and some may be a vegetarian. (1 Cor. 8:7-13).] **3 Let not him that eateth despise him that eateth not; and let not him which eateth not judge him that eateth: for God hath received him.** [What a person eats or does not eat is not the important thing. If a person has trusted in Christ that is the main thing. God has received us both (1 Cor. 12:12, 21-25).] **4 Who art thou that judgest another man's servant? to his own master he standeth or falleth. Yea, he shall be holden up: for God is able to make him stand.** [Each person is accountable to God (Psa. 73:22-26; 1 Cor. **4:3**-5; Mat. 7:1-5; Rom. 2:1) God has declared all who are in Christ as NOT guilty (Rom. 4:22, 24, 25; 8:33, 34). We stand 100% righteous in God's sight because we are in Christ (Gal. 3:26-28) not because we have more understanding or are somehow more "spiritual" than anyone else but because of what Christ has done (Rom.3:22-24).] **5 One man esteemeth one day above another: another esteemeth every day alike. Let every man be <u>fully persuaded in his own mind.</u>** [The Sabbath was a sign between the LORD and Israel to set them apart from other nations whoever did not keep it was to be killed (Ex. 31:12-15). The Sabbath represents the millennium. Now in our day of Gentile opportunity (Rom. 11:13, 25 we are not under Israel's laws (Rom 6:14, 9:4) and all days are alike and important (Col. 2:16, 17). <u>We cannot force someone to be saved or to come to understand right division.</u> If they have no interest we should look for those who do, but not to give up on them too soon. We do not want to harden them to the gospel or to turn them off to the message of grace. Perhaps they will listen in the future. Even if the time never comes, so be it. He will learn when he gets to heaven. Since God does not force saved people to read their Bibles and they answer to God, how much more, then, should we not force weaker brethren to learn the truth of God's word. When we do, we are trying to take control over God's Servant, when God knows what is best for them. We should be "fully persuaded" in our minds that we are NOT Israel we have no special days (Gal. 4:10, 11; Col. 2:16, 17; Phil. 2:15, 16).] **6 He that regardeth the day, regardeth it unto the Lord; and he that regardeth not the day, to the Lord he doth not regard it. He that eateth, eateth to the Lord, for he giveth God thanks; and he that eateth not, to the Lord he eateth not, and giveth God thanks.** [Some people who are not aware of the dispensation we are living in today may think that they would be more acceptable to God if they shared in Israel's holy days (Gal. 4:9-11). Whatever we do, we do it unto the Lord, our only Judge (Col. 3:23-25).] **7 For none of us liveth to himself, and no man dieth to himself. 8 For whether we live, we live unto the Lord; and whether we die, we die unto the Lord: whether we live therefore, or die, we are the Lord's.** [We represent Christ as His ambassadors.] **9 For to this end Christ both died, and rose, and revived, that he might be Lord both of the dead and living.** [From spiritually dead and alive. Lord of lost and the saved. Notice that Christ both rose and revived. He was dead (His soul was separated from His body) but then simultaneously His Spirit returned to His body and He rose in His glorified body which was able to go through the grave clothes (linen wrappings). He was the first to put on a glorified immortal body since He can walk through walls and ascend in the air. Have you ever wondered why His disciples did not recognize Him? I believe it was because He looked different in His glorified body, and we will too. People will be able to recognize us but we may not have blood in our special immortal body (1 Cor. 15:50).]

10 But why dost thou judge thy brother? or why dost thou set at nought thy brother? for we shall all stand before <u>the judgment seat of Christ</u>. [Christ will judge us all the Judgment Seat of Christ based on (14:17-19). We are not judge each other, or even ourselves (<u>1 Cor. 3:8-15; 4:3-5</u>). God's word is "like a fire" the <u>perfect standard measure by which all things will be judged, Jer. 23:29</u>; God does the work through us, and we get the reward, so we will then give Him all the glory! We are training here, for reigning there! (2 Cor. 1:14, 5:9, 10; Col. 3:24, 25, 2 Tim. 2:20). Our motivation is love, gratitude and understanding, and God's thinking compels us to allow Him to do good works through us (Gal. 2:20). We are His "purchased possession" (Eph. 1:14), bought with His blood (Acts 20:28; 1 Cor. 6:19, 20) <u>so living for Him is our reasonable service" (Rom. 12:1) it is our duty, but He still graciously gives us a reward. That is grace! Grace is unearned and undeserved favor. Our operating system is grace, not the Law.</u>] **11 For it is written, As I live, saith the Lord, <u>every knee shall bow to me, and every tongue shall confess to God.</u>** [Everyone will bow their knee to Christ and confess that He is LORD. Israel shall glory in Him and so shall we. Isa. 45:23; We will bow at His Judgment Seat. Some may not have confessed Him as Lord in life, but they will (Phil. 2:10, 11).] **12 So then every one of us shall give account of himself to God**. [We dedicate or consecrate ourselves to God by presenting our bodies a living sacrifice, and living as a Christian should. Not because we have to, but because we want to please God and represent Him well to others. We are personally responsible to God for our actions.] **13 Let us not therefore judge one another any more: but judge this rather, that no man put a stumblingblock or**

an occasion to fall in his brother's way. [We are not to do anything that stumbles another person, but instead be concerned with his spiritual well-being. Rather we are to judge them as weaker and seek to make them stronger. We can use the mind of Christ to judge all things (then we judge righteously).] **14 I know, and am persuaded by the Lord Jesus, that there is nothing unclean of itself: but to him that esteemeth any thing to be unclean, to him it is unclean.** [Under grace we have liberty to do all things (Gal. 5:1), but not everything is expedient or profitable (1 Cor. 6:12). But if someone things something is unclean it is for them.] **15 But if thy brother be grieved with thy meat, now walkest thou not charitably. Destroy not him with thy meat, for whom Christ died.** [Do not ruin another man's spiritual walk by what you eat or drink (Cor. 8:7-13). Christ died for them. "For, brethren, ye have been called unto liberty; only use not liberty for an occasion to the flesh, but by love serve one another" (Gal. 5:13).] **16 Let not then your good be evil spoken of:** [Let not our good suffer because of our thoughtlessness. Our "good" is the wonderful, liberating sound doctrine found in Paul's epistles (Col. 1:20-26).] **17 For the kingdom of God is not meat and drink; but righteousness, and peace, and joy in the Holy Ghost.** [These are the things that matter to God. Let's focus on the things God is doing, not on petty things such as what man eats or drinks. What we ourselves eat should be irrelevant to us. God's will is: for people to be saved and to come to the knowledge of the truth (1 Tim. 2:4). When people are saved they receive God's righteousness (3:21, 22) and have peace with God (5:1). When they come to the knowledge of the truth, they "rejoice ever more" (1 Thess. 5:16) over being forgiven of their sin, being seated with Christ in the heavenly places, given all the spiritual blessings, and Christ living in them. That is why Paul says, "If meat make my brother to offend, I will eat no flesh while the world standest, lest I make my brother to offend" (1 Cor. 8:13). Let us concentrate on eternal things.]

18 For he that in these things serveth Christ is acceptable to God, and approved of men. [Those who thoughtfully, lovingly, and courteously serve others with righteousness, peace, and joy are acceptable to God, and approve of men.] **19 Let us therefore follow after the things which make for peace, and things wherewith one may edify another.** [Sometimes we have to go along with things we know really do not matter in order to keep peace so we can have a chance to edify. For example, we may not want to serve pork chops to a brother or sister who believe they are to follow Israel's dietary laws. So as to not offend them and to have more of a chance to edify the person on eternal matters later, so we may serve them chicken instead. We are adult sons of God and stronger brothers because of the sound doctrine we have learned; we are to operate on a higher spiritual plane, walking by faith not by sight.] **20 For meat destroy not the work of God.** [Do not destroy the work of God because of food. God is working in the weak believer to make him stronger.] **All things indeed are pure; but it is evil for that man who eateth with offence.** [It is fine to eat all foods, but not everyone knows this and may be offended.] **21 It is good neither to eat flesh, nor to drink wine, nor any thing whereby thy brother stumbleth, or is offended, or is made weak.** [We should voluntarily abstain from certain dietary practices for the sake of the weaker brother.] **22 Hast thou faith? have it to thyself before God. Happy is he that condemneth not himself in that thing which he alloweth. 23 And he that doubteth is damned if he eat, because he eateth not of faith: for whatsoever is not of faith is sin.** [If we think we can eat something we can keep it to ourselves, but if a weaker brother thinks they are eating something that is against God's law that could wound their conscience (2:15). It is sin to go against our conscience.]

EDIFY

Him that is weak in the faith receive ye, but not to doubtful disputations. Let us therefore follow after the things which make for peace, and things wherewith one may edify another.
Romans 14:1, 19 KJV

Jesus sent Paul

Romans Chapter 15 Paul's ministry to the Gentiles
15:1-7 We should be patient when teaching the weaker brother or sister Pauline sound doctrine.
15:8-12 Christ was a minister to the circumcision (the Jews) to confirm the promises made to the fathers. Christ's earthly ministry was to the Jews so that they could then save the Gentiles. Gentiles that are saved in Israel's program will not be at the same level as Israel, but below. Today there is no difference between Jews and Gentiles (Gal. 3:28). There is a pattern that progresses in these verses quoted by Paul. The Gentiles hear the word (Psa. 18:49); Gentiles rejoice with the Jews (Deut. 32:43); All the Gentiles praise God (Psa. 117:1); The Gentiles trust Christ and enjoy His reign (Isa. 11:10). In Israel's program Gentiles need to believe in the King of the Jews and bless the Jews. Today we are saved by believing the gospel directly without going through Israel and apart from the law. **Notice what Paul says next** "I myself also am persuaded of you, my brethren, that ye also are full of goodness, filled with all knowledge" (15:14) **Paul expects the Romans to understand that he has been talking about Israel's glorious program. Because he explained about Israel's blindness in Ch. 11. Paul treats them as a father does an adult son. He encourages them as to who they are in Christ. We must look at the letter to the Romans as a whole and not narrowly focus our mind on just one passage or chapter**. Under the **law** we obey out of fear of punishment, but under **grace** we obey out of love and gratitude. It is a mistake to think that every time God is speaking about Gentile salvation that He is speaking about us. (Every promise in the book is not mine.) In Time Past and in the Ages to Come Gentiles are saved by believing that Jesus is the Messiah the King of the Jews and blessing Israel. In the Present, Gentiles are saved by believing directly on Christ and what He has done (without going through Israel, apart from Israel) how that Christ died for OUR SINS, was buried, and rose again.
15:13-32 Paul then talks about his plans to go to Jerusalem with a monetary gift before coming to see the Romans and asks them to pray for him.

Romans 15:1 We then that are strong ought to bear the infirmities of the weak, and not to please ourselves. [The "infirmities" in this context is the following of religious rules "by those weak in Pauline sound doctrine. We all used to be mixers of Peter and Paul or weaker brothers, but now we are stronger brother/sister if we understand the mystery given to Paul. When we understand Paul's sound doctrine we are more likely to walk in the spirit and put on "the Lord Jesus Christ, and make not provision for the flesh, to fulfill the lusts thereof" (13:14). We should not chastise the weaker brothers, but to bear with them and not to please ourselves. We are to be willing to sacrifice our wants for the purpose of ministering to them. Christ went to Israel in spite of their unbelief because that is what the Father wanted Him to do, and we should be willing to help those who are weak in Pauline truth (immature in sound doctrine) and have become stuck under the law because they follow Peter believing that the body of Christ began in Acts 2, instead of Acts 9. (The dispensation of grace began when Christ saved Paul on the road to Damascus and ends at the Rapture).] **2 Let every one of us <u>please his neighbour</u> for his good to edification.** [Every one means all of us brothers and sisters in the faith. We who are strong in the faith should be careful when helping those who are weak in sound doctrine (Gal. 6:1-5). To edify means to "build up." God's word rightly divided is able to build us up (Acts 20:32). Women edifying another outside the local church setting is not "usurping authority." Priscilla and Aquila edified Apollos. We "should minister grace to the hearers" Eph. 4:29; "Let no man seek his own, but every man another's wealth" (1 Cor. 10:24).] **3 For even Christ pleased not himself; but, as it is written, <u>The reproaches of them that reproached thee fell on me.</u>** [This is a quote from Psa. 69:9. Christians are to follow the example of Christ, who did not live to please Himself (Phil. 2:5-8). Christ bore the reproach of those who crucified Him even begging the Father to forgive their ignorance, "for they know not what they do" (Luke 23:34). So we should be able to bear a little shame from a weaker brother who may be resistant to sound doctrine because they don't understand it or those who criticize us. Notice how Paul points us to Jesus as our example when we know that Paul suffered a lot of reproach from the Jews and also from the Corinthian brethren.] **4 <u>For whatsoever things were written aforetime were written for our learning, that we through patience and comfort of the scriptures might have hope.</u>** [What Paul just quoted in Psa. 69:9 is for our learning. We can learn from all the Bible rightly divided. Paul also suffered reproach (1 Cor. 9:19-23). All of us have had to suffer reproach at some time, and we should be willing to do it for the lost so they may be saved, and those weak in Pauline sound doctrine. We gain spiritual comfort of the scriptures by experience. The Bible is spiritual nourishment from our Head "in whom are hid all treasures of wisdom and knowledge" (Col. 2:2-3). We must view the Bible from a Pauline perspective. All the Bible is "for us," but not all of the Bible is "to" or "about us." Even so, I still believe that God was killing two birds with one stone so to speak, and that He was sharing information with Israel that He knew the body of Christ could profit from. That is why Paul says that "All scripture . . . is profitable (2 Tim. 3:16, 17). We will only get the profit out of the Bible that God has for us if we study it diligently rightly dividing (2 Tim. 2:15).] **5 Now the God of patience and <u>consolation</u> grant you to be <u>likeminded</u> one toward another according to Christ Jesus:** [The God of patience provides comfort as we in the body of Christ follow Paul.] **6 That ye may with <u>one mind</u> and <u>one mouth</u> glorify God, even the Father of our Lord Jesus Christ.** [Saying the same thing, as we follow our one apostle Paul's doctrine, "the preaching of Jesus Christ, according to the revelation of the mystery" (Rom. 16:25).]

7 ¶ Wherefore receive ye one another, as Christ also received us to the glory of God. [Paul begins this paragraph talking about us receiving the weaker believer. For this reason, receive one another, as Christ also received us (Gentiles in the body of Christ in mystery) to the glory of God.] **8 Now I say that <u>Jesus Christ was a minister of the circumcision</u> for the truth of God, <u>to confirm the promises made unto the fathers</u>: 9 And that the <u>Gentiles might glorify God for his mercy</u>; as it is written, For this cause <u>I will confess to thee among the Gentiles</u>, and <u>sing unto thy name</u>.** [Christ was a minister to the circumcision, the believing Jews, Peter's group (Matt. 10:5, 6) in the previous dispensation. Christ's earthly ministry to Israel confirmed the promises God made unto Abraham, Isaac, and Jacob, and their descendants. Christ came to Israel so that the nation of Israel could be saved and then be a "kingdom of priest" <u>to save Gentiles in prophecy</u> (Ex. 19:5, 6; Isa. 61:6). <u>God intended to use His nation to bless all nations with the opportunity of salvation</u>. God told Abraham "in thee shall all families of the earth be blessed" (Gen. 12:3). Christ let the woman of Canaan know that the Gentiles will be blessed after the overflow of Israel's fullness, their table with the crumbs (Matt. 15:24-28). There is a parallel in the two programs because <u>Gentiles can be saved in both</u>, but the Gentiles in Israel's program will not be on the same level with Israel because the middle wall of partition will be up. Christ wants Israel to confess [declare] Him to the Gentiles in prophecy and sing His name (Psa. 18:49).] **10 And again he saith, Rejoice, ye Gentiles, with his people.** [Israel, Deut. 32:43] **11 And again, Praise the Lord, all ye Gentiles; and laud him, all ye people.** [Psa. 117:1] **12 And again, Esaias saith, There shall be a root of Jesse,** [Jesus Christ] **and he that shall rise to reign over the Gentiles; in him shall the Gentiles trust.** [Isa. 11:10. There is a pattern that progresses the Gentiles hear the word (Psa. 18:49); Gentiles rejoice with the Jews (Deut. 32:43); All the Gentiles praise God (Psa. 117:1); The Gentiles trust Christ and enjoy His reign (Isa. 11:10).] **13 <u>Now the God of hope fill you with all joy and peace in believing, that ye may abound in hope, through the power of the Holy Ghost.</u>** ["Now" Paul switches to joy in the present dispensation. God has always wanted to save the Gentiles in every dispensation. The wonderful thing is that today Jews can be saved into the body of Christ in God's time of opportunity for the Gentiles by joining them. But in the kingdom God will give the Gentiles 1,000-year opportunity to be saved in Israel's program.] **14 And I myself also am persuaded of you, my brethren, that ye also are <u>full of goodness</u>, <u>filled with all knowledge</u>, able also to admonish one another.** [Paul knows that the saints in Rome already knew that Christ wanted to save Gentiles in Israel's program and in

His program to the body of Christ. Daniel Webster's 1828 dictionary definition of "admonish" is "to correct, notify of a fault; to reprove with mildness." If we notice someone has a wrong understanding, we are to correct them privately. Paul knew that the believers in Rome were mature knowledgeable saints, but he still wanted them to have all the fundamental knowledge which he lays out in Romans. They know that Paul has a special commission to reach the Gentiles with the gospel and to share the mystery will all believers apart from Israel.] **15 Nevertheless, brethren, I have written the more boldly unto you in some sort, as putting you in mind, because of the grace that is given to me of God, 16 That I should be the minister of Jesus Christ to the Gentiles, ministering the gospel of God, that the offering up of the Gentiles might be acceptable, being sanctified by the Holy Ghost.** [Christ appointed Paul to be His minister (Acts 26:16). Paul wanted the Gentile believers in mystery to be acceptable to the Godhead. He wants us to be the best we can be. What an Apostle's heart he had; it will be a privilege for all of us to meet him. The "gospel of God" appears 7 times in the King James Bible, 6 in Paul's writings and once in Peter's (1 Peter 4:17). The gospel of God is the basic prophesied information of Christ's death, burial and resurrection for sins. Both Peter and Paul preached the basic gospel of the Redeemer for both groups. But Peter emphasized the gospel of the kingdom and Paul the gospel of Christ. Peter said that Christ was the King of the Jews to sit on the throne in the coming kingdom. Paul preached Christ crucified and risen and our justification by faith (Rom. 4:24, 25). So what is the difference between Paul's gospel and Peter's. Paul said Christ died for OUR SINS (Jews and Gentiles in mystery) apart from Israel. Paul never said that the body of Christ would live in a kingdom on earth but in heavenly places (Eph. 2:6, 2 Cor. 5:1). Gospel means "good news." There is more than one gospel in the Bible but there is only one that saves today, Paul's.]

17 I have therefore whereof I may glory through Jesus Christ in those things which pertain to God. [Paul has reason to glory because of the office Christ has given him. He is His minister.] **18 For I will not dare to speak of any of those things which Christ hath not wrought by me, to make the Gentiles obedient, by word and deed, 19 Through mighty signs and wonders,** [2 Cor. 12:12] **by the power of the Spirit of God; so that from Jerusalem, and round about unto Illyricum, I have fully preached the gospel of Christ.** [Paul concentrates on the authority and commission Christ gave him. Paul is to make the Gentiles obedient or to believe by faith (Rom. 1:5) in what Christ gave Paul to write and do, so that after salvation we can also do and serve God. "Those things, which ye have both learned, and received, and heard, and seen in me, do and the God of peace shall be with you" (Phil. 4:9). Paul is our pattern, so we should copy what he does. In order to live a godly life, we must have the sound doctrine found in Paul's epistles built up in our inner man. When we do that we have peace and are in God's will. The Spirit of God worked in Paul and He works in us. The gospel of Christ is found in 1 Cor. 15:3, 4. After the uproar in Ephesus which was a mob that chanted for two hours and basically wanted to tear Paul apart (Acts 19:29-32, 40), Paul went to Macedonia, then to Illyricum, then down to Corinth. Most maps miss this but the map in God's Secret includes it.] **20 Yea, so have I strived to preach the gospel, not where Christ was named, lest I should build upon another man's foundation:** [Christ is the foundation for both prophecy and according to the revelation of the mystery (16:25). Paul was commissioned to preach to those heathen (unsaved Jews and Gentiles) who had not heard about a chance for salvation, while Peter and his group ministered to the saved Jews, the circumcision, who had believed the gospel of the kingdom (Gal. 2:9). This is the way Paul did not build on Peter's foundation (message). The Jews would not go to the Gentiles so Jesus sent Paul (Acts 11:19).] **21 But as it is written, To whom he was not spoken of, they shall see: and they that have not heard shall understand.** [Isa. 52:15. Christ spoke to Paul by revelation, and the Holy Spirit also used the Old Testament scriptures.] **22 For which cause** [preaching to those who had not heard] **also I have been much hindered from coming to you.** [Paul had been busy preaching to the heathen.] **23 But now having no more place in these parts,** [Having been forced to leave Ephesus because of the uproar caused by the silversmiths (Acts 19:29-32, 40), and having covered the other ground preaching the gospel (so that in Col. 1:5, 6, 23) he says everyone had heard.] **and having a great desire these many years to come unto you; 24 Whensoever I take my journey into Spain, I will come to you:** [They are next on his list.] **for I trust to see you in my journey, and to be brought on my way thitherward by you, if first I be somewhat filled with your company. 25 But now I go unto Jerusalem to minister unto the saints.** [Paul arrived in Jerusalem in Acts 21:17 so this is another clue that the book of Romans was written in Acts 20:1-3.] **26 For it hath pleased them of Macedonia and Achaia to make a certain contribution for the poor saints which are at Jerusalem.** [In 2 Cor. 8-9:15, Paul speaks about the collection that was being taken for the saints in Jerusalem which helps us to know that Romans was written after that. He is rather funny the way He used the Macedonian giving to encourage the Corinthians to give and visa-versa.] **27 It hath pleased them verily; and their** [saints at Jerusalem] **debtors they are. For if the Gentiles have been made partakers of their spiritual things,** [How are we partakers of Israel's spiritual things? (His Spirit, adoption, eternal life). Because spiritually the little flock saints are "in Christ" and "Christ is in them." Now Christ is in us and we are in Him. Peter and the remnant have been placed on hold, their program has been postponed because of the unbelief of their nation.] **their duty is also to minister unto them in carnal things.** [Material things, since God has postponed Israel's program and is giving Gentiles an opportunity to believe directly on what Christ has done apart from going through Israel. The saints in Jerusalem had bravely stood up for God, not man, but now they were poor since they had obeyed Christ command to sell all that they had (Luke 12:33, Acts 2:45, 4:34, 35). They were anticipating going into the Tribulation and would not be able to buy or sell because they would not have the mark of the beast. Also for the purpose of having the little flock's good will and blessing so that there would be no strife or hindrance between the two groups of believers. The Christians would be edified, being able to do their duty and give, and the saints in Jerusalem would experience Christian love in action.] **28 When therefore I have performed this, and have sealed to them this fruit,** [Gift of money.] **I will come by you into Spain. 29 And I am sure that, when I come unto you, I shall come in the fulness of the blessing of the gospel of Christ.** [Apparently, Jesus Christ had communicated to Paul that he would receive the full revelation of the mystery by the time he arrived in Rome, even if he had not written everything down yet. Paul would be able to share this with the saints at Rome when he arrived.]

30 Now I beseech you, brethren, for the Lord Jesus Christ's sake, and for the love of the Spirit, that ye strive together with me in your prayers to God for me; [Prayer is work because the flesh does not want to do it. Paul asked for prayer regarding three things: (1) him to be delivered from being killed by unbelieving religious Jews in Judaea, (2) that the believing remnant will accept the gift, and (3) that he may come to them in Rome with joy by the will of God, and be refreshed with them after trying to save his kinsmen.] **31 [1] That I may be delivered from them that do not believe in Judaea; [2] and that my service which I have for Jerusalem may be accepted of the saints; 32 [3] That I may come unto you with joy by the will of God, and may with you be refreshed. 33 Now the God of peace be with you all**. **Amen.** [Was Paul's prayers answered? Yes! Paul arrived alive in Rome and the gift was accepted (Acts 21:15-17, 28:16). Paul prays that the God's peace will be with them. Knowing His Spirit in us (Rom. 8:9) and our blessed hope of the Rapture gives us peace.]

Romans Chapter 16 Benediction about the revelation of the mystery
16:1-27 Personal greetings and the benediction about the mystery.

Romans 16:1 I commend unto you Phebe our sister, [a saint that carried the letter to Rome.] **which is a servant of the church which is at Cenchrea:** [a seaport near Corinth.] **2 That ye receive her in the Lord, as becometh saints,** [in the gracious manner that becomes saints (Phil. 1:27).] **and that ye assist her in whatsoever business she hath need of you** [help her in every possible way]: **for she hath been a succourer** [helper] **of many, and of myself also. 3 Greet Priscilla and Aquila my helpers in Christ Jesus:** [This couple had met Paul in Corinth after being told to leave Rome and after helping Paul in Ephesus they had moved back to Rome (Acts 18:2, 18, 26; 2 Tim. 4:19).] **4 Who have for my life laid down their own necks:** [Why does Paul mention Priscilla first? Perhaps in the uproar (Acts 19:40) Priscilla may have been braver or she may have been stronger in the doctrine.] **unto whom not only I give thanks, but also all the churches of the Gentiles.** [Without Paul the Gentile churches would have no further revelation from Jesus for His heavenly group] **5 Likewise greet the church that is in their house.** [They had a house church and Paul mentions three or more in this letter.] **Salute my wellbeloved Epaenetus, who is the firstfruits of Achaia unto Christ.** [Among the first to believe, probably a member of the household of Stephanas (1 Cor. 16:15).] **6 Greet Mary, <u>who bestowed much labour on us.</u>** [She worked hard to serve Paul and his friends, possibly the mother of John Mark, Acts 12:12.]

7 Salute Andronicus and Junia, my kinsmen, and my fellowprisoners, who are of note among the apostles, who also were in Christ before me. [When Paul talks about <u>Andronicus and Junia</u> he makes it clear that they were "in Christ" (saved) before him. They were saved by the preaching of the little flock; this is how they are "in Christ" before Paul. Since we know that Paul is the first one in the body of Christ (1 Tim. 1:16). What was the gospel that they had trusted? The gospel of the kingdom. They repented (changed their minds) and believed that Jesus Christ was the King of the Jews and were baptized with water and the Holy Ghost. They met Paul in prison (perhaps in Philippi, Acts 16:25). They were respected by the 12 apostles. Christ told Peter and the little flock that they will be in Him and He will be in them (John 14:20, 17:23). However, those saints realized that God had changed dispensations and had begun working through a new apostle, Paul. They wanted to be part of what God is now doing so they joined Paul. Barnabas and Silas are examples of other "little flock" saints who also helped Paul. Paul mentions that his face for a while was unknown to the "churches of Judae which were <u>in Christ</u>" (Gal. 1:22). Everyone who is saved is "in Christ" and not in Adam. This is how we have so "much more" in Christ because we have the gift of

His righteousness (Rom. 5:17). In the fullness of times God will gather everyone who is "in Christ" into the new heaven and the new earth (Eph. 1:10).] **8 Greet Amplias my beloved in the Lord. 9 Salute Urbane, our helper in Christ, and Stachys my beloved. 10 Salute Apelles approved in Christ. Salute them which are of Aristobulus' household.** [Possibly another house church.] **11 Salute Herodion my kinsman.** [Either a Jew or a relative of Paul.] **Greet them that be of the household of Narcissus, which are in the Lord.** [Possibly another house church.]

12 Salute Tryphena and Tryphosa, [Probably twins women.] **who labour in the Lord.** [These women helped others to be saved and to come to the knowledge of the truth of sound doctrine getting the gospel out. Women are to be faithful to share what they have learned about Pauline truth just like men are. Many women helped in the ministry (Phil. 4:3). Notice who is sanctifying believers and cleansing us by His word in these verses: "Husbands, love your wives, even as Christ also loved the church, and gave himself for it; That he [Christ] might sanctify and cleanse it with the washing of water by the word, That he might present it [the Church] to himself a glorious church, not having spot, or wrinkle, or any such thing; but that it should be holy and without blemish" (Eph. 5:25-27). The Bible is clear (especially in the pastoral epistles) that women should not be pastors and we all agree with that. The King James Bible is our final authority. When Paul said teach other faithful men who in turn would teach other faithful men, he did not mean that women should not also be faithful to teach others so they may be saved, come to the knowledge of Pauline sound doctrine, and understand all of the Bible. Both men and women can be beguiled by false doctrine (2 Cor. 11:3). We all constantly have to be on our guard to remain both Biblical and dispensational correct. Paul does not discount 50% of the human race. He says that we "are all one in Christ" (Gal. 3:28). Each person is important to God. He wants all to be saved. Even the North Koreans.] **Salute the beloved Persis,** [A woman.] **which laboured much in the Lord. 13 Salute Rufus chosen in the Lord, and his mother and mine.** [Mark 15:21, this mother mothered Paul.] **14 Salute Asyncritus, Phlegon, Hermas, Patrobas, Hermes, and the brethren which are with them.** [Possibly another house church.] **15 Salute Philologus, and Julia, Nereus, and his sister, and Olympas, and all the saints which are with them.** [Possibly another house church.] **16 Salute one another with an holy kiss.** [Affectionate kiss on the cheek.] **The churches of Christ salute you.**

17 ¶ Now I beseech you, brethren, mark them which cause divisions and offences contrary to the doctrine which ye have learned; and avoid them. [Phil. 3:17-19. Paul implores them to mark (identify, name) and avoid anyone that would take them away from following the sound doctrine they have learned from him. Teachers of false doctrine should be avoided (those who believe that the body of Christ began in Acts 2). Most of these pastors preach Acts 2 out of ignorance, they just don't know any better. We must remember that we were like them. For they that are such serve not our Lord Jesus Christ, but their own belly; and by good words and fair speeches deceive the hearts of the simple.] **18 For they that are such serve not our Lord Jesus Christ, but their own belly;** [Unless the ministry is Pauline they are NOT serving Christ, 2 Cor. 11:13-15. They just want to promote themselves and their mixed up beliefs. They do not know the truth and they care more about money to feed themselves rather than feeding others spiritual truth.] **and by good words and fair speeches deceive the hearts of the simple.** [They may sound eloquent and their spiritualizing of God's word and cute stories may sound like they are saying something of value, but they are not following Paul.] **19 For your obedience is come abroad unto all men.** [Your faithful following of Paul's sound doctrine.] **I am glad therefore on your behalf:** [Paul is happy to hear that.] **but yet I would have you wise unto that which is good,** ["Good" means Paul's sound doctrine stored up in the inner man. Just like Christ we can have faith in God's plan. God has told us to live by allowing Christ to live through us. "Christ liveth in me" (Gal. 2:20). So now we live by the faith of the Son of God, offering our bodies as living sacrifice.] **and simple concerning evil.** [False doctrine.] **20 And the God of peace shall bruise Satan under your feet shortly.** [Christ can live through us and bruise Satan and his false ministers under our feet by His sound doctrine working in us. God can use all that we have learned in Romans chapters 1-16. Satan and his workers cannot stand Paul's powerful truth. It is in Paul's epistles that Christ triumph over him is made known (Col. 2:15). But Satan does what he can to conceal Pauline truth. When a group of believers are strong together in the truth with Christ working through them laboring to get the message out (1 Tim. 2:4) Satan is bruised. Satan hates the final authority of the King James Bible because his lies cannot prevail against it. What does Paul mean by shortly? It will be shortly compared with eternity. He did not know that our dispensation would continue for nearly 2,000 years. Paul says that the truth will do damage to Satan. God's knowledge is power. However, when Satan and his angels are cast out and we replace them, then Satan will be truly bruised under out feet (Rev. 12:7-9). It will be shortly compared to all eternity. **The grace of our Lord Jesus Christ be with you Amen.** [Paul has concluded the main portion of the letter. He often says "Amen" which means "so be it" at the end of his letters. His letters begin with his name and end with grace (2 Thess. 3:17).]

21 ¶ Timotheus my workfellow, and Lucius, and Jason, and Sosipater, my kinsmen, [Possibly Luke, or the Lucius in Acts 13:1.] **salute you. 22 I Tertius,**

who wrote this epistle, salute you in the Lord. [The secretary or amanuensis who wrote down the dictated letter says hello. Paul only wrote Galatians with his own hand Gal. 6:11.] **23 Gaius mine host, and of the whole church, saluteth you. Erastus the chamberlain of the city saluteth you, and Quartus a brother.** [Probably the Gaius in 1 Cor. 1:14. Perhaps it is the Gaius of Derbe that traveled with him in Acts 20:4 and or the Gaius of Acts 19:29: Erastus was the City Treasurer in Corinth. He is mentioned as being in Corinth in 2 Tim. 4:20. So that is another clue that the letter was probably written in Acts 20:2, 3.] **24 The grace of our Lord Jesus Christ be with you all. Amen.**

25 ¶ Now to <u>him that is of power to stablish you</u> according to <u>my gospel,</u> [God can stablish the believer by three things: (1) "My gospel," (2) "The preaching of Jesus Christ, according to the revelation of the mystery," and (3) "By the scriptures and the prophets" meaning all scripture, both the Old and New Testament, outside Paul's epistles rightly divided (as the scriptures relate from a Pauline perspective). "My gospel" is the imputed righteousness of Christ, justification by faith. When we believe Paul's gospel a transaction occurs, God places our sins on Christ and imputes or imparts the Son of God's righteousness to us (Rom. 3:22-26, 4:22-25; 1 Cor. 15:3, 4; 2 Cor. 5:21). When we have the righteousness of Christ God declares us perfectly righteous and justified so we can then come before the Holy Father without being obliterated. We have been translated out of Adam into Christ and out of Satan's kingdom into the kingdom of His dear Son (1 Cor. 15:22; Col. 1:13, 14). Paul calls it "my gospel" to distinguish it from the gospel of the kingdom given to the twelve. "My gospel" is the "gospel of Christ" and the "gospel of grace," and the audience Paul preached to is the uncircumcision. Paul's gospel is the only gospel that saves today. Paul is the only apostle of the Gentiles who says that Christ died for OUR SINS believing Gentiles in mystery. Paul makes it clear Christ died to be a "ransom for all" (1 Tim. 2:6). In this age anyone can be saved by believing what Christ has accomplished for him.] **and <u>the preaching of Jesus Christ, according to the revelation of the mystery, which was kept secret since the world began,</u>** [Paul calls his doctrine the "mystery" because it was kept secret until it was revealed to him. Jesus Christ Himself revealed the mystery to Paul. He did not receive it from another man such as Peter, and he didn't need another man to teach him (Gal. 1:1, 11, 12). The mystery revelation was not known until Christ first revealed it to Paul in Acts 9. The mystery was unsearchable (Eph. 3:8, read Eph. 3:1-9.) No creature was as surprised as Satan when Christ returned after a year in heaven and saved His worst enemy on the road to Damascus. "What?" Satan said, "that is not what the scriptures say? That is un-prophesied! That was not what was supposed to happen next! Where is God's wrath on His people?" God defeated Satan by keeping a secret: the formation of the body of Christ in the dispensation of grace. Compare this to what Peter says in Acts 3:19-21. The mystery is the entire body of doctrine given to Paul by revelation from the ascended, glorified Lord Jesus Christ (Romans to Philemon).] **26 But now is made manifest,** [God has now revealed it through Paul, Eph. 3:1-9.] **and by the scriptures of the prophets,** [The rest of the Bible, prophecy, the scriptures outside of Paul's writings (Romans to Philemon), in both the Old Testament and New Testament scriptures (rightly divided). To be more clear Genesis to Acts 9 and then Hebrews to Revelation. Further and more advanced knowledge was given to Paul. Paul often quotes the Old Testament and by the inspiration of the Holy Spirit he sometimes changes words to give more revelation. (Paul could do that but we cannot we are to believe what is written.) God is the author of the Bible so all of the Bible could be in red letters.] **according to the commandment of the everlasting God, made known to all nations for the obedience of faith:** [God has commanded that all nations believe the gospel that He gave to Paul. Then come to the knowledge of the truth (1 Tim. 2:4). The revelation that God is now forming the body of Christ, (the one new man, Eph. 2:15) during the dispensation of grace, to reign with Christ in the heavenly places. So all people can believe the sound doctrine Christ gave us through Paul.] **27 To God only wise, be glory through Jesus Christ for ever. Amen.** [God alone is wise. Paul constantly exalts our Saviour the Lord Jesus Christ and gives Him all the glory and so should we because He has done everything that was necessary to save us. First, God's will is for "all men to be saved" (1 Tim. 2:4) by believing the gospel (1 Cor. 15:3, 4). Second, "to come to the knowledge of the truth" (1 Tim. 2:4) by learning the sound doctrine that is found in Paul's 13 letters (2 Thess. 2:15; 1 Tim. 1:3; 2 Tim. 2:7). Then third, for us to learn the rest of the truth in the Bible found outside Paul's epistles, because "all scripture . . . is profitable" (2 Tim. 3:16, 17).]

> Paul said...The grace of our Lord Jesus Christ be with you all. Amen. Now to him that is of power to stablish you according to my gospel, and the preaching of Jesus Christ, according to the revelation of the mystery, which was kept secret since the world began, But now is made manifest, and by the scriptures of the prophets, according to the commandment of the everlasting God, made known to all nations for the obedience of faith: To God only wise, be glory through Jesus Christ for ever. Amen.
> Romans 16:24-27 KJV

First Corinthians Commentary
Chapter 1 Not living up to their standing in Christ
1:1-9 Introduction: The believers standing in grace
1:10-17 Not thinking like God. Divisions in the body due to human wisdom
1:18-25 Human wisdom contrasted with God's wisdom
1:26-31 Corinthian believers not of the wise, Christ is our wisdom

1:1 <u>Paul, called to be an apostle of Jesus Christ through the will of God</u>, and Sosthenes our brother, [The former chief ruler of the synagogue was now a brother and probably took the dictation of this letter from Paul who took it from Christ. He was the second such leader to be saved by Paul in Corinth. Paul founded the church at Corinth in Acts 18:1-18, and was commissioned to be Christ's apostle as recorded in Acts 9:1-16, 22:7-10, 26:14-18.] **2 Unto the church of God** [God's church] **which is at Corinth, to them that <u>are sanctified in Christ Jesus, called to be saints,</u> with all that <u>in every place</u> call upon the <u>name of Jesus Christ our Lord, both theirs and ours:</u>** [Paul tactfully reminds the Corinthians that they are "<u>sanctified [set apart] in Christ Jesus</u>," they are "in him" (2 Cor. 5:21). The "theirs" is the believing remnant (Peter's group) of Israel (Gal. 6:16). Peter's group was already sanctified in the previous dispensation by faith and the body of Christ will have an inheritance among them, an "inheritance among them which are sanctified by faith that is in me" (Acts 26:18). He is not only our Lord; He is their Lord also. There were followers of Peter (Cephas) in the assembly at Corinth (1:12).] **3 Grace be unto you, and peace, from God our Father, and from the Lord Jesus <u>Christ</u>.** [Today God offers grace and peace to those who believe what He says His Son has done for us. We are living in the dispensation of grace (Eph. 3:2) when the gospel of the grace of God (Acts 20:24) is in effect.]

4 ¶ I thank my God always on your behalf, for the grace of God which is given you by Jesus <u>Christ</u>; [Paul thanks God on their behalf that God graciously gave them spiritual gifts so that the Jews in the synagogue next door would be saved.] **5 That in every thing ye are enriched by <u>him</u>, in all <u>utterance</u>, and in all <u>knowledge</u>;** [They were rich in the gift of tongues (speaking other languages) and supernatural knowledge (13:8) of what Christ had revealed to Paul before the revelation given to him was complete.] **6 Even as the testimony of <u>Christ</u> was confirmed in you:** [These gifts were evidence of their salvation and that God was working in and through them.] **7 <u>So that ye come behind in no gift</u>; waiting for the <u>coming of our Lord Jesus Christ</u>:** [1 Cor. 5:5; 2 Cor. 1:14; Phil. 1:6, 1:10; 2:16; Col. 1:22, 23; 1 Thess. 5:23. The Corinthian church was wonderfully blessed with more sign gifts than any other of the churches Paul had founded. The Greek for gifts is Charisma. The coming of our Lord Jesus Himself for His body to catch us up is the Rapture.] **8 Who shall also <u>confirm you unto the end,</u>** [Phil. 1:6] **that ye may be <u>blameless in the day of our Lord Jesus Christ.</u>** [Blameless is to have Christ's imputed perfect righteousness in the day of the coming of the Lord v. 7 (see those references).] **9 God is faithful, by whom ye were called unto the <u>fellowship of his Son Jesus Christ our Lord.</u>** [We are in the fellowship of the mystery (Eph. 3:9).]

10 ¶ Now I beseech you, brethren, by the name of our Lord Jesus <u>Christ</u>, that ye all speak the <u>same thing</u>, [When we all say what God says to us through Paul then we speak the same thing.] **and that there be no divisions among you; but that ye be perfectly joined together in the <u>same mind</u>** [Thinking like Christ 2:16 and making decisions like He would] **and in the <u>same judgment.</u>** [Paul uses the word "same" three times to emphasize the goal of saying the same thing, thinking the same, and judging the same. Paul has reminded them of who they are in Christ, then he launches into a discussion of their sins, dealing first with the matter of division in the church. He clearly states the correct goal: to be perfectly joined together making the decisions Christ would make. The unity in Eph. 4:1-6. The body of Christ is a team.] **11 For it hath been declared unto me of you, my brethren, by them which are of the <u>house of Chloe</u>, that there are contentions among you.** [Paul said he had heard from Chloe that they were contending with one another and causing division. Now he is saying to them that he heard that they are following individual personalities. They are not to follow men, nor Christ's earthly ministry given in Matthew, Mark, Luke and John, but Christ's heavenly ministry through Paul. They needed to take their eyes off each other and onto Christ.] **12 Now this I say, that every one of you saith, <u>I am of Paul</u>; and <u>I of Apollos</u>; and <u>I of Cephas</u>; and <u>I of Christ.</u>** [Paul did not want them to follow individuals, but Christ's heavenly ministry through Paul. Not Christ's earthly ministry given in Matthew, Mark, Luke and John.] **13 Is Christ divided? was Paul crucified for you? or were ye baptized in the name of Paul? 14 I thank God that I baptized none of you, but Crispus and Gaius;** [Crispus was the first ruler of the synagogue to be converted in Acts 18:8, the rest of the Jews should have followed. Gaius was probably Paul's host on his visit to Corinth in Acts 20:3 when he wrote Romans.] **15 Lest any should say that I had baptized in mine own name.** [They would have accused Paul next.] **16 And I baptized also the household of Stephanas: besides, I know not whether I baptized any other.** [Paul was not keeping track of who he baptized.] **17 <u>For Christ sent me not to baptize, but to preach the gospel</u>: not with wisdom of words, lest the cross of Christ should be made of none effect.** [<u>Water baptism</u> makes the cross of none effect. Paul also clearly states that Christ did not send him to water baptize (he only did so with a few) but to preach. Paul describes our spiritual baptism into Christ in 12:13.]

18 ¶ For the preaching of the cross is to them that perish foolishness; but unto us which are saved it is the power of God. [Paul says the "power of God" three times in First Corinthians (1:18; 1:24, 2:5). Paul was not ashamed to preach "the gospel of Christ: for it is the power of God unto salvation to everyone that believeth" (Rom. 1:16) because it works. Faith in what Christ has done has the power to translate the believer out of Adam (and bondage to sin and Satan and eternal death) and into Christ (and freedom from the penalty and power of sin and eternal life, Col. 1:13). Paul preached Christ crucified wherever he went and so should we.] **19 For it is written, I will destroy the wisdom of the wise, and will bring to nothing the understanding of the prudent.** [Paul quotes Isa. 29:14, 15 and says that God will destroy man's wisdom.] **20 Where is the wise? where is the scribe? where is the disputer of this world? hath not God made foolish the wisdom of this world?** [God's magnanimous act of the cross dwarfs everything else.] **21 For after that in the wisdom of God the world by wisdom knew not God, it pleased God by the foolishness of preaching to save them that believe.** [What is actually "foolish"? Paul quotes Isa. 19:12, 33:18. Men with their wisdom could not find God, but God can reach them by the preaching of the truth of His word (Rom. 1:16, 10:17, and 2 Thess. 2:14). People who think they know everything will not realize their need for a Saviour.] **22 For the Jews require a sign, and the Greeks seek after wisdom:** [God spoke to Jews with signs Psalm 74:9, and the Greeks had their philosophers like Plato. God made a covenant of sight with Israel Ex. 34:10. Because of the law contract, God would chastise Israel (Lev. 26) with signs like no rain, famine, enemies, etc. But in this dispensation of grace, we walk by faith in His word (2 Cor. 5:7). God does not chastise us with weather and enemies but we have an enemy (1 Thess. 2:18) and live in a present evil world (Gal. 1:4).] **23 But we preach Christ crucified, unto the Jews a stumblingblock, and unto the Greeks foolishness;** [The Jews stumbled at the cross (John 1:11, Rom. 9:32, 33; 1 Peter 2:8). Not many believed when Paul preached in Athens but mocked him (Acts 17:32).] **24 But unto them which are called, both Jews and Greeks, Christ the power of God, and the wisdom of God.** [Christ is the power and wisdom of God. The Father wagered everything on His Son's ability to go through with His plan of redemption. He saved two groups of believers by one cross. His plan to save all mankind was not revealed until it was revealed to us by Paul (1 Cor. 2:6-8; 1 Tim. 2:6). Today, Christ is saving both Gentiles and Jews into the body of Christ (Gal. 3:28).] **25 Because the foolishness of God is wiser than men; and the weakness of God is stronger than men. 26 For ye see your calling, brethren, how that not many wise men after the flesh,**

not many mighty, not many noble, are called: 27 But God hath chosen the **foolish things** [The preaching of the cross by believers.] **of the world to confound the wise; and God hath chosen the weak things of the world to confound the things which are mighty;** [The cross demonstrates God's wisdom in solving the sin problem. God saves ordinary people who believe, which confuses the wise of the world.] **28 And base things of the world, and things which are despised, hath God chosen, yea, and things which are not, to bring to nought things that are:** [The despised are Paul and his followers by them God brings to nothing the things done by Satan inspired men or Satan who thought he was wise and mighty (Ezek. 28:3).] **29 That no flesh should glory in his presence. 30 But of him are ye in Christ Jesus, who of God is made unto us wisdom, and righteousness, and sanctification, and redemption: 31 That, according as it is written, He that glorieth, let him glory in the Lord.** [Paul wants them to glory in Christ, not men. Christ is everything to us, so let us glory in Him (Jer. 9:24; 2 Cor. 10:17).]

Compare the Bibles below:

ARE YOU SAVED OR ARE YOU "BEING" SAVED?

I Corinthians 1:18

KJV	For the preaching of the cross is to them that perish foolishness; but unto us which **are saved** it is the power of God.
NKJV	For the message of the cross is foolishness to those who are perishing, but to us who **are being saved** it is the power of God.
NIV	For the message of the cross is foolishness to those who are perishing, but to us who **are being saved** it is the power of God.
ESV	For the word of the cross is folly to those who are perishing, but to us who **are being saved** it is the power of God.
NLT	The message of the cross is foolish to those who are headed for destruction! But we who **are being saved** know it is the very power of God.

For by grace **are ye saved** through faith... - Ephesians 2:8

And grieve not the holy Spirit of God, whereby **ye are sealed** unto the day of redemption. - Ephesians 4:30

Chapter 2 The Mystery, God's hidden wisdom and spiritual truth
(2:1-16) God's Spirit, mind, wisdom, and power must work through us.

2:1 And I, brethren, when I came to you, came <u>not with excellency of speech or of wisdom, declaring unto you the testimony of God</u>. [Christ accomplished the <u>Father's plan of redemption</u> on Calvary (His death, burial, and resurrection on the third day according to the scriptures for all mankind's sins). God alone redeemed mankind.] **2 For <u>I determined not to know any thing among you, save Jesus Christ, and him crucified</u>.** [Paul's focus was Christ and what He had done and did not waste any time talking about anything else.] **3 And I was with you in weakness, and in fear, and in much trembling.** [Paul arrived in Corinth after a seeming defeat in Athens where he made only a few converts. He humbly shared all that Christ had revealed to him. He probably told them the testimony of his salvation. <u>His fear was that they would not believe, and Paul trembled at the thought of them not going to heaven</u>. He took his commission very seriously and zealously did his very best for Christ. Christ entrusted him with the mystery and to be the masterbuilder of this new body of believers destined for heaven (3:10).] **4 And <u>my speech</u> and <u>my preaching</u> was not with <u>enticing</u> [persuasive] <u>words of man's wisdom, but in demonstration of the Spirit and of power:</u>** [Paul allowed the power of Christ to work, speak, and live through him. He used words that were easy to understand.] **5 That your faith should not stand in the wisdom of men, but in the <u>power of God</u>.** [I have circled and colored this phrase "power of God" every time God uses it in my Bible. (1 Thess. 1:5). <u>Paul was "not ashamed of the gospel of Christ; for it is the power of God unto salvation to everyone that believeth" (Rom. 1:16). Paul knew the gospel of Christ worked.</u> Faith in Christ's cross-work has the power to save a sinner and translate him out of Adam into Christ (Col. 1:13). God's Plan was to save two groups of believers (Eph. 1:9, 10).]

6 Howbeit <u>we speak wisdom among them that are perfect:</u> yet <u>not the wisdom of this world</u>, nor of the princes of this world that come to nought: [Paul speaks to the spiritually mature that have God's wisdom and will understand. In contrast the wise men of the world whose father is Satan will come to nothing (Eph. 2:1-3, 6:12).] **7 <u>But we speak the wisdom of God in a mystery, even the hidden wisdom, which God ordained before the world unto our glory:</u>** [The hidden wisdom of God was <u>a mystery or secret</u> that was not mentioned in the Bible until Christ revealed it to Paul. <u>God hid the fact of His two-fold eternal purpose to reclaim both heaven (using the body of Christ) and earth (using the nation of Israel) from Satan and his cohorts. Most Christians are ignorant of this truth which is outlined in Ephesians chapters 2 and 3.</u> Because of their ignorance of Paul's distinct apostleship to the Gentiles, many pastors are unknowingly trying to "bring in the kingdom," instead of preparing the believers to "reign with Christ in heaven." God's solved the sin problem by the cross. The Lord Jesus Christ redeemed both the believers in heaven (mystery) and on earth (prophecy).] **8 Which none of the princes of this world knew: for had they known it, they would not have crucified the Lord of glory.** ["The princes of the world" were empowered by Satan (and the "principalities . . . powers rulers of darkness . . . spiritual wickedness in high places" (Eph. 6:12) to crucify Christ. Satan did not know about the hidden wisdom of God since it was not made known in scripture until Paul (Eph. 3:1-9). The crucifixion sealed Satan's doom, Christ took back heaven and earth (Col. 1:20, 2:15). Paul speaks the wisdom of God, not "the wisdom of this world" (2:6, see Eph. 2:1-3), nor anything that can be learned from the "princes of this world" (men that are highly esteemed because of their worldly "wisdom" like scientists and philosophers, Eph. 6:12) who come to nothing. Paul is speaking the wisdom that God kept hidden, a mystery or secret that was not mentioned in the Bible until Christ revealed it to Paul.] **9 But as it is written, Eye hath not seen, nor ear heard, neither have entered into the heart of man, the things which God hath prepared for them that love him.** [God's wonderful plan to redeem the body of Christ had no entered into man's heart. Whenever Paul says it is written he quotes Old Testament. Notice that Isaiah says "waiteth for him" (Isa. 64:4) while Paul by the Holy Spirit says "love him." The believing remnant of Israel (Peter's group) is still waiting to "be born again" at Christ's Second coming when they will be resurrected and receive their glorified bodies. We will receive our glorified bodies at the Rapture. We have been quickened with Him (Eph. 2:1). God has a plan for us to live with Christ in us now and in eternity. In the dispensation of grace God is forming the body of Christ being prepared to live in the heavenly places. We "love him" – believe Him, trust what God says in His word that Christ has done for us. We are grateful to Him that we are saved from the penalty and bondage (power) of sin – and will not get what we deserve. Because of this hope "the love of God is shed abroad in our hearts by the Holy Ghost" (Rom. 5:5). God knew that love is the greatest motivator of all time. God gave the body of Christ "all spiritual blessings in heavenly places in Christ" (Eph. 1:3). Our gratitude and our love for Him and His love for us "constraineth us" to serve Him out of love. We love Him and others out of a grateful heart for what the Father and Christ have done for us. In this dispensation we are "not under the law, but under grace" (Rom. 6:14). Israel on the other hand, had put themselves under the law contract with God when they promised to keep His commandments (Ex. 19:8, 24:7) and the law demands obedience out of fear, not love (Ex. 20:20.] **10 But God hath revealed them unto us by his Spirit: for the Spirit searcheth all things, yea, the deep things of God.** [God has revealed His mystery to us now, it is no longer hidden (Rom 16:25, 26). It is too late for Satan, he has already lost both heaven and earth, even though Christ has not taken possession of them yet.] **11 For what man knoweth the things of a man, save the spirit of man which is in him? even so the things of God knoweth no man, <u>but the Spirit of God.</u>** [Here is a parallel man's spirit in him knows what is in man; likewise, only God's Spirit knows what is in God.] **12 Now <u>we have received, not the spirit of the world, but the spirit which is of God</u>; that we might know the things that are freely given to us of God.** ["Spirit" when it refers to God was not always capitalized by the King James translators. God freely gives us His Spirit so we can be spiritual men and understand His plan of salvation and that we will live in heaven by faith.] **13 Which things also we speak, not in the words which man's wisdom teacheth, but which the <u>Holy Ghost teacheth; comparing spiritual things with spiritual.</u>** [God's truth passes from the mind of God to His people through His word. God's spiritual words are to be compared in one place with related words found in another place to gain the most profit out of them (cross-referenced).] **14 But the natural man receiveth not the things of the Spirit of God: for they are foolishness unto him: neither can he know them, because <u>they are spiritually discerned.</u>** [<u>The Bible is a closed book to anyone who is not saved. His Spirit is needed to understand it (Job 32:8), because it is spiritually discerned.</u>] **15 But <u>he that is spiritual judgeth all things</u>, yet <u>he</u> himself is judged of no man.** [A saved person can judge or examine what God says, and all things. God alone judges the believer and no one judges God, 4:3-5.] **16 For who hath known the mind of the Lord, that he may instruct him? But <u>we have the mind of Christ.</u>** [We have the "mind of Christ" now. Adam in Eden was created in God's image and thought like Him. So when he named the animals that is exactly what God would have named them. <u>How do we have the mind of Christ?</u> By reading and studying His word. No one can tell God what to do. <u>God wants us to think like Him and is conforming us to Christ</u> (Rom. 8:29, 12:1, 2; Phil. 2:5).]

No one knew about the benefits of the cross of Christ until they were revealed to our apostle Paul (1 Corinthians 2:6-8 KJV).

Chapter 3 Rewards in heaven for Christian service
3:1-8 Carnal and worldly vs. spiritual growth and maturity
3:9-23 Rewards for being "labourers together with God"

3:1 And I, brethren, could not speak unto <u>you as unto spiritual, but as unto carnal,</u> even as unto <u>babes in Christ.</u> [The Corinthians were worldly or carnal (in the flesh) acting like unbelievers.] **2 I have fed you with <u>milk, and not with meat:</u> for hitherto ye were <u>not able to bear it, neither yet now are ye able.</u>** [They were Baby Christians who were only able to comprehend the simplest truths "milk." Paul was not able to tell them deep spiritual truths. Heb. 5:11-14.]

3 ¶ For <u>ye are yet carnal</u>: for whereas there is among you <u>envying, and strife, and divisions, are ye not carnal, and walk as men</u>? [They were envying each other and competing instead of working in unity. The purpose of the church is to edify (or build up) one another in love. We are a team! In the past when the Church was in its infancy we needed apostles but not anymore since Paul completed the Bible (Eph. 4:11-16; Col. 1:23-25, 2:2, 3).] **4 For while <u>one saith, I am of Paul; and another, I am of Apollos; are ye not carnal?</u>** [Some said I follow Paul, while others said we follow Apollos, when they should be one Church, one body in Christ. They should follow the Christ that Paul preached, not men. Read Acts 18:18-28 to learn more about Apollos and Paul.] **5 <u>Who then is Paul, and who is Apollos, but ministers by whom ye believed,</u> even <u>as the Lord gave to every man</u>?** [Paul says we are both just ministers by which you believed even as the Lord gives the increase. How the Spirit conforms our will with God's is not fully understood, see Acts 16:14. We are not to focus on men.] **6 <u>I have planted, Apollos watered</u>; but <u>God gave the increase.</u>** [Paul planted or founded the church in Corinth, then Apollos, who was mighty in the Scriptures, came and watered or helped them in their spiritual growth.] **7 So then neither is he that planteth any thing, neither he that watereth; but <u>God that giveth the increase.</u>** [The person God uses are nothing because it is God's power (by His Spirit) that makes a person willing to believe God. This is a miracle that only God understands how it works. It has to do with conforming our will to His, by faith. The Spirit's role in using God's word so the unbeliever is willing to put his faith on Christ is not fully understood (Col. 2:12). Paul was saying Apollos and I are only ministers, what Christ has done is what really matters. We should not elevate ministers, and neither should we disrespect them.] **8 Now <u>he that planteth and he that watereth are one</u>: and every man shall receive <u>his own reward according to his own labour.</u>** [Paul and Apollos are one on the same level as ministers. Every person who labors in what God is doing (1 Tim. 2:4) will receive a reward according to what he has done. This reward is probably a job, that is his position in heaven.]

9 For we are <u>labourers together with God</u>: ye are God's husbandry, ye are God's building. [We are working together with what God is doing as His messengers. As part of the body of Christ, the Corinthians are God's farmers, and His building (or Temple). Many farmers are needed to prepare the soil, plant, water, pull weeds, cultivate, harvest. Each receives wages and shares in the harvest. The goal is for the church to be at its spiritual best.] **10 According to the grace of God which is given unto me, as a wise <u>masterbuilder, I have laid the foundation, and another buildeth thereon. But let every man take heed how he buildeth thereupon.</u>** [God graciously gave Paul the position of masterbuilder and the ministry of laying the foundation for the body of Christ. Then Apollos came along and built on what Paul had begun. But everyone should be careful how they build on Paul's foundation.] **11 <u>For other foundation can no man lay than that is laid, which is Jesus Christ.</u>** [The foundation that Paul builds on is Jesus Christ according to the revelation of the mystery, or Christ's ministry from heaven which is distinct from His earthly ministry to Israel.] **12 Now <u>if any man build upon this foundation gold, silver, precious stones, wood, hay, stubble;</u>** [The gold is <u>wisdom</u>, the silver is <u>understanding</u>, and the precious stones are <u>knowledge</u> (of what God is doing at present 1 Tim. 2:4). All three words are found in Proverbs 2:1-5: "My son, if thou wilt receive my words [what God says], and hide my commandments with thee; So that thou incline thine ear unto <u>wisdom</u>, *and* apply thine heart to <u>understanding</u>; Yea, if thou criest after <u>knowledge</u>, *and* liftest up thy voice for understanding; If thou seekest her as silver, and searchest for her as *for* hid treasures; <u>Then shalt thou understand the fear of the LORD, and find the knowledge of God.</u>" These things last (Prov. 3:13-15; 16:16, 20:15) while wood, hay, and stubble (the wisdom of men, the world, and false doctrine) will burn up.]

13 <u>Every man's work shall be made manifest</u>: for the <u>day</u> shall declare it, because <u>it shall be revealed by fire</u>; and <u>the fire shall try every man's work of what sort it is.</u> [There will be rewards in heaven for faithful service built on the right foundation. At the Judgment Seat of Christ, there will be rewards for service done in this life on earth. Christ will try our work as by fire to see if it is good or bad (2 Cor. 5:10). <u>The fire of His word (Romans to Philemon)</u> and eyes will purify us by burning away any impurities. "<u>Is not my word like as a fire?</u>" (Jer. 23:29). Christ has eyes "like unto a flame of fire" (Rev. 2:18). Fire takes away and cleanses anything that is not pure. "Take away the dross from the silver, and there shall come forth a vessel for the finer" (Prov. 25:4). In a sense, our lives are like a race to see how much labor we can do with His Spirit working in us while on earth. Knowing that His will is to have "all men saved and to come to the knowledge of the truth" (1 Tim. 2:4). As ambassadors, we are sharing the gospel with the lost and those who think they are saved but have not trusted in Christ's work alone but added to their salvation (Rom. 4:5). We are also helping the weaker brother (Rom. 14) who mixes Peter and Paul (Israel's prophetic program with the mystery) to come to Pauline dispensationalism. We are so blessed to have come to the knowledge of this truth. We want as many as possible to be saved and join us in this knowledge before the Rapture. God wants us to <u>do our best</u> to have something of value at the Judgment Seat of Christ, (1 Cor. 9:24-27; 2 Tim. 4:7, 8). Paul also says that the Philippians and Thessalonian believers are his crown, Phil. 4:1; 1 Thess. 2:19.] **14 <u>If any man's work abide which he hath built thereupon, he shall receive a reward.</u>** [If any <u>man's work for service done on earth</u> (2 Cor. 5:10) does not burn up he will receive a reward.] **15 <u>If any man's work shall be burned, he shall suffer loss: but he himself shall be saved; yet so as by fire.</u>** [If a person's work is burnt up he will have loss of reward, but still get into heaven.]

16 <u>Know ye not that ye are the temple of God, and that the Spirit of God dwelleth in you?</u> [Paul reminds the Corinthian church that they are members of one another as a group, a holy temple for God to live in (Eph. 2:20-22). Notice the "ye" refers to the plural you meaning a group, not an individual. The King James Bible makes this distinction while modern Bibles do not. The Church, the body of Christ is a Temple for God to live in. This is a <u>corporate body</u>, while in 1 Cor. 6:19 Paul speaks of the temple being the physical <u>body of the individual</u>.] **17 If any man <u>defile the temple of God, him shall God destroy</u>; for <u>the temple of God is holy, which temple ye are.</u>** [Paul warns those who defile the temple of God by speaking against the body of Christ. In Psalm 79:1, unbelievers have come into Jerusalem's holy temple. God will destroy false teachers who attempt to defile the body of Christ from it's pure faith (Col. 2:4, 8, 18). Paul warned about wolves from without, and men from within who would draw disciples after themselves and not Christ (Acts 20:29, 30). God will bring them to ruin (Gal. 5:10). But in 2 Cor. 11:3, 4, 13, 14, 22, Paul said some Hebrews had come in to defile the Church. "For if he that cometh preacheth another Jesus [Christ's earthly ministry, not heavenly], whom we have not preached, or if ye receive another spirit [legalism, not grace], which ye have not received, or another gospel [the gospel of the kingdom, not the gospel of grace], which ye have not accepted, ye might well bear with him" (2 Cor. 11:4).]

18 ¶ <u>Let no man deceive himself. If any man among you seemeth to be wise in this world, let him become a fool, that he may be wise.</u> [A fool is one who considers himself wise. If any man has the world's wisdom and thinks he is wise, he is deceiving himself. We should be willing to be a fool for Christ like Paul because then we will be wise. The wise of the world think that the cross is foolishness (1:23); while God calls their wisdom foolishness (3:19).] **19 <u>For the wisdom of this world is foolishness with God. For it is written, He taketh the</u>**

wise in their own craftiness. [Job 5:13, Psa. 94:1, 2, 11. Satan thought he was wise and that no secret could be hid from him. "Behold, thou art wiser than Daniel; there is no secret that they can hide from thee" (Ezek. 28:3). Satan thought that if God's people, the Jews, crucified their Messiah that God would hate them and that he would gain the earth. But God caught Satan in his own craftiness and ransomed Jacob from him by keeping a secret (Jer. 31:11). God had a Glory Plan to glorify His Son in heaven and earth that He never mentioned until Paul (Eph. 1:9-12).] **20 And again, <u>The Lord knoweth the thoughts of the wise, that they are vain.</u>** [God knows that man's wisdom is empty.] **21 Therefore <u>let no man glory in men</u>. For <u>all things are yours</u>; 22 Whether <u>Paul, or Apollos, or Cephas, or the world, or life, or death, or things present, or things to come; all are yours;</u>** [Peter's ministry was to the circumcision. Some of the "little flock" believers had realized that God was now working through Paul and were helping him (such as Barnabas, Silas, and Luke). We will inherit with Christ all things.] **23 And ye are Christ's; and Christ is God's.** [<u>The wisdom of this world is foolishness to God. We are not to glory in men, but glory in God who has given us all things in Christ.</u>]

The following verses in Acts 18 help us to understand more about Apollos: 18:23 And after he [Paul] had spent some time there, he departed, and went over all the country of Galatia and Phrygia in order, strengthening all the disciples. [Paul went on his third Apostolic journey.]

24 ¶ And a certain Jew named Apollos, born at Alexandria, an eloquent man, and mighty in the scriptures, came to Ephesus. [Meanwhile Apollos comes to Ephesus.] **25 This man <u>was instructed in the way of the Lord; and being fervent in the spirit, he spake and taught diligently the things of the Lord, knowing only the baptism of John. 26 And he began to speak boldly in the synagogue: whom when Aquila and Priscilla had heard, they took him unto them, and expounded unto him the way of God more perfectly.</u>** [This couple privately caught Apollos up with the Lord Jesus' earthly through the twelve and His heavenly ministry through Paul.] **27 And when he was disposed to pass into Achaia, the brethren wrote, exhorting the disciples to receive him: who, when he was come, helped them much which had believed through grace:** [Apollos wanted to go to Achaia so the couple told him about the churches there, and wrote a letter of recommendation for Him.] **28 For he mightily convinced the Jews, and that publickly, shewing by the scriptures that Jesus was Christ.** [Apollos publically convinced many of the Jews in Corinth from scripture that Jesus was the Christ so they could be saved and join the body of Christ.]

Chapter 4 Stewards of the Mysteries, apostolic example
4:1-21 Apostolic function, example, and authority

4:1 Let a man so account of us, as of the <u>ministers of Christ, and stewards of the mysteries of God</u>. [Paul is the steward "of the mysteries" but graciously includes Apollos a secondary apostle as also being a steward of the mysteries because he is a worker in the faith given to Paul. We identified several secondary apostles to the body of Christ, in our study of chapter 3. The twelve apostles are not in the body of Christ but have a different destiny (Matt. 19:28). Paul and Apollos were ministers of Christ's heavenly, not His earthly ministry.] **2 Moreover it is required in <u>stewards</u>, that a man be found <u>faithful</u>.** [A steward <u>is a manager of his master's wealth</u> (for example Abraham's servant Eliezer, and Joseph in Potiphar's house). Paul "managed" and relayed God's hidden wisdom in person and in his letters. The mysteries God revealed to him concern His heaven-bound people.] **3 But with me it is a very small thing that <u>I should be judged of you, or of man's judgment</u>: yea, <u>I judge not mine own self</u>.** [Paul will be judged by his own Master according to his faithfulness.] **4 For I know nothing <u>by myself</u>; yet am I not hereby justified: but <u>he that judgeth me is the Lord</u>.** [Paul did not know this information by himself it was revealed to him. He faithfully shared the revelation of the mysteries he received from Christ with us (Gal. 1:11, 12). Paul is not justified by the work he does for Christ. What matters is what Christ does through the believer. We cannot be reluctant about taking a stand for the word of God rightly divided. We cannot be influenced by the fashion of this world. Because if we are, then our edification process is hampered. Instead, we should welcome the sufferings of Christ. Paul's only concern was pleasing God, not men. God is his judge, Paul cares nothing about the judgment of men, and does not even dare to judge himself. We are not to compare ourselves with one another, we serve Christ. Christ is our power source.] **5 Therefore judge nothing before the time, <u>until the Lord come</u>, who both will <u>bring to light the hidden things of darkness</u>, and will <u>make manifest the counsels of the hearts: and then shall every man have praise of God</u>.** [At the Judgment Seat of Christ, God will reveal the secrets of men's hearts (our motives and intentions, Heb. 4:12). The rewards we receive will probably be our job assignments in the heavenly places. Paul mentions himself first because Christ made him our "pattern" (1 Tim. 1:16) to follow and imitate. Paul and Apollos are only messengers it is Christ who is everything. The Lord Jesus Christ is the one who should be exalted.]

6 And these things, brethren, I have in a figure <u>transferred</u> to myself and to Apollos for your sakes [Paul uses himself and Apollos mere human messengers as our examples]**; that ye might <u>learn in us not to think of men above that which</u>**

is written, that no one of you be <u>puffed up for one against another</u>. [Paul and Apollos are only messengers and examples, it is Christ who is everything.] **7 For who maketh thee to differ from another? and <u>what hast thou that thou didst not receive? now if thou didst receive it, why dost thou glory, as if thou hadst not received it?</u>** [If Paul and Apollos were examples and a blessing to the Corinthians they should be grateful to God and not men. All that we have comes from Him. Even our spiritual understanding.]

8 Now ye are full, now ye are rich, ye have <u>reigned as kings without us: and I would to God ye did reign, that we also might reign with you.</u> [Paul uses loving sarcasm. You Corinthians brag about one another as if you were kings on thrones. How wonderful it must be to reign like kings and look down on others. Still Paul says, I wish that you really were genuine kings, and I wish we could reign with you.] **9 For I think that God hath set forth us the apostles last, <u>as it were appointed to death:</u> for we are made <u>a spectacle unto the world, and to angels, and to men.</u>** [Paul says God seems to have put us apostles last, as if appointed to death. I must be a despised apostle, a spectacle (gazingstock in an arena, Heb. 10:33) or extraordinary exhibit to the world and to angels. Since the mystery of the formation of the body of Christ in the dispensation of the grace of God was not revealed in the Bible until Paul revealed it, curious angels are learning from Paul and us in the body of Christ. Angels observe us so we should be careful to behave well (Eccl. 5:6; Eph. 3:10). Man was made a little lower than the angels, but because Christ is in us we will be elevated above them (Heb. 2:7-10).] **10 <u>We are fools for Christ's sake,</u> but ye are wise in Christ; <u>we are weak,</u> but <u>ye are strong; ye are honourable, but we are despised. 11 Even unto this present hour we both hunger, and thirst, and are naked, and are buffeted, and have no certain dwellingplace; 12 And labour, working with our own hands: being reviled, we bless; being persecuted, we suffer it: 13 Being defamed, we intreat</u>** [while being falsely accused and spoken badly of, we ask you anxiously to accept our message]: **<u>we are made as the filth of the world, and are the offscouring of all things unto this day.</u>** [<u>Paul and Apollos</u> blessed them while they reviled (spoke against) them. We should be willing to be a fool for Christ's sake. For example, when he told the Jews that circumcision doesn't matter he was not very popular with them and they beat him. He suffered many things even while writing this letter. He and Apollos both worked to support themselves. The world cannot understand this kind of sacrifice and calls that person a fool. Paul could have been a great Rabbi, but he gave it up to be a minister of Christ (Phil. 3:1-11). Paul was a fool; they were wise. They said Paul was weak in person; but thought they were strong. They were honorable, Paul was despised; but they thought they were impressive using the world's wisdom. We should rely on God's word, not the world's wisdom. We must be willing to be despised, thought of as scum of the earth. We should bless others while being reviled by them.] **14 I write not these things to shame you, but as my beloved sons I warn you.** [The Corinthians treated Paul less than what he deserved. Paul said he didn't write this letter to shame them but to warn them, because they were his beloved sons. He reminded them that he had begotten them in Christ when he gave them the gospel and showed them from scripture who Jesus was and what He had done. After that Paul patiently nursed them along for more than 18 months. Paul was their spiritual father, even if they had ten thousand instructors.] **15 For though ye have ten thousand instructors in Christ, yet have ye not many fathers: for in Christ Jesus I have begotten you through the gospel.** [There were too many chiefs and not enough Indians. Everyone thought they were a leader or teachers. Teachers need to have a solid understanding of the word of God rightly divided.] **16 Wherefore I beseech you, be ye followers of me.** [Paul implores them to follow him (11:1; Phil. 3:17).]

17 For this cause [division, because they do not understand that they need to follow Paul] **have I sent unto you Timotheus, who is my beloved son, and faithful in the Lord, who shall bring you into remembrance of my ways which be in Christ, as I teach every where in every church.** [Even now he was hoping that they would change their minds about who Paul was and follow him, and "his ways" (1 Tim. 1:16). Notice how Paul says "in Christ" Paul constantly gives Christ the credit for anything good that he does. Paul sent Timothy to them because he fully understood Paul's distinctive ministry and apostleship. Paul sent this letter from Ephesus with him. In Second Corinthians we find out that they did not respect Timothy so Paul had to dispatch Titus. Timothy was timid, but Titus spoke with confidence. Titus was finally able to give Paul a good report about how this letter had convicted them and changed their minds about Paul. They finally realized that Paul loved them enough to corrected them and to point them back to the fact that he was their Christ's appointed apostle, and they were behind him all the way.] **18 Now some are puffed up, as though I would not come to you.** [Paul had to be firm he mentions that phrase "puffed up" several times in this letter (4:6, 18, 19, 5:2) referring to the Corinthians attitude of superiority and carnal pride. The leaven (or yeast) of sin had crept into the church and puffed them up (5:6). They were inflated with "false spirituality" and showmanship. A carnal Christian often brags, but there is no demonstration of God's Spirit working through them (2:4). Therefore, Paul found it necessary to warn them saying fancy talk is cheap, but he is interested in their power. They said his letters are stern, but in person he is weak.] **19 But I will come to you shortly, if the Lord will, and will know, not the speech of them which are puffed up, but the power.** [They were thinking that Paul would not come to them. But, Paul did come to them (2 Cor. 2:1, 2 and 12:14)] **20 <u>For the kingdom of God is not in word, but in power. 21 What will ye? shall I come unto you with a rod, or in love, and in the spirit of meekness?</u>** [It must have grieved Paul to have to write this letter correcting the carnal Corinthians, but that is what they needed. Paul did it because he loved them. It was necessary for their own good. They needed to stop being divided and to realize that Christ had appointed him to be the apostle and was giving him revelation for the body of Christ. Did they want him to come with a <u>spanking stick</u> of correction when he came, or in <u>love</u>, and in the <u>spirit of meekness</u>? Meekness is power under control. It is being obedient to what God says.]

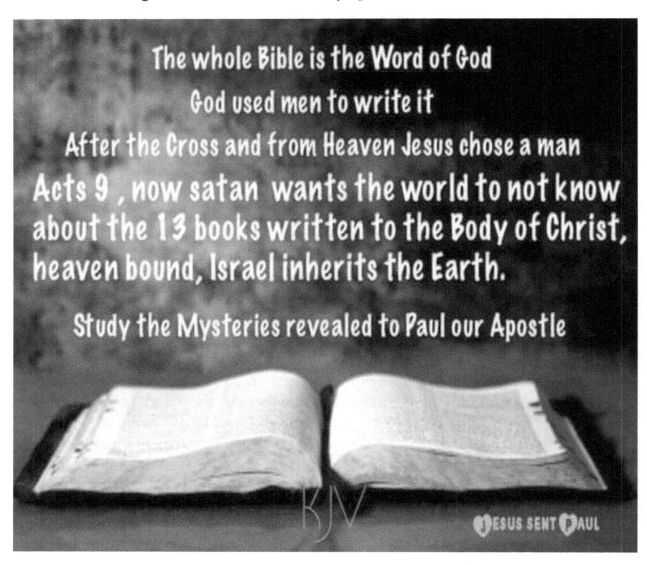

Chapter 5 Wrong living, immorality rebuked
5:1-13 Judging a member living in open sin (fornication)

5:1 It is <u>reported commonly</u> that there is <u>fornication among you</u>, and such fornication as is <u>not so much as named among the Gentiles</u>, that one should have his father's wife. [It was <u>common knowledge</u> "that a man should have his father's wife" to Paul by those of Chloe's household and probably confirmed by the three who brought the letter of church questions to Paul (16:17). This sin was even shocking among the Gentiles. To allow a church member to live in open sin hurts them as well as the reputation of the church. A man had relations with his father's wife. The woman involved (his stepmother) was not a member of the church or Paul would have dealt with her as well. Not only is this type of incest against what God says (Lev. 18:8) but it is covetousness (wanting what someone else has) and extortion (taking something that belongs to someone else). Sexual relations are not to be between a man and a woman, but between a husband and his wife. The marriage bed is "undefiled" (Heb. 13:4). James describes how wrong thinking produces sinful actions. "Let no man say when he is tempted, I am tempted of God: for God cannot be tempted with evil, neither tempteth he any man: But every man is tempted, when he is drawn away of his <u>own lust</u>, and <u>enticed. Then when lust hath conceived, it bringeth forth sin: and sin, when it is finished, bringeth forth death</u>" (James 1:14, 15). The lust is of the flesh, eyes, and pride of life (1 John 2:16). "This wisdom descendeth not from above, but is earthly [physical body], sensual [soul], devilish [spirit]" (James 3:15). Before we were saved who was our father? Satan was. At salvation God rescued us from that darkness (Col. 1:13; Eph. 2:1-3) and not only saved those who trust Christ, but sealed them with the Holy Ghost (Eph. 1:13, 14). God changes our thinking so we can live right and serve him. Paul is a wonderful example of a man with a regenerated spirit (Titus 3:5). He went from an angry, exceedingly mad man who hauled away men and women to prison, to wanting to save the jailer who put his lashed body in stocks in the inner prison (Acts 8:1, 16:23-31, 26:9-11). The fornicator's sin was a total disgrace even among the Gentiles. Can you remember someone in prophecy that also did that? Jacob's firstborn son Rueben did so. Therefore, he did not receive the birthright of a double portion. Joseph (the firstborn of Rachel) received that blessing so that both his sons Manasseh and Ephraim received an inheritance (portion) in the land of Israel (Gen. 49:3, 4).]

2 And ye are <u>puffed up</u>, and have not rather <u>mourned</u>, that he that hath done this deed might be <u>taken away from among you</u>. [Church members were "puffed up" glorying because they thought they were so "open minded" <u>tolerating the fornicator</u>. They should have been <u>mourning</u> that this person may not be saved if he was committing such gross immoral sin or they may need to excommunicate this person out of their assembly because his conduct may affect other church members.] **3 For I verily, as absent in body, but present in spirit, have <u>judged already</u>, as though I were present, concerning him that hath so done this deed, 4 In the name of our Lord Jesus Christ, when ye are gathered together, and my spirit, with the power of our Lord Jesus Christ,** [Paul had already judged the situation. This man was making bad choices (lust and pleasure for a moment) not realizing what his heart attitude should be because of all that Christ had done for him.] **5 To <u>deliver such an one unto Satan for the destruction of the flesh</u>, that the spirit may be saved in the <u>day of the Lord Jesus</u>.** [Notice how Paul does not say soul but spirit, because this man's problem is wrong thinking (just like the Corinthians). <u>Deliver him to Satan</u> means to <u>cut him off from church fellowship so he must live in the world</u>. Let him go from the assembly so he can destroy his flesh with the pleasures of this world so that he realizes his need for the Saviour and fellowship. The world is controlled by Satan (2 Cor. 4:4; Gal. 1:4) and is vain (empty). Sensual sin and perversion will bite in the end just like intoxication drink (Prov. 23:13-15, 26-35). <u>The purpose of such discipline is not to lose a member</u>, but rather first to <u>make sure they are saved</u> (will be raptured). But if he is saved, to bring him to repentance that he might be <u>saved from the loss of reward on the day of judgment</u>. Wandering saints need to be warned for their own good. Paul says in his letters that several types of believers should not be in the church. Members who have a reputation for <u>flagrant sin</u> (1 Cor. 5:9-11), those who <u>cause division</u> (Titus 3:10, 11), those who perpetuate <u>false doctrine with error</u> (Rom. 16:17; 1 Tim. 1:20), and those who <u>refuse to work</u> (2 Thess. 3:6-12). Mature believers should lovingly seek to restore those who are suddenly overtaken by sin (Gal. 6:1). Paul kept his own vessel in control (9:27).]

6 <u>Your glorying is not good</u>. Know ye not that a little leaven leaveneth the whole lump? 7 <u>Purge out therefore the old leaven</u>, that ye may be a <u>new lump</u>, as <u>ye are unleavened</u>. For even <u>Christ our passover is sacrificed for us</u>: 8 Therefore <u>let us keep the feast, not with old leaven</u>, neither with the leaven of malice and wickedness; <u>but with the unleavened bread of sincerity and truth</u>. [Paul begins the bread analogy. Paul said <u>purge out old leaven</u> (the fornicator) so the church can be <u>a new unleavened lump</u> of dough. In prophecy leaven is a symbol of sin. Before the Passover the Jews were to go through their homes and remove all leaven (Ex. 12:14-20). Likewise, the church should clean house and remove the leaven, the fornicator. Would you open your home to anyone? Do you not realize that one member living in open sin can defile the entire church? For Christ is the unleavened bread (without sin) our Passover sacrifice. Therefor we can celebrate what He has done for the Church every day (Col. 2:16). Do not purge the offender out because of hatred but because you care for this man. For we can even treat the fornicator without leaven (sin) and malice (evil) and without wickedness, but in sincerity and truth. While he was malicious and wicked.]

9 I wrote unto you in an epistle not to company with fornicators: 10 Yet <u>not altogether with the fornicators of this world</u>, or with the <u>covetous, or extortioners, or with idolaters</u>; for then must ye needs go out of the world. 11 <u>But now I have written unto you not to keep company, if any man that is called a brother</u> be a <u>fornicator, or covetous, or an idolater, or a railer, or a drunkard, or an extortioner</u>; with such an one no not to eat. [<u>Paul now clarifies a letter that he had written before. I used to believe it was a letter that was not scripture, but it could be the Thessalonian letters to the Gentiles (1 Thess. 4:3; 2 Thess. 3:6)</u>. Paul said, "And <u>if any man obey not our word by this epistle, note that man</u>, and have no company with him, that he may be ashamed" (2 Thess. 3:14). Paul clarifies his instruction saying they are not to associate with a person who calls themselves <u>a believer</u> and blatantly sins. If he "calls" himself a believer, he may or may not be a believer (only God knows the heart). However, we find out in 2 Cor. 2:6-8 that this man was a true believer and did repent and realized his error, but that the leadership of the church was reluctant to let him back into the church. We expect the unsaved to sin. But even the world expects Christians to be different. Church members should not be like the world. One reason the church has so little influence in the world today is that <u>the world has too much influence in many local churches</u>. We are not to even eat with church members who have ruined their testimony by open sin and have never made things right with the church and the Lord. If the church tolerates the sin they are condoning the sin.]

12 <u>For what have I to do to judge them also that are without?</u> do not ye judge them that are within? [Paul says that he is concerned with the body of Christ, not unbelievers, and that believers should judge the actions of believers. <u>It shocks some believers when they hear that they are supposed to judge others.</u>] **13 But them that are without God judgeth. Therefore put away from among yourselves that wicked person.** [We are not to judge those without Christ, God will do that. But we are to expel those who live in open sin, and will not change their minds and decide to stop sinning and live unto God, from the local assembly. Church discipline must not be done hastily but all parties involved must be permitted to state their case. Sometimes weaker brethren will accuse a strong King James Bible believers and right divider because they are ignorant of these facts. On other occasions it is Satan who tries to bring division among the believers (2 Cor. 2:11). There must be prayer and the word of God must be consulted. There must be sincere Christian love (Gal. 6:1). Only God can judge the thoughts and intents of the heart (4:5) but we are to judge other believer's actions (2:15). Paul says that what that man did was wicked. <u>Now Paul says straight out that the fornicator should be put out of the church.</u> When we are in the flesh we are useless as laborers for God. This is what Satan wants. Our enemy is very sneaky. "For to be <u>carnally minded is death;</u> but to be spiritually minded is <u>life</u> and <u>peace</u>" (Rom. 8:6). <u>When believers are "carnally minded" they live and act like the lost. The carnal are in the flesh (the sin nature) and not useful sons of God.</u> For the body of Christ, the answer for how to live the Christian life is in our doctrine, Romans to Philemon.]

> And such were some of you: but ye are washed, but ye are sanctified, but ye are justified in the name of the Lord Jesus, and by the Spirit of our God. All things are lawful unto me, but all things are not expedient: all things are lawful for me, but I will not be brought under the power of any.
> 1 Corinthians 6:11-12 KJV
> PAUL IS THE APOSTLE TO THE BODY OF CHRIST

Chapter 6 Disputes in the courts. The Holy Ghost in us.
6:1-8 Christians are forbidden to go to law against each other before unbelievers. We are to judge this present world in this life, and we will judge angels.
6:9-11 Our bodies are holy because they are washed, sanctified, and justified.
6:12-18 Our bodies belong to the Lord.
6:19, 20 Our bodies are the temple of the Holy Ghost.

6:1 Dare any of you, <u>having a matter against another, go to law before the unjust, and not before the saints?</u> [Paul is saying do you not understand how hazardous and dangerous it is to ask unbelievers instead of believers to judge between you?] **2 Do ye not know that the <u>saints shall judge the world?</u> and if the world shall be judged by you, are ye unworthy <u>to judge the smallest matters?</u>** [We are to judge all things pertaining to this life (2:5, 6:3). Paul asks, are you not able to judge the little disputes among yourselves? People today often use lawsuits as a get rich scheme. I remember some lady sued McDonald's because she spilled her hot coffee. People like to blame others for their stupid decisions and not take responsibility for their own actions. Paul is not saying that there is anything wrong with the courts of law because government structure was instituted by God for our good (Rom. 13). But unsaved judges do not have the ability to decide spiritual matters. The church members in Corinth were ruining their testimony and disgracing the name of the Lord by going to public courts.]

3 <u>Know ye not that we shall judge angels?</u> how much more things that <u>pertain to this life?</u> [When Paul says to judge the world he means in this life, in the world today. The church is to judge the world and things that pertain to this life. Paul essentially says, "can't you judge the small matters among yourself, even the fornicator." We are supposed to know what is going on in the world politics, laws, weather, etc. But we are not to get entangled by them (2 Tim. 2:4). <u>Our goal is to keep singled eyed on what God wants to accomplish, and not to get caught up with those who are blind to the things of God. If we really want to know what is going on, it is more important to read the Bible than the newspaper.</u> Paul probably prayed for Nero's salvation, and I prayed for Obama's. We are commanded to pray for our leaders (1 Tim. 2:1, 2), so let us be diligent to pray for wisdom, discernment and right action for President Trump. The Corinthians and us should practice being able to judge now because we will <u>judge holy angels when we are in heaven.</u> The word "judge" means to rule. This realization should make worldly disputes seem less important.] **4 If then <u>ye have judgments of things pertaining to this life, set them to judge who are least esteemed in the church</u>.** [If the church members have no courage to judge a matter because they are worried about their reputation, then pick the least esteemed in the church to do it (because anyone can do the job). You are too afraid to make unpopular decisions! Being a parent (like Paul was their spiritual father) is not a popularity contest. What matters is the well-being of the church members.] **5 I speak to your shame. Is it so, that there is not a wise man among you? no, <u>not one that shall be able to judge between his brethren?</u>** [Shame on you says, Paul. Is there not one wise enough to be a mediator or arbitrator between brethren? If two parties cannot reach an agreement, then they can quietly bring the matter before a spiritually mature Christian in the church. This person should prayerfully, privately, and discreetly be able to judge the matter.] **6 But <u>brother goeth to law with brother, and that before the unbelievers.</u>** [You are suing each other in front of unbelievers!] **7 Now therefore there is utterly <u>a fault among you, because ye go to law one with another. Why do ye not rather take wrong?</u> why do ye not rather <u>suffer yourselves to be defrauded?</u>** [Their thinking is not right. <u>Defraud means</u> taking something that rightfully belongs to someone else without consent. It is better to let ourselves be defrauded than to go bring lawsuits in public courts before unbelievers. Forget the wrong things people do to you, let them go! Too many Christians get wrapped up and consumed trying to protect their rights and get a little money from other Christians which takes away from serving God.] **8 Nay, <u>ye do wrong, and defraud, and that your brethren.</u>** [Do you not understand how wrong it is to defraud a brother in Christ? You are brethren, so love one another. We should not insist on having our rights. We should say "you first" and then the other should reply, "No, I insist you first." Show love to one another, we are family (Gal. 6:10).]

9 Know ye not that <u>the unrighteous shall not inherit the kingdom of God? Be not deceived:</u> neither <u>fornicators,</u> nor idolaters, nor adulterers, nor effeminate, nor abusers of themselves with mankind, 10 Nor thieves, nor covetous, nor drunkards, nor revilers, nor extortioners, shall inherit the kingdom of God. [Paul says do you not know that the unrighteous (unbelievers) will not inherit the kingdom of God? So why do you bring your complaints to them? The kingdom of God is made up of two realms: heaven (to be populated by the body of Christ) and earth (to be populated by the kingdom of heaven on earth believers). Who wants them to be deceived? That is right that old Serpent of old, Satan. Then Paul lists eleven awful sins beginning with fornication that the unrighteous unbelievers are now and believers used to be (6:6, Eph. 5:1-10, Gal. 5:19-22).] **11 And <u>such were some of you:</u> but ye are <u>washed,</u> but ye are <u>sanctified,</u> but ye are <u>justified in the name of the Lord Jesus,</u> and by the Spirit of our God.** [They used to be like these unbelievers but now they have the imputed righteousness of Christ (2 Cor. 5:21) and their position is perfect and complete in Him (Col. 2:10) they have been declared just before God by the Spirit of our God

(Gal. 2:16).] **12 All things are lawful unto me, but all things are not expedient: all things are lawful for me, but I will not be brought under the power of any.** [We are not under the law but under grace. We have liberty (freedom). Nothing is prohibited but Paul is not going to allow himself to be ruled by his appetites and be brought under control of evil things. Paul is responsible. God believes in us. He shows us grace. God is confident that by treating us as adult sons and lovingly allowing us free will to decide, that we will choose to serve Him and do right. God knows that love is the best motivator. He loved us first (1 John 4:19).] **13 Meats for the belly, and the belly for meats: but God shall destroy both it and them.** [Lusts are like dainty morsels of meat (Prov. 23:1-8). God will destroy the meats and the unrighteous unbelievers.] **Now the body is not for fornication, but for the Lord; and the Lord for the body.** [Our bodies belong to the Lord, and the Lord for the body. We should serve the Lord with our body now (Rom. 6:18, 12:1). We can be motivated by God's grace to do right. Grace teaches us to live "soberly, righteously, and godly, in this present world" (Titus 2:12).] **14 And God hath both raised up the Lord, and will also raise up us by his own power.** [Paul puts their eyes on the main thing. What matters is that God has raised up the Lord and will raise us up by the same power. We have been promised eternal life. The Father raised up Jesus Christ (Gal. 1:1; 2 Cor. 4:14). The Son raised Himself up (John 10:17). The Holy Spirit raised Jesus from the dead and will also raise us up (Rom. 8:11).]

15 Know ye not that your bodies are the members of Christ? shall I then take the members of Christ, and make them the members of an harlot? God forbid. [Paul is still talking about the evils of fornication he began in chapter 5. Notice how he uses questions to make them think and his points easy to understand. We also detect his obvious outrage.] **16 What? know ye not that he which is joined to an harlot is one body? for two, saith he, shall be one flesh.** [In Gen. 2:24 God says that we are one flesh when we have physical relations with others. People look for love in all the wrong places, when God has already loved us (Rom. 5:8, 8:32).] **17 But he that is joined unto the Lord is one spirit.** [But we are one spirit with the Lord being spiritually joined with Him (Eph. 5:25-32). Paul occasionally uses the marriage analogy with us the body of Christ, but we are the one new man (Eph. 2:15) a "he" while Israel is the Bride of Christ a "she." Christ is our "head," but Israel's royal "Bridegroom."] **18 Flee fornication. Every sin that a man doeth is without the body; but he that committeth fornication sinneth against his own body.** [Fornication is a sin against the Lord who we belong to and against ourselves, therefore escape from it, avoid it!] **19 What? know ye not that your body is the temple of the Holy Ghost which is in you, which ye have of God, and ye are not your own?** [Our bodies are the temple of the Holy Ghost and we do not belong to ourselves. The entire Godhead is in us (Eph. 4:6; Col. 1:27). We who are "in Christ, he is a new creature" (2 Cor. 5:17) individually and corporately (Gal. 6:15). Israel is also "born again" individually by faith in what God says (1 Peter 1:23) and will be born again corporately at Christ's Second Coming (Isa. 66:8).] **20 For ye are bought with a price: therefore glorify God in your body, and in your spirit, which are God's.** [Christ Redeemed both groups of believers with His blood on the cross (Col. 1:14; 1 Peter 1:18, 19). Both His earthly kingdom believers and His kingdom in heaven believers. Therefore, we should glorify God in our body and spirit which belong to Him (Eccl. 12:7; Luke 23:46; Rom. 12:1).]

GOD HAS TWO DIFFERENT PEOPLE

WITH TWO DIFFERENT AND SEPARATE PROGRAMS

All saved people, saints of all ages, are IN CHRIST.
However, apostle Paul was the first to be saved and sealed
IN THE BODY OF CHRIST. To say that the 12 are IN THE BODY, is to say
the 12 are not part of Israel's covenants and that they will
not be able to function according to prophecy in order to reign
with Christ in the Millenium Kingdom as part of a
Kingdom of priests. But, that's simply not what the KJV Bible
rightly divided teaches us.

Chapter 7 Concerning marriage
7:1-7 God has established marriage. It is better to marry than to burn.
7:8-24 Marriage between believers and unbelievers.
7:25-40 Advice to the unmarried and their parents.

7:1 Now concerning the things whereof ye wrote unto me: It is good for a man not to touch a woman. [One reason why Paul remained celibate was so that he might devote himself completely to the service of Christ.] **2 Nevertheless, to avoid fornication, let every man have his own wife, and let every woman have her own husband.** [However, marriage can help the husband and wife avoid fornication because their intimate needs are filled. Other reasons for marriage are companionship and affection and to prevent immorality. Part of the duty of a husband and a wife is to give themselves to intimate relations with one another.] **3 Let the husband render unto the wife due benevolence:** [Doing good, bringing joy, and pleasure.] **and likewise also the wife unto the husband. 4 The wife hath not power of her own body, but the husband: and likewise also the husband hath not power of his own body, but the wife.** [The husband's body belongs to the wife and the wife's body to the husband. We are not to practice self-gratification, but gratification within the confines of marriage. Paul clearly teaches monogamy between one husband and one wife. Furthermore, it was important for husbands to be satisfied at home and not run up to the Temple of Aphrodite on top of the mountain overlooking the city of Corinth with its thousand temple prostitutes.] **5 Defraud ye not one the other, except it be with consent for a time, that ye may give yourselves to fasting and prayer; and come together again, that Satan tempt you not for your incontinency.** [Withholding intimate relations is a type of defrauding of the spouse unless done by mutual consent for a short time of prayer and fasting. But then come together again so that Satan cannot tempt either one from seeking satisfaction elsewhere. Incontinence means unable to contain themselves.] **6 But I speak this by permission, and not of commandment.** [Paul says I am telling you this by permission from Christ, not by commandment.] **7 For I would that all men were even as I myself. But every man hath his proper gift of God, one after this manner, and another after that.** [Paul wishes that everyone had the gift of celibacy. Paul may have been married at one time since he was probably a member of the Sanhedrin (he cast his vote against the believers in the little flock in Acts 26:10) and marriage was a requirement for that office. But he was now celibate and serving the Lord. Paul says I have the gift of celibacy but I know that everyone has different gifts.]

8 ¶ I say therefore to the unmarried and widows, It is good for them if they abide even as I. 9 But if they cannot contain, let them marry: for it is better to

marry than to burn. 10 And unto the married <u>I command</u>, yet not I, but the Lord, <u>Let not the wife depart from her husband: 11 But and if she depart, let her remain unmarried, or be reconciled to her husband: and let not the husband put away his wife.</u> [If someone has the desire for intimate relations and a life partner let them marry that is not sinning. The Lord told Paul that a wife should not depart from her husband. If she leaves for a while she should not marry another but may go back and reconcile with her husband. Paul is permitting not commanding separation. A husband is not to put away his wife. We are not under the law but under grace (Rom. 6:14).] **12 But to the rest speak I, <u>not the Lord</u>: If any brother hath a wife that believeth not, and she be pleased to dwell with him, let him not put her away. 13 And the woman which hath an husband that believeth not, and if he be pleased to dwell with her, let her not leave him. 14 For <u>the unbelieving husband is sanctified by the wife, and the unbelieving wife is sanctified by the husband: else were your children unclean; but now are they holy</u>. 15 But if the unbelieving depart, let him depart. A brother or a sister is <u>not under bondage in such cases</u>: but God hath called us <u>to peace</u>. 16 For what knowest thou, O wife, whether thou shalt <u>save thy husband</u>? or how knowest thou, O man, whether thou shalt <u>save thy wife</u>?** [Husbands and wives of unbelievers should remain with unsaved partners and do their best to win them to Christ. We are to live in peace with them. I heard a pastor say that he led his wife to the Lord because he did not presume that she was saved even though she was in the church choir and did many other "Christian" things. We have to ask our spouses what they are trusting in to get them into heaven. If it is not in Christ alone then they are not saved. The other partner and their children are sanctified by the believer because through them they have an opportunity to be saved by observing the believer. But if the unbeliever leaves then through abandonment the marriage relationship is broken and the partner has a chance for divorce and remarriage.] **17 But as God hath distributed to every man, <u>as the Lord hath called every one, so let him walk</u>. And so ordain I in all churches. 18 Is any man <u>called being circumcised? let him not become uncircumcised. Is any called in uncircumcision? let him not be circumcised.</u>** [Remain in the physical condition you are in when you are saved. Some teach that this verse refers to the little flock and the body of Christ believers; but I believe Paul is talking about physical circumcision. Circumcision is nothing today because the cross-work of Christ is everything (Gal. 2:3; 5:1-6). "We contributed nothing to our salvation except the sin that made it necessary" as Johnathan Edwards said. There is no distinction in the body of Christ among believers, between Jews and Gentiles we are all one in Christ (Gal. 3:28). <u>I believe that Paul is saying that just like the color of someone's skin does not matter in marriage neither does their religious background matter. All that matters is that they have trusted in Christ for their salvation</u>. We are made of one blood (Acts 17:26). In Israel's program circumcision mattered (Gen. 17). God was mad with Moses for not having his son circumcised (Ex. 4:25). Today, Israel is not the preferred nation, the "middle wall of partition" is down (Eph. 2:14). Israel of today is in apostasy not believing in their Messiah. After the Rapture God will resume His dealings with Israel. Today, both Jews and Gentiles are saved by believing Paul's gospel (1 Cor. 15:3, 4). Today to be water baptized or physically circumcised is a sign of unbelief in what God is doing. Our baptism and circumcision are both spiritual and take place the moment we believe (1 Cor. 12:13, Col. 2:9-15). Since we can't feel this, we accept it by faith in what the Bible says. When we identify with Christ's death and resurrection through faith God performed an operation without hands and circumcised or cut the connection between our soul and our body (flesh), freeing us from the power of our flesh. The fleshly nature was rendered dead and powerless, so if the believer sins now he does so by choice. God made us spiritually alive with Christ forgiving us of all our trespasses. He blotted out all the sins that we had committed, all the wrong things that we had done against God. He took them out of the way and nailed them to the cross. *Notice that Christ in whom the Godhead dwells bodily spoiled (plundered, or took us back from Satan and his devils). Jesus was victorious and triumphed over Satan. He openly shamed him and his cohorts with one gigantic costly sacrifice of obedience to the Father demonstrating the manifold wisdom of God. Jews and Gentiles can marry in the Lord in this age (Col. 3:11). Furthermore, there are no health reasons for being circumcised according to the American College of Pediatrics. Remember in many countries in Europe none of the men are circumcised (except the Jews) and they do not have an increased health problem because of that. Sexual contact and uncleanliness are what causes sexually transmitted disease. In fact, uncircumcision may have a protective purpose and assist with increased sensitivity. Remember that Adam was made perfectly to live forever and he had foreskin. The circumcision of the Jews involves just the tip of the foreskin and not all of it (like in America). Circumcision was a token of the covenant between God and His nation (Gen. 17:11). It was a sign for Israel to trust in God, not their flesh (like Abraham did when he had Ishmael). Even for Israel, they were to have a circumcision of the heart. But we are not under the law, but under grace.] **19 Circumcision is nothing, and uncircumcision is nothing, but the keeping of the commandments of God.** [Christ has done everything to save us, so whether a man is circumcised or not, does not matter. We obey the commandments Christ gave us through Paul and to be circumcised was not one of them (14:37). Circumcision was one the covenants that belong to Israel (Rom. 9:4).] **20 Let every man abide in the same calling wherein he was called. 21 Art thou called being a servant? care not for it: but if thou mayest be made free, use it rather. 22 For he that is called in the Lord, being a servant, is the Lord's**

freeman: likewise also he that is called, being free, is Christ's servant. [Believers are to stay where they are when they were saved as far as their socio-economic workplace goes. But if you have an opportunity to improve your workplace take it. Servants are free in Christ, and free men are His servants. If you are a slave and have an opportunity to be free take it. Servants can marry others in the Lord. There are no socio-economic prohibitions in marriage.] **23 Ye are bought with a price; be not ye the servants of men.** [Paul says "bought with a price" for the second time (6:20) so serve God.] **24 Brethren, let every man, wherein he is called, therein abide with God.**

25 ¶ Now concerning virgins I have no commandment of the Lord: yet I give my judgment, as one that hath obtained mercy of the Lord to be faithful. 26 I suppose therefore that this is good for the present distress, I say, that it is good for a man so to be. 27 Art thou bound unto a wife? seek not to be loosed. Art thou loosed from a wife? seek not a wife. [Concerning virgins (male or female) Paul says let a man remain a virgin (Rev. 14:4). The present distress was the sufferings during the foundation of the body of Christ. If you are married stay that way, if you are unmarried stay that way.] **28 But and if thou marry, thou hast not sinned; and if a virgin marry, she hath not sinned. Nevertheless such shall have trouble in the flesh: but I spare you.** [If a virgin marries they have not sinned. But for the sake of the female Paul says she will have trouble in the flesh. Marriage brings responsibilities. Women have so much work to do in the home. No human is able to meet another human's need completely. Humans are imperfect so we both need to be patient with each other. It is nice to have a companion in this life. Only God can meet our every need. The woman was to be a coregent with Adam (Gen 1:26-28), but because Eve sinned, the husband rules over the wife. Christ's righteousness upon salvation is greater than the sin of Adam and Eve (Rom. 5). There is still a hierarchy between equals as we will learn in chapter 11. In the kingdom, Christ will rule with His Bride (Israel's believers).] **29 But this I say, brethren, the time is short: it remaineth, that both they that have wives be as though they had none; 30 And they that weep, as though they wept not; and they that rejoice, as though they rejoiced not; and they that buy, as though they possessed not; 31 And they that use this world, as not abusing it: for the fashion of this world passeth away.** [Time is short because our lifetimes are short, we do not know when we will be raptured, and this world is passing away and will be replaced (2 Peter 3:7-13). Serve God as if you did not have a wife. It is time for those who weep because of widowhood or abandonment to serve God as if they had no sorrow. Those who rejoice (newlyweds) to work as if they did not. Businessmen do not let your business take you away from working for the Lord. Do not let your possessions possess you. This world is a very vain (empty) fashion show (Psa. 90:10). "All the world's a stage, and all the men and women merely players: they have their exits and their entrances; and one man in his time plays many parts, his acts being seven ages" William Shakespeare.] **32 But I would have you without carefulness. He that is unmarried careth for the things that belong to the Lord, how he may please the Lord: 33 But he that is married careth for the things that are of the world, how he may please his wife. 34 There is difference also between a wife and a virgin. The unmarried woman careth for the things of the Lord, that she may be holy both in body and in spirit: but she that is married careth for the things of the world, how she may please her husband.** [But be not full of care. If you are unmarried you will care for the things that belong to the Lord, how we can please Him. But the married care for the things of the world, how they can please their spouse.] **35 And this I speak for your own profit; not that I may cast a snare upon you, but for that which is comely, and that ye may attend upon the Lord without distraction. 36 But if any man think that he behaveth himself uncomely toward his virgin, if she pass the flower of her age, and need so require, let him do what he will, he sinneth not: let them marry.** [In that culture it was customary for the father to decide who the daughter should marry. Paul speaks for our best interest. Paul does not want us to feel trapped. He just says that it is best to stay single so we can serve the Lord without distraction. Jesus said something similar: "For there are some eunuchs, which were so born from their mother's womb: and there are some eunuchs, which were made eunuchs of men: and there be eunuchs, which have made themselves eunuchs for the kingdom of heaven's sake. He that is able to receive it, let him receive it" (Matt. 19:12). If a father wants his daughter to marry and she has come of age, he can go and find her a husband and let them marry which is not a sin.] **37 Nevertheless he that standeth stedfast in his heart, having no necessity, but hath power over his own will, and hath so decreed in his heart that he will keep his virgin, doeth well. 38 So then he that giveth her in marriage doeth well; but he that giveth her not in marriage doeth better.** [So the father that gives his virgin in marriage does well, but the father that decided in his heart to be responsible for and to provide for his virgin daughter so she can remain single and serve the Lord does better.] **39 The wife is bound by the law as long as her husband liveth; but if her husband be dead, she is at liberty to be married to whom she will; only in the Lord. 40 But she is happier if she so abide, after my judgment: and I think also that I have the Spirit of God.** [Marriage is for life. The wife should stay married "till death do you part." If her husband dies, she is free to marry whom she wants, but only to a believer (2 Cor. 6:14-18). Paul says he has the Spirit of God as he writes and that the widow will be happier if she stays single. We may marry whom we will only in the Lord. Regarding marriage and divorce, we are under grace. If there is physical abuse in the marriage or dangerous activity like drug and alcohol abuse, or sexual infidelity (which may lead to deadly venereal disease like AIDS) then the spouse should be able to exit the marriage for their own safety. Christ taught that adultery was grounds for divorce (Matt. 19:7-9). Even God divorced Israel for a season because of her spiritual adultery (Jer. 3:8; Isa. 50:1). But God did not have relations with another during that time but remained faithful to His people (Rev. 19:7, 21:9-14).]

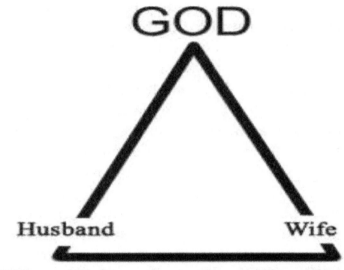

When further from God, the distance between husband and wife is greater.

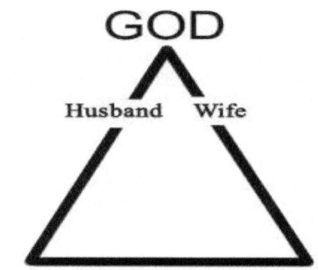

When closer to God, the husband and wife will be closer to each other.

Chapter 8 The weaker brother, idols, and our liberty
8:1-13 Meat offered to idols, Christ our example, and the weaker brother.

8:1 Now as <u>touching things offered unto idols</u>, we know that <u>we all have knowledge. Knowledge puffeth up</u>, but <u>charity edifieth</u>. [Paul is answering their questions regarding meat (food) offered to idols. While it is true that knowledge can "puff" us up. Paul does not mean that we should not do all we can to know God and what He says through His word. This is why he prays for the Ephesians and Colossians that they may have knowledge (Eph. 1:17; Col. 1:9, 10). Paul's goal was knowledge of Jesus (Phil 3:10; 2 Cor. 10:5). But knowledge must be balanced by charity (love in action) which builds up. How often does our flesh want to be exalted? All the time. Therefore, we must as Paul says, "I die daily" (15:31). It is not about me or us, it is about Christ. We must die to ourselves, and live unto Christ. It is "not I, but Christ" (Gal. 2:20). We reverence the Godhead, are in awe of His word, and are grateful that He graciously gives us eternal life and not what we deserve. We must do all for the glory of God. Our motive should always be to exalt the Lord Jesus Christ, and bless the body of Christ. It takes only one millisecond to go from walking in the Spirit to living in the flesh that is why Paul says "I keep under my body, and bring it into subjection" (9:27). But in our zeal and liberty, we must be careful not to stumble the weaker brother.

In the context, this "knowledge" is the understanding that eating meat offered to idols does not matter. What matters is what Christ has done. But we must not use our liberty to stumble someone whose conscience may think it is wrong to eat that meat. These chapters (8-10) address the weaker brother principle found in Romans chapter 14 to 15:3.

I used to be a weaker brother before I learned how to rightly divide the word of truth (2 Tim. 2:15). At that time, I did not eat my favorite part of my pizza, the sausage, because I was a mixer and thought the Jewish dietary laws somehow pertained to me. I mixed Peter and Paul, law and grace, the things that belonged to Israel with those of the body of Christ because I thought that the Church, the body of Christ, began in Acts 2. I had not yet learned that the body of Christ began in Acts 9. I did not know that there was more than one church in the Bible. I did not know that there was more than one church in the Bible. The church in the wilderness (Acts 7:38), the Messianic Judaism church in Matthew (16:16-18; Psalm 22:22; Heb. 2:12) and then the body of Christ (Eph. 1:22, 23).

In Acts 10:15, God showed Peter that He was no longer making the distinction between clean and unclean animals or people (the clean represented the Jews and the unclean, the Gentiles). What happened? Why the change? Peter did not understand why until Paul told him in Acts 15 and Galatians 2. God has postponed His prophetic dealings with the nation of Israel because they rejected their Messiah for the third time in Acts 7 with the stoning of the Holy Ghost filled Stephen. Israel committed the blasphemy of the Holy Ghost, and are in apostasy.

2 And if any man think that he knoweth any thing, he knoweth nothing yet as he ought to know. [We can think we know something when we really just have a very limited concept of how things are, compared to God. For one thing, Paul had not received the full revelation of the mystery yet (1 Cor. 13:12) and for another thing, every one of us must be careful not to fall into the temptation of wrong a motive (Gal. 6:1-5).] **3 But if any man love God, the same is known of him.** [Loving God for what He has done is the knowledge that counts. God sees our hearts and knows those who belong to Him. "Nevertheless the foundation of God standeth sure, having this seal, The Lord knoweth them that are his. And, Let every one that nameth the name of Christ depart from iniquity" (2 Tim. 2:19). The Bible says that the Lord knows us and has sealed us unto the day of redemption (Eph. 4:30). A sealed person is a saved person. We cannot tell who is saved by looking at them. So how can we know? By their testimony. By who and what they say they are trusting in for their salvation.] **4 As concerning therefore the eating of those things that are offered in sacrifice unto idols, <u>we know that an idol is nothing in the world, and that there is none other God but one</u>**. [There is but only one God. Since there is no power in an idol the meat is not affected in any way.] **5 For though there be that are called gods, whether in heaven or in earth, (as there be gods many, and lords many,)** [There were many temples for the Greek gods in Corinth, like the Temple of Apollos. These false gods were merely called gods, they were really not gods but a result of men's imagination and superstition in trying to explain their existence. Perhaps some of the gods were a result of worshipping constellations or pieces of meteors. They made their likeness in stone (marble), wood, and metal.] **6 But to us there is but one God, the Father, of whom are all things, and we in him; and one Lord Jesus Christ, by whom are all things, and we <u>by him.</u>** [The knowledgeable Christian knows that there is only one God, the Father who made all things and that we are in Him (Col. 3:3). There is but one Lord Jesus Christ who made all things, and we have life because of Him.] **7 Howbeit there is not in every man that knowledge: for some with conscience of the idol unto this hour eat it as a thing offered unto an idol; and their conscience being weak is defiled.** [Weak meaning becoming fearful. Some weaker brothers can have their conscience bother them; their conscience can be defiled. So they criticized the others who felt at liberty to eat the meat. This is often the case today, it is the weaker non-Pauline believers who think they are being spiritual when they abstain from certain things. These are the ones who are offended. This kind of separation is not due to spirituality; it is due to ignorance. Read Rom. 14-15:3. In Romans 14:23, Paul says that going against our conscience is sin. So let us define the word. Conscience (Noah Webster, 1828 Dictionary): Internal or self-knowledge, or judgment of right and wrong; or the faculty, power or principle within us, which decides on the lawfulness or unlawfulness of our own actions and affections, and instantly approves or condemns them.] **8 But meat commendeth us not to God: for neither, if we eat, are we the better; neither, if we eat not, are we the worse.** [What we eat or do not eat does not matter to God (Col. 2:20-23). We can eat disgusting things if we want to, what matters is if we have trusted in Christ. Paul clearly says that idols are not real, and that meat offered to idols could not hurt anyone. There is no demonic influence in that quality meat.] **9 But take heed lest by any means this liberty of yours become a stumblingblock to them that are weak.** [Some believers do not have this knowledge. They do not realize that food is not sinful in itself. The Corinthian believer could go and get the meat at the temple shop and eat it without any problem. But what about their weaker brother? Were they concerned with how it will affect him? Paul says in 10:23, all things are lawful but not all things are expedient, all things do not edify.]

10 For if any man see thee which hast knowledge sit at meat in the idol's temple, shall not the conscience of him which is weak be emboldened to eat those things which are offered to idols; [If someone sees you eating food at the temple, he might feel bold and imitate you, but later his conscience might convict him because he is weak in knowledge. There are many things that we should not do because of love for others.] **11 And through thy knowledge shall the weak brother perish, for whom Christ died?** [Our knowledge and liberty can be dangerous to others and cause them to stumble or perish. What a tragedy if a believer were to defile their conscience, or a lost sinner reject Christ because a selfish Christian wants to assert "his rights" and have his way without thinking how it may affect another person. Christ died for him, He sacrificed Himself, and we should be able to make a small sacrifice and forgo eating the temple food for our weak brother or sister in the faith. Those who do not understand God's grace for today and Paul's distinctive apostleship are the weaker brothers.] **12 But when ye sin so against the brethren, and wound their weak conscience, ye sin against Christ.** [When we are responsible for a believer falling away from Christ, we are affecting Christ Himself. Our liberty can wound another's conscience which is to sin against Christ. It is not a question of right or wrong, but how will it affect the weak brother. It is better to go without meat. We need to learn to do without, out of love for others.] **13 Wherefore, if meat make my brother to**

offend, I will eat no flesh while the world standeth, lest I make my brother to offend. [Paul is saying, if my brother will offend God by copying me, by sinning against his conscience then I will avoid eating those things. Paul said I would rather go without eating flesh as long as I live than to offend a brother. "Let no man seek his own, but every man another's wealth" (1 Cor. 10:24). Paul has given the Corinthians guidelines to follow. If they had friends that would be stumbled by seeing them eat that prime piece of meat at the temple meat shop, then they should stop going there. The weaker brother principle applies in many areas in our lives: what we eat and drink, the movies or plays we watch, the books we read, the music we listen to, etc. How ever since God said that His will is that all men be saved and come to the knowledge of the truth (1 Tim. 2:4), then saving others and helping weak brethren to come to understand Paul's distinctive ministry to the heaven bound body of Christ is the most important. The Lord Jesus Christ was patient with His disciples and we must be patient with all who will listen to us because we used to be mixers in the past. The greatest need of the Church today is to not only be biblical but also dispensational, or they will never understand the Bible. God cares about our conduct and how we treat others especially those in the body (Gal. 6:10). <u>God has called us to live on a higher plane above sin and self</u>. As we will see in chapter 13, charity is what should motivate our Christian conduct, and moment by moment we must make wise selfless decisions for His glory.]

JESUS SENT PAUL

Am I not an apostle? am I not free? have I not seen Jesus Christ our Lord? are not ye my work in the Lord? For though I preach the gospel, I have nothing to glory of: for necessity is laid upon me; yea, woe is unto me, if I preach not the gospel! For if I do this thing willingly, I have a reward: but if against my will, a <u>dispensation of the gospel</u> is committed unto me.
1 Corinthians 9:1, 16-17 KJV

OUR DOCTRINE Romans thru Philemon

Chapter 9 Paul defends his apostleship and grace giving
9:1-27 Paul uses himself as an example of helping weaker brothers (the Corinthians) by not insisting on his "rights."

9:1 <u>Am I not an apostle?</u> <u>am I not free?</u> <u>have I not seen Jesus Christ our Lord?</u> <u>are not ye my work in the Lord?</u> [Paul just asked four questions. Apostle means sent. Paul was an apostle. He had liberty. He had seen the Lord who sent him to the Gentiles with a message (Acts 9:17, 27; 26:12-18). In fact, Paul was the last one to see the Lord Jesus (15:8). One of the qualifications of an apostle is to be a witness of the Lord Jesus Christ (Acts. 1:22). Jesus said, "Verily, verily, I say unto you, He that receiveth whomsoever I send receiveth me; and he that receiveth me receiveth him that sent me" (John 13:20). Paul says that Christ appointed him to be an apostle and personally taught him what he needed to know. Paul did not learn about his ministry from another man. The Lord Jesus Christ kept him separate from the twelve apostles on purpose (Gal. 1:1, 11-20). To not believe Paul was whom Jesus Christ sent to the body of Christ, is to deny what Christ is doing today. Paul was the first person into the body of Christ, he is the "pattern" for us to follow (1 Tim. 1:16). Paul magnified his office of being "the apostle of the Gentiles" (Rom. 11:13). The Corinthian believers were evidence of his apostleship.] **2 If I be not an apostle unto others, yet doubtless I am to you: for the <u>seal of mine apostleship are ye in the Lord.</u>** [Paul says even if others do not consider him to be their apostle there is no doubt that he is their apostle because the Corinthians are his proof. Paul reminded them where they came from and how they changed in 6:9-11. But Paul gave them the gospel knowing it had the power to save them, just like his encounter with Christ had saved him. Paul was undeserving of Christ's loving sacrifice and so are we. Knowing this should make us willing to share the truth of the gospel with anyone, not just the people we are comfortable with.] **3 <u>Mine answer to them that do examine me is this,</u>** [Paul will now begin a long answer to those who say that he is not an apostle like the 12. Paul uses himself as an example for them to follow. He says that he did not assert "his rights" out of love for the Corinthians and because it could hinder the gospel. He did not want their money, even if it was right for them to support him, he wanted them. He wanted them to have eternal life by the power of the gospel of Christ. Now he wants them to grow up and be mature in their service to Christ.]

4 Have we not <u>power to eat and to drink</u>? [Sure they had the power to eat and drink even things offered to idols.] **5 Have <u>we not power to lead about a sister, a wife, as well as other apostles, and as the brethren of the Lord, and Cephas?</u>** [Paul and Barnabas could have married, but they chose to remain single for the sake of the gospel (so they would be free to serve). They did not use this power (authority), but curtailed their liberty. Peter, the other apostles, and the brothers of Christ (like James and Jude) all took their wives along when they preached.] **6 Or I only and Barnabas, have not we power to forbear working?** [It is interesting that Paul mentions Barnabas instead of Apollos. Perhaps Barnabas had visited Corinth and that they knew him. Paul and his friends were entitled to their support, but supported themselves wherever they went (2 Thess. 3:8, 9).] **7 Who goeth a warfare any time at his own charges? who planteth a vineyard, and eateth not of the fruit thereof? or who feedeth a flock, and eateth not of the milk of the flock?** [Paul uses the example of human custom to reimburse those who earn it: the soldier, the farmer, and the shepherd (Prov. 27:18). No soldier supports himself, but receives supplies and wages from the government. After all his hard work the farmer has a right to the produce. The shepherd expects to get milk and meat from the flock. Likewise ministers of spiritual things are entitled to compensation.] **8 Say I these things as a man? or saith not the law the same also?** [Paul is not saying this as a man. God says the same thing in the law.] **9 For it is written in the law of Moses, Thou shalt not muzzle the mouth of the ox that treadeth out the corn. Doth God take care for oxen?** [God says this about oxen for man's good (Deut. 25:4; 1 Tim. 5:18).] **10 Or saith he it altogether for our sakes? For our sakes, no doubt, this is written: that he that ploweth should plow in hope; and that he that thresheth in hope should be partaker of his hope.** [God says that both he that plows (plants) and he that reaps should enjoy sharing in the harvest.]

11 If we have sown unto you spiritual things, is it a great thing if we shall reap your carnal things? [Paul applies the analogy of reaping and sowing to spiritual things and material things (Gal. 6:6).] **12 If others be partakers of this power over you, are not we rather? Nevertheless we have not used this power; but suffer all things, lest we should hinder the gospel of Christ.** [Paul had heard that the Corinthians were supporting other apostles and preachers. So he asks "are we not more worthy of your support?" Paul had a right to be supported for his work, but he did not exercise this "right." He had not asked them for anything because he did not want to hinder the gospel. He supported himself by his tent making trade.] **13 Do ye not know that they which minister about holy things live of the things of the temple? and they which wait at the altar are partakers with the altar?** [Paul uses the example of the old testament priests having a part of the sacrifices and offerings to further drive home his point (perhaps for the sake of the Jews in the assembly).] **14 Even so hath the Lord ordained that they which preach the gospel should live of the gospel.** [God has ordered that those who have received a spiritual blessing should support those who bless them spiritually. Those who preach the gospel are to live by means of the gospel. We are to graciously support those who bless us spiritually. Many grace pastors today chose to support themselves like Paul.] **15 But I have used none of these things: neither have I written these things, that it should be so done unto me: for it were better for me to die, than that any man should make my glorying void.** [Paul had not claimed his right to live off the gospel, and he is not telling the Corinthians this because he wants them to pay him anything. Paul says that he would rather die than have someone take away his reward.] **16 For though I preach the gospel, I have nothing to glory of: for necessity is laid upon me; yea, woe is unto me, if I preach not the gospel!** [Preaching the gospel is what Christ required Paul to do. Paul was compelled to preach it. He has no choice in the matter. He is under orders, Christ has given him a job to do, a ministry. Paul is the masterbuilder of the body of Christ in the dispensation of the grace of God (3:10).] **17 For if I do this thing willingly, I have a reward: but if against my will, a dispensation of the gospel is committed unto me.** [If Paul carries out his assigned ministry willingly he will get a reward, but he has no choice about the job Christ has given him. Paul is to dispense the gospel (the body of sound doctrine Christ has given for him to deal out). To dispense means to distribute, give out, provide. A pharmacy dispenses medication, a vending machine dispenses drinks and snacks, a gas station dispenses gasoline. The word "dispensation" is found four times in the King James Bible (1 Cor. 9:17; Eph. 1:10, 3:2; Col. 1:25). Guess which apostle is the only one to use this word? Yes, Paul. This is because we have to divide the truth to the body of Christ (God's heavenly people) from the rest of the Bible (God's earthly people). Paul says this in 2 Tim. 2:15. In this present age, God is dispensing grace and peace. How did Paul open this letter? See 1:3 and Gal. 1:3. It is not just a nice greeting from Paul when he says grace and peace, it is what God is dispensing today. This dispensation that we are living in is holding back His WRATH and FURY. God is not angry with anybody because Christ died for our sins and paid the sin debt of all mankind. The Father's approval of His Son's payment was demonstrated by His resurrection. Death could not hold His sin-less Son. God is not imputing our sin to us now (2 Cor. 5:19). It is not sin that sends a person to hell, but unbelief. To be saved we need to believe the gospel clearly stated in 1 Cor. 15:3, 4. Without faith it is impossible to please God (Heb. 11:6).]

18 What is my reward then? Verily that, when I preach the gospel, I may make the gospel of Christ without charge, that I abuse not my power in the gospel. [Paul says, I am compelled to preach the gospel and cannot do anything but preach it! So what is my reward? I will have a reward if I preach it for free, without cost to anyone. If Paul received financial compensation, he could perhaps be tempted to abuse his authority and take a bribe.] **19 For though I be free from all men, yet have I made myself servant unto all, that I might gain the more.** [Paul was free from the control of all men. He did not owe anyone anything. He was not on any man's payroll. Still he made himself a servant to everyone so that he could win them to Christ.] **20 And unto the Jews I became as a Jew, that I might gain the Jews; to them that are under the law, as under the law, that I might gain them that are under the law; 21 To them that are without law, as without law, (being not without law to God, but under the law to Christ,)** [Christ is Paul's authority, his Master. He is under His law (Rom. 8:2). Christ's life is operating in him.] **that I might gain them that are without law. 22 To the weak became I as weak, that I might gain the weak: I am made all things to all men, that I might by all means save some.** [Paul did not offend people; he set aside personal privileges out of love on purpose. Paul carefully used tact to make contact with people. Paul was born a Jew (so he used that to win the Jews), and Paul was a Roman citizen (so he used that to win the Gentiles). He was uniquely suited as the perfect apostle to the body of Christ made up of both Jews and Gentiles. He became all things to all people so that he might save some. He knew he would not win everyone to Christ, but he wanted to save as many as possible and help them to have sound doctrine.] **23 And this I do for the gospel's sake, that I might be partaker thereof with you.** [Paul worked hard for the gospel's sake, so that he could be a bodybuilder for Christ (building the body of Christ so that he could spend eternity with many). In contrast, Israel's program involves nation building. In Israel's program the nation had to confess their sins as a nation: "If we [the nation of Israel] confess our [national] sins, he is faithful and just to forgive us [the nation of Israel] our sins, and to cleanse us from all unrighteousness" (1 John 1:9 as commanded in Lev. 26:40-42). But we in the body of Christ, just thank God that for Christ's sake He has already paid and forgiven us of that sin.]

24 Know ye not that they which run in a race run all, but one receiveth the prize? So run, that ye may obtain. [Run to win! We do not work for our salvation; that is a gift given by the grace of God. But after we are saved Christ motivates us to do the work He has prepared us for (Eph. 2:10). Once we understand God's will. What is it? Yes, that is right, 1 Tim. 2:4 (win souls and share the mystery). Then we are in a race to do as much as we can, as well as we can, for Christ and His people (the body of Christ). He encourages the Corinthians and us to run to win. Many run in a race but only one wins the price. But, we can all participate in the spiritual race of giving out the word of God rightly divided.] **25 And every man that striveth for the mastery is temperate in all things. Now they do it to obtain a corruptible crown; but we an incorruptible.** [The "we" is Paul, Barnabas, and the Corinthian believers. Our crown is not a perishable laurel wreath, but a job with responsibility in heaven. Paul used an illustration from the Greek games familiar to the reader, for the Isthmian Games (similar to the

Olympics) were held near Corinth. The contestants that train to be a master in their sport are moderate in all things, not excessive. They had to discipline themselves and work hard to win a prize. Paul reminds the Corinthians again to focus on their eternal rewards, not the temporal. Temperate means moderate. Paul wisely paces himself so he can have quality fruit. God wants all believers to have something to show at the Judgment Seat of Christ (2 Cor. 5:10).] **26 I therefore so run, not as uncertainly; so fight I, not as one that beateth the air:** [Paul is not shadowboxing. Paul says, he lives his life on purpose, calculating out what is the best use of his time for Christ.] **27 But I keep under my body, and bring it into subjection: lest that by any means, when I have preached to others, I myself should be a castaway.** [Paul is out on the racetrack running so that he will get a reward. Just like an athlete Paul wisely keeps himself disciplined and under control. He is careful to not do what he tells others not to do. "Castaway" means unapproved by God (disqualified of getting a reward). Paul did not want to lose his reward for faithful service. Salvation is a free gift, but God wants all of us to work for Him in our various roles to receive a reward. I love to teach the word of God to equip believers to be strong in sound doctrine so they can serve Christ, and teach others (2 Tim. 2:2). What has God motivated you to do for Him and the body of Christ?]

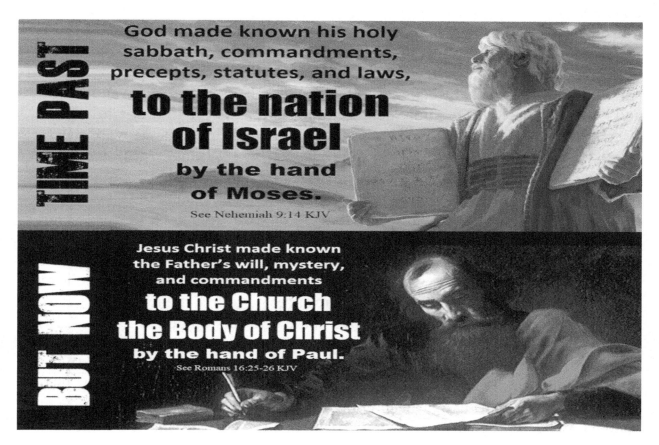

Chapter 10 Israel as an example of what not to do
10:1-15 Flee from the sins Israel fell into in the past.
10:16-11:1 Believers must be 100% separated unto God. No idol worship!
Make sure there is not a hint of a desire in you to worship idols (the table of devils). We cannot be partakers of the Lord's table, and of the table of devils. Paul finishes the weaker brother principle laid down in chapter 8.

10:1 Moreover, brethren, I would not that ye should be <u>ignorant, how that all our fathers were under the cloud</u>, and <u>all passed through the sea</u>; 2 And were all <u>baptized unto Moses</u> in the cloud and in the sea; 3 And did all eat the same <u>spiritual meat</u>; 4 And did all drink the same <u>spiritual drink</u>: for they drank of that <u>spiritual Rock</u> that followed them: and <u>that Rock was Christ</u>. [Paul speaks as a Jew and uses Israel as an example of what not to do. There were many Jews in the church at Corinth since they had come over from the Synagogue next door. They realized that God was now working with Paul. These had seen that <u>God had given Paul and those in that assembly Israel's signs</u>. Paul says he does not want them to be ignorant (unaware) that their fathers (Abraham, Isaac, Jacob, and the twelve tribes) were under Christ's care for their needs in the wilderness. This was during their exodus from Egyptian bondage on their way to the promised land. The Israelites were "baptized unto Moses in the cloud and in the sea" (identified with Moses' group as they passed on dry ground through the Red Sea, there is no water in this baptism. Just like in Rom. 6:3, 4 when we identify with Christ's death, burial, and resurrection). They all ate the same spiritual food (Manna, Ex. 16:31) and drank of the spiritual Rock that followed them. Paul, who was given further and more advanced information identifies and states, "<u>that Rock was Christ</u>" (Ex. 17:5, 6; Num. 20:7-13, 27:14). Almost every time the Bible uses the word rock or stone it is referring to Christ (Ex. 33:22; Deut. 32:17, 18; Dan. 2:34; Psa. 118:22; Matt. 7:25, 16:18, 21:42 -46; 1 Peter 2:5-10; Acts 4:11). <u>Both, the church in the wilderness with Moses and the Messianic church Christ began with Christ as their Rock.</u> Christ said He would build the <u>kingdom on earth church on Peter's confession of faith</u> (Matt. 16:16). In contrast, for us in the body of Christ, Jesus is the Head of the body. The church in the wilderness (Acts 7:38) and the kingdom church are the believers that will live in the <u>earthly kingdom</u>. Those who believed God from Adam to Abraham will also be resurrected to live in the earthly kingdom. <u>But the body of Christ will live in the heavenly kingdom</u> (2 Tim. 4:18).]

5 But with <u>many of them God was not well pleased</u>: for they were <u>overthrown in the wilderness</u>. [But God was not pleased with many of them because of their unbelief; not only during their wanderings but also when they were about to conquer and enter the land of Canaan. The Israelites were overthrown in the wilderness (they were disqualified because of their lack of faith). They took part in the spiritual food and drink, but they still died. They had to wander in the wilderness for forty years while that generation who had unbelief died (Num. 14:26-33). The ten spies died immediately (Num. 14:36-38).] **6 Now these things were our examples, to the intent we should not lust after evil things, as they also lusted.** [God wrote this so that we could learn not to repeat Israel's poor choices. Their bad example is also repeated in the book of Hebrews as a bad example to those who will go through the Tribulation (Heb. 3:8, 17). We should learn from their mistakes and not lust after evil things as they did. Paul says "neither" four times so that believers should not follow any of Israel's bad examples. Covetousness is idolatry (Col. 3:5). Those people wanted things that were outside the will of God for them at that particular time. The mixed multitude were not satisfied with the Manna, and longed for the food in Egypt, the "cucumbers, and the melons, and the leeks, and the onions, and the garlick. But now our soul is dried away: there is nothing at all, beside this manna, before our eyes" (Num. 11:5, 6).]

7 Neither be ye idolaters, as were some of them; as it is written, The people sat down to eat and drink, and rose up to play. [Paul says "neither" four times that believers should not follow Israel's example. Paul says do not be idolaters like the Israelites who rose up to play (Ex. 32:6). They worshipped the golden calf (while Moses was up on the mountain receiving the Ten Commandments from God). Who does the molten calf represent? Right, the once anointed cherub that once covered God's throne, Satan (2 Chron. 11:15; Ezek. 28:14, 1:10, 10:14; Rev. 4:7). The Adversary always wants to foil God's plan, and counterfeit what He is doing. He was against Moses, against Christ and the little flock, and then against Paul.] **8 Neither let us commit fornication, as some of them committed, and fell in one day three and twenty thousand.** [Paul now warns against fornication like they did when Balaam told the king of Moab to cause his people to fornicate with the Jews so that Israel would bow down to their gods. Therefore, 23,000 died in one day. Num. 25:9 says 24,000 because that is the total of the deaths since more died later.] **9 Neither let us tempt Christ, as some of them also tempted, and were destroyed of serpents.** [Also do not tempt God as the Israelites who spoke against His plan for them and what Moses was doing, saying, have you brought us to the wilderness to die? They were ungrateful for the miracle of Manna saying, "our soul loatheth this light bread" (Num. 21:5, 6). So God sent fiery serpents to bite them so that they died. – Therefore, Moses was commanded to make a brass serpent and put it on a pole so that anyone who was bitten who looked at it by faith, lived (Num. 21:7-9).] **10 Neither murmur ye, as some of them also murmured, and were destroyed of the destroyer.** [Paul warns the Corinthians not to murmur or complain like Korah and those who joined with him; they murmured and God sent a plague (the destroyer is Jesus, the Judge) that killed about fifteen thousand (Num. 16:36-50). God hates complaining.] **11 Now all these things happened unto them for ensamples: and they are written for our admonition, upon whom the ends of the world are come.** [God did not like it when Israel murmured so Paul warns believers not to murmur and complain. Then Paul reiterates that these things were written for our admonishing (as warnings). We cannot fake it. God knows our hearts. They ate spiritual food and drink but they suffered the second death "the ends of the world" because of their lack of faith.] **12 Wherefore let him that thinketh he standeth take heed lest he fall.** [All people have had similar temptations. Paul warns that believers should not be overconfident that they will not be tempted to fall into these sins. Once a person is saved they cannot lose their salvation, but they can still sin and have a fruitless life without any rewards at Christ's Judgment Seat.] **13 There hath no temptation taken you but such as is common to man: but God is faithful, who will not suffer you to be tempted above that ye are able; but will with the temptation also make a way to escape, that ye may be able to bear it.** [God knows that we still have the sin nature in our flesh. He who keeps us is faithful and will not allow us to be tempted to the point of falling from grace, without giving us an opportunity to escape the temptation. God is faithful. God is very interested in us and what we say and do. God did physical signs for Israel such as parting the rivers, sending or not sending rain, winning their battles, etc. For the body of Christ, God gives us all the spiritual blessings up front (Eph. 1:3). He is concerned with our spiritual growth, the edification of our soul and spirit. Christ lives in us. We are not to grieve His Holy Spirit with our poor conduct. God will give us the grace not to succumb to this list of sins that the nation of Israel did (un-belief, lust for evil things, idol worship, lewd behavior, fornication, speaking against Christ, murmuring). One way we can live above sin and self is to renew ourselves in His word daily (Col 3:16; Rom. 10:17, 12:2; Eph. 5:25-27). We can be tempted, but if we allow the "mind of Christ" (2:16) to reprogram our minds we will think correctly (like Him). This is how it works: we read His word and understand it with our minds (spirit) then we believe what we have understood with our heart (soul) then His word is internalized by going from our mind to our heart by faith so it can work effectually in us (1 Thess. 2:13). When we understand and believe His perfect word (KJV) rightly divided we can function the way God intended us to and be useful to Him.]

14 ¶Wherefore, my dearly beloved, flee from idolatry. [Paul calls the Corinthians my dearly beloved and says flee from idolatry. Joseph is an example of someone that was able to flee from fornication. May I say that a bar is not a place for a former alcoholic, neither is the donut shop the place for someone determined to lose weight. Neither is the TV remote or social media the place for someone who wants to study the Bible. Idolatry is anything we value more than God. <u>Flee from exalting anything above the Lord Jesus Christ. Without Him we are nothing and have no hope.</u> So everything else crumbles. But with us in Christ and Him in us we can be useful to God and others. One of the main ways to grow in faith is by studying the word (Rom. 10:17 says?). By studying the Bible, we will learn to know God. If we study the Bible rightly divided, we will be able to be renewed in our minds and transformed to be like Him (Rom. 12:2).] **15 I speak <u>as to wise men; judge ye what I say</u>.** [Paul uses a little holy sarcasm when he says that he speaks as to wise men. Then he challenges them to judge that what he says is true.] **16 <u>The cup of blessing</u> which we bless, <u>is it not the communion of the blood of Christ? The bread</u> which <u>we break,</u> is it not the <u>communion of the body of Christ?</u>** [Paul says that we bless and share in Christ's death (His blood and broken body). <u>Separation to God is essential. Paul illustrates this as he contrasts the Lord's table and Satan's table to idols.</u> Satan always makes a counterfeit of what God does. Paul says that devils are behind the food offered to idols (we already read that in Deut. 32:17, 18). Paul makes it clear that he has taught them to remember the Lord by drinking wine and eating bread with His sacrifice in mind. I know that this is a controversial subject even among grace believers so, I ask you to hear me out. Paul is referring to the wine, "the cup of blessing" as representing Christ's blood, and the "bread" His body that was broken for us (we will cover this more in chapter 11). The idea that the wine and bread really are Christ's blood and body, trans-substantiation, as mentioned in the Catholic and Lutheran ceremonies, is totally false. Because Christ was speaking symbolically (John 6:47-58). The "body of Christ" in this verse is Christ's physical body.] **17 For <u>we being many are one bread, and one body</u>: for we <u>are all partakers of that one bread</u>.** [In this verse the first "one bread" (being many) and "one body" are the members of the body of Christ (12:27), while the last "one bread" is Christ. How can we be certain that the first "one bread" does not include Peter and his group? Because in Galatians 6:16 Paul makes a distinction between the two groups (also see Matt. 19:28). Israel as a nation stumbled at the cross, then fell in Acts 7 at the stoning of Stephen. Peter and his group, the believing remnant, was given a one-year opportunity to preach to Israel to get them to believe on their Messiah. Christ pleaded with the Father to forgive them on the cross (Luke 23:34) reducing their sentence from murder to manslaughter. Jesus Christ also pleaded with the Father to give the Jews one more year to believe (Luke 13:6-9). When Stephen preaches he essentially says your time is up. Peter and his group did not fully know that their program was interrupted, put on hold, closed to new recruits, and postponed until Paul told them in Acts 15:1-29 and Gal. 2:1-10. During the diminishing (Rom. 11:11, 12) Paul went to the Jews scattered abroad to tell them that Jesus is the Christ (Rom. 10:8) and if they want to be saved for them to believe the gospel he preaches (1 Cor. 15:3, 4). When did Paul know that Israel as a nation had fallen? When he heard Christ say, "delivering thee from the people [unbelieving Israel]" (Acts 26:17). PAUL KNEW THAT ISRAEL HAD FALLEN <u>ON THE VERY DAY THAT HE WAS SAVED IN ACTS 9</u>, but the Holy Spirit by the pen of Luke, did not disclose that information until Acts 26. Christ sent Paul to the unbelieving Gentiles so they would <u>now</u> have an opportunity to be saved apart from Israel. The Gentiles could be saved apart from blessing Israel as commanded in Genesis 12:1-3. We live in a new and different dispensation formerly kept secret. The dispensation of grace, the mystery, has been revealed through Paul, but Satan still wants to conceal it.] **18 Behold Israel after the flesh: are not they which eat of the sacrifices partakers of the altar? 19 What say I then? that the idol is any thing, or that which is offered in sacrifice to idols is any thing? 20 But I say, that the things which the Gentiles sacrifice, they sacrifice to devils, and not to God: and I would not that ye should have fellowship with devils.** [Israel after the flesh are those who were not spiritually circumcised by receiving the Holy Ghost like Peter's group. Paul said that the priests who sacrificed to God could eat what had been offered on the altar. Paul is not saying that an idol is anything, but that he does not want them to take part in Satan's counterfeit communion service (Lev. 17:7; Psa. 115:4-8). There is no power in the idol, but the devil is behind them. Paul says to make sure that no part of you has any fellowship with devils, by esteeming the idol, rather than God.] **21 Ye cannot drink the cup of the Lord, and the cup of devils: ye cannot be partakers of the Lord's table, and of the table of devils. 22 Do we provoke the Lord to jealousy? are we stronger than he?** [We cannot worship both God and an idol. We cannot partake of both the Lord's table and the table of idols. God wants all of our worship. Do not make Him jealous by spiritual adultery, He knows your heart (Deut. 32:21). Christ said we cannot serve two masters (Matt. 6:24). Make sure no part of you cares about idols! <u>We must separate ourselves 100% to God alone.</u>]

23 All things are lawful for me, but all things are not expedient: all things are lawful for me, but all things edify not. [Paul is under grace, not the law. He is free to do as he wants – but not everything is profitable to him or others. Our liberty is limited by love.] **24 Let no man seek his own, but every man another's wealth.** [Paul summarizes the weaker brother principle which has to do with what is best for others. When we seek to esteem others better than ourselves we are showing love. (Paul will say more about "charity," God's kind of unconditional sacrificial love, in chapter 13).] **25 Whatsoever is sold in the shambles, that eat, asking no question for conscience sake:** [Now Paul will give some very practical advice. Do not be overly picky and legalistic. Eat whatever you like in the food courts without asking where it came from (eat, don't ask).] **26 For the earth is the Lord's, and the fulness thereof. 27 If any of them that believe not bid you to a feast, and ye be disposed to go; whatsoever is set before you, eat, asking no question for conscience sake.** [Everything belongs to God, even the cows, and all food (Ex. 9:29). If some unbelievers have you over for a meal eat what they serve. There is no rule that we should not eat certain meat, but out of love for someone whose conscience is weak we should not eat it. At the Jerusalem Council, James asked the Gentiles that had turned to God to abstain from idols, fornication, "and things strangled, and from blood. For Moses of old time hath in every city them that preach him, being read in the synagogues every sabbath day" (Acts 15:19-21) so the Gentiles could save the Jews into the body of Christ.] **28 But if any man say unto you, This is offered in sacrifice unto idols, eat not for his sake that shewed it, and for conscience sake: for the earth is the Lord's, and the fulness thereof:** [But if anyone says that the food was offered to idols do not eat it for his weak conscience sake. Everyone does not know that God owns everything. So you could wound his weak conscience by your knowledge and strong conscience in this matter. We may not want to serve our Jewish guests pork chops or bacon.] **29 Conscience, I say, not thine own, but of the other: for why is my liberty judged of another man's conscience?** [We are free to eat what we want and someone that does not know that should not judge us.] **30 For if I by grace be a partaker, why am I evil spoken of for that for which I give thanks?** [Paul asked, why should someone speak evil of something I eat when I have thanked God for it (1 Tim. 4:1-6)? Food is nothing. What Christ has done is everything.] **31 Whether therefore ye eat, or drink, or whatsoever ye do, do all to the glory of God.** [Whatever we do, we do it all for the glory to God (Col. 3:23-25). It glorifies God when we care about how our conduct may affect our weaker brother. It is better to go hungry than to cause a weaker brother to stumble.] **32 Give none offence, neither to the Jews, nor to the Gentiles, nor to the church of God: 33 Even as I please all men in all things, not seeking mine own profit, but the profit of many, that they may be saved.** [There were three kinds of people in the world at the time of this letter: lost Jews, lost Gentiles, and the church of God (Paul's group and Peter's group). Like Paul, do not offend others by the food you eat and serve, but seek to please and profit others, so more are saved. Today there are two kinds of people saved and unsaved.]

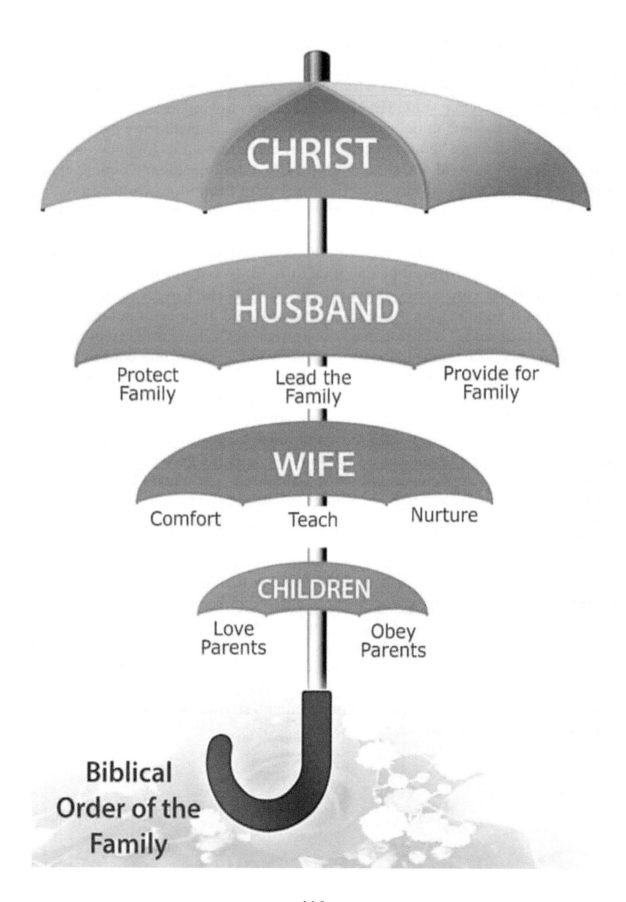

CHRIST

HUSBAND

Protect Family   Lead the Family   Provide for Family

WIFE

Comfort   Teach   Nurture

CHILDREN

Love Parents   Obey Parents

Biblical Order of the Family

Chapter 11 Christian order and the Lord's Supper
11:2-16 Order in the local church at Corinth
11:17-34 Disorder at the Lord's Table (Supper) rebuked

11:1 Be ye <u>followers of me, even as I also am of Christ.</u> [Limit your liberty for the sake of another as Christ and I have done. To follow Paul is to follow Christ's heavenly ministry. Christ made Paul His minister to the body of Christ (Acts 26:16; Rom. 11:13, 15:16; Eph. 3:7; Col. 1:25).] **2 Now I praise you, brethren, that ye remember me in all things, and <u>keep the ordinances, as I delivered them to you.</u>** [Paul encourages the Corinthians to follow instructions he has given them. They should <u>keep the ordinances as he delivered them</u>. Paul then begins to talk about order in the church. Some women were praying in tongues too much, and some men were competing with others for a chance to speak.] **3 But I would have you know, that <u>the head of every man is Christ; and the head of the woman is the man</u>;** [her husband] **<u>and the head of Christ is God.</u>** [Paul lays down the <u>chain of command among equals</u> Father God, Christ, man, woman (Eph. 5:23). Authority is for the sake of order, to eliminate confusion. There were too many chiefs and not enough Indians. We are to "study to be quiet" (1 Thess. 4:11). The Head gives direction and the final say. Be sure to respect the head. Every man is <u>not</u> the head of the woman, Paul will make it clear that the husband is the head of the wife. For the sake of order, in marriage, the wife should allow the husband to make the final decision. A wife is to respect her husband (Eph. 5:33). He, in turn, must be willing to die for her (Eph. 5:25). Christ said I and my Father are one (John 10:30), but he also said, "My father is greater than I" (John 14:28). Christ voluntarily took a lower place while He was here on earth (Phil. 2:5-7). As a woman submits to her husband, she practices submitting to her Master, the Lord Jesus Christ. She gives Him all the glory; for He alone is worthy, and we will praise His name forever. Paul will now apply the headship principle to wearing the customary veil in Corinth.] **4 <u>Every man praying or prophesying, having his head covered, dishonoureth his head. 5 But every woman that prayeth or prophesieth with her head uncovered dishonoureth her head</u>:** [husband] **<u>for that is even all one as if she were shaven.</u>** [Notice that Paul says that <u>women were praying in the church and prophesying</u> but needed to do so with a veil on their heads. These were gifts in that church for both men and women. (It is interesting that all the 120 men and women in the Upper Room all received the Holy Ghost on Pentecost.) Prostitutes in the immoral city of Corinth, did not wear a veil announcing their availability for sinful pleasures. Therefore, to appear ladylike the women should wear veils in church.] **6 For <u>if the woman be not covered, let her also be shorn: but if it be a shame for a woman to be shorn or shaven, let her be covered.</u>** [veil] [Although it is not customary in our country to wear veils, in some countries veils and shawls are considered modest apparel for women to show respect to their husbands. For both men and women ambassadors for Christ, what we wear and how we conduct ourselves should honor our ultimate Head, the Lord Jesus Christ. We are not to be "conformed to this world: but be ye transformed by the renewing of your mind, that ye may prove what is that good, and acceptable, and perfect, will of God" (Rom. 12:2). Paul says that the woman should be modest and cover her head with a veil to distinguish herself from the prostitutes out of respect for her husband and the culture in Corinth. Many were the priestesses at the temple to Aphrodite. They were essentially prostitutes. They had "shaven" (bald) heads or "shorn" (short hair) and did not wear veils like the fine ladies.] **7 For a man indeed ought not to cover his head, forasmuch as he is the image and glory of God: but the woman is the glory of the man.** [Moses covered his face with a veil so that the people of Israel would not discover that the glow of his face (that he received when he spoke with God) was fading away (Ex. 34:33-35; 2 Cor. 3:7). But when Moses spoke with God, his head was uncovered. Paul says men should <u>not</u> cover their heads. There should not be anything between a man and Christ.] **8 For the man is not of the woman; but the woman of the man. 9 Neither was the man created for the woman; but the woman for the man.** [The woman was made to be Adam's help meet (Gen. 2:18, 22). Both were made in God's image (Gen. 1:27; 5:1). The woman was made to complete the man, to make his life richer, fuller, and more exciting! To be his help meet, companion, and the other part of him. No man is complete without a woman except in special cases when God has given special grace to a man for a special work. Paul said this in 7:7 and the Lord in Matt. 19:12. Apparently, some of the women in the church at Corinth were saying, "Since, all things are lawful for me, therefore, I won't cover my head with a veil." Paul says that since the veil is a sign of submission to their husbands and to God, in the culture at Corinth, the women in the church should wear the veil. But Paul does not apply that custom to other churches (11:16). However, Paul does say elsewhere that women should dress modestly (1 Tim. 2:8-10). "Holy hands" are hands ready to accept what God has said, not fighting against Him with clenched fists. Peter also wants women to dress modestly (1 Peter 3:1-4). Peter also says that the husbands should treat the woman as the weaker vessel, like fine porcelain china (1 Peter 3:7). (Women are weaker physically. But, as a mother of three and a retired nurse-midwife, I am able to say that mothers have to be tough because childbearing is very painful, difficult work, requiring immense strength, and stamina.) Women should dress modestly yet be appealing; we can fix our hair and wear a little makeup occasionally.] **10 For this cause ought the woman to have power** [authority] **on her head because of the angels.** [Angels are another reason why women should wear a veil in Corinth. The angels are watching our conduct. They know if we honor our husband with our

118

submissive respectful behavior and by what we wear.] **11 Nevertheless <u>neither is the man without the woman, neither the woman without the man, in the Lord</u>. 12 For as the <u>woman is of the man, even so is the man also by the woman</u>; but all things of God.** [The woman was made from Adam's rib (Gen. 2:22), but the woman gives birth to the man. The man needs the woman and the woman needs the man. We both have strengths that we bring to the marriage. We are one flesh, one team. This is what our Lord said about marriage: Matt. 19:4-6.]

13 Judge in yourselves: is it <u>comely</u> that a <u>woman pray</u> unto <u>God uncovered</u>? [un-veiled] [Comely means handsome, beautiful, elegant. Paul does not think that it is ladylike for the woman not to keep the Corinthian custom of wearing a veil. A woman who is teaching a Bible class or praying should do so in modest dress and bring attention to the LORD and His word, the Bible.] **14 Doth not <u>even nature itself teach you, that, if a man have long hair, it is a shame unto him</u>**? [Most male animals have short hair, with a few exceptions like the lion. Men should not look like women and vice versa. In Bible times, the Nazarite vow was an act of consecrating oneself to God. It was symbolized by long, uncut hair. This meant that the Nazarite was willing to bear shame for God's name. Even at that time, long hair on men was considered shameful. Because of this verse, I believe Jesus had short hair. Unfortunately, many paintings show him with long hair. In many ways, long hair on men is a sign of rebellion and is narcissistic; think of Absalom (2 Sam. 18:9-14).] **15 But if a woman have <u>long hair, it is a glory to her</u>: for her hair is given her for <u>a covering</u>.** [Paul changes course a little because he does not want to impose veil wearing on all his churches. He now says that the woman's hair is her covering. Long hair is "a glory to her" but we are free to wear our hair in any way that is becoming in this age. Because it is what Christ did for us that is important, not our hair length. For a while, I had to have short hair because my hair was breaking. I found out that the cause was the high protein diet that I was on. Protein breaks down to amino acids which need to be buffered by calcium carbonate, which the body robs from the hair and bones if there is a low carbohydrate intake. So my hair and bones were more fragile on a high protein, low carb diet. Once I went on a high starch, low meat diet, my hair, nails, and bones all became stronger and longer. Remember, the woman who dried Jesus's feet with her hair? She was, in essence, saying, You, are of more worth than the glory of my hair, it can wipe your feet, I glorify You above all else (Luke 7:36-50.] **16 But if any man seem to be contentious, <u>we have no such custom, neither the churches of God</u>**. [Some men may insist on having long hair. Paul concludes by saying that the church should not make rules in connection with the matter of women's dress or men's hair. Paul says that he is not giving one rule for all other churches to follow.]

119

17 ¶ Now in this that I declare unto you I praise you not, that ye come together not for the better, but for the worse. [Paul now rebukes the Corinthians for their abuse of the Lord's Table. Paul says that the Corinthians were coming together for the worse, not the better. They had a meal that preceded the ordinance of the Lord's Supper, which is the same as the Lord's table. Paul only mentions the celebration of the Lord's supper in this epistle, but how often does God have to tell us something before we obey? I hope you will say once. Still, we are under grace, not the law, and different churches celebrate the Lord's death in different ways. We are commanded to remember the day of Christ's death, not the day of His birth. We, of course, can individually remember the Lord's death every waking moment, but Paul is referring to a local church group activity. It is something the body of Christ should do together with gratitude because His death for our sins at Calvary is what we all have in common. His death and resurrection are what binds us together. We celebrate it because Christ accomplished our redemption. He was victorious in paying the costly price for our penalty after living a perfect life, and dying a perfect death. It was His merit, love, and courage. Some churches celebrate it monthly and some quarterly. Some just share the meal, and others just the bread and grape juice. Since the event took place during the week of unleavened bread, the juice was unfermented. It is called the "fruit of the vine," never wine in the gospels. Paul is concerned about order and unity. They should have come together out of love for each other.] **18 For first of all, when ye come together in the church, I hear that there be divisions among you; and I partly believe it. 19 For there must be also heresies among you, that they which are approved may be made manifest among you**. [He said they were eating in cliques, dividing themselves from one another. (He had most likely heard this from Chloe's household). He said that those who do so commit heresies, while those who do not sit in cliques, are approved. Heresies mean unsound doctrines or opinions. Remember when Peter and Barnabas withdrew from the Gentiles when certain men from James came and Paul withstood Peter to the face? He did it because Peter knew that God was not making a difference between Jews and Gentiles in the new dispensation He had begun. Peter's action built the middle wall of partition again (Gal. 2:11-21; 3:28). By separating himself and eating only with the Jews, Peter was denying that the middle wall of partition was down.] **20 When ye come together therefore into one place, this is not to eat the Lord's supper. 21 For in eating every one taketh before other his own supper: and one is hungry, and another is drunken.** [When you come together you should be thinking that this is for the purpose of celebrating the Lord's Supper and having fellowship with others, not feeding yourselves. People were bringing their own food and not sharing it with those who were poor and hungry. Some were even drunk! They were in no condition to remember Christ or the body of Christ.] **22 What? have ye not**

houses to eat and to drink in? or despise ye the church of God, and shame them that have not? What shall I say to you? shall I praise you in this? I praise you not. [WHAT! Paul is appalled. Being drunk is a sin (Gal. 5:21; Eph. 5:18). If they were not going to share in a time of fellowship they should have eaten at home. The fellowship was broken. Don't you have homes where you can eat before you come? Do you despise other believers and shame those who do not have as much money as you? Furious Paul asks, "shall I praise you in this? I praise you NOT." Breaking bread together meant sharing, not every person having their own. The Lord's supper was a physical picture of what Christ had done for them.]

23 For I have received of the Lord that which also I delivered unto you, That the Lord Jesus the same night in which he was betrayed took bread: [Paul says that he delivered to them what the Lord Jesus personally told him. The same night that he was betrayed of Judas, at the end of the meal Jesus took bread and broke it and gave it to the twelve. *Notice that Judas took part in this remembrance ceremony after Jesus had washed his and the others' feet (John 13:10-12, 27; Luke 22:19-22).] **24 And when he had given thanks, he brake it, and said, Take, eat: this is my body, which is broken for you: this do in remembrance of me.** [The Lord had to drink the cup of God's wrath because of all mankind's sins. But, for us what the Lord did is a cup of blessing (10:16) because without His sacrifice we have no hope. In giving instruction about the Supper, Paul quotes the Lord. We should remember how He offered His body in our place (2 Cor. 5:21).] **25 After the same manner also he took the cup, when he had supped, saying, This cup is the new testament in my blood: this do ye, as oft as ye drink it, in remembrance of me.** [Now that the Testator is dead, His will can be carried out. He was a perfectly satisfying sacrifice that the Father accepted on our behalf.] **26 For as often as ye eat this bread, and drink this cup, ye do shew the Lord's death till he come.** [As often as we eat the bread and drink the juice, we are celebrating His death till He comes in the air to catch us up. This was new information given to Paul.] **27 Wherefore whosoever shall eat this bread, and drink this cup of the Lord, unworthily,** [Their unworthy conduct, drunk and not reverent, was denying what the bread and cup represent.] **shall be guilty of the body and blood of the Lord.** [No one should eat or drink the cup unworthily with drunken, gluttonous, unruly behavior.] **28 But let a man examine himself, and so let him eat of that bread, and drink of that cup.** [A man should examine his own conduct in light of the word of God and consider what Christ has done for him. He should be sure to see the picture of Christ's suffering for him in the broken bread and blood-red juice and behave right. After that, he can drink the cup.] **29 For he that eateth and drinketh unworthily, eateth and drinketh damnation to himself,** [The word "damnation" here is not going to hell, it was being "judged wrong" and reaping the fruit of their own sinful conduct (Gal. 6:7, 8). Christ has already died for the sins they are now committing. "Unworthily" (an adverb) refers to their behavior, not them. They were drunk and gluttons at the Lord's Supper. It was unworthy, sinful conduct during the remembrance ceremony for Christ's death for their sins] **not discerning the Lord's body.** [The Corinthians had a problem with discernment because whoever eats the bread without reverence and gratitude, does not understand the great sacrifice that the Lord Jesus Christ made on our behalf. He also does not show love to the Lord's body (the body of Christ) "the one bread, and one body" (10:17).] **30 For this cause many are weak and sickly among you, and many sleep.** [The Corinthians were spiritually and physically weak and sickly because of their lifestyle; and needed to wake up to who they were in Christ and walk circumspectly (Eph. 5:14-16).] **31 For if we would judge ourselves, we should not be judged.** [When we do wrong we should judge or correct ourselves. If they would judge themselves to be wrong, then they would not need to be judged by someone else (Paul). We should judge our own conduct so that we do not have to be judged by others (2:15, 5:5, and Gal. 6:1). They should have been able to judge the fornicator in 5:5. Paul is speaking of them correcting their own behavior and the behavior of others, he is not talking about their standing, but their state (conduct). Their standing is that we are "complete in him" (Col. 2:10), but they should behave like the saints they are.] **32 But when we are judged, we are chastened, of the Lord that we should not be condemned with the world.** [God does not chasten us according to the law today, but He cares about their conduct. We are chastened, judged, or corrected by His word, by other people, or the conviction of the Holy Spirit. God also lets us suffer the consequences of our poor choices. In this case, God is using Paul's letter to chasten the Corinthians. Paul reproved them for the purpose of reforming them, it was a remedial instruction to correct their conduct. Believers are able to admonish each other (Rom. 15:14; 2 Thess. 3:15). Paul said, "All scripture . . . is profitable for doctrine, for reproof, for correction, for instruction in righteousness: That the man of God may be perfect, throughly furnished unto all good works (2 Tim. 3:16, 17).]

33 Wherefore, my brethren, when ye come together to eat, tarry one for another. [Paul says that when they come together to commemorate Christ's death, they should wait to eat until everyone has the bread and juice or food before eating.] **34 And if any man hunger, let him eat at home; that ye come not together unto condemnation. And the rest will I set in order when I come.** [Their conduct is bringing condemnation on them. If they are too hungry to wait to eat, then they should eat at home before they act like drunk, selfish, gluttons (condemnation). They were out of order in many ways. There are other things Paul will set in order when he comes. Paul tells Timothy how to instruct those who "oppose themselves" (2 Tim. 2:24-26). We must be "gentle," "patient," and "apt to teach." Paul never questions the Corinthian's salvation, only their conduct. They often behaved the way they did before they were saved. The Corinthians thought that all things were lawful for them. Paul tells them to be polite and gracious and to wait to eat. They should have some regard for the other saints. The word of God should be used to help others.

What was the Corinthians problem? Their sanctification. They were living below their identity as Christians. <u>They were guilty of conduct unbecoming of a saint</u>. They were "carnal" and "babes." Their conduct did not match their identity in Christ. "Because the carnal mind is enmity against God" (Rom. 8:7). Carnal believers are dead while they are living, "she that liveth in pleasure is dead while she liveth" (1 Tim. 5:6). "For if ye live after the flesh, ye shall die" (Rom. 8:13). We must wake up from this death. "Awake thou that sleepest, and arise from the dead, and Christ shall give thee light" (Eph. 5:14). Christ will invigorate us with His word rightly divided. Grace teaches us how we should live. "Teaching us that, denying ungodliness and worldly lusts, we should live soberly, righteously, and godly, in this present world" (Titus 2:12). To conclude, I personally believe that the Lord's Supper should be practiced, perhaps at the end of a fellowship meal. Because of what Christ has done, there are no believers who are unworthy of partaking in the Lord's Supper (Rom. 3:24, 5:1). But, as Paul said, we should do it in a worthy manner. Pastor Bryan Ross from Grace Life Bible Church in Michigan has YouTube studies and notes that were helpful to me in preparing this lesson. Were the Corinthians sinning in their observance of the Lord's Supper? Yes. What does the Supper commemorate? Christ's death for our sins. Paul had to rebuke the Corinthians because they had failed to judge this matter for themselves. Being drunk is a sin (Gal. 5:21; Eph. 5:18). Gluttony is also a sin Proverbs 23:21 For the drunkard and the glutton shall come to poverty: and drowsiness shall clothe a man with rags. In chapter 11 Paul, told the Corinthians that they were disgracing the Lord's Supper.]

Chapter 12 The purpose of gifts in this early church
12:1-11 Paul and the members at Corinth had different spiritual gifts.
12:12-31 The function of the supernaturally bestowed gifts and unity in the body of Christ.

12:1 <u>Now concerning spiritual gifts</u>, brethren, <u>I would not have you ignorant</u>. **2 Ye know that <u>ye were Gentiles, carried away unto these dumb idols</u>, even as ye were led.** [The Corinthians had come out of idolatry and were worshipping the true God. The powerless idols were dumb and could not speak (1 Thess. 1:9).] **3 Wherefore <u>I give you to understand, that no man speaking by the Spirit of God calleth Jesus accursed: and that no man can say that Jesus is the Lord, but by the Holy Ghost</u>.** [Paul gives them instructions on how to discern if someone is speaking for God when they prophesy (and not a false teacher) as mentioned in verse 10. <u>Accursed means doomed to destruction</u>. No one can say anything against Christ if they are speaking by the Spirit. But, by the Holy Ghost they can say Jesus is Lord. Today, the gift of prophecy is not in effect because we have the complete word of God (in English it is in the King James Bible). However, we must still discern what God's word says and which Bible teachers are worth listening to. The marks of a good Bible teacher are: a saved King James Bible believer who teaches the word of God rightly divided.] **4 <u>Now there are diversities of gifts, but the same Spirit</u>.** [The same Spirit gave different gifts to people.] **5 And there are <u>differences of administrations, but the same Lord</u>.** [The Lord administered the gifts differently.] **6 And there are <u>diversities of operations</u>, but it is the <u>same God</u> which <u>worketh all in all</u>.** [God operated the gifts differently. The gifts had different functions. *Notice how the entire Godhead is mentioned: the same Spirit (4) the same Lord (5) and the same God (6). Each Person of the Godhead is Spirit. God is Spirit and must be worshipped in Spirit and truth (John 4:24). The context will tell us which one of the Godhead is being referred to.] **7 <u>But the manifestation of the Spirit is given to every man to profit withal</u>.** [Gifts were divinely given by the Spirit for the purpose of profiting all the members in the early church (Rom. 12:3-8).] **8 For to <u>one is given by the Spirit the word of wisdom; to another the word of knowledge by the same Spirit</u>; 9 To <u>another faith by the same Spirit; to another the gifts of healing by the same Spirit</u>; 10 To <u>another the working of miracles; to another prophecy; to another discerning of spirits; to another divers kinds of tongues; to another the interpretation of tongues</u>:** [To illustrate what he means Paul lists some gifts given by the Spirit: word of wisdom, knowledge, faith, healing, working of miracles, prophecy, discerning of spirits, divers kinds of tongues, and interpretation of tongues (translating of the foreign language spoken). Notice that discerning of "spirits" is lower case because it is the spirit in the man, whether he or she is speaking God's words. Paul told us that women were also praying in tongues and prophesying (11:5). When the Holy Ghost fell on the 120 men and women in the Upper Room they all spoke in divinely given tongues, and were understood by those who spoke those different languages (Acts 1:15, 2:4-12). Tongues, a spiritual gift, is being able to speak a language that you have never formally studied to learn.] **11 But all these worketh that one and the selfsame Spirit, dividing to every man severally as he will.** [That list of gifts, all work by the same Spirit who distributes several gifts as He will.] **12 For as the body is one, and hath many members, and all the members of that one body, being many, are one body: so also is Christ.** [We are one body made up of many members working in unison. All are important, no one is more important than the other (Rom. 12:3-8). The members are all controlled by the same Head, Christ (Eph. 1:22, 23; Col. 1:18, 24, 2:19).] **13 For by one Spirit are we all baptized into one body, whether we be Jews or Gentiles, whether we be bond or free; and have been all made to drink into one Spirit.** [We have a spiritual baptism without water (Rom. 6:3, 4; Eph. 4:5). The instant we believe; we are spiritually placed into the body of Christ. The body of Christ is Christ's heavenly group of Jews and Gentiles. (Gal. 3:28). We all partake of the same Spirit.] **14 For the body is not one member, but many**. [The body of Christ is made up of many members. Paul will now use the human body analogy for the body of Christ.] **15 If the foot shall say, Because I am not the hand, I am not of the body; is it therefore not of the body?** [The foot is still part of the body.] **16 And if the ear shall say, Because I am not the eye, I am not of the body; is it therefore not of the body?** [Each different part is still of the body.] **17 If the whole body were an eye, where were the hearing? If the whole were hearing, where were the smelling?** [Paul says that God gave different gifts so that all could benefit from each other's gifts. We grow like a living body, or organism (Eph. 4:15, 16).] **18 But now hath God set the members every one of them in the body, as it hath pleased him**. [God has placed every member in the body the way He wants.] **19 And if they were all one member, where were the body?** [If everyone was an eye there would not be a complete body.] **20 But now are they many members, yet but one body.** [If everyone had the same gift the body of Christ would be limited. But since everyone is different, and has different gifts, the body of Christ can function as a unit.] **21 And the eye cannot say unto the hand, I have no need of thee: nor again the head to the feet, I have no need of you.** [We all need of each other. We are a team.] **22 Nay, much more those members of the body, which seem to be more feeble, are necessary:** [We even need those members who seem to be weak. The members that we think are less important are really more needed.] **23 And those members of the body, which we think to be less honourable, upon these**

125

we bestow more abundant honour; and our uncomely parts have more abundant comeliness. [Paul says we should bestow more honor on those we think are less honorable, then the less appealing members will become more attractive. Many of you know I have a daughter with Down Syndrome. Like Hitler and abortionists many in society would exterminate people like her thinking they are less valuable. But I have learned, and continue to learn so much from her about how to give and show unconditional love and care for others. She is the cheerful greeter for our Bible Study. When Nam (from Vietnam) came here for the first time, Grace ran to meet her at the door with a big hug saying "I love you." I could see Nam melt and relax. I could tell she felt special immediately. Grace excels in social skills and naturally has a doctorate degree in communicating love. I can only hope to achieve to her level. She is a joy to be around. If you ever come to visit, you can have a great, big Gracie hug.] **24 For our comely parts have no need: but God hath tempered the body together, having given more abundant honour to that part which lacked:** [The attractive members have no need of more honor. God had duly mixed the body of Christ together, so that there was a mixture of gifted people and He gives more abundant honor to the parts that seem to be less. It is not spiritual uniformity, but spiritual unity. It is not a homogenous mixture, but more like a fruit salad. All the different fruits make the salad so nice.] **25 That there should be no schism in the body; but that the members should have the same care one for another.** [When some members do not follow Christ's apostle Paul, there is strife and division (like there was in Corinth). We should love each other like a family. There should not be any division, only unity. We should not prefer one person above another. There should be genuine camaraderie.] **26 And whether one member suffer, all the members suffer with it; or one member be honoured, all the members rejoice with it.** [We suffer if one of us suffers, and we rejoice and cheer if one of us is honored. There is no room for self-interest.] **27 Now ye are the body of Christ, and members in particular.** [We are one group or team, made up of distinct and different members.] **28 And God hath set some in the church, first apostles, secondarily prophets, thirdly teachers, after that miracles, then gifts of healings, helps, governments, diversities of tongues.** [Paul ranks gifts in the early church in the order of importance. It was first apostles, second prophets, then teachers, workers of miracles, gifts of healing, helps, government, and speaking in different tongues which were languages, last. Our apostle Paul was the first member of the body of Christ (1 Tim.1:16). The prophets were able to speak God's words (after they had been revealed to Paul). The prophets could also discern which letters by Paul were inspired by the Holy Spirit, and the order they should be placed in the Bible. There are no apostles, prophets, miracle workers, tongues or any other spiritual gifts today. We do not need supernatural gifts today because we have something much better, we have the complete word of God and the Holy Spirit in us (Eph. 3:16-21).] **29 <u>Are all apostles? are all prophets? are all teachers? are all workers of miracles? 30 Have all the gifts of healing? do all speak with tongues? do all interpret?</u>** [No. Even in Corinth, not everyone had the same gifts. They did not all speak in tongues for example.] **31 <u>But covet earnestly the best gifts: and yet shew I unto you a more excellent way.</u>** [Paul said, desire the best gifts. Yet he will show them a more excellent way.]

Our spiritual growth is of more value than our material wealth and needs to be given our highest priority.

THEWORDFORTHEDAY

Chapter 13 Using sign gifts in love and their impending cessation
13:1-13 Ministry gifts must be exercised in love and when they will cease.

13:1 Though I speak with the tongues of men and of angels, and have not charity, I am become as sounding brass, or a tinkling cymbal. [If a believer does not have Christ's love working in and through him then even if they are marvelously eloquent with their words, they are like the noise of an irritating toot of a brass horn or a tinkling cymbal. God has given us free will. We are saved by choosing to believe what God says. This involves the mind (spirit), heart (soul), and will (the action of a yielded body). After salvation, there is no self-condemnation when we "walk not after the flesh, but after the Spirit" (Rom. 8:1). We are not under the Mosaic law (Rom. 6:14), but the law of the "spirit of life in Christ Jesus" (Rom. 8:2) operates in us. Before I came to right division I did not have many of the graces displayed in my life. Because I thought the body of Christ began in Acts 2, I had put myself under the law. The law then made my sin nature (my flesh) come alive and abound exceedingly. Paul says in Rom. 7:9, "I was alive without the law once" (when he was under grace), "but when the commandment came, sin revived and I died" (when he put himself back under the law, sin came alive in him). It was not until I started to understand the Bible rightly divided that I started seeing fruit in my life (Gal. 2:20, 5:22-26). The fruit of the spirit (graces) has eternal value because it is something we allowed Christ to do through us. This is another reason why everyone should learn how to rightly divide the word of truth.] **2 And though I have the gift of prophecy, and understand all mysteries, and all knowledge; and though I have all faith, so that I could remove mountains, and have not charity, I am nothing.** [Prophecy without charity profits nothing. Without charity, understanding all of God's mysteries has no eternal value. Paul said that supernatural knowledge can "puff up" (8:1). In Matt. 17:20, 21, the "mountain" represents a kingdom. In the Tribulation, Antichrist will be setting up his one world government and one world religion. The "little flock" or believing remnant, will be praying and fasting to be able to say to that mountain "remove hence to yonder place." Compare it with Rev. 8:8. Here we notice that the second trumpet judgment of a great mountain burning with fire is cast into the sea. The city called Babylon will be destroyed in one hour (Rev. 18:16-20). If we have faith enough to remove mountains but do not have charity, we are nothing.] **3 And though I bestow all my goods to feed the poor, and though I give my body to be burned, and have not charity, it profiteth me nothing.** [If we give all that we have including our lives, without Christ working in us, there is no value.] **4 Charity suffereth long, and is kind; charity envieth not; charity vaunteth not itself, is not puffed up,** [Compare charity with the love and unity in Rom. 12:9-16. Paul describes the characteristics of charity: longsuffering (patient), kind, without envy, it does not exalt itself and is not prideful. The word "vaunteth" refers to an outward display of self-importance. Charity rises above petty squabbles. Love realizes that the enemy wants to divide the believers and decides not to let him. Charity is generous in the way it treats others. It is easy to love the loveable; but how difficult it is to love those who have injured or attacked us. Paul said, "being reviled, we bless; being persecuted, we suffer it" (4:12; Rom. 12:17-21). Envy is a terrible sin. Cain envied his brother and killed him. There is no room for envy in the body of Christ. There is so much work that needs to be done in these last days in the dispensation of grace. We know what God's will is for "all men to be saved, and to come unto the knowledge of the truth" (1 Tim. 2:4). So many are not saved because they have not heard the clear gospel message of what Christ has done for us (1 Cor. 15:3,4) or have added their own works to His. Furthermore, there are so few who have come to the knowledge of the word of God rightly divided (2 Tim. 2:15). The truth for the body of Christ is found in Paul's writings, Romans to Philemon and is the Mystery. This truth must be divided from the rest of the Bible which is truth about Israel's King and His earthly kingdom (Prophecy). In the next dispensation, Christ will set up His one world government and one world religion. At this late hour in the dispensation of grace, it is all hands on deck. We should all be so busy about our own ministry that we do not have time to criticize someone else's.] **5 Doth not behave itself unseemly, seeketh not her own, is not easily provoked, thinketh no evil;** [Paul is indicting the Corinthians for not having charity and unity. Paul is telling them what charity is and saying you are not doing it. Charity is not self-centered but esteems others above themselves. They were being self-centered. The Corinthians needed to remember what Christ did for them on the cross. When we were yet sinners and His enemies, Christ died for us (Rom. 5:8, 10). Charity does not get angry easily, it thinks the best about people, and is not suspicious, accusatory, or paranoid.] **6 Rejoiceth not in iniquity, but rejoiceth in the truth;** [Finds no joy in evil, but is happy about the truth. We want people to live with us in heaven (and not go to that awful other place). We are thrilled when someone says (after 9, or 28, or 54 years of being a Christian) "I finally came to understand how to divide the Bible and the message of grace." We want people to have the truth, joy, and clarity we have under grace and not be in bondage in a performance-based religious system.] **7 Beareth all things, believeth all things, hopeth all things, endureth all things.** [Charity carries the burden for others. Charity believes that it is possible for anyone to be saved "and to come to the knowledge of truth" (the word of God rightly divided). Charity endures all things without complaint. Christ and Paul both suffered for us.] **8 Charity never faileth: but whether there be prophecies, they shall fail; whether there be tongues, they shall cease; whether there be knowledge, it shall vanish away.** [Love will not be done away with. What we do with Christ living through us lasts forever. But prophecies will not last and tongues will stop. Special supernatural knowledge will vanish away. Paul wrote this Corinthian letter from Ephesus in Acts 19. He knew that Christ would finish giving him the revelation of the mystery (Rom. 15:29, 16:25, 26). After he had the complete revelation, it was given for him to finish writing the word of God (Col. 1:25). Words that are written down can be referred to and do not depend on someone's memory about what was said. Once the provoking ministry to Israel was finished, the sign gifts would end. Luke then stopped writing the book of Acts. Let us look at the last several verses after Paul arrived in Rome, in Italy (Acts 28:17-31). Please keep in mind that the kingdom of God is made up two realms, heaven and earth. But first, let us look at when and where Christ through Paul set Israel aside: at Antioch, in Pisidia (Acts 13:46), at Corinth, in Greece (Acts 18:6), and in Rome, Italy (Acts 28:28). Paul set the Jews aside in three different countries. He let them know that God would save the Gentiles in spite of them, and without them. So now that the Acts period is over, so are the sign gifts.] **9 For we know in part, and we prophesy in part.** [By this time in his Acts ministry, when Paul wrote First Corinthians (Acts 19), he had only received part of the revelation of the mystery from the Lord. Christ had said in Acts 9 (but recorded in Acts 26) that he would appear to him and progressively give him further revelation (Acts 26:16; 2 Cor. 12:1, 7).] **10 But when that which is perfect is come, then that which is in part <u>shall be done away</u>.** [When Paul would finally have the complete revelation of the mystery, the supernatural sign gifts would not be needed.] **11 When I was a child, I spake as a child, I understood as a child, I thought as a child: but when I became a man, I <u>put away childish things</u>.** [Paul refers to the body of Christ as a child. The child speaks (tongues), understands (knowledge), and thinks (prophecy) like a child. But when the child is a fully grown man, the childish things (spiritual gifts) will be put away. We should not desire to go back to the childish things of sign gifts. They have been put away.] **12 <u>For now we see through a glass, darkly; but then face to face: now I know in part; but then shall I know even as also I am known</u>.** [Corinth was famous for its metal mirrors, so Paul uses them as an illustration. A person could only see a dim reflection of themselves in those mirrors. When Paul has the full revelation of the mystery from Christ, then all will be able to read and learn about what Christ is doing now. Then we in the body of Christ shall be able to <u>see ourselves perfectly</u> (know all that God has said to us) and be able to be conformed to His image (Rom. 8:29) by the effectual working of His word in us.] **13 And now abideth <u>faith</u>, <u>hope</u>, <u>charity</u>, these three; <u>but the greatest of these is charity</u>.** [God used the gifts to start the Church, but now it runs on its own. The sign gifts ceased, as Paul said they would at the end of Acts 28. Now faith, hope, and charity remain; but the greatest of these is charity. Charity is our motivation. Today the word of God is complete and there is no more revelation to be added to the Bible. The only other place in the Bible where Paul talks about a mirror is in 2 Cor. 3:18. We behold the glory of the Lord, when we look into His word. We need the Holy Spirit to give us enlightenment, in order to understand it. Paul prayed for the believers to be enlightened (Eph. 1:15-23).]

Charity suffereth long, and is kind; charity envieth not; charity vaunteth not itself, is not puffed up, Doth not behave itself unseemly, seeketh not her own, is not easily provoked, thinketh no evil;
1 Corinthians 13:4-5
KJV

Chapter 14 Regulation of spiritual gifts in the local assembly
14:1-26 Prophesy is the superior gift. Paul contrasts tongues and prophesy.
14:27-40 Order in the church in regard to spiritual gifts.

14:1 <u>**Follow after charity, and desire spiritual gifts, but rather that ye may**</u> <u>**prophesy.**</u> [Paul said to follow him as he follows Christ (11:1), but now he says to follow after charity. Charity is the kind of love we can only display when Christ is working through us. Christ wanted the same for His followers in His earthly ministry (John 13:34). Prophecy is the message, while to prophesy is to give the message. In 12:31, Paul said "covet earnestly the best gifts" and now he says that prophesy is the best gift.] **2 For he that speaketh in an unknown tongue speaketh not unto men, but <u>unto God</u>: for no man understandeth him; howbeit in the spirit he speaketh mysteries.** [God understood the foreign languages that were supernaturally spoken, but not the other people unless they spoke that same language. In his spirit that person was speaking mysteries to God.] **3 But he that prophesieth speaketh unto men to edification, and exhortation, and comfort.** [Someone who is speaking God's words, build up the body of Christ with words of encouragement and comfort from God. "Edification is to build up by instruction. "Exhortation" is to give encouragement, advice, and counsel. "Comfort" is to relieve, console, and support.] **4 He that <u>speaketh in an unknown</u>** <u>**tongue edifieth himself**</u>**; but he that <u>prophesieth edifieth the church</u>.** [Tongues are for the speaker's own good, if he understands what he is saying. It was the lesser gift of the five mentioned in 12:28. But, to prophesy is for the good of the church.] **5 I would that ye all spake with tongues, but rather that ye prophesied: for greater is he that prophesieth than he that speaketh with tongues, except he interpret, that the church may receive edifying.** [Paul wants everyone to be able to speak in tongues, but he would rather have them prophesy. Prophesy is greater than tongues. Because unless the speaker, or someone with the gift of interpretation, interprets what he is saying no one will understand him.]

6 Now, brethren, if I come unto you speaking with tongues, what shall I profit you, except I shall speak to you either by revelation, or by knowledge, or by prophesying, or by doctrine? [Paul is saying, "What profit will you have if I speak in foreign tongues that you do not understand, unless I speak something that you can understand by revelation, knowledge, prophesying or doctrine (teaching)?"] **7 And even things without life giving sound, whether pipe** [flute] **or harp, except they give a distinction in the sounds, how shall it be known what is piped or harped?** [Unless there is a distinct sound of a musical instrument, no one can make sense of it.] **8 For if the trumpet give an uncertain sound, who shall prepare himself to the battle?** [Unless a trumpet gives a clear sound, no one will charge into the battle.] **9 So likewise ye, except ye utter by the tongue words easy to be understood, how shall it be known what is spoken? for ye shall <u>speak into the air</u>.** [If no one can understand what you are saying, you might as well speak into the air.] **10 There are, it may be, so many kinds of voices in the world, and none of them is without signification.** [There are many different voices or real languages in the world and all are important.] **11 Therefore if I know not the meaning of the voice, I shall be unto him that speaketh a barbarian, and he that speaketh shall be a barbarian unto me.** [But if I (Paul) do not know that language I will be like a barbarian (an uncivilized foreigner) to the other person, and he to me.] **12 Even so ye, forasmuch as ye are zealous of spiritual gifts, seek that ye may excel to the edifying of the church.** [The Corinthians overemphasized tongues. It is best to do things that edify the church.] **13 Wherefore let him that speaketh in an unknown tongue pray that he may interpret.** [The person who speaks in a tongue that no one understands, should pray that God will help him interpret it.] **14 For if I pray in an unknown tongue, my spirit prayeth, but my understanding is unfruitful.** [Paul, used himself as an example, he said that if he prays in a tongue to God his spirit is praying, but his understanding is unfruitful.] **15 What is it then? I will pray with the spirit, and I will pray with the understanding also: I will sing with the spirit, and I will sing with the understanding also.** [What is it then to be fruitful? It is being able to pray with both the spirit and understanding. I will sing, says Paul, with both the spirit and understanding.] **16 Else when thou shalt <u>bless with the spirit</u>, how shall he that occupieth the room of the unlearned say Amen at thy <u>giving of thanks</u>, seeing he understandeth not what thou sayest?** [Or else when you bless God in the spirit, how shall a person who is learning be able to agree with your thankfulness to God, when he doesn't understand what you are saying?] **17 For thou verily <u>givest thanks well</u>, <u>but the other is not edified</u>.** [Truly you are saying thank You to God well, but the other doesn't understand what for.] **18 <u>I thank my God, I speak with tongues more than ye all</u>:** [Paul is grateful that he spoke more languages than all of them. He needed them in his travels and ministry.] **19 Yet in the church I had rather speak <u>five</u> words with my understanding, that by my voice I might teach others also, <u>than ten thousand words in an unknown tongue</u>.** [Paul said that he would rather speak <u>five words</u> that can teach others than ten thousand words that no one understands. An example of five words is "Christ died for our sins."] **20 Brethren, <u>be not children in understanding</u>: howbeit in malice be ye children, but in understanding be men.** [The Corinthians are "complete in him" (Col. 2:10) but they need to grow spiritually. Malice is the intent to bring harm to someone. Paul wants them to be children in that, but he doesn't want them to be children or "babes" in their understanding.] **21 In the law it is written, With men of <u>other tongues</u> and other lips will I speak unto this**

people; and yet for all that will they not hear me, saith the Lord. [Even if God speaks to the people in a language they can understand they will still refuse to listen to His voice (Deut. 28:45, 46).] **22 Wherefore tongues are for a sign, not to them that believe, <u>but to them that believe not</u>: but prophesying serveth not for them that believe not, but for them which believe.** [Tongues were a sign to the unbelievers of Israel (1 Cor. 1:22; Acts 10:44-46), while prophesy is for believers. In the Tribulation, tongues will be a sign to the unbelieving in Israel again (Mark 16:17).] **23 If therefore the whole church be come together into one place, and all speak with tongues, and there come in those that are unlearned, or unbelievers, will they not say that ye are mad?** [If the whole church is gathered and unbelievers and those who are learning Paul's sound doctrine enter and hear the chaos of everyone speaking in various languages, will they not say these people are crazy?] **24 But if all prophesy, and there come in one that believeth not, or one unlearned, he is convinced of all, he is judged of all:** [But if everyone is prophesying, the unbeliever and unlearned will be convicted and instructed by God's words.] **25 And thus are the secrets of his heart made manifest; and so falling down on his face he will worship God, and report that God is in you of a truth.** [The secret things in their hearts are exposed by hearing God's word (Rom. 10:17) and they will agree that God's Spirit is speaking to them by those who prophesy. He will recognize his need to decide to believe the gospel or to grow spiritually. At the Great White Throne Judgment of sinners God will judge unbelievers by what Paul calls <u>my gospel</u>. "In the day when God shall judge the <u>secrets</u> of men by Jesus Christ according to <u>my gospel</u>" (Rom. 2:16).] **26 <u>How is it then, brethren? when ye come together, every one of you hath a psalm, hath a doctrine, hath a tongue, hath a revelation, hath an interpretation. Let all things be done unto edifying.</u>** [Paul said that everyone was given different gifts (12:10, 28-30) so why are the Corinthians saying they <u>all</u> have the <u>same gifts</u>? Everyone had a song, a teaching, a tongue, a revelation, and an interpretation; at Corinth it was a competition for the limelight.]

27 If any man speak in an unknown tongue, let it be by two, or at the most by three, and that by course; and let one interpret. [Paul, now begins to delineate the rules for speaking in tongues. Tongues and the sign gifts must be used with orderly restraint and only if an interpreter is present. There should be groups of two or three and one of them should be the interpreter.] **28 But <u>if there be no interpreter, let him keep silence in the church</u>; and let him speak to himself, and to God.** [If there was no interpreter, the tongue speaker should keep quiet. He could speak later at home to himself and God.] **29 Let the prophets speak two or three, and let the other judge.** [Let the prophets speak in groups of two or three, with one judging or discerning the spirits (12:10).] **30 If any thing be revealed to**

another that sitteth by, let the first hold his peace. [If anything is revealed to someone who is sitting nearby, let him not blurt out what came to him but let him wait to speak. Let the first speaker pause and allow him to insert what was revealed to him.] **31 For ye may <u>all prophesy one by one</u>, that <u>all may learn, and all may be comforted</u>**. [Everyone should take turns prophesying so everyone can hear, learn, and be comforted.] **32 And the spirits of the prophets are subject to the prophets.** [You should control your spirits, and they should be subject to you; you are not to be ruled by them or be impulsive.] **33 For <u>God is not the author of confusion, but of peace, as in all churches of the saints</u>**. [God is a God of order and peace, not confusion.] **34 Let your women keep silence in the churches: for it is not permitted unto them to speak; but they are commanded to be under obedience, as also saith the law.** [The context is speaking in tongues and prophesying. Women were not to take part in praying in tongues and prophesying in the church (11:5). When Eve sinned, all women were made subject to their husbands by God (Gen. 3:16). Today there are no sign gifts so women may speak in church and ask questions at an appropriate time.] **35 And if they will learn any thing, let them ask their husbands at home: for it is a shame for women to speak in the church.** [Paul also put the responsibility on the husband. If the wife had any questions she should ask her husband at home. It seems that because of <u>the culture</u> the men talked among themselves and the women were sitting in another place. If the women had a question they could ask their husbands at home what was said. Perhaps the women were abusing the gift of tongues and using them out of place. They may have been getting carried away with them and being too emotional. Both men and women if acting out of place in the church, tear it down instead of build it up. Both can be deceived.] **36 What? came the word of God out from you? or came it unto you only?** [The word of God did not come to the Corinthians alone, but it came to Paul first.] **37 If any man think himself to be a prophet, or spiritual, let him acknowledge that the things that I write unto you are the commandments of the Lord.** [If any man thinks himself to be a prophet or spiritual, let him acknowledge that Paul is writing the things that the Lord commanded him to write. Because Paul is their apostle appointed by Christ (1 Tim. 6:3-5).] **38 But if any man be ignorant, let him be ignorant.** [If anyone does not want to agree with the fact that the Lord is speaking through Paul, then let them remain "ignorant," destitute of knowledge and uninformed of what Christ is doing in His heavenly ministry through him.] **39 Wherefore, brethren, covet to prophesy, and forbid not to speak with tongues.** [Have an earnest desire to prophesy but do allow the speaking of tongues.] **40 <u>Let all things be done decently and in order</u>.** [Paul wants the church to be orderly. Today, since knowledge of the Bible does not depend on spiritual gifts any one can teach it. God uses imperfect people to do so.]

Chapter 15 Concerning the hope of resurrection
15:1-34 Proof of the resurrection.
15:35-49 Process of the resurrection.
15:50-58 Pending victory over death as the motivation for faithful service.

15:1 Moreover, brethren, I [Paul] **declare unto you the gospel which I preached unto you, which also ye have received, and wherein ye stand;** [Paul had declared the gospel to them and they had received it. They were already justified and standing by faith in Christ. Christ has done all that is necessary for our salvation; it is a free gift that can only be received by faith. We stand (positional salvation, justification) when we have His righteousness imputed to us (Rom. 4:25; 2 Cor. 5:21). The gospel is not something we do; it is something Christ has already done.] **2 By which also ye are saved, if ye keep in memory what I preached unto you, unless ye have believed in vain.** [If they were "saved" what does Paul mean? As we know, every time the word "saved" is used in the Bible it does not mean from hell. This refers to being saved from deception and false doctrine if they continue in the truth of the gospel that Paul taught them 9practical sanctification). Look ahead to verses 12-14, some were saying that they would not be resurrected, that the dead would not rise. Paul says they will be saved from this "evil communication" see verse 33. Paul will show that both Christ's death for our sins and His resurrection are essential components of the gospel of our salvation. Without the resurrection, we believe in vain and without profit, because Christ's resurrection is tied to our own.] **3 For I delivered unto you first of all that which I also received, how that Christ died for our sins according to the scriptures;** [Paul repeats what he told them in Corinth when they were saved. He had shared what Christ had revealed to him. Christ died by crucifixion for not only Israel's sins (as prophesied), but for all mankind's sins (not prophesied).] **4 And that he was buried, and that he rose again the third day according to the scriptures:** ["Buried" confirms His death and the placing of His body in the tomb. He rose again because the Father accepted His perfect blood sacrifice as full payment for all sins that have, are, and will be committed. "According to the scriptures" means just as prophesied in the word of God. Christianity rests on facts. His death, burial, and resurrection are facts and they were confirmed by many eyewitnesses. The grave could not hold Him; the empty tomb is proof that He rose. See what Luke, Paul's companion beginning in Acts 16, wrote in Luke 24:45-48.]

5 And that he was seen of Cephas, then of the twelve: [Christ appeared to Peter who denied Him three times, and then to the twelve (Mathias being one of them, James was not dead yet). Twelve is a collective term. Paul is separate from the twelve; he is the one apostle to the one body of Christ.] **6 After that, he was seen**

of above five hundred brethren at once; of whom the greater part remain unto this present, but some are fallen asleep. [Paul is the only one who reveals that Christ was seen by more than 500 at one time. Most of those eyewitnesses of His resurrection were still alive.] **7 After that, he was seen of James; then of all the apostles.** [Christ was seen by James, then by all the apostles including Thomas.] **8 And last of all he was seen of me also, as of one born out of due time**. [Paul saw Christ apart from the twelve (in Acts 9). Paul is a separate apostle, for a separate ministry. He was "born out of due time" (Gal. 1:1, 11, 12). All believers have Christ in them (John 17:26; Col. 1:27).] **9 For I am the least of the apostles, that am not meet to be called an apostle, because I persecuted the church of God.** [Paul says that he is the least of the apostles and not fit to be called an apostle because he persecuted that church, the believing remnant of Israel or "little flock" (Acts 8:1-3; Gal. 1:13; 1 Tim. 1:13). This remnant will receive the kingdom and sit on the twelve thrones (Luke 12:32; Matt. 19:28, 21:43).] **10 But by the grace of God I am what I am: and his grace which was bestowed upon me was not in vain; but I laboured more abundantly than they all:** [the 12] **yet not I, but the grace of God which was with me**. [Because of God's grace Paul is the apostle of the Gentiles (Rom. 11:13). He says, Christ did not give me this grace for nothing, because I worked more fervently than all of them, but it was not me, but the grace of God that was with me. Paul is always careful to acknowledge the power of Christ in him.] **11 Therefore whether it were I or they, so we preach, and so ye believed.** [Most of the believers at Corinth <u>were saved</u> by the gospel (<u>good news</u>) that Paul preached but some were also saved by Apollos, and others by Peter and his group. Both Peter and Paul preached the death, burial and resurrection of Christ. But Peter did it as a murder indictment, <u>bad news</u> (Acts 2:23, 4:10, 5:30; 1:12). Peter preached the gospel of the kingdom: that Jesus of Nazareth, was the Messiah to sit on David's throne in the kingdom (Acts 2:29-38).]

12 Now if Christ be preached that he rose from the dead, how say some among you that there is <u>no resurrection of the dead?</u> [Paul asks, if the twelve and the 500 eyewitness and I, all say that Christ rose from the dead why are some of you denying what we preach? As we know, Paul and the twelve were willing to die for the truth of the resurrection.] **13 But if there be no resurrection of the dead, then is Christ not risen:** [Paul will now demonstrate the importance of the resurrection by a series of "ifs." Everyone's resurrection is dependent on the fact that Christ was the first to be resurrected in a glorified body. Paul revealed that Christ's sacrifice paid for all sins. Christ's resurrection and ours are linked together.] **14 And if Christ be not risen, then is <u>our preaching vain, and your faith is also vain.</u>** [If Christ is not risen, then our preaching is useless, and your faith is worthless.] **15 Yea, and we are found false witnesses of God; because we**

have testified of God that he raised up Christ: whom he raised not up, if so be that the dead rise not. [Paul says, we are found false witnesses because we said that God raised Christ from the dead – if He did not, then there is no resurrection of the dead.] **16 For if the dead rise not, then is not Christ raised:** [Paul argues, if there is no resurrection of dead believers, then that means Christ did not rise.] **17 And if Christ be not raised, your faith is vain; ye are yet in your sins.** [They would be still in their sins if the Father had not accepted Christ's payment. If Christ did not rise, their faith has no eternal value.] **18 Then they also which are fallen asleep in Christ are perished.** [Then those who have died believing in Christ (whose bodies are now asleep) will not live again.] **19 If in this life only we have hope in Christ, we are of all men most miserable.** [If we only have hope of this life, then we are all doing this for nothing, wasting our time, and should be miserable.] **20 But now is Christ risen from the dead, and become the firstfruits of them that slept.** [But the truth is that Christ rose from the dead (remember Paul saw Him several times). Jesus is the first of those who died in faith to have a glorified body.] **21 For since by man came death, by man came also the resurrection of the dead.** [The reason Christ had to die was because death came by Adam. Christ became a man and was resurrected to undo what Adam had done so that others could have eternal life.] **22 For as in Adam all die, even so in Christ shall all be made alive.** [We have to be "in Christ" to be saved. This is the proof text of the resurrection.] **23 But every man in his own order: Christ the firstfruits; afterward they that are Christ's at his coming.** [The order of the resurrection was that Christ is the firstfruits from the dead (Col. 1:18, 19). Jesus was "firstfruits" of those that will have a glorified body. "They that are Christ's at his coming" the kingdom saints at His Second Coming.] **24 Then cometh the end, when he shall have delivered up the kingdom to God, even the Father; when he shall have put down all rule and all authority and power. 25 For he must reign, till he hath put all enemies under his feet. 26 The last enemy that shall be destroyed is death.** [After His millennial reign and the final rebellion, Christ will have secured all the believers to live in heaven and on earth. Then those who compose both realms (His kingdom) will be delivered to the Father. Christ will put down all opposition. All the enemies, including death will be cast into the Lake of Fire (Rev. 20:9-15).] **27 For he hath put all things under his feet. But when he saith all things are put under him, it is manifest that he is excepted which did put all things under him.** [In Psalm 110:1, the Father speaks to the Son, "The LORD said unto my Lord, Sit thou at my right hand, until I make thine enemies thy footstool." The Father is excluded from what is placed under His Son's feet.] **28 And when all things shall be subdued unto him, then shall the Son also himself be subject unto him that put all things under him, that God may be all in all.** [When all is done, the Son will be subject to the Father who put all things under Him. That God may be all in all.] **29 Else what shall they do which are baptized for the dead, if the dead rise not at all? why are they then baptized for the dead?** [What good is it for all who have been baptized (identified with) into Christ's death (Rom. 6:3-9) if they will not rise?] **30 And why stand we in jeopardy every hour?** [Why are we risking our lives if we will not be resurrected?] **31 I protest by your rejoicing which I have in Christ Jesus our Lord, <u>I die daily</u>.** [Paul says, I affirm so that you can have this joy yourselves. I remind myself every day that I am dead to the flesh daily. I am dead <u>to sin and self</u> (Rom. 6:2) and alive unto God. To overcome our evil flesh, we need to know, reckon, and yield to the fact that God says we are dead to sin, crucified with Christ; but alive unto God through Him (Gal. 2:20). We are spirit, soul, and body (1 Thess. 5:23). We know (mind/spirit), reckon (believe in our heart, soul), yield (our bodies a sacrifice, and take right actions). It is a relief that our lives are not about us, but about Him. This old earth and heaven and everything in it will all burn up. God will make a new heaven and earth. Our value is life with Him in the new heaven and new earth.] **32 If after the manner of men I have fought with beasts at Ephesus, what advantageth it me, if the dead rise not? let us eat and drink; for to morrow we die.** [If I had to fight with those beast-like men at Ephesus (Titus 1:12), what profit is my struggle if the dead do not rise? (The mob uproar in Acts 19:40, had not happened yet, but Paul was already dealing with those adversaries.) Let's just eat, drink and be merry if there is nothing more to life than the present. But this life is not all there is.] **33 <u>Be not deceived: evil communications corrupt good manners</u>.** [The corrupt communication that the resurrection would not happen was having an effect on their conduct.] **34 Awake to <u>righteousness, and <u>sin not</u>; for some have not the knowledge of God: I speak this to your shame.** [Paul says "awake" from this deceptive false teaching. Is there not a wise man among you? Speak no evil saying there is no resurrection. This evil communication and thinking is sin. Paul wants to throw cold water on them so they will wake up and think and act like the righteous saints they are. They need to follow what Christ teaches them through Paul. He blames the Corinthians for the lack of understanding of what God is doing and His word.]

35 ¶ But some man will say, <u>How are the dead raised up?</u> and <u>with what body do they come?</u> [Some were asking about the specifics of resurrection, so Paul begins to answer that.] **36 Thou fool, that which thou sowest is not quickened, except it die:** [They should know that something can't come alive if it hasn't first died.] **37 And that which thou sowest, thou sowest not that body that shall be, but <u>bare grain</u>, it may chance of wheat, or of some other grain:** [We are going to get different bodies than what we have now (Christ also spoke on this subject, John 12:24). God may use the bare grain such as an atom of the one we have now.]

139

38 But God giveth it a body as it hath pleased him, and <u>to every seed his own</u> <u>body</u>. [God will do what pleases Him, and each seed has its own body. The glorified body retains the identity and individuality of the believer.] **39 All flesh is not the same flesh: but there is one kind of flesh of men, another flesh of beasts, another of fishes, and another of birds. 40 There are also celestial bodies, and bodies terrestrial: but the glory of the <u>celestial is one</u>, and the glory of the <u>terrestrial is another</u>.** [Just like there are different kinds of flesh; men, beasts, fish, birds, so there are different types of glorified bodies. The heaven bound saints and the earth bound saints will both have glorified bodies but they will each be different. One kind is celestial (suited for heaven) and another is terrestrial (suited for the earth).] **41 There is one glory of the sun, and another glory of the moon, and another glory of the stars: <u>for one star differeth from</u> <u>another star in glory</u>.** [Celestial bodies differ in glory. Each star shines with a different intensity (Dan. 12:3). In astronomy, the lower the number is, the greater its magnitude. So a zero is the brightest, and a five is the dimmest star we can see with the naked eye.] **42 <u>So also is the resurrection of the dead. It is sown in</u> <u>corruption; it is raised in incorruption</u>:** [This is how the resurrection of the dead is also. Each person will shine with different wattage. Christ in us will be our light. Our corrupt bodies are raised without corruption.] **43 It is sown in dishonour; it is raised in glory: it is sown in weakness; it is raised in power: 44 It is sown a natural body; it is raised a spiritual body. There is a natural body, and there is a spiritual body.** [Our bodies are sown in dishonour and weakness, but raised with power. – It is sown a natural body, but raised a spiritual body.] **45 And so it is written, <u>The first man Adam was made a living soul; the last</u> <u>Adam was made a quickening spirit</u>.** [Adam became a living soul (Gen. 2:7). But Christ became a quickening spirit who gives life and light to those who trust in what He has done. The last Adam reversed the curse the first Adam brought into the world. We will have His light in us as we shine in the heavens.] **46 <u>Howbeit</u> <u>that was not first which is spiritual, but that which is natural; and afterward</u> <u>that which is spiritua</u>l.** [Just like the spiritual (Christ) was not first, but the natural (Adam) was first so it is for us; we are natural, then spiritual.] **47 <u>The first man is</u> <u>of the earth, earthy: the second man is the Lord from heaven</u>.** [Adam was of the earth, earthy. The second man is the Lord from heaven.] **48 As is the earthy, such are they also that are earthy: and as is the heavenly, such are they also that are heavenly. 49 And <u>as we have borne the image of the earthy, we shall</u> <u>also bear the image of the heavenly</u>.** [We were earthy and made in Adam's likeness. But God "will change our vile body, that it may be fashioned like unto his glorious body" (Phil. 3:21).] **50 Now this I say, brethren, that <u>flesh and blood</u> <u>cannot inherit the kingdom of God</u>; neither doth corruption inherit incorruption.** [We cannot inherit the kingdom of God in our flesh and blood

bodies. Remember that we have been made joint-heirs with Christ "and will be glorified with him" (Rom. 8:17). It is not because of any merit of our own, but by His. Also remember that the kingdom of God consists of both the heavenly and earthly realms. There will be a new heaven and a new earth for only the believers.]
51 Behold, <u>I shew you a mystery</u>; <u>We shall not all sleep, but we shall all be changed,</u> [Paul now reveals a mystery, or divine secret about the rapture. This mystery is exclusive to the body of Christ in the dispensation of grace; that not everyone will die, but all will be changed.] **52 <u>In a moment, in the twinkling of an eye, at the last trump: for the trumpet shall sound, and the dead shall be raised incorruptible, and we shall be changed.</u>** [This change will occur as fast as a "twinkling of an eye," in a fraction of a second, with two sounds of a trumpet. At the first trump (the sound that the trumpet makes) "the dead in Christ shall rise first" (1 Thess. 4:16, 17). Then with the second trump, "we shall be changed." Notice how Paul includes himself, because Christ did not tell him when the rapture would take place. The trump may be the voice of our Lord, as mentioned in the resurrection of the kingdom on earth saints at His Second Coming (John 5:25-29; see Rev. 1:10).] **53 <u>For this corruptible must put on incorruption, and this mortal must put on immortality</u>.** [We will put on immortal bodies that will last forever.] **54 <u>So when this corruptible shall have put on incorruption, and this mortal shall have put on immortality, then shall be brought to pass the saying that is written, Death is swallowed up in victory. 55 O death, where is thy sting? O grave, where is thy victory?</u>** [When we have our eternal bodies, that is when our death and our grave will be conquered. For the kingdom on earth saints it will be at His return to earth, not the air (Isa. 25:8; Hos. 13:14).] **56 <u>The sting of death is sin; and the strength of sin is the law.</u>** [Death is the result of sin (Rom. 6:23). The thing that makes sin stronger and more obvious, is the law.] **57 <u>But thanks be to God, which giveth us the victory through our Lord Jesus Christ.</u>** [Christ has removed our sins and the sting of death. Paul thanks God for His plan of redemption. Our Lord Jesus Christ won this victory over sin and death for us.]
58 <u>Therefore, my beloved brethren, be ye stedfast, unmoveable, always abounding in the work of the Lord, forasmuch as ye know that your labour is not in vain in the Lord.</u> [Paul now applies the sure fact of the resurrection to the believer's conduct. We can be steadfast because we have eternal life. Christ overcame both sin and death. On the cross He overcame sin; at His resurrection, He overcame death. In light of this truth, we should be steadfast (stable) un-moved by bad doctrine, abounding in good work for the Lord, because we know our labor is not in vain in the Lord. The things that we have done with Christ working through us will be of value at the judgment seat of Christ (2 Cor. 5:10). As ambassadors (2 Cor. 5:18-20), we can do God's will (1 Tim. 2:4). Because the tomb was empty, Paul's preaching was not in vain (14) and their faith and ours is

not in vain (14), and our labor is not in vain (58). This life is a place of service and preparation for our eternal life to come. Our rewards in heaven are determined by what we do in this life here on earth.]

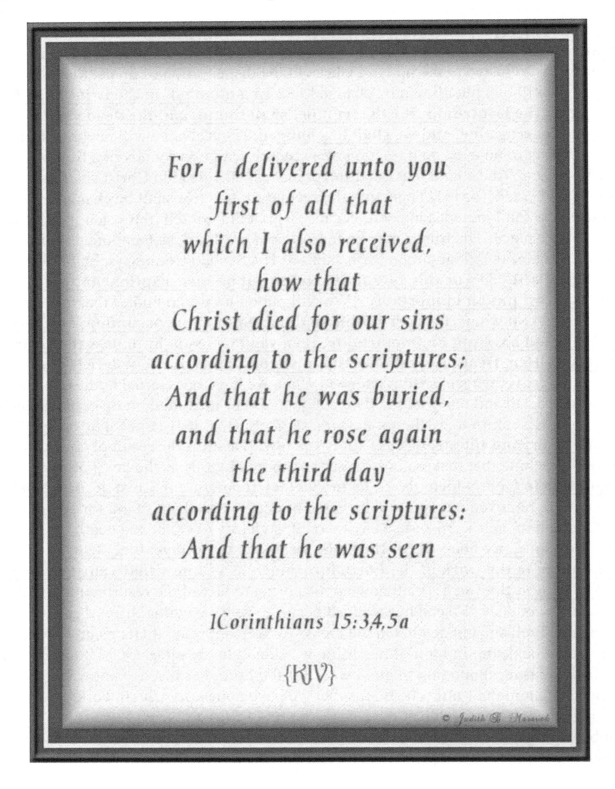

For I delivered unto you
first of all that
which I also received,
how that
Christ died for our sins
according to the scriptures;
And that he was buried,
and that he rose again
the third day
according to the scriptures:
And that he was seen

1Corinthians 15:3,4,5a

{KJV}

© Judith B. Monaco

Chapter 16 Concerning the collection for the saints and farewell
16:1-24 Instruction for the collection for the poor saints in Jerusalem and salutations.

16:1 Now concerning the <u>collection for the saints</u>, as I have given order to the churches of Galatia, even so do ye. [Paul went to Galatia again in Acts 18:23 and told them that they should take up a collection for the poor saints in Jerusalem.] **2 Upon the <u>first day of the week let every one of you lay by him in store</u>, as God hath prospered him, that there be no gatherings when I come.** [The church members generally met on Sundays, the day the Lord Jesus Christ rose from the dead. Collect on that day.] **3 And when I come, whomsoever ye shall approve by your letters, them will I send to bring <u>your liberality unto Jerusalem</u>.** [The Corinthians were to pick someone trustworthy to take the offering to Jerusalem.] **4 And if it be meet that I go also, they shall go with me.** [If it was fitting for Paul to go also, they could go together.] **5 Now <u>I will come unto you</u>, when I shall pass through Macedonia: for I do pass through Macedonia.** [Paul plans to come to Corinth when he goes through Macedonia (Rom. 15:19).] **6 And it may be that I will abide, yea, and <u>winter with you</u>, that ye may bring me on my journey whithersoever I go.** [Paul probably wintered with them in Acts 20:3.] **7 For I will not see you now by the way; but I trust to tarry a while with you, if the Lord permit. 8 But I will tarry at <u>Ephesus</u> until Pentecost.** [He planned to stay till spring. Paul wrote this letter from Ephesus.] **9 For a <u>great door and effectual is opened unto me</u>, and there are many adversaries.** [The great open door for ministry was probably his teaching at the school of Tyrannus (Acts 19:9). The enemies were the silver and copper smiths who made the shrines to the goddess Diana (Acts 19:24).] **10 Now <u>if Timotheus come</u>, see that he <u>may be with you without fear: for he worketh the work of the Lord, as I also do</u>.** [Do not give Timothy a hard time. He works for the Lord like me.] **11 Let no man therefore despise him: but <u>conduct him forth in peace</u>, that he may come unto me: for <u>I look for him with the brethren</u>.** [Be kind to him and help him on his way, so he can come back to me with the others.] **12 As touching our brother <u>Apollos, I greatly desired him to come unto you with the brethren: but his will was not at all to come at this time; but he will come when he shall have convenient time</u>.** [The Corinthians wanted Paul to send the eloquent Apollos, but he said he was too busy, but will come when he has a chance. He was probably busy ministering the word.] **13 <u>Watch ye, stand fast in the faith, quit you like men, be strong</u>.** [Stand fast in the faith and doctrine that Paul has given them. Keep looking for the Lord to return for us, stay strong in the faith, behave like adults, be strong (not babies).] **14 Let all your things be done with charity**. [We are to do everything with charity (unconditional love for others).] **15 I beseech**

you, brethren, (ye know the house of <u>Stephanas, that it is the firstfruits</u> of Achaia, and that they have addicted themselves to the ministry of the saints,) [In Romans 16:5, Paul said that Epaenetus was the first fruit of Achia so he was probably a member of the household of Stephanas. The first family to be saved in Greece are addicted to the ministry of the saints in the body of Christ. They are so enthusiastic about what God is doing and serving Him, by serving the believers.] **16 That ye submit yourselves unto such, and to every one that helpeth with us, and laboureth**. [Treat these leaders, and similar leaders, and everyone who works with us with respect and yield to their wise authority.] **17 <u>I am glad of the coming of Stephanas and Fortunatus and Achaicus: for that which was lacking on your part they have supplied.</u>** [Paul was glad that these three men came and treated him with respect by giving him a list of questions the church was asking him. They wanted his instruction, advice, and words of wisdom for the believers at Corinth. They were courteous and showed Paul the regard that many of the Corinthians did not, to their shame (4:14).] **18 For <u>they have refreshed my spirit and yours: therefore acknowledge ye them that are such.</u>** [Treat people like these with respect, because of their good conduct you have been blessed.]

19 ¶ The <u>churches of Asia salute you. Aquila and Priscilla salute you much in the Lord</u>, with the church that is in their house. [Salutations from Paul's several churches in Asia Minor (in Ephesus, in Galatia, in Colosse, and Laodicea, and so on). Aquila and Priscilla, whom they knew, had a church in their home again and send their greetings.] **20 All the brethren greet you. Greet ye one another with an holy kiss.** [Paul wants them to be affectionate to one another.] **21 The <u>salutation of me Paul with mine own hand.</u>** [Paul signs the letter himself. He began doing so after the forged letter to the Thessalonians (2 Thess. 3:17, 18).] **22 If any man love not the Lord Jesus Christ, let him be Anathema Maranatha.** [Paul uses some Aramaic words. He says, <u>do not associate with a brother who does not love the Lord Jesus Christ (5:11-13). Let him be accursed our Lord come. Believers are to follow the one Christ sent (4:16, 17).</u>] **23 The grace of our Lord Jesus Christ be with you.** [He begins and ends the letter with grace, for the grace of the Lord Jesus Christ to be with them.] **24 <u>My love be with you all in Christ Jesus.</u> Amen.** [Paul wrote this letter out of love for them (the local church) and for the Church (the body of Christ) who he was helping Christ to build (3:10, 9:17).]

Second Corinthians Commentary
Chapter 1 Double trouble and the God of all comfort.
1:1-7 Why does God permit His people to suffer?.
1:8-11 That we might have confidence in God alone.
1:12-14 That we might put our faith in what God has said.
1:15-24 Paul explains his delay.

1:1 ¶ Paul, an apostle of Jesus Christ by the will of God, and Timothy our brother, unto the church of God which is <u>at Corinth</u>, with all the saints which are in <u>all Achaia</u>: [Paul emphatically states that <u>it is by the will of God that he is an apostle</u>. Paul did not have a choice about being an apostle. <u>The risen, ascended, glorified Lord Jesus Christ from heaven chose Paul to be His apostle to build the body of Christ in the dispensation of grace</u> (Acts 9:15, 22:10, 26:16; 1 Cor. 9:16, 17). Timothy may have been the one to write this dictated letter to the Corinthians and to other believers in Achaia (southern Greece).] **2 <u>Grace</u> be to you and <u>peace</u> from God our Father, and from the Lord Jesus Christ.** [<u>We are living in the time of Israel's temporary national blindness which will end at the rapture</u>. It is a time when God the Father and the Lord Jesus Christ are dispensing grace and peace (Eph. 3:2). After that God will resume His dealings with Israel (Acts 15:14-16; Rom. 11:25, 26).]

3 ¶ Blessed be God, even the Father of our Lord Jesus Christ, the Father of mercies, and the <u>God of all comfort</u>; [Out of a grateful heart, Paul praises the Father of our Lord Jesus Christ, the Father of mercies, the God of all comfort.] **4 Who comforteth us in <u>all our tribulation</u>, that we may be able to comfort them which are in <u>any trouble</u>, by the comfort wherewith we ourselves are comforted of God.** [Paul was comforted so that he can comfort others. God comforts us in all our tribulations so that we can comfort others. Paul mentions comfort four times in this one verse. I knew a family whose 14-month-old baby boy died because he strangled on the Venetian blind cord the father installed and meant to shorten the day before. His death caused great sorrow. But the family was later able to minister to others whose children had accidentally died. Children who die before the age of accountability go to heaven to be with the Lord (2 Sam. 12:23). This is better than growing up and rejecting who Christ is and what He has done because the result of that is eternal torment. Notice that Paul says the God of <u>all</u> comfort and <u>any</u> trouble. God can comfort believers no matter what happens. He is able to turn the sour lemons life deals us into lemonade. Hopefully, we will learn from both our failures and successes.]

5 For as the sufferings of Christ abound in us, so our consolation also aboundeth by Christ. [Just like the sufferings of Christ abound in us so does God's consolation. We suffer as we try to reconcile others to God by sharing the gospel of Christ (1 Cor. 15:3, 4) and when we try "to make all men see what is the fellowship of the mystery, which from the beginning of the world hath been hid in God, who created all things by Jesus Christ" (Eph. 3:9). We suffer as we seek to do the will of God (1 Tim. 2:4). We are guaranteed to suffer. "Yea, and all that will live godly in Christ Jesus shall suffer persecution" (2 Tim. 3:12). One of the greatest sufferings in this life is the pain in our hearts that comes from knowing that many of our loved ones have not really trusted in Christ alone for their salvation – so they are not saved and will suffer forever in the Lake of Fire. Our hearts ache for them. They stubbornly refuse what God says in His word rightly divided. They think that somehow the good that they have done will outweigh the bad. And that God will somehow let them into heaven.

Some believe that this life is all there is. They may, like John Lennon, foolishly say: "Imagine there's no heaven It's easy if you try No hell below us Above us only sky." Lennon now knows that he was wrong. Eternity is a long time to be wrong. We don't want that for our family, friends, or even our worst enemy. "The fool hath said in his heart, *There is* no God" (Psalm 14:1). Many of our family and friends shun us grace believers, not knowing that we are Christ's ambassadors, His representatives, and our soul's desire is that they be reconciled to God and be saved (2 Cor. 5:18-20). Everything is about Christ and what He has done. We suffer and are fearful for those who reject Him and us. They tell us: "We don't want to hear about Jesus, the Bible, or Paul. We just want to eat drink and be merry." They reject Him, His word, and us. They try to find joy in food, drink, drugs, experiences, while they chase the mighty dollar. But the truth is that no one can really be merry without Christ. He saved us. He is our all. He is the source of true joy. Eternal life is found in the Person of Jesus Christ, not in religion. Our performance or religious traditions cannot save us. God Himself had to do it.

We suffer for His sake and for His glory. Some other reasons for our sufferings:
1) We live in a sin-cursed world among the children of disobedience (Gal. 1:4; Eph. 2:2).
2) Satan tries to bring division between the members of the body of Christ. He attacks the message and the messenger. He discourages the messenger (2:11).
3) We must suffer the consequences of our own stupid decisions (Gal. 6:7, 8).]

6 And whether we be afflicted, it is for your consolation and salvation, which is effectual in the enduring of the same sufferings which we also suffer: or

whether we be comforted, it is for your consolation and salvation. [Paul our "pattern" (1 Tim. 1:16) was afflicted and <u>consoled</u> so we can do the same. The key for us in the body of Christ is to imitate Paul (Phil. 4:9); to handle opposition and be eager learners of sound doctrine given by Christ to us through Paul. "Salvation" <u>here is saved from the effects of sufferings</u>. God does not send or remove tribulations, but will help us in them. Christ is intimately working in us just like He did in Paul. Paul suffered a great deal to preach the mystery to everyone, and lay the foundation for building the body of Christ in the dispensation of grace (Col. 1:23-29). But Christ had said that he would suffer (Acts 9:16).] **7 And our hope of you is stedfast, knowing, that as ye are <u>partakers of the sufferings, so shall ye be also of the consolation</u>**. [Paul is confident that Christ will work in us just like He has in Paul. We are "partakers" in the "<u>sufferings of Christ</u>," (Phil. 3:10; Col. 1:24) but we are also partners in the ability to console others. Our ultimate consolation is the rapture (1 Thess. 4:13-18).] **8 For we would not, brethren, have you ignorant of our <u>trouble which came to us in Asia</u>, that we were pressed out of measure, above strength, insomuch that we despaired even of life: 9 But we had the sentence of death in ourselves, that we should <u>not trust in ourselves, but in God which raiseth the dead</u>:** [Ephesus was such a strategic location to spread the gospel from. Paul and his companions despaired and were pushed to the edge of what they could endure in "the uproar" there. They were pressed out of measure (Acts 19:23) above strength and feared for their lives. After all, Paul had poured himself into the ministry to all of Asia Minor for three ears (two of which he taught in the School of Tyrannus), so all heard the gospel of Christ; then, <u>in one day his adversaries put an end to his ministry</u>. If Paul had confronted the mob, they would have torn him apart at Ephesus. They wanted to kill him. The silver and copper smiths wanted them to continue with their idolatry of the goddess Diana. They worshipped a piece of a meteor that dropped from the sky rather than the God who made all things and died for them (Acts 19:35). The Ephesians believed it was a piece from the god and planet Jupiter (the Roman god that is equivalent to the Greek sky god Zeus). Jupiter means "bright" interestingly, one of his ancient epithets of Jupiter according to the online Encyclopedia Britannica was "Lucetius" which means "light-bringer" which is closely tied to Lucifer/Satan who wants to be worshipped in heaven and earth. At the Tower of Babel, God gave the nations up to the idolatrous worship of the heavens and creation (Gen. 11:4, 5; Rom. 1:18-25; 1 Cor. 8:5). <u>Paul was very discouraged about the destruction of his ministry in Asia. He worried that he would also lose those in Corinth and Achaia. The dark clouds of double trouble piled on top of each other. They became more threatening when Titus did not show up when and where Paul expected him</u>. Paul had fears without and within (7:5). He was "cast down" (7:6). The situation seemed hopeless and Paul just had to trust that God would work things out. God had begun building a new group to live in heaven. We should not trust in ourselves, but in the powerful God "who raises the dead." God has the power, salvation is a gift and a miracle where we are translated out of Adam into Christ (1 Cor. 1:18; Col. 1:13, 14). Because Christ rose, we will rise also (1 Cor. 15:22). This life is about determining where we spend eternity and what our rewards or job description will be when we get there.] **10 Who delivered us from so great a death, and doth deliver: in whom we trust that he will yet deliver us;** [Notice the three tenses of our deliverance. Christ paid for the penalty of our sin. He freed us when He died on the cross in our place (5:21). He is delivering us from the power of sin (Rom. 6:14). He will deliver us from the presence of sin at the rapture or adoption, "the redemption of the body" (Rom. 8:23).] **11 Ye also helping together by prayer for us, that for the gift bestowed upon us by the means of many persons thanks may be given by many on our behalf.** [Paul is thankful for the prayers of the saints for him and his companions and the "gift" of Paul's deliverance from the mob at Ephesus. It enabled him to continue his work as the apostle of Jesus Christ to His body. Priscilla and Aquila had risked their lives so that all the churches could be grateful to them and the others who also helped at that time (Rom. 16:3, 4).]

12 ¶ For our rejoicing is this, the testimony of our conscience, that in simplicity and godly sincerity, not with fleshly wisdom, but by the grace of God, we have had our conversation in the world, and more abundantly to you-ward. [Many at Corinth questioned Paul's sincerity, motives, and apostolic authority. "Our conversation" means "behave ourselves." Paul rejoiced that he could give the testimony that his conscience was clear (2:17; 1 Cor. 1:17, 18). He had ministered with simplicity and godly sincerity, not fleshly wisdom or enticing words, but by the grace of God everywhere and to them (Acts 24:16; 1 Cor. 2:1-5).] **13 For we write none other things unto you, than what ye read or acknowledge; and I trust ye shall acknowledge even to the end;** [Paul says he writes to them what he has always plainly said to them, and hopes they will acknowledge what he has said until the end of the dispensation of grace.] **14 As also ye have acknowledged us in part, that we are your rejoicing, even as ye also are ours in the day of the Lord Jesus**. [Only a part of them acknowledged Paul and his friends at Corinth which gave him confidence that the other part would too. Paul says that at the Judgment Seat of Christ, "the day of the Lord Jesus," they will rejoice in each other. This is a day of blessing when believers receive rewards for service done while on earth (1 Cor. 1:8, 3:10-15; 5:5; Phil. 1:6, 10, 2:16). After the Judgment Seat of Christ (where all impurities will be burned off), the Lord Jesus will take us to appear before the Father (Col. 3:4). In contrast, the "dreadful day of the LORD" (Mal. 4:5) is a day of judgment of the unbelieving

Jews and Gentiles in prophecy (Isa. 2:12; Joel 1:15; Rev. 19:19-21) which will be complete after the Great White Throne Judgment when Satan, the lost, and death have been cast into the "lake of fire" (Rev. 20:14, 15). In 2 Thess. 2:3, Paul tells the Thessalonians, you have not missed the rapture because the "man of sin" has not been revealed. You will not know who he is because the dispensation of grace is restraining the day of the LORD. "And now ye know what [the dispensation of grace] withholdeth that he [Antichrist] might be revealed in his time. For the mystery of iniquity doth already work [Satan is "god of this world" (4:4) since the fall of man in the Garden]: only he [the body of Christ] who now letteth will let [restrain], until he [the one new man, the body of Christ] be taken out of the way" (2 Thess. 2:6, 7). The Tribulation and that Wicked will be revealed after the rapture (2 Thess. 2:8-10; 1 Thess. 4:16, 17). In the book of Revelation, the apostle John was called up through a door into heaven and described what he saw: the events of the Tribulation (Rev. 6-19), the Second Coming of Christ (Rev. 19:11-16), and His millennial reign (Rev. 20:3-6). Satan will be chained in the bottomless pit during the millennium. At the end of the millennial reign, Satan will be loosed and there will be a final rebellion (Rev. 20:7-10). The day of the Lord ends with the Great White Throne Judgment (Rev. 20:11-15). Then "the day of God" begins with the new heaven and new earth (2 Peter 3:10-13). Paul says that God begins a new dispensation called the fulness of times (Eph. 1:9, 10). The New Jerusalem comes down on the new earth (Rev. 21:1, 2). For this reason, the day of the Lord has a broader scope than the day of wrath; the 70th week of Daniel.]

15 ¶ And in this confidence I was minded to come unto you before, that ye might have a second benefit; 16 And to pass by you into Macedonia, and to come again out of Macedonia unto you, and of you to be brought on my way toward Judaea. 17 When I therefore was thus minded, did I use lightness? or the things that I purpose, do I purpose according to the flesh, that with me there should be yea yea, and nay nay? 18 But as God is true, our word toward you was not yea and nay. [Paul explains his delay. Paul is confident that more of them will acknowledge him as their chosen apostle. He wants to come and give them a second benefit (more revelation of the mystery) to add to the partial they had. He visited them one last time at Corinth for three months (Acts 20:3) and shared with them the revelation that he taught at the School of Tyrannus and wrote in the letter to the Romans. Paul had honestly planned to sail to them, to swing by them on his way to Macedonia, then come again to them on his way to Jerusalem. He says, do you think I made this plan lightly? Do you think I walk in the flesh? Paul walked by faith (5:7). Some were accusing him of saying yes and no (like a politician). He meant what he said. But as God is true, he had said he would not come now, because it was wiser to wait.] **19 For the Son of God, Jesus Christ,**

who was preached among you <u>by us</u>, even by me and Silvanus and Timotheus, was not yea and nay, but in him was yea. 20 For all the promises of God in him are yea, and in him Amen, unto the glory of God <u>by us</u>. [For the Son of God, Jesus Christ, who we preached is the big "Yes." <u>We can rely on the promises of our faithful gracious God. All the promises of God are yes and amen in Christ. He is true to His word preached by Paul and his friends to His glory (Acts 18:5).</u> Paul was the spokesman chosen by Christ in His heavenly ministry. Silvanus (Silas) and Timothy were secondary apostles (1 Thess. 1:1, 16). <u>What are some of the promises God has made to the body of Christ?</u> Once saved always saved (Rom. 8:31-39), we are sealed with the Holy Ghost (Eph. 4:30), joint-heirs with Christ (Rom. 8:17), eternal life in heaven (2 Cor. 5:1), we are His workmanship (Phil. 1:6; Eph. 2:10), Christ lives in us (Gal. 2:20; Col. 1:27).] **21 Now he which stablisheth us with you <u>in Christ</u>, and hath anointed us, is God; 22 Who hath also <u>sealed us, and given the earnest of the Spirit in our hearts.</u> 23 Moreover I call God for a record upon my soul, that to spare you I came not as yet unto Corinth. 24 <u>Not for that we have dominion over your faith, but are helpers of your joy: for by faith ye stand.</u>** [Paul said God is the one who stabilizes us with you "in Christ." He anointed us by His Spirit. God chose Paul, Silvanus, Timotheus, and us to serve Him. <u>When we fear God, fill our minds with His word, and live to please him, we have peace and confidence in the midst of troubles.</u> God is involved in our salvation. God sealed us with His Spirit in our hearts, the earnest or down payment (Eph. 1:13, 14). Some at Corinth were critical that Paul said he would come, but delayed. They complained and accused him of not keeping his word. God is my witness upon my soul, says Paul, that the reason I held off coming to you was to spare you. Paul waited because he wanted to know how they were doing from Timothy and then Titus. <u>He decided he would not give them another painful rebuke</u> (2:1-4). He says, we are not in charge of your faith, <u>we are helpers of your joy.</u> God treats them as adult sons. By faith in Christ, they have their standing in Christ having received His imputed righteousness. <u>When we understand that the body of Christ began with Paul's salvation in Acts 9, and not in Acts 2, we have clarity and joy because we understand the Bible better. All apparent contradictions disappear as we understand that God interrupted "prophecy" and inserted the "mystery." God is forming the body of Christ in the dispensation of grace. God is forming a new creature, a heavenly people group. We are all one and there is neither Jew nor Gentile (Gal. 3:28). God has revealed an un-prophesied mystery to us through Paul, but Satan still wants to conceal it.</u>]

Chapter 2 Forgive the repentant brother and Satan's devices
2:1-3 Paul continues to explain his delay in coming.
2:4-11 Forgive and comfort the contrite saint; we are aware of Satan's devices.
2:12-17 Paul was worried about Titus and the ministry at Corinth, but God always causes us to triumph in Christ. We speak the truth of what Christ from heaven says.

2:1 But I <u>determined</u> this with myself, that I would not come again to you in heaviness. [So Paul did come to them in heaviness, but had decided he did not want to do that again (12:14, 13:1, 2). Believers decide (1 Thess. 3:1, 4:3; Titus 3:12). He did not want to have to confront them. He delayed his visit to them on purpose.] **2 For if I make you sorry, who is he then that maketh me glad, but the same which is made sorry by me?** [Paul asks can I expect you to make me glad if I have made you sorry?] **3 And I wrote this same unto you, lest, when I came, I should have sorrow from them of whom I ought to rejoice; having confidence in you all, that my joy is the joy of you all**. [Paul is writing another letter to bring comfort and healing to their relationship. So they can clear things up before he comes and have mutual joy of each other. Paul is confident that they will share his joy because the first letter had good results.]

4 For out of much affliction and anguish of heart I wrote unto you with many tears; not that ye should be grieved, but that ye might know the love which I have more abundantly unto you. [Paul opens his heart to the saints, he leads by example, we should also be willing to open our hearts to our brothers and sisters. He was greatly grieved by what was going on in their assembly; not only concerning the fornicator (1 Cor. 5:1-13) but he also cared enough to want to correct their many problems. He did it out of his great love for them as their spiritual father. He wanted them to be restored to doing what is right before God for their benefit. Because the first letter was a success he writes again so that they can clear things up before he gets there.] **5 But if any have caused grief, he hath not grieved me, but in part: that I may not overcharge you all**. [In 1:14, Paul says that <u>only a part of the Corinthians acknowledged Paul's apostleship and ministry</u>. This grieved him. But he will not blame them all for not following him. Paul had charged the Corinthians with neglecting to deal with the blatant offender. They permitted gross immorality in the church. They had, in fact, shut their eyes to the case of incest in the congregation which was not even practiced among the heathen. Yet, they were puffed up and acting as if they were very spiritual. Paul told them to put away that wicked person from the assembly, so others would not be enticed. He said "deliver such an one unto Satan for the destruction of the flesh, that the spirit may be saved in the day of the Lord Jesus" (1 Cor. 5:5). When that man is in the world with sin and disease he may realize his need for Paul's sound doctrine. This is what happened, he changed his thinking. He wanted back into the church where Jesus who died for that sin also is proclaimed.] **6 Sufficient to such a man is this punishment, which was inflicted of many**. [Paul said, sufficient to such a man (one who causes grief) is the punishment that had been done when he was put out of the assembly. His punishment was enough.] **7 So that contrariwise ye ought rather to forgive him, and comfort him, lest perhaps such a one should be swallowed up with overmuch sorrow**. [This act of discipline brought him to the point of being <u>truly sorry</u> and having a desire to change his ways, but now the church went to the opposite extreme, they were not willing to let him back in. Paul says, on the contrary, forgive him, <u>comfort </u>him, so he doesn't get overwhelmed with sadness not only for his sin, but because he is left outside the fellowship. Satan wants us to believe that we cannot be forgiven, that our only way out is suicide. But we know we can never lose our salvation even by the things we do ourselves (Rom. 8:38, 39). When someone is sorry we should forgive them. In Israel's program Satan is the "accuser of our brethren" (Rev. 12:10). For us in the body of Christ, he likes to remind us of our past sins. Satan works spiritually because he knows that is what God is doing. He says, "you're not good enough." He wants to rob us of our joy and usefulness to God. But our sins were already dealt with at the cross. Jesus has paid for our sins with His own blood. "In whom we have redemption through his blood, even the forgiveness of sins" (Col. 1:14). Another reason God allows us to suffer is so that we can grow spiritually through our trials. Every hardship that we endure can make us better inside. With every trail, God gives us a way of escape (1 Cor. 10:13).] **8 Wherefore I beseech you that ye would confirm your <u>love</u> toward him**. [Paul begs them to confirm their love for him. There is the doctrine of separation and of restoration. They had separated him from their assembly to protect the local church, but now they can restore him.] **9 For to this end also did I write, that I might know the proof of you, whether ye be obedient in all things**. [They did well to obey Paul before in what he said in his letter, now he wants them to obey him again by forgiving.] **10 To whom ye forgive any thing, I forgive also: for if I forgave any thing, to whom I forgave it, for your sakes forgave I it <u>in the person of Christ</u>;** [Whoever they forgive, Paul forgives in the Person of Christ. Paul has also forgiven the Corinthians for their past reluctance to deal with the fornicator.] **11 Lest Satan should get an advantage of us: for we are not ignorant of his devices**. [Satan causes sin and division. Satan probably enticed the man to sin with the woman, but the Christian man chose to take the bait. In 1 Cor. 6:9-11, Paul had reminded them not to live like the worldly children of disobedience, that they had once been (Eph. 2:1-3). Satan wants to cause division in the church. The adversary had wanted them to exalt men's personalities and even Christ's earthly ministry over Christ's heavenly ministry (1 Cor. 1:12). Satan wants there to be cliques, and factions in the body of Christ. But God wants us to have unity (Eph. 4:1-6). Satan knows the strategy of divide and conquer. Satan tried to discredit the messenger, Paul, in the eyes of his followers. A wave of distrust in Paul's apostolic authority had swept through the church at Corinth, so Paul defended himself saying: "Receive us; we have wronged no man, we have corrupted no man, we have defrauded no man" (2 Cor. 7:2). If we forgive others, then we eliminate the wedge that Satan is trying to drive between us (Eph. 4:32).]

12 Furthermore, when I came to Troas to preach Christ's gospel, and a door was opened unto me of the Lord, [Paul says the "gospel of Christ" eleven times (Rom. 1:16, 15:19, 29; 1 Cor. 9:12, 18; 2 Cor. 4:4, 9:13, 10:14; Gal. 1:7; Phil. 1:27; 1 Thess. 3:2) and "Christ's gospel" once (2:12). Luke was probably from Troas and may have had a home or friends there. Notice the "we" and "us" when Luke joins Paul, Silas, and Timothy at Troas in Acts 16:6-10. Paul preached "Christ's gospel" given to Paul from Christ in heaven, not on earth (Matt. to John). This gospel is the same as the gospel Paul calls "my gospel" or "our gospel" to distinguish his message from that of the 12 apostles. Notice how the Lord had opened the door. We should be ready when the Lord opens a door for us to share the gospel or right division. I like to ask people, "Do you know what the five most important words in the world are? They are: "Christ died for our sins" and a few more important words are: "and rose again the third day according to the scriptures" (1 Cor. 15:3, 4). If you believe this you will be saved instantly.] **13 I had no rest in my spirit, because I found not Titus my brother: but taking my leave of them, I went from thence into Macedonia**. [Paul opens his heart and talks about his own doubts and fears. Like in an autobiography we look into the inner workings of our apostle. He said God had given him an opportunity to preach the gospel at Troas, but because he was anxious about Titus (and the Corinthians) he was restless in his spirit and did nottake advantage of the opportunity but moved on to Macedonia.] **14 Now thanks be unto God, which always causeth us to triumph in Christ, and maketh manifest the savour of his knowledge by us in every place**. [With a grateful heart Paul thanks God that we always triumph in Christ. Believers have His great wisdom and knowledge working in us like a pleasant smell, perfume, or fragrant incense.] **15 For we are unto God a sweet savour of Christ, in them that are saved, and in them that perish**: [To God the message and messenger are a sweet-smelling aroma or perfume of Christ to those who are saved, and those that are not (1 Cor. 1:18).] **16 To the one we are the savour of death unto death; and to the other the savour of life unto life. And who is sufficient for these things?** [To the unbeliever we are an odor of death unto death; and to the believer the perfume of life unto life. Sharing the gospel with others is a great responsibility, we use His powerful word, and pray for we are not sufficient in ourselves. We don't want people to go where there is torment forever and ever and where "they have no rest day nor night" (Rev. 14:11). We want to serve God, with Christ doing the work through us. Let us remember that "our sufficiency is of God," not ourselves (3:5).] **17 For we are not as many, which corrupt the word of God: but as of sincerity, but as of God, in the sight of God speak we in Christ**. [The word "corrupt" is very interesting, it means: 1. To change from a sound to a putrid state which is accompanied by a fetid smell. 2. To change from good to bad. 3. To waste, lose purity, or spoil. 4. To defile, pollute, or render impure. 5. To pervert; to falsify; to infect with errors; as, to corrupt the sacred text. False teachers corrupt the word of God by teaching the Mosaic system or Christ's earthly ministry. Paul and his friends did not change or pervert God's words or message. They sincerely and plainly preached what Christ had revealed to His spokesman Paul in God's sight "in Christ" (1 Cor. 2:1-5; 4:2). Peter also said that people were seeking to "wrest" the scripture Paul spoke (2 Peter 3:15, 16). Paul's purpose was not a means for making a living, but to build and edify the body of Christ. Paul was sincere in motive, message, and method. Paul did not do his ministry by his own power or in the flesh, but by Christ's power in the Spirit.

Satan is in the business of opposing everything that God does, and that includes corrupting God's word. Satan is behind the more than three hundred modern counterfeit Bibles which are being published. These Bibles omit words, add words, and change words. These Bibles are devoid of the Holy Spirit. They lie and deceive those who read them. The people who read them have never done any research into which Bible is correct. They just follow the crowd. God only has one Bible in English that is His perfect preserved word in the King James Bible. In order to have a copyright at least 20% of the KJV needs to be changed. So in the process of making new Bibles God's words are changed. The NKJV is the most deceptive sneaky Bible of all because it claims to be the genuine King James Bible without the "thees" and thous" and is just a Satanic counterfeit that is full of lies. Those pronouns are needed to know exactly who is being spoken to. Many of the modern Bibles are based on the false Greek text concocted by Westcott and Hort, in 1881. There is a very helpful article about the King James Bible in the appendix of God's Secret. In chapter 11 we will find out that "Satan himself is transformed into an angel of light" and has his own "apostles of Christ" (11:13-15) and "ministers of Christ" (11:23).

The three major ploys of Satan:
    Attack the Message.
    Attack the Messenger.
    Discredit the Messenger.

Satan **attacks the message** "I marvel that ye are so soon removed from him that called you into the grace of Christ unto another gospel: Which is not another; but there be some that trouble you, and would pervert the gospel of Christ" (2 Cor. 2:17; Gal. 1:6, 7).

Satan physically, emotionally, and mentally tried to **attacked the messenger**, Paul (2 Cor. 11:24-29; 12:7). Paul said that believers should not be frightened by the afflictions of their adversaries but expect them because it is a privilege to suffer for His sake (Phil. 1:28, 29). Our afflictions are light compared with Christ's and works to produce dependence on God and godliness in us (2 Cor. 4:17). The Jews constantly tried to destroy Paul's ministry, when he was in a location and after he left. They wanted to catch him when he left Corinth after his last visit there (Acts 20:3). He told the Ephesians that the Jews had laid in wait for him (Acts 20:19) and that after he left them that grievous wolves would come in among them and even of themselves men would arise to try to draw away disciples after themselves (Acts 20:28-30). Ministry is about exalting the Person of the Lord Jesus Christ, not a human. Paul said that we are not to follow personalities. The Corinthians should not follow Apollos, Peter, Paul, or even Christ in His earthly ministry (1 Cor. 1:12), but Christ in His ministry from heaven to the body of Christ (Col. 2:17-19).

Satan tried to **discredit the messenger**, Paul, in the eyes of his followers. A wave of distrust in Paul's apostolic authority had swept through the church at Corinth and Paul defended himself: "Receive us; we have wronged no man, we have corrupted no man, we have defrauded no man" (2 Cor. 7:2).]

Satan's policy of Evil is to attack the message, the messenger, and discredit and intimidate the messenger.

Chapter 3 Able ministers of the New Testament and the Spirit
3:1-18 The glorious ministry of the Spirit of the Lord versus the Old Covenant.

3:1 Do we begin again to commend ourselves? or need we, as some others, epistles of commendation to you, or letters of commendation from you? [Paul just finished saying that we speak "in Christ" the true words of Christ and that he and his co-workers do not corrupt the word of God. He asks, with a little sarcasm, do we need to tell you why we are worth listening to again? Do we need letters of recommendation for and from you, like some others? Aquila and Priscilla wrote a letter of introduction and recommendation for Apollos to give to the church at Corinth when he decided to visit there after he left them at Ephesus (Acts 18:27). Perhaps some teachers arrived at Corinth with letters of recommendation from the apostles at Jerusalem. As we found out last week Satan wanted to discredit Paul in the eyes of his followers. One faction at Corinth said that Paul was not a legitimate apostle like the 12 who had been with Jesus. Paul did not need letters of approval from anyone. The salvation and changed life of the Corinthians was the proof. Even our own salvation is proof of Paul's apostleship. The grace doctrine in Romans to Philemon working in us is proof of Paul's ministry. Paul used this accusation as an opportunity to compare the old covenant with the holy Spirits ministry of Christ's gospel in the dispensation of grace.] **2 Ye are our epistle written in our hearts, known and read of all men**: [You Corinthians are our letter of recommendation written in our hearts for all to read.] **3 Forasmuch as ye are manifestly declared to be the epistle of Christ ministered by us, written not with ink, but with the Spirit of the living God; not in tables of stone, but in fleshy tables of the heart.** [After all, their salvation was a result of Paul and his friends preaching the gospel to them and planting that church (Acts 18:1-17). Paul said in 2:14, that he shared Christ's gospel in every place, and so should we. God's knowledge and power was the cause of the triumph (Eph. 3:7). The result is saved souls and people who understand the mystery in which we live as revealed by Christ through Paul to us (1 Cor. 9:2; Eph. 3:2; Col. 2:2-4). They were Christ's letters ministered "by us" written, not with ink, but by the Spirit of the living God, not on tablets of stones, but in their hearts of flesh. Paul says that the Spirit of the living God writes Jesus Christ "according to the revelation of the mystery" (Rom. 16:25) in the believer's heart.]

4 ¶ And such trust have we through Christ to God-ward: [Paul trusts that God is doing this work in them. He is our mediator.] **5 Not that we are sufficient of ourselves to think any thing as of ourselves; but our sufficiency is of God;** [Paul says we are not sufficient for this work in ourselves, our sufficiency is of God.] **6 Who also hath made us able ministers of the new testament; not of the**

letter, [Law] **but of the <u>spirit</u>: for <u>the letter killeth</u>, but the <u>spirit giveth life</u>**. [God made them able ministers of the new testament, not of the law, but of the Spirit. The Law is holy and good, but it cannot give life. "Is the law then against the promises of God? God forbid: for if there had been a law given which could have given life, verily righteousness should have been by the law" (Gal. 3:21). The law kills, it condemns us by showing us our sin (Rom. 3:19, 20), but the Spirit of Christ is life. <u>We benefit from the effect of the law in that it shows us that we are not able to live up to God's standards and need a Saviour</u>. When we believe what Christ has done we receive the Holy Spirit. Each Person of the Godhead is Spirit. The Father is Spirit, the Son is Spirit, and the Holy Ghost is Spirit. All the members of the Godhead are in us (Eph. 4:6; Col. 1:27; 2 Tim. 2:14). So holy Spirit can refer to any member of the Godhead, the context will tell us who. Remember that God is one in three Persons, God the Father, God the Son, and God the Holy Ghost (1 John 5:7). <u>The "new testament" differs from the New Covenant</u>. A testament <u>is a will that goes into effect when someone dies</u>. Christ lived the perfect life. His shed blood was the perfectly satisfying sacrifice for all sins and the Father proved it by raising Him from the dead. His "last will and testament" went into effect after He died on Calvary (Heb. 7:22). Because Christ was the propitiation that paid mankind's sin debt, God can now dispense grace to us (Eph. 2:11-13). The Law condemns us to hell as sinners and yet Christ's finished crosswork saves us by making us saints. After His death, His wealth or "treasure" is His life in the believer (2 Cor. 4:7, 10, 11). Christ gives His righteousness, His Spirit, His Divine nature, to anyone who believes what He told them to believe. This is the only way anyone who has ever lived or will ever live, can come before the holy Father. All mankind is saved by faith (Heb. 11:6), not by works of the law. "But that no man is justified by the law in the sight of God, it is evident: for, The just shall live by faith" (Gal. 3:11). But in Israel's program works are required to accompany one's faith, such as water baptism (Mark 16:16). "Ye see then how that by works a man is justified, and not by faith only" (James 2:24).

A <u>covenant</u>, on the other hand, <u>is a contract or agreement</u>. Often God is the One who makes and keeps a one-sided contract; but the keeping of the Law was something that Israel on their part said they would do, but failed miserably to keep. "And all the people answered together, and said, All that the LORD hath spoken we will do. And Moses returned the words of the people unto the LORD" (Ex. 19:8, 24:3, 7). The children of Israel should never have said they would keep the Old Covenant, the Ten Commandments. Later, God promised that one day He would make a New Covenant with His people. The coming of the Holy Ghost at Pentecost was a foretaste of the New Covenant (Heb. 6:5). God described this contract with His Bride, the nation of Israel, saying He would give them His Spirit and cause them to obey His law perfectly (Ezek. 36:21-28; Jer. 31:31-36). But in Hebrews we read that the New Covenant is not in effect yet, because the Tribulation precedes the kingdom on earth (Heb. 2:8, 12:24-26). The New Covenant (Heb. 8:8-13, 10:15-17) will be in effect after His Second Coming. <u>None of the covenants belong to the body of Christ, they all belong to Israel</u> (Rom. 9:4; Eph. 2:11, 12). Paul never quotes Jer. 31:31 and applies it to us. Members of the body of Christ, can obey the law perfectly too (1 Tim. 1:9), not by working at it, but as a natural or automatic by product of walking in the Spirit (Gal. 5:16, 22, 23), as we put "on the Lord Jesus Christ, and make not provision for the flesh, to fulfil the lusts thereof" (Rom.13:14). We are to "Walk in the Spirit, and ye shall not fulfil the lust of the flesh" (Gal. 5:16). This is how we can live above sin and self and please God. But, we can make a wrong decision to live and act like the world (carnal Christians) and be imperfect at any time. We can go from being in the Spirit to being in the flesh in an instant. We still sin. Have you ever been offended when someone cut you off on the Freeway? But Israel will be caused to live perfectly 100% of the time. They will be in their glorified body in the kingdom, but we are still in our fleshly bodies which harbor the sin nature, that can raise its ugly head (Rom. 7:18).]

7 But if the ministration of death, written and engraven in stones, was glorious, so that the children of Israel could not stedfastly behold the face of Moses for the glory of his countenance; which glory was to be done away: [The ministration of the Law was glorious. God wrote the Ten Commandments on stone tables. Moses had been in God's presence when He wrote on the tables the second time.] **8 How shall not the ministration of the <u>spirit</u> be rather glorious? 9 For if the ministration of condemnation be glory, much more doth the <u>ministration of righteousness exceed in glory</u>**. [Paul asks, If the glory was wonderful when God gave the law to Israel through Moses, shall not the work of the Spirit of Christ in us be even more glorious? The law that condemns was glorious, but the Spirit of His perfect life-giving righteousness exceeds that glory.] **10 For even that which was made glorious had no glory in this respect, by reason of the glory that excelleth. 11 For if that which is done away was glorious, much more that which remaineth is glorious**. [The imputation of His perfectly righteous Spirit excels the glory of the Law. "For Christ is the end of the law for righteousness to every one that believeth" (Rom. 10:14). It is only because of His righteousness that anyone can come before the Holy Father. When Christ died His Spirit went to the Father, His soul to Abraham's bosom, and His body remained in the tomb. After the Father declared His propitiation fully satisfying by raising Him from the dead on the third day, all believers can receive His imputed righteousness by faith (Rom. 3:21-31, 4:23-25). Everyone in all dispensations are saved by faith, but the instructions that they had to believe were different (build an ark, have descendants and a land, etc.).] **12 Seeing then that we have such hope, we use great plainness of speech**: [Since we have hope of being accepted by the Father because of Christ's righteous Spirit, we speak with great plainness of speech (no fancy words or eloquence) so everyone can understand. The full meaning of the finished work of Calvary was given to Paul.]

13 And not as Moses, which put a vail over his face, that the children of Israel could not stedfastly look to the end of that which is <u>abolished</u>: [The Old Covenant is abolished. Paul said, <u>we do not cover the truth</u> like Moses had to cover his face so the children of Israel would not see the glory fading (Ex. 34:29-35). In Israel's program, the Law (Old Covenant) came through Moses, but Jesus Christ brought in a better New Covenant (Heb. 10:1). The law could not save or give life; but revealed the holiness of God, the perfect, clear cut, holy high standard of God which only Christ kept perfectly (Acts 13:38, 39; Matt. 5:17). Jesus never sinned in thought, word, or deed. He fulfilled all scripture. Christ saved mankind through the sacrificial system begun by God in the Garden (Gen. 3:21) and further incorporated and elaborated in the books of the law given to Moses (Ex. 29; Lev. 4). <u>Everyone needs to be clothed in the righteousness of Jesus Christ</u>. Adam was saved when he believed God, and called his wife the "mother of all living" (Gen. 3:20). Eve was saved when she believed God thinking that she had given birth to the Redeemer (Gen. 4:1). One day the kingdom of earth believers will have their glorified bodies that will shine (Dan. 12:2, 3; Matt. 13:43). Satan was blind-sided when Christ became the perfect sacrifice for both: God's kingdom on earth believers and God's heavenly kingdom believers. His kingdom includes both realms (Eph. 1:9, 10).] **14 But their minds were blinded: for until this day remaineth the same vail untaken away in the reading of the old testament; which vail is done away in Christ.** [Israel's minds as a nation have been temporarily blinded, but individual Jews can be saved if they believe Paul's gospel (Rom. 10:8). We are living at the time of Israel's national temporary blindness (Rom. 11:25). Elymas who was blinded for a season in Acts is a type of the nation of Israel (Acts 13:6-12).] **15 But even unto this day, when Moses is read, the vail is upon their heart**. [They do not see Christ when they read the Old Testament.] **16 Nevertheless when it shall turn to the Lord, the vail shall be taken away**. [The "it" is their heart. I used to wonder which verse to use to win Jews to Christ. When a Jew believes the gospel given to Paul by the glorified Lord Jesus Christ from heaven (1 Cor. 15:3, 4) they are saved and can understand the Bible.] **17 Now the Lord is that <u>Spirit</u>: and where the <u>Spirit</u> of the Lord is, there is liberty**. [Paul tells us plainly who the Spirit is; it is the Spirit of the Lord. He gives us liberty from sin and the law. He deals with us on the basis of grace, NOT the bondage of the law, and values free will (Rom. 6:14; Gal. 5:1).] **18 But we all, with open face beholding as in a glass the glory of the Lord, are changed into the same image from glory to glory, even as by the <u>Spirit</u> of the Lord.** [We behold His glory when we look into the glass (mirror, the word of God) and let it dwell in us richly (Col. 3:16). His word has the power to change us (to reprogram us) to be like Him. It is our glory to be made into His image (Rom. 8:29; Col. 3:10, 11). God's word will change us to be like Jesus. We want to look into the mirror and see Jesus' face looking back at us. As we read and study His word, we learn to think like Christ and have His mind (1 Cor. 2:12-16). With the help of His Spirit we understand His word with our minds (spirits) and then believe it in our hearts (souls), and act on it in our bodies. The more we learn the more we know; the more we know, the more we want to know. His word is our spiritual food for spiritual growth. God's word just keeps getting more wonderful and exciting as we study it, till we just can't get enough. Our glory "in Christ" will never fade, it just grows from glory to glory. Because our sufficiency is of God, we are able (equipped) ministers of Christ (via Paul) to the saved and to the lost. We can proclaim Christ's death for our sins, burial, and resurrection so others can receive forgiveness (atonement) <u>now</u> (Rom. 5:10, 11). The nation of Israel will need to wait till Christ's Second Coming before they will receive their atonement (Zech. 12:10; Acts 3:19-21; Rom. 11:27).]

But if our gospel be hid, it is hid to them that are lost: In whom the god of this world hath blinded the minds of them which believe not, lest the light of the glorious gospel of Christ, who is the image of God, should shine unto them.

2 Corinthians 4:3-4 KJV

Chapter 4 The treasure is the life of Jesus in our earthen vessels
4:1-18 Paul was able to endure sufferings because the "life of Jesus" was in him.

4:1 Therefore seeing we have this ministry, as we have received mercy, we faint not; [God has made Paul and us, able ministers of the new testament according to the revelation of the mystery. We are under a new law (Rom. 8:2). His righteous Spirit in us does what the Old Testament Law could not do. There is nothing wrong with the Ten Commandments; the problem is with our sinful and weak flesh. We could not keep that Law; it showed us our sin. For "by the law is the knowledge of sin" (Rom. 3:20). We needed a Redeemer. The Lord Jesus Christ's shed blood redeemed two groups of people: those who will live in heaven, and those who will live on earth. God has been merciful to both groups. Paul committed the blasphemy of the Holy Ghost at the stoning of Stephen. God changed dispensations showed mercy to Paul (Matt. 12:31, 32; 1 Tim. 1:12-16). Paul is our pattern and the first one into the body of Christ. Gentiles had no hope before the dispensation of the grace of God. In time past, Gentiles were "without Christ, being aliens from the commonwealth of Israel, and strangers from the covenants of promise, having no hope, and without God in the world: But now in Christ Jesus ye who sometimes were far off are made nigh by the blood of Christ" (Eph. 2:12, 13). So Paul says, we faint not. "Faint not" means not giving up. We keep giving out the word of God plainly with enthusiasm. We soldier on in the face of opposition wanting others "to be saved and come to the knowledge of the truth" (1 Tim.2:4). We also want "to make all men see what is the fellowship of the mystery, which from the beginning of the world hath been hid in God, who created all things by Jesus Christ" (Eph. 3:9). There was a secret "hid in God" from before the foundation of the world (Eph. 1:4). Christ in us is also one of the mysteries given by the glorified Lord Jesus Christ to Paul (Col. 1:27). Paul is the steward of the mysteries (1 Cor. 4:1) of this dispensation. We want others to have what we have – His Spirit and His increasing glory.] **2 But have renounced the hidden things of dishonesty, not walking in craftiness, nor handling the word of God deceitfully; but by manifestation of the truth commending ourselves to every man's conscience in the sight of God**. [Paul is speaking of his current ministry as the apostle of the Gentiles. And admitting that he had given up his prior ministry (as a lost man, the Pharisee, Saul of Tarsus) of serving Satan in a corrupt Judaistic religious system. He and his co-workers are honest, not crafty. They handle God's word without deceit, revealing the truth of God's mystery which Christ gave to Paul to every man's conscience while God watches. Their conscience should recognize the truth (5:11, 13:8). The "truth" is the mystery. Everyone must make a decision to believe or reject what Christ has done and what Paul said about the mystery given from Christ in heaven to us (Eph. 3:2).] **3 But if our gospel be hid,**

it is hid to them that are lost: **4 In whom the <u>god of this world</u> hath <u>blinded the minds of them which believe not</u>, lest the light of the <u>glorious gospel of Christ, who is the image of God, should shine unto them</u>**. [<u>The "gospel" is the imputed righteousness of Christ, justification by faith, and the entire mystery doctrine given to Paul</u>. If the mystery of the formation of the body of Christ in the dispensation of God's grace is hid, it is hid to those who are lost. Those who do not believe the gospel (good news and the doctrine given to Paul) is because Satan has blinded their minds. Notice that it is "their minds." <u>The battle for salvation and dispensational biblical understanding is in the mind</u>. Satan does not want the light of the glorious gospel of Christ, who is the image of God (because He is God), to shine unto the lost. <u>Some are lost and without Christ and others are saved but ignorant of what Christ is doing now</u>. <u>Satan doesn't want the lost to know that Jesus Christ already paid for all mankind's sins (past, present, and future) nearly 2,000 years ago</u>. All that any sinner has to do to receive eternal life is to BELIEVE what Christ has already DONE. Upon believing the gospel, we became part of the body of Christ, counted as crucified, dead, buried, risen, and seated with Him in heaven. Our group inherits heaven, not the earth. There are three things to believe and only the first is required for salvation: (1) faith in Christ alone for salvation (1 Cor. 15:3,4). (2) faith that God has preserved His word (Psa. 12:6, 7) in English it is in the King James Bible and (3) faith in Christ's heavenly ministry to the body of Christ through His apostle Paul in the dispensation of grace (Rom. 11:13; Eph. 3:2). This life is about where we will spend eternity and what our rewards or job description will be when we get to heaven. Satan is the "prince of the power of the air" (Eph. 2:2). He became the "god of this world" by default when Adam sinned. He was able to offer "the kingdoms of the worlds" to Christ (Matt. 4:8; Luke 4:5). Satan is happy when denominational churches avoid Paul's letters, mix law and grace, Peter and Paul, and mistakenly say the body of Christ is "spiritual Israel." Did Peter preach the same message as Paul? No! Peter preached the same gospel of the kingdom as Jesus preached (Matt. 4:17, 23, 9:35, 19:28; Mark 1:14, 15; Luke 9:1, 2, 12:31, 32; Gal. 2:7-9). Paul preached that God is forming the body of Christ to dwell in the heavenly places. God wants to populate both heaven and earth with true believers. He has put His dealings with the nation of Israel on hold and postponed the kingdom until after our rapture. He has interrupted "prophecy" and inserted the "mystery." Through Paul, Christ is declaring His ministry from heaven to the body of Christ. His ministry on earth will resume after His ambassadors have been removed.]

5 For we preach not ourselves, but Christ Jesus the Lord; and ourselves your servants for Jesus' sake. [Paul and his co-workers represent Christ and preach Him, not themselves, as they serve the Corinthian believers.] **6 For God, who**

commanded the light to shine out of darkness, hath shined in our hearts, to give the light of the knowledge of the glory of God in the face of Jesus Christ. [The same God who said, "Let there be light" (Gen. 1:3) has enlightened Paul and his companion's hearts to give them a brilliant clear understanding of what Christ from heaven is doing now. Jesus is the Creator who spoke and commanded His light to shine has shined in our hearts severing us from spiritual darkness. The Second Person of the Godhead is the Word of God, the Spokesman (John 1:1-4; Col. 1:16). As we read His word, God shines in our hearts to give us the light of the knowledge of the glory of God in the face of what Jesus Christ has done. Jesus has made a way for us to be accepted, not just Israel (Eph. 1:4, 6; John 14:6; Heb. 10:19, 20). God is revealing the knowledge of who He is and what He is doing to us through His word. He is forming a new group of people (the body of Christ) to live in the heavenly places during the dispensation of grace for His glory.]

7 ¶ **But we have this treasure in earthen vessels, that the excellency of the power may be of God, and not of us**. [Paul will define what the treasure and earthen vessels are in the next few verses (4:11). The treasure is the life of Jesus in us. The "earthen vessels" are our "mortal bodies." Our resource, or power supply, is the life of Jesus in us. In the triune God is hid all the treasures of wisdom and knowledge (Col. 2:2, 3).] **8 We are troubled on every side, yet not distressed**; [On the one hand, Paul's three-year ministry in Ephesus ended in one day with a mob revolt. On the other hand, he doesn't want his work in Corinth in jeopardy. Paul is writing to those in Corinth who follow him so they will have ammunition to refute those in the assembly who speak against Christ's ministry through him (5:12). Because Paul knew that his truth was the truth of Christ, he was not distressed.] **we are perplexed, but not in despair**; [Paul may have been puzzled about what God was doing, but He trusted Him and did not lose hope.] **9 Persecuted, but not forsaken**; [Paul was persecuted by the unbelieving Jews and the idol worshipping pagans he was trying to save; but he knew that God was with him.] **cast down, but not destroyed**; [Paul felt like he had been thrown down as in wrestling, but he was still alive. Paul felt low but, he would never give up.] **10 Always bearing about in the body the dying of the Lord Jesus, that the life also of Jesus might be made manifest in our body**. [Paul and his friends remind themselves daily that Christ died for them and they died with him (1 Cor. 15:31). He paid our sin debt in full as the perfect sacrifice on Calvary, so now we can live a new life with Him as our resource (Rom. 6:2-4). He lives out His life through the believer (Gal. 2:20; Col. 1:27). This is the mystery of godliness (1 Tim. 3:16). His life made known through us. Christ is revealing Himself to the world through believers. When we exchange these clay pots for our glorious eternal space suits, His life will shine out of us. Our celestial bodies will glow with varying degrees of

brightness (1 Cor. 15:38-41).] **11 For we which live are alway delivered unto death for Jesus' sake, that the <u>life also of Jesus</u> might be made manifest in our mortal flesh.** [Notice that the phrase "life also of Jesus" is repeated twice but the first time it says "body" and the next "mortal flesh." This is an example of the Bible's built in dictionary. Body is equal to mortal flesh which are the earthen vessels. We are dead to sin, but alive unto God (Rom. 6:11). We have His life in our mortal bodies right now which is being manifested to the world.] **12 So then death worketh in us, but life in you.** [With a little note of sarcasm Paul says, death is working in us but life in you Corinthians. They were willing to die to self (1 Cor. 15:31), and allow Christ to use their bodies so the Corinthians could live (Rom. 12:1).] **13 We having the same spirit of faith, according as it is written, I believed, and therefore have I spoken; we also believe, and therefore speak**; [Paul says, we share the same spirit of faith. Whenever Paul says it is written we look to find where it is written in the Old Testament, in this case, Psalm 116:10. Paul has been afflicted, but because he believes the truth, he is speaking to them.] **14 Knowing that he which raised up the Lord Jesus shall raise up us also by Jesus, and shall present us with you.** [We know that God who raised up Christ will raise up us also by Jesus, and present us with you (Rom. 8:11). After the Judgment seat of Christ for service done in this body, Christ will present us to the Father (Col. 3:4; 2 Cor. 5:10).] **15 For all things are for your sakes, that the abundant grace might through the thanksgiving of many redound to the glory of God.** [Paul says, we are doing what we do for your sakes, so that the abundant grace that God has shown us will redound (return) with greater force to God's glory by everyone's thanksgiving when we are in heaven (9:11). He can hardly wait for the time when he and the Corinthians and the rest of the body of Christ glorify the Lord Jesus in heaven. <u>We will glorify the Lord Jesus Christ, and the Godhead forever</u>. We are so grateful that God had a plan to save us from our sin.] **16 For which cause we faint not; but though our outward man perish, yet the inward man is renewed day by day.** [The "cause" is wanting to give glory to God as the Body of Christ in heaven. For this reason, Paul presses on (faints not) to help the Corinthians understand the gospel. We have a glorious eternal future together with Him. Our outward man (our physical bodies) is deteriorating/dying but our inward man (soul and spirit) is being renewed daily by His transforming life giving word being applied to our hearts and minds by the living Spirit of Jesus in us.] **17 For our light affliction, which is but for a moment, worketh for us a far more exceeding and eternal weight of glory;** [Paul was willing to suffer afflictions for Christ, the Corinthians, and the body of Christ (Col. 1:24). The unseen glory dwarfed Paul's present affliction – so he called them "light" (Rom. 8:18). Many saints really have hardships. But these afflictions are often working in us to strengthen our faith in His word and make us willing to present our "bodies a living sacrifice" for Christ to live through which is our reasonable service (Rom. 12:1, 2). In chapter 12, we will learn His "grace is sufficient" for His "strength is made perfect in weakness" (12:9). The work that we have allowed Christ to do through us will bring more glory to God. The Lord Jesus Christ suffered greatly, bore our sins in His own body, and died for our salvation. Because He paid for our sins, believers receive His righteousness. Because of God's holiness no one could touch mount Sinai when God was there without dying (Ex. 19:12). This is why those in "Abraham's bosom" (Luke 16:22) had to wait till the redemption by His blood was complete and accepted (as demonstrated by His resurrection). Without the shedding of blood there is no remission of sin (Rom. 3:25; Heb. 9:22). Everyone needs the righteousness of Christ to come before God.] **18 While we look not at the things which are seen, but at the things which are not seen: for the things which are seen are temporal; but the things which are not seen are eternal**. [Our confidence is not in what we see on earth, but in what we do not see in heaven (Heb. 11:1). The things that we see here on earth are temporary, while our heavenly home is eternal (2 Cor. 5:1). We can endure anything if we know we will have eternal life with our Saviour. We look forward to glorifying our God and Lord Jesus Christ for all eternity. We dare to believe what God says about us and our future in His word.]

HEAVEN IS MY ETERNAL HOME

"For we know that if our earthly house of this tabernacle were dissolved, we have a building of God, an house not made with hands, eternal in the heavens."
2 Corinthians 5:1 KJV

Jesus sent Paul · Romans – Philemon

Chapter 5 The reconciliation of the world and the new creature
5:1-10 We have a house eternal in the heaven, so live to please Christ.
5:11-19 Because Christ died for all, God has reconciled the world.
5:20-21 Because He took our place, reconciling others is our ambassadorship.

5:1 For we know that if our earthly house of this tabernacle were dissolved, we have a building of God, an house not made with hands, eternal in the heavens. [We know (we don't just guess) that we have a building or spiritual housing for our inner man (spirit and soul) after our present tabernacle (tent) is dissolved (die). The glorious body we will receive will be like Christ's (Phil. 3:21). Our housing made by God, will be specialized celestial bodies that can function and live "eternal in the heavens." But, the earthly kingdom believers will also receive eternal terrestrial bodies (1 Cor. 15:40; 1 John 3:2). Abraham, Isaac, and Jacob dwelt in tents because they were looking for "a city which hath foundations, whose builder and maker is God" (Heb. 11:9, 10). This is the "many mansions" Christ spoke about (John 14:2), the New Jerusalem (Rev. 21:2, 3). God formed the heaven and earth to be inhabited by Himself and those who love Him (Isa. 45:18). He is the "possessor of heaven and earth" (Gen. 14:19).] **2 For in this we groan, earnestly desiring to be clothed upon with our house which is from heaven: 3 If so be that being clothed we shall not be found naked** [without an immortal body]. **4 For we that are in this tabernacle do groan, being burdened: not for that we would be unclothed, but clothed upon, that mortality might be swallowed up of life**. [We groan in our earthen vessels waiting for our glorified bodies. Our body is like a house for our inner man (soul and our spirit). If we are unclothed (without a body) we are dead. We desire immortality; not that our tents be dissolved by death but that we be clothed upon at His appearing in the air. We would prefer not to have to go through death. All creation is groaning, waiting for the curse to be removed by God (Rom. 8:18-23) and for the restoration of Creation to its intended eternal splendor. We yearn to be at home with the Lord and we set our affections on things above (Phil. 1:19-24; Col. 3:2).] **5 Now he that hath wrought us for the selfsame thing is God, who also hath given unto us the earnest of the Spirit**. [We are God's workmanship; He made us to be immortal. He has given us the down payment of the holy Spirit in us as proof that we will have eternal life with Him.] **6 Therefore we are always confident, knowing that, whilst we are at home in the body, we are absent from the Lord**: [We are always confident of our promised eternal life since we know He has given us the down payment of His Spirit in us. We know that while we are at home in these bodies, we are absent from being with the Lord in heaven. We would not survive without this tent. Jesus is at the right hand of God (Rom. 8:34).] **7 (For we walk by faith, not by sight:)** [We walk by faith in what God tells us in His word, since we do not see Jesus now. We trust the certain fact that we will be with the Lord Jesus for all eternity.] **8 We are confident, I say, and willing rather to be absent from the body, and to be present with the Lord**. [We are confident that we will be with Him, but would prefer to be with Him now.] **9 Wherefore we <u>labour</u>, that, whether present or absent, we may be accepted of him**. [Paul says we labor so our work will be accepted by God. Likewise, we as adult sons, should do right even when no one is looking (but God sees everything).] **10 <u>For we must all appear before the judgment seat of Christ; that every one may receive the things done in his body, according to that he hath done, whether it be good or bad</u>**. [We know that we must all stand before His judgment seat to have our service done while on earth tested (1 Cor. 3:10-15; Rom. 14:7-13). We will have a reward for the good, the bad will be burned off by fire (<u>the sound word Christ gave to Paul is the fire</u>). Adult sons work in the family business, so we must be sure to do the will of our Father (1 Tim. 2:4). Our work is evaluated based on what sort it is (quality, is it gold?). We want our work to be valuable, pleasing, and acceptable not by keeping the law (a performance based acceptance system) but by faith in what Christ says in His word to us through Paul. The work that we did in our flesh will be burnt off, but the work that we allowed Christ to do through us will last.]

11 ¶ Knowing therefore the terror of the Lord, we <u>persuade men</u>; but we are made manifest unto God; and I trust also are made manifest in your consciences. [The "terror of the Lord" is God's perfect holiness and His justice which demands the Great White Throne Judgment of the lost. God will also judge Paul and all believer's service on earth. We are "manifest to God," He knows our hearts (1 Samuel 16:7; Heb. 4:12). Paul is trying to persuade them to follow what Christ is doing through him and to have them do something of eternal value for God. Many Corinthians were glorying in appearances. They boasted about their various attractive preachers and criticized Paul. God knows Paul and his friends are true, and he hopes the conscience of the Corinthians will also know they are true. Conscience is that part of us that knows truth from a lie, right from wrong. Truth resonates in us (4:2, 13:8). In the end we let God do the judging (1 Cor. 4:1-7).] **12 For we commend not ourselves again unto you, <u>but give you occasion to glory on our behalf, that ye may have somewhat to answer them which glory in appearance, and not in heart</u>**. [Paul had commended them in First Corinthians (1 Cor. 9:1). We walk by faith in the "mystery." We are giving you reasons and answers for them who doubt what Christ is doing through us. There were people at Corinth that were seduced by attractive smooth talkers, and did not glory in the sincere, genuine apostle.] **13 For whether we be <u>beside ourselves</u>, it is to God: or whether we be sober, it is <u>for your cause</u>**. [Festus accused him of this, "Paul, thou art <u>beside</u> thyself; much learning doth make thee <u>mad</u>" (Acts 26:24). Some at

Corinth may have made that same accusation. Paul says if we appeared mad (not in our right minds) it is for God, but if we are accounted to be in our right mind it is for your sakes.] **14 For the love of Christ constraineth us; because we thus judge, that if one died for all, then were all dead: 15 And that he died for all, that they which live <u>should not henceforth live unto themselves</u>, but unto him which died for them, and rose again**. [Jesus' love for us compels us to live for Him and serve Him (Rom. 6:11, 18). Because Christ loved us and died and rose for all. We all died with Him, and we now live for Him. His salvation is a salvation from sin and self. Christ's death saved us from the doom of sin, but His death also means we should no longer live unto ourselves. We who have obtained eternal life by faith in Him should no longer live for ourselves but for Him who died and rose. Who we were in Adam before we believed died. We identify with Christ's death, burial, and resurrection (Rom. 6:4, 5; Gal. 2:20). We have His life in us (2 Cor. 4:10). The fact that Christ died for all mankind, even the Gentiles in "mystery," was not revealed until Paul (compare these verse to see that in His earthly ministry, Christ came to die for Israel: 1 Tim. 2:6 with Isa. 53:8; Matt. 1:21, 20:28; Mark 10:45). It is our reasonable service not to live for ourselves, but to live for Him who loved us (Rom. 12:1, 2).] **16 Wherefore henceforth know we no man after the flesh: yea, though we have known Christ after the flesh, yet now henceforth know we him no more**. [From now on we do not know someone "after the flesh." Although we have known about Christ in His earthly ministry (who He was and did, John 1:14). But now, we do NOT know Him after His earthly ministry any longer. Now we know Him according to His ministry from heaven. "Jesus Christ, according to the revelation of the mystery" (Rom. 16:25). <u>It is the life of Jesus (His Spirit) working in us that matters and the sound doctrine given to Paul.</u>] **17 Therefore if any man be <u>in Christ</u>, he is a new creature: <u>old things are passed away</u>; behold, <u>all things are become new</u>**. [What are the "old things" that have passed away? <u>Who we were in Adam has passed away and we are new creatures "in Christ.</u>" Who we were in Adam before we believed that Christ died for our sins. The "<u>old things</u>" passed away the instant we trusted exclusively in what Christ did for us on Calvary. God the holy Spirit saw our hearts of faith. We were translated out of darkness in Adam, into Christ (Col. 1:13). At salvation five things happen. To describe these, we can use the acrostic CRIBS: <u>circumcised spiritually</u> (Col. 2:11, 12), <u>regenerated</u> (Titus 3:5), <u>indwelt by God</u> (Col. 1:27), <u>baptized into Christ</u> (1 Cor. 12:13), and <u>sealed with the holy Spirit</u> (Eph. 1:13). (Borrowed from Pastor Richard Jordan's New Creature YouTube video.) When we believed we identified with Christ's death, burial, and resurrection and became new creatures with His divine Spirit in us. Our "old man" (old Adam) or sin nature, the flesh, was crucified and died (Gal. 2:20). Sin lost its power over us (Rom. 6:2-6, 14, 17,18). Since we were individually baptized into the body of Christ by His Spirit (1 Cor. 12:13; Gal. 3:26-28); <u>we are new creatures individually and corporately</u>. The "<u>all things are become new</u>" refers to the fact that we were made new creatures "in Christ" by faith. This became possible when God ushered in the new dispensation in which we are now living, the <u>dispensation of the grace of God</u>. We are "in Christ" "according to the revelation of the mystery" (Rom. 16:25) we are part of a new creature, the body of Christ (1 Cor. 12:27; Rom. 12:5). We have been baptized into the "one new man" (Eph. 2:15, 16) the body of Christ, which is also a new creature, organism, or group made up of new creatures. God builds the new Creature one individual at a time. A person is either "in Adam" or "in Christ" (1 Cor. 15:22). The middle wall of partition is down in this dispensation; there is no distinction between the circumcision and the uncircumcision in the new creature (Gal. 6:15). Israel does not have a preferred nation status today. The two distinctions today are "without Christ" and lost, or "in Christ" and saved. The Father sees us dead in Him, risen in Him, and seated with Him (Eph. 2:6, 7). In Israel's program believers are "born again" when they believe that Jesus is Messiah, the Redeemer, and will be "born again" as a nation at His Second Coming (Ex. 4:22; Isa. 66:8). Paul said that some were "in Christ" before him (Rom. 16:7). Everyone needs to be "in Christ" to come before God, even those in prophecy. <u>We are new creatures in a new dispensation</u>.] **18 And all things are of God, who hath reconciled us to himself by Jesus Christ, and hath given to us the ministry of reconciliation**; ["All things are of God." God has a group of people to live on earth, but it was God's glory plan to reveal the secret mystery of another group of people to live in heaven. So that "in the fulness of times he might gather together in one all things in Christ, both which are in heaven, and which are in earth; even in him" (Eph. 1:10). God planned to interrupt prophecy and insert the mystery between the 69th and 70th week of Daniel. God knew that His people would reject Christ and crucify Him at the hands of the Romans by His foreknowledge (Acts 2:23; Psa. 2:1-3). He knew that His nation's religious leaders would blaspheme and reject the Holy Ghost (Matt. 12:31, 32; Acts 7). God planned to use <u>one</u> of the ringleaders to be His apostle to the Gentiles (Acts 9:15; 1 Tim. 1:16; Rom. 11:13). This apostle would reveal all that Christ accomplished by the cross. God reconciled us to Himself by the God-Man, Jesus Christ, and now He has given us the ministry of reconciling others to Him (Rom. 6:18). Christ was not only the mediator for Israel, but also for us in the body of Christ (1 Tim. 2:5; Heb. 9:15).] **19 To wit, that God was in Christ, reconciling the world unto himself, not imputing their trespasses unto them; and hath committed unto us the word of reconciliation**. [To wit (know) that God was in Christ. The Father and the Son worked in unison to reconcile the world. Jesus had to become a man so that He could shed human blood once (Heb. 9:12, 22, 26-28). His blood was so effective because it was God's blood (Acts 20:28). God the

Father was with Christ helping Him by the counsel of His word; as Jesus lived a life of dependence on Him while on earth. The justice of God demanded a blood sacrifice. The Lord Jesus Christ paid the sin debt of all mankind, because only He (as the God-Man) could be the perfectly satisfying sacrifice. God in Christ has reconciled the world to Himself. Reconciled means brought into friendship from a state of disagreement or being enemies. When Adam sinned the justice of God demanded that the sin be punished. The justice of God made it so that God had to turn His face away from sinful mankind. The Father's wrath was poured out on His Son because of the sin of all mankind. But now that Jesus Christ has fully satisfied the justice of God (Isa. 53:10, 11), the Father can dispense grace and peace to us. The sin debt was paid for nearly 2,000 years ago. God is not imputing our trespasses unto us. Christ paid for our sins and made peace possible between God and man. God has been offering grace and peace since Acts 9 (Col. 2:13). God is holding out His hand to us in friendship so we should grasp ahold of it and shake it. Jesus said I love you when He died for us (Rom. 5:8). The Father said I love you when He spared not His own Son (Rom. 8:32). It is as though God is saying, I want to be your friend, come to Me by faith in what My Son has already done, and receive forgiveness and eternal life with us. All a sinner has to do to receive salvation is to believe (1 Cor. 15:3, 4). <u>Only those people who have believed who Christ is and what He has done receive His imputed righteousness and are forgiven</u>. God has given believers the word of reconciliation. We are justified by the cross, not at the cross (Eph. 2:16). "At" means when, but "by" means how.] **20 Now then we are ambassadors for Christ, as though God did beseech you by us: we pray you in Christ's stead, be ye reconciled to God.** [Like Paul, we are ambassadors for Christ (Eph. 6:20). As ambassadors, we represent Christ to others. It is as if God begs and implores others to be saved through us. We earnestly urge them on His behalf and in His place to be reconciled to God.] **21 For he hath made him to be sin for us, who knew no sin; that we might be made the righteousness of God in him**. [<u>The word "sins" means the wrong things we do, while "sin" means our sin nature. In this verse, Christ was made sin for us, to destroy our sin nature</u>. JESUS CHRIST NEVER SINNED. HE TOOK OUR PLACE AND DIED THE DEATH WE DESERVED – THEN HE LET US TAKE HIS PLACE BEFORE HIS FATHER BY GIVING US HIS RIGHTEOUSNESS. God solved the sin problem with the substitutionary death of His Son. Paul revealed how God the Father can remain JUST and be the JUSTIFIER of those who have His Son's righteousness. "To declare, I [Paul] say, at this time [during the dispensation of grace] his righteousness: that he might be JUST, and the JUSTIFIER of him which believeth in Jesus" (Rom. 3:26). Paul summed this up by a real live example in Philemon 17, 18: "If thou count me therefore a partner, receive him as myself. If he hath wronged thee, or oweth thee ought, put that on mine account." Jesus Christ says to the Father "receive him as Myself, if he owes you anything, put it on My account, I will pay for it." He took our sins, and gave us His righteousness. What a great deal for us. But a costly sacrifice for the Father and His beloved Son (Isa. 53:10, 11). Paul said, "But God forbid that I should glory, save in the cross of our Lord Jesus Christ" (Gal. 6:14).]

Chapter 6 Receive not the grace of God in vain
6:1-10 Paul has the marks and heart of a true ambassador to the Church.
6:11-7:1 Be not unequally yoked with those who glory in appearances.

6:1 We then, as workers together with him, beseech you also that ye receive not the grace of God in vain. [Paul and his coworkers work together with God, and beg the saints not to have received the grace of God without being willing to share it with others.] **2 (For he saith, I have heard thee in a time accepted, and in the day of salvation have I succoured thee: behold, now is the accepted time; behold, now is the day of salvation.)** [Believers were heard and accepted by God; in the day of salvation God helped them. We heard the gospel and were saved, so now we should help others. God is dispensing grace to all people today, so this is the time for all people to be saved. God wants us to be His ambassadors who tell others that Christ died and rose again (5:15). These are the two foundational stones: His atonement and resurrection, on which the hope of all mankind rest. In 1 Cor. 15:3, 4 the Bible says "according to the scriptures" twice, because the word of God is more important than the word of man. Sadly, mankind likes to reverse this order and elevate their word over God's word. When Christ was "made sin for us," He did so in obedience to the Father, not in rebellion. He carried out His Father's plan. He laid aside His glory, not His deity when He became a man. By faith in what Christ did for us, we can receive His righteousness. He paid it all; all to Him we owe! He is worthy of all praise!] **3 Giving no offence in any thing, that the ministry be not blamed:** [*Notice the colon. In the next several verses Paul explains in detail how he was careful not to give any offence in anything so that the ministry could not be blamed. As ambassadors doing God's will (1 Tim. 2:4) we should not offend anyone either. Paul told Titus, use "Sound speech, that cannot be condemned; that he that is of the contrary part may be ashamed, having no evil thing to say of you" (Titus 2:8). We are to be gracious, wise, patient, and loving as we share the gospel of salvation, which Bible is the preserved word of God (since Satan has modern counterfeit Bibles which hide God's truth), and the truth that Christ is now forming the body of Christ to live in the heavenly places. He has two ministries, two groups of people, and two realms, heaven and earth that He is populating with believers. Paul is the apostle to the body of Christ. We must be kind when we share "the knowledge of the truth" and be willing to suffer.] **4 But in all things approving ourselves as the ministers of God, in much patience, in afflictions, in necessities, in distresses,** [Paul has been appealing to the conscience (4:2, 5:11, 13:8) of the Corinthians. He expects their conscience to recognize truth when they hear it. Truth resonates with our spirit. Our spirit understands the truth of God's word, and then our will decides to believe it with our hearts. Having laid out the dispensational truth of what God is doing today, Paul continues his appeal for them to follow him to follow Christ. Patience here means enduring like a good soldier in battle. There is a spiritual warfare going on. Believers are in enemy territory. We must "war a good warfare" (1 Tim. 1:18). Paul continues his job description and lists a series of physical, mental, and spiritual trials which he endured. As ambassadors we should be willing to endure the same ones "our pattern" did. Paul endured afflictions, necessities, and distresses out of obedience, not disobedience.]

5 In stripes, in imprisonments, in tumults, in labours, in watchings, in fastings; [This list is physical. Paul went through more suffering than anyone else other than the Lord Jesus. He will go into more detail in chapter 11. Tumults are riots. Such as the one at Ephesus. "Watchings" may be going to see or sending others to find out how the local church is doing, and praying for them. Paul often had to go without food.]. **6 By pureness, by knowledge, by longsuffering, by kindness, by the Holy Ghost, by love unfeigned,** [This list is mental and spiritual. Pure motives. Knowledge of what God is doing. Longsuffering here is patience. By kindness, the grace doctrine working effectually in us who believe God's word (1 Thess. 2:13) teaches us to be kind (Col. 3:12). By the Holy Ghost helping them. By love that is not fake, but real.] **7 By the word of truth, by the power of God, by the armour of righteousness on the right hand and on the left,** [The tools we use as ambassadors are spiritual and powerful. The word of truth, the power of God's Spirit in us. We are surrounded by the armour of His righteousness since we are positioned "in Christ" and His soldiers.] **8 By honour and dishonour, by evil report and good report: as deceivers, and yet true;** [Paul now lists a series of contrasts that he and his friends experienced. Some honored them, while others will dishonor them. Some gave an evil report of them, others a good one. Some said they were deceivers, others that they were true. Many of us have found this to be an honest assessment of our ambassadorship if we are a King James Bible believer who rightly divides the word of God, and understands and shares the mystery (Eph. 3:9).] **9 As unknown, and yet well known; as dying, and, behold, we live; as chastened, and not killed;** [They were unknown to many but well known to others including God and Satan (Acts 19:14, 15). They died in Christ, but were alive unto God (Rom. 6:11). They were chastened or punished by the unbelieving Jews and Gentiles for doing right and speaking the truth, but not killed.] **10 As sorrowful, yet alway rejoicing; as poor, yet making many rich; as having nothing, and yet possessing all things.** [Paul and his companions were sad when people did not believe them, but they rejoiced that seeds had been planted. They were poor, but made others rich by telling them how to have eternal life and all spiritual blessings (Rom. 6:23; Eph. 1:3). Paul often had nothing but the clothes on his back, yet he had the riches of Christ (Eph. 1:7, 18, 2:7, 3:16; Col. 2:2). They possessed sound doctrine and were joint-heirs with Christ (Rom. 8:17).

When we die the only thing we can take with us is our inner man and the sound doctrine which is stored up in it.] **11 O ye Corinthians, our mouth is open unto you, our heart is enlarged.** [Paul and his friends suffered these things for their sakes (5:13). "Our mouth is open" we tell you all the truth that Christ has revealed to us. Our hearts are so large with love that you can all fit.] **12 Ye are not straitened in us, but ye are straitened in your own bowels.** [With an open heart, Paul begs them to separate from false teachers and follow him. He does not mean that we should separate from sinners, but from the influence of those who teach false doctrine. You are not restrained by us, but you are confined by your own choice. They needed to listen to Paul and his coworkers, not silver-tongued "false apostles."] **13 Now for a recompence in the same, (I speak as unto my children,) be ye also enlarged.** [Paul says my heart is open to you, open your hearts to me in return. He wants their hearts to be enlarged to him. He speaks to them as his beloved children. Often children will love their parents back, especially when they get older and realize all that the loving parents did for them. Paul hopes that when their faith increases that their hearts will be enlarged to him (10:15). It is Christ's life in us that gives us love in our hearts, and enlarge our affection for others.] **14 Be ye not unequally yoked together with unbelievers: for what fellowship hath righteousness with unrighteousness? and what communion hath light with darkness?** [Paul does not want them to be yoked together with someone that doesn't believe the "mystery" of what Christ in heaven is doing through Paul's ministry. Paul will ask a series of 5 rhetorical questions. They "glory in appearances" (5:12). It may appear as if we should follow Christ in His earthly ministry, but that is what He did for Israel, not the body of Christ (Rom. 15:8). We walk by faith (5:7) trusting His heavenly ministry to us. Paul wants them to obey the instructions the glorified Lord from heaven had given to them through him. An ox and an ass cannot pull together to make a straight path/furrow (Deut. 22:10). The righteous have no fellowship with the unrighteous, just like true Pauline believers of Christ have no fellowship with false ministers. One is full of light and the other of darkness. Sometimes false counterfeit apostles and ministers are difficult to spot (11:13, 14).] **15 And what concord hath Christ with Belial? or what part hath he that believeth with an infidel?** [What agreement or resemblance is there between Christ (Pauline believers) and Belial (an Old Testament term for Satan), his spirit is in the children of disobedience and wrath (Deut. 13:13; Eph. 2:2, 3). An "infidel" is an unbeliever.] **16 And what agreement hath the temple of God with idols? for ye are the temple of the living God; as God hath said, I will dwell in them, and walk in them; and I will be their God, and they shall be my people.** [You are the temple of God. God lives in believers. Idols represent the false religious system. It is false to follow Christ's earthly ministry today. Paul quotes (Lev. 26:11, 12) but the holy Spirit applies this to God in the believer. God is in them and wants to walk or live His life in and through them. This is how He will be our God and we will be His people. In the dispensation of grace, Gentile believers are "His people," not the people of Israel. (Although individual Jews who believe Paul's gospel will become members of the body of Christ.) The way to flee from idolatry is to follow Paul (1 Cor. 10:14, 15).] **17 Wherefore come out from among them,** [those who glory in appearances (5:12), the false apostles and false believers] **and <u>be ye separate, saith the Lord, and touch not the unclean thing; and I will receive you,</u>** [Paul quotes Isa. 52:11, telling the Corinthians to stop listening to or idolizing false apostles, but to listen to him and his coworkers. Paul says that the Lord commands believers to <u>separate from those who refuse to follow him</u>. What they are teaching is unclean, and useless to God. We are not to support them with our finances or our presence. We are to come out from false churches, and separate from false pastors and teachers who do not follow Paul.] **18 And will be a Father unto you, and ye shall be my sons and daughters, saith the Lord Almighty.** [Walk by faith in the words Christ has given to Paul. Paul is not speaking of salvation, but sanctification. All his letters are to believers. We are also to separate from false teachers and ministers. Come out from those who follow Christ's earthly ministry. The "unclean thing" is anything that is against the truth of what God is doing now – Christ's ministry from heaven through Paul. We need to turn to God's word to us through Paul so that God can be our Father to us and we can serve Him like sons and daughters. False religion is idolatry. A Baptist or Pentecostalist may be saved, but unless he or she is a Pauline dispensationalist, they will not be able to function the way God intends them to. We can't be useful sons or daughters to God unless we realize the distinctive ministry of the apostle Paul. We must rightly divide the word of truth (2 Tim. 2:15) between: "mystery" to the believers that will live in heavenly places, from "prophecy" for the believers who will live on earth. This is how a believer can be useful son of God.]

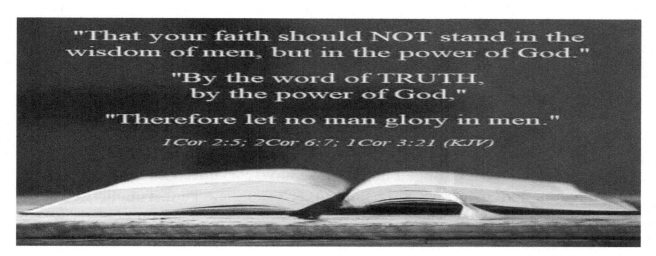

"That your faith should NOT stand in the wisdom of men, but in the power of God."

"By the word of TRUTH, by the power of God,"

"Therefore let no man glory in men."

1 Cor 2:5; 2 Cor 6:7; 1 Cor 3:21 (KJV)

Chapter 7 The heart of Paul and how God comforted him
7:1-6 Separate from false doctrine. Comfort at the arrival of Titus.
7:7-12 Comfort of the Corinthian's obedience, hopes for more obedience.
7:13-16 Comfort of their reception of Titus and him.

7:1 Having therefore these promises, dearly beloved, let us cleanse ourselves from all <u>filthiness of the flesh and spirit</u>, perfecting holiness in the fear of God. [The "<u>promises</u>" are: eternal life in heaven, Christ's life in us, rewards in heaven, and to be sons and daughters of God. God will deal with us in a Father to son relationship when we know how to work for Him. We need to know what God is doing so we can labor with Him effectually. This does not mean that if we do not come out and be separate that you will lose your salvation. It does mean that we will not function as useful sons and daughters if we don't. We need to be willing to commit to what God says rightly divided, and not be reluctant to leave those who teach that the body of Christ began in Acts 2. By staying under false doctrine you are saying I don't believe your word rightly divided. I am covering all my bases. I am staying under the wrong doctrine just in case. <u>Although you may actually be His son, God cannot treat you as a father would treat his son, if you don't understand what He is doing today</u>. You must take step one, before you can take step two. The way to flee from idolatry is to follow Paul (1 Cor. 10:14, 15). We are to cleanse ourselves of "<u>filthiness of the flesh and spirit</u>." From wrong thinking and actions which come if we follow those "who glory in appearances, and not in heart" (5:12). We are to purge ourselves from **false doctrine**. Wrong thinking is a result of following the Mosaic law (3:7) and Christ's ministry when He was in the flesh (2 Cor. 5:16; Rom. 15:8) instead of Paul and His grace (Titus 2:11, 12). There is nothing wrong with either the law or Christ's ministry on earth, it is just that that is not what God is doing now. Sanctification is the ongoing process of making right decisions as we follow our apostle Paul. As we understand and believe the mystery and the sound doctrine given to Paul, we are "<u>perfecting holiness</u>." We trust that "the word of God, which effectually worketh also in you that believe" (1 Thess. 2:13) will produce fruit unto holiness (Gal. 5:22, 23; Col. 1:5, 6). God wants us to be holy and transformed into the likeness of His Son by His word and His Spirit in us. Satan does not want us to know that we are in Him, and He is in us. He doesn't want us to know what God is doing now. We have His life in us (4:11) so we are able to decide to think and do right.]

2 Receive us; we have wronged no man, we have corrupted no man, we have defrauded no man. [Receive and believe us. The "us" are Paul, Timothy, Titus and his other co-workers. Make room for us in your hearts. Paul says clearly we have not wronged, caused anyone to be defiled, or taken advantage of anyone. Paul and his coworkers have spoken the truth of the mystery to them (2:17, 4:2).] **3 I speak not this to condemn you: for I have said before, that ye are in our hearts to die and live with you.** [Paul is not saying this to find fault with them. He is making an appeal to them to believe him and his coworkers are true ministers of Christ. He has said before that their heart's desire is to die and live with them in heaven (4:14-16). The "cause" is God's glory plan to populate heaven and earth with two different groups of believers in Christ. These believers will glorify God's Son, the Son will glorify the Father, and the Holy Ghost will glorify both. All believers will have a part in this glory celebration for all eternity.] **4 Great is my boldness of speech toward you, great is my glorying of you: I am filled with comfort, I am exceeding joyful in all our tribulation.** [Paul says he speaks to them with great unrestrained fearless boldness. He is full of comfort and overflowing with joy. They made all their tribulations worth it.] **5 For, when we were come into Macedonia, our flesh had no rest, but we were troubled on every side; without were fightings, within were fears.** [When we came to Macedonia we were restless in our bodies, there were struggles without and fears within. Paul was anxious about the spiritual condition of the Corinthians. He was worried sick about Titus. He probably also wondered how things would turn out in Ephesus after his nearly three-year ministry there ended abruptly in one day. Joys, sorrows, fears and questions crowded his mind. The Lord had entrusted him with the <u>sound doctrine</u> and the <u>ministry of the Gentiles</u> (1 Tim. 1:9-12).]

6 Nevertheless God, that comforteth those that are cast down, comforted us by the coming of Titus; [But God, who comforts the downcast, comforted us with the coming of Titus (2:12, 13).] **7 And not by his coming only, but by the consolation wherewith he was comforted in you, when he told us your earnest desire, your mourning, your fervent mind toward me; so that I rejoiced the more.** [We were not only comforted by our warm reunion with Titus, but by how he was consoled and comforted by your genuine sorrow, and eager mind toward me, which made me rejoice even more. Many who mourned over their sins, were on fire for Paul again and had an earnest desire to see him. Paul wanted them to realize that his apostleship was from the Lord.] **8 For though I made you sorry with a letter, I do not repent, though I did repent: for I perceive that the same epistle hath made you sorry, though it were but for a season.** [Paul had been wondering that maybe the letter he sent was too stern, and that perhaps he should not have sent it. But the letter had been effective. It had done it's work in their hearts; they had real sorrow for a little while. <u>First Corinthians Summary</u>: In First Corinthians, Paul corrects their thinking, conduct, and service to God. What matters is Christ crucified, not the wisdom of men. He calls them "carnal" and "babes" as he deals with the division among them, their overemphasis on temporary sign gifts, and going to public courts to solve their disputes. He says it is better to suffer the wrong. He told them that God had a secret plan to form the body of Christ that Satan didn't know about because it was not in the Bible. If Satan had known, he would not have allowed Christ to be crucified. He told them about the Judgment Seat of Christ. He said that they were puffed up with pride and should have dealt with the fornicator by putting him out of their local assembly. He informed them that he was the steward of the mysteries, the masterbuilder (1 Cor. 3:10) of the dispensation that God had entrusted him with (1 Cor. 9:17). He defended his apostleship and wanted them to follow him (1 Cor. 4:16, 17, 11:1) as he follows Christ. Paul is always careful to give all the glory to Christ who is in him. Then he answered their questions about marriage, eating food offered to idols, and the resurrection. They should not be unbelievers like Israel in the wilderness. He corrected them regarding respectfully celebrating the Lord's death with the Lord's supper and to restore order in the church. He told them that sign gifts would end when he had received the full revelation of the mystery from Christ. We are to do everything with charity. Finally, he said that just as the resurrection of Christ was a proven witnessed fact, so will our resurrection (Rapture) be. He ended the letter telling them that he would visit, but not yet, because he had a great ministry opportunity in Ephesus. In the meantime, he wanted them to take up a collection for Peter and his group in Jerusalem. Paul said that if any man considered himself spiritual "let him acknowledge that the things that I write unto you are the commandments of the Lord" (1 Cor. 14:37).] **9 Now I rejoice, not that ye were made sorry, but that ye sorrowed to repentance: for ye were made sorry after a godly manner, that ye might receive damage by us in nothing.** [Now I rejoice not that you were made sorry, but that you sorrowed to the point that you changed your minds and dealt with the offender. You had godly sorrow that lead to God. The letter worked effectually in you. We wrote it so we would not leave you with spiritual damage, uncorrected, and continuing to do wrong. It is loving to correct people when they are in error.] **10 For godly sorrow worketh repentance to salvation not to be repented of: but the sorrow of the world worketh death.** [Godly sorrow works to save you from error, which has no regrets: but the sorrow of the world leads to death. The "salvation" is salvation from false doctrine: the teaching of the Mosaic system (3:7) and Christ's earthly ministry (5:16). We have been reconciled to God and He is offering us His friendship, grace and peace (5:19). Godly sorrow puts our eyes back on Christ and what God the Father has and is doing, and not on ourselves. The sorrow of the world is characterized by self-pity, blaming others and ourselves which may result in depression, self-absorption, and suicide (Prov. 18:2). But, godly sorrow draws us to God, not away from Him.] **11 For behold this selfsame thing, that ye sorrowed after a godly sort, what carefulness it wrought in you, yea, what clearing of yourselves, yea, what indignation, yea, what fear, yea, what vehement desire, yea, what zeal,**

yea, what revenge! In all things ye have approved yourselves to be clear in this matter. [The letter cleared their minds of wrong thinking, which resulted in wrong actions. Paul tells them, your sorrow was the godly kind when you realized your error. You demonstrated regret by prohibiting the fornicator from being in your assembly. By putting him out of the assembly you vindicated yourselves of condoning the fornicator's sin. You became indignant of his sin, feared God, and wanted to do right by Him. Your vehement zeal led you to carry out the appropriate punishment of the offender (this is the revenge). You proved your obedience by clearing yourselves of the guilt of condoning the incest (1 Cor. 5:1).]**12 Wherefore, though I wrote unto you, I did it not for his cause that had done the wrong, nor for his cause that suffered wrong, but that our care for you in the sight of God might appear unto you.** [I did not write the letter for the sake of the person that did wrong, nor for the sake of the person that was wronged, but for your sakes. The letter was to let you know the loving care we have for you before God.] **13 Therefore we were comforted in your comfort: yea, and exceedingly the more joyed we for the joy of Titus, because his spirit was refreshed by you all.** [We were comforted by your comforting of Titus. His joy of you made us overflow with even more joy when we united with him. You refreshed his spirit. Paul was happy because of the respectful way Titus was received and believed.] **14 For if I have boasted any thing to him of you, I am not ashamed; but as we spake all things to you in truth, even so our boasting, which I made before Titus, is found a truth.** [I wrote you a stern letter without reserve, but behind your backs I boasted of you to Titus. I am not ashamed of bragging about you because it turned out that you proved me right. Paul is proud of them! We should also say warm things to others.] **15 And his inward affection is more abundant toward you, whilst he remembereth the obedience of you all, how with fear and trembling ye received him.** [Titus' job was to get the Corinthians to believe that Christ is working His heavenly ministry through Paul. Titus was happy that they were now zealous to follow Paul. They had respectfully welcomed him and listened to what he had to say about Christ's ministry to them through Paul. The abundant love Titus has in his heart for you is evident. He remembered your concern and willingness to obey my apostolic instruction in the letter. You welcomed him with trepidation and trembling. Paul had once trembled with godly fear for the sake of their salvation (1 Cor. 2:3).] **16 I rejoice therefore that I have confidence in you in all things.** [Paul is relieved and rejoiced that they have made some wise choices. Many had turned their back to him. They wisely obeyed his apostolic authority and directions. His love and care for them in his letters was working. They proved right in the matter of the fornicator so Paul hoped they will do right in other things (2 Cor. 2:9). He is confident that they are on the right track moving in the right direction of following Paul to follow Christ

(John 13:20; 1 Cor. 11:1). Although his ministry at Ephesus had been dealt a big blow, it seemed that Corinth was doing well. Paul wanted the Corinthians to be reconciled to him and his ministry. The Corinthians comforted Titus, who comforted Paul, and now Paul comforted them. He knew that his next visit to them would be an enjoyable one.]

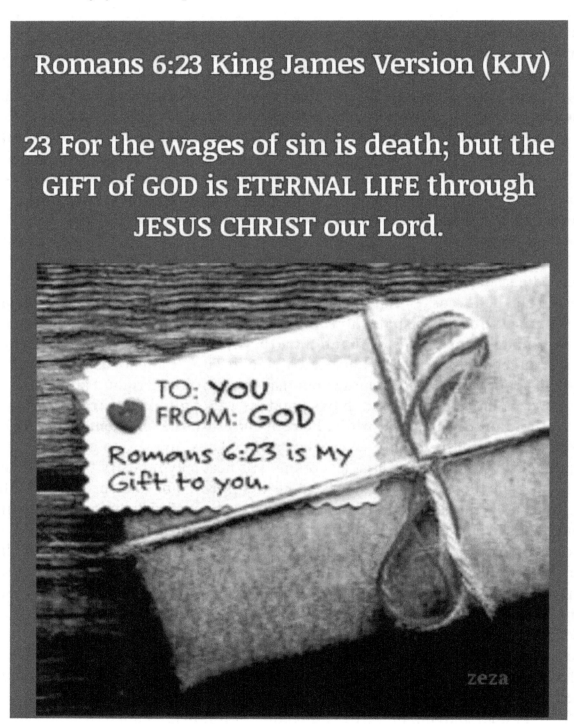

Chapter 8 Grace giving
8:1-6 The example of the churches in Macedonia.
8:7-15 The example of Christ. Giving proportionately.
8:16-24 Three trusted representatives to carry the money.

8:1 Moreover, brethren, we do you to wit of the <u>grace</u> of God bestowed on the churches of Macedonia; [Paul wants the Corinthians to know about how the grace of God is working in Macedonia. Notice "churches" is plural and may include the churches in Philippi, Thessalonica, and possibly Berea (Acts 20:4). It was in the heart of God to care for His little remnant of believers in Jerusalem.] **2 How that in a great trial of affliction the abundance of their joy and their deep poverty abounded unto the riches of their liberality.** [These churches were giving liberally out of their abundance of joy and deep poverty despite being persecuted.] **3 For to their power, I bear record, yea, and beyond their power they were willing of themselves;** [Paul gives them credit for deciding to give to God on their own.] **4 Praying us with much intreaty that we would receive the gift, and take upon us the fellowship of the ministering to the saints.** [They begged and urged for their donation to be taken so that they could partner in blessing the poor saints in Jerusalem.] **5 And this they did, not as we hoped, but first gave their own selves to the Lord, and unto us by the will of God.** [They did this beyond what we could have hoped for, Paul said First they committed themselves to the Lord, and then to us by the will of God.] **6 Insomuch that we desired Titus, that as he had begun, so he would also finish in you the same <u>grace</u> also.** [Thrilled about their desire to contribute they want Titus, who has helped them to be solid grace believers, to also finish this same grace in the Corinthians (8:1).] **7 Therefore, as ye abound in every thing, in faith, and utterance, and knowledge, and in all diligence, and in your love to us, see that ye abound in this grace also.** [God gave the Corinthians more sign gifts than any of the other churches. God gave Paul and the Corinthians sign gifts to show the Jews that God was now working with them (1 Cor. 1:22). The people of Israel said, "they have our gifts, so God must be working with them!" The Gentiles said, "We have the spiritual gifts God gave to the Jews, so God must be working with us!" The Corinthian church "abounded" in the temporary spiritual gifts because it was next door to a Jewish synagogue. "Utterance" is the gift of speaking in tongues or other languages (that they had not previously learned). "Knowledge" is the gift of "special knowledge" of what God was doing that He revealed first to Paul and then to them. Remember, that these sign gifts ended along with Paul's provoking ministry to the Jews at the end of Acts 28 (Acts 28:28; Rom. 11:11), after Paul had received the complete revelation of the mystery, even though it was not all written down yet (Rom. 15:29; 1 Cor. 13:8-10). For more information, see my book *First Corinthians: A Commentary*.

Spiritual signs are different from the Spiritual graces. The list in Gal. 5:22, 23 are the graces of the Spirit, not signs. Paul wants them to be sure to abound in all diligence, in love for Paul and his workers, and in "grace giving" which are also a result of the Spirit in the believer.] **8 I speak not by commandment, but by occasion of the forwardness of others, and to prove the sincerity of your love.** [Paul is not speaking to them by commandment of the Lord, but because of the initiative of the other churches who had taken it upon themselves to be involved in God's work. God wants to use them to provide for His poor saints in Jerusalem. The other churches had already completed their offering. They had put their money up so the Corinthians should do the same. Paul is not requiring them to give (like under the law), he is inviting them to prove their sincere love of what God is doing by giving voluntarily. The saints in Jerusalem were poor because Christ had told them to sell all that they had (Luke 12:31-34). They sold what they had and had "all things in common" (Acts 4:32). They would not be able to buy or sell during Jacob's trouble because they could not take the "mark of the beast" (Rev. 13:17, 18). Jesus had asked the rich young ruler to show his faith in the gospel that the kingdom of God was at hand by selling all that he had too (Luke 18:18-27). But, because Israel fell (Acts 7; Rom.11:12) God postponed the Tribulation and began the "mystery." So now the persecuted saints in Jerusalem were poor.] **9 For ye know the grace of our Lord Jesus Christ, that, though he was rich, yet for your sakes he became poor, that ye through his poverty might be rich.** [Paul gives the grace of our Lord Jesus Christ as an example of giving. The Son of God laid aside His glory, not His deity and became a man and then humbled Himself and became obedient unto death (Phil. 2:5-8). As a man He could shed man's blood and die. He satisfied the justice of God. He was the propitiation, a fully satisfying sacrifice. He shed His perfect blood so that by faith believers can have His righteousness. This is how the Father can remain just and justify the believer. The Father sees the believer dressed in the righteousness of His Son, and can accept him. "Whom God hath set forth to be a propitiation [fully satisfying sacrifice (Isa. 53:10, 11)] through faith in his blood, to declare his righteousness for the remission of sins that are past, through the forbearance of God; To declare, I say, at this time his righteousness: that he [the Father] might be just, and the justifier of him which believeth in Jesus" (Rom. 3:25, 26). We have atonement now. "And not only so, but we also joy in God through our Lord Jesus Christ, by whom we have now received the atonement" (Rom. 5:11). He gave His life as a ransom for all (1 Tim. 2:6). No one can out-give God; He "spared not his own Son" (Rom. 8:32). He suffered in our place, as our substitute (2 Cor. 5:21). But the Lord also rose, and so will we (4:14). The sinner who trusts that Christ's blood paid for their sins do not get the wages of sin, which is death, but the gift of God, which is eternal life (Rom. 6:23).] **10 And herein I give my advice: for this is**

expedient for you, who have begun before, not only to do, but also to be forward a year ago. [**Paul gives practical advice – he does not command them.** To expedite their giving, they should just continue to carry out the pledges they made a year ago. In First Corinthians, <u>Paul had told them exactly when, the frequency, and how to collect an offering for Jerusalem</u>: every Sunday a portion of their excess – as God had helped them to prosper should be gathered (1 Cor. 16:1-3). This contribution is for the "poor saints in Jerusalem." Because the nation of Israel fell, "salvation is come unto the Gentiles . . . the riches of the world . . . the riches of the Gentiles" (Rom. 11:11, 12). The Gentiles, people of all nations now have an opportunity to have eternal life by faith in what Jesus has done. We, Gentiles, have access to God now, which we did not have before (Eph. 2:11-13). It was not the believing remnant's fault that the nation of Israel did not believe them. The little flock did their part. Gentiles have an opportunity to be spiritually blessed during this dispensation of God's grace and Israel's national blindness (Eph. 3:2; Rom. 11:25). So they can bless the "little flock" because God wants them to (Rom. <u>15:25-28</u>). *<u>It is important to note that the "little flock" did not continue, but died out in the first century</u>. Believers have His love now. Today Israel is in apostasy. We do not need to bless that nation. But the Jews need to hear the gospel of Christ as much as anyone else. We should witness to all people, both Jews and Gentiles. But we should give to people and groups that will handle money wisely. We are not obligated to pay a debt we never incurred.] **11 Now therefore perform the doing of it; that as there was a readiness to will, so there may be a performance also out of that which ye have.** ["Perform the doing of it" in a few words Paul gets to the heart of the matter. Since you had a will to donate, now do what you have said. Words are good, but actions are better. Give out of what you have.] **12 For if there be first a willing mind, it is accepted according to that a man hath, and not according to that he hath not.** [A willing mind is necessary first; thoughts precede actions. Give according to what you have, not according to what you do not have. Paul advocates proportionate giving, a percentage of a person's income. This is the only fair way of giving since people have varying amounts. A flat tax without loopholes is also the fairest and best way to tax people and businesses. A "tithe" is a tenth; a proportion that precedes the law (Gen. 14:20). In Israel's program, the Jews gave up to 30% of their produce for religious and governmental service. Still, a tenth is a fair amount for rich and poor in any dispensation. We are not under the law, but under grace and we can give more if we want to. Giving is a privilege. It is natural to want to support a ministry that blesses us (Gal. 6:6). We have even received checks which have helped us to pay for some books that we bless poor people with. I have always said that the best way to bless this ministry is to buy our books and to give them out to family and friends who need to be saved and to know the truth.] **13 For I mean not that**

other men be eased, and ye burdened: [Paul said, my purpose is not to burden you so others can have it easier.] **14 But by an equality, that now at this time your abundance may be a supply for their want, that their abundance also may be a supply for your want: that there may be equality:** [The "their" is the Macedonian churches. Paul wants all the churches to give so that the burden to supply the needs of the saints in Jerusalem will be spread out. The Corinthians can make up for what the Macedonians could not give, and they can make up for what you (Corinthians) do not give.] **15 As it is written, He that had gathered much had nothing over; and he that had gathered little had no lack.** [Paul uses an example from the Old Testament of gathering manna (Ex. 16:16-18), everyone ended up with an equal amount, one homer. No one had anything left over, and no one had less than the other. There are three books of worship: the Bible, the hymn book, and the pocketbook. By giving a percentage of what they have, they will each feel the same pinch.] **16 But thanks be to God, which put the same earnest care into the heart of Titus for you.** [Paul thanks God for the diligent care Titus has in his heart for them to also give to the poor saints.] **17 For indeed he accepted the exhortation; but being more forward, of his own accord he went unto you.** [Titus volunteered to go back to Corinth to finish the collection there so that it would be ready when Paul arrived.] **18 And we have sent with him <u>the brother</u>, whose praise is in the gospel throughout all the churches;** [Paul sent another brother with Titus who had a clear, grateful, understanding of the gospel (the good news Christ gave to Paul) and the praise of all the churches.] **19 And not that only, but who was also chosen of the churches to travel with us with this grace, which is administered by us to the glory of the same Lord, and declaration of your ready mind:** [Paul sent another brother with Titus who was praised of all the churches and for his understanding of the gospel (the good news Christ gave to Paul). Paul does not mention any names so we do not know who the men are but they may be some of the ones in <u>Acts 20:4</u>. This brother was chosen by the churches to travel with Paul and his friends when they go to Jerusalem to deliver the money (grace).] **20 Avoiding this, that no man should blame us in this abundance which is administered by us:** [By having several people in charge of the abundant offering we will avoid any blame.] **21 Providing for honest things, not only in the sight of the Lord, but also in the sight of men.** [We want to demonstrate an honest handling of the funds, in the sight of the Lord, and in the sight of men.] **22 And we have sent with them <u>our brother</u>, whom we have oftentimes proved diligent in many things, but now much more diligent, upon the great confidence which I have in you.** [We are also sending along a third brother who is one of you, who has often proved to be very diligent in many things. But now he is even more diligent since he has the same confidence that I have in you, that you understand what Jesus is doing for you through me. Paul does not mention any names so we do not know who this is, but it may be Erastus (Acts 19:22; Rom. 16:23; 2 Tim. 4:20).] **23 Whether any do enquire of Titus, he is my partner and fellowhelper concerning you: or our brethren be enquired of, they are the messengers of the churches, and the glory of Christ.** [If anyone should ask, Titus is my fellow partner and helper in the ministry and so are the other two messengers of the churches for the glory of Christ.] **24 Wherefore shew ye to them, and before the churches, the proof of your love, and of our boasting on your behalf.** [For this reason show them and the churches that you love the ministry of Jesus Christ by proving it with your contribution. This also proves that we were right to brag about you.]

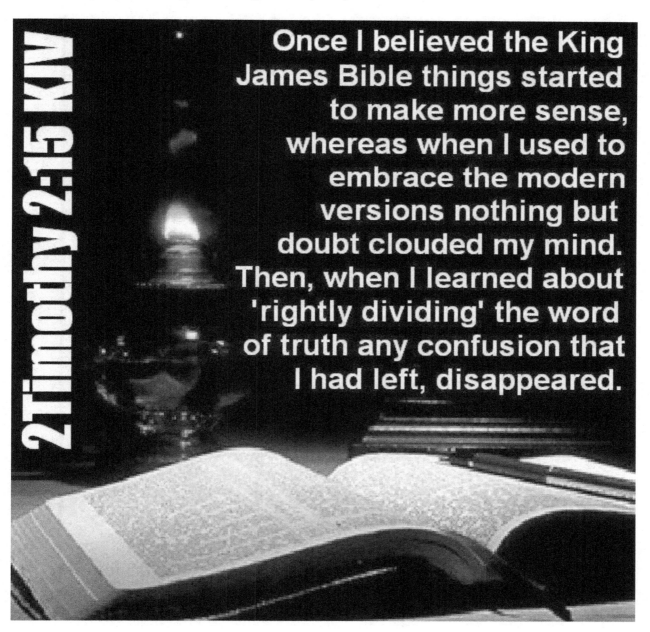

KING JAMES BIBLE FACTS
Authorised King James Version 1611

1. 54 translators worked for 7 years to complete the King James Bible translation in the year 1611.

2. 67% of American adults own a King James Bible.

3. Guy Fawkes threatened the completion of the King James Bible when he tried to blow up King James and the Parliament, but failed.

4. 66 books in the Bible with 40 different authors. Written over a span of 1,500 years.

5. The King James Bible is not copyrighted unlike the newer translations.

6. "LORD" or "Lord" appears 7,736 times.

7. Psalm 118 is the center of the Bible, verse 8 is the middle verse: "It is better to take refuge in the Lord than to trust man."

8. It takes 70 hours to read the whole Bible aloud.

9. "Do not be afraid" appears 365 times, one for every day.

10. King James I of England brought forth the English translation

11. "Thy Word" appears 7 times in the New Testament & "His Son" appears 7 times in the Bible.

12. The word "God" appears in every book of the Bible except Esther and Song of Solomon

Chapter 9 Be generous because God has lavished His grace on us
9:1-5 Your willingness to give encouraged others.
9:6-11 Giving brings blessings to ourselves.
9:12-15 Giving brings glory to God. No one can outgive God.

9:1 For as touching the ministering to the saints, it is superfluous for me to write to you: 2 For I know the forwardness of your mind, for <u>which I boast of you to them of Macedonia</u>, that Achaia was ready <u>a year ago</u>; and your zeal hath provoked very many. 3 Yet have I sent the brethren, lest our boasting of you should be in vain in this behalf; that, as I said, ye may be ready: 4 Lest haply if they of Macedonia come with me, and find you unprepared, we (that we say not, ye) should be ashamed in this same confident boasting. [Paul says you are well aware of the great need of the saints in Jerusalem. They sold all they had and shared among themselves. Then came the great famine predicted by Agabus (Acts 11:28). Paul had used the Macedonians to encourage the Corinthians to give, now he says that the Corinthian's willingness to give a year ago had encouraged the Macedonians. (The mention of "a year ago" is how we know that the Corinthian letters were penned a year apart.) Paul says that he sent the three brethren (his fellowhelper, Titus, and the two messengers in 8:23) to collect their bounty before he and the Macedonians arrive. Paul says, that he and his friends do not want to be embarrassed for having bragged about their pledge.] **5 Therefore I thought it necessary to exhort the brethren, that they would go before unto you, and make up beforehand your bounty, whereof ye had notice before, that the same might be ready, as a matter of bounty, and not as of covetousness.** [Paul explains that he thought it best to finish the collection and have it ready before they arrive so that it will reflect their bountiful generosity, and not to seem as if Paul is only interested in taking their money.]

6 But this I say, He which soweth sparingly shall reap also sparingly; and he which soweth bountifully shall reap also bountifully. [Paul makes and analogy with a farmer (9:6-11) because he wants a bountiful generous harvest from the Corinthians which will glorify God. Giving materially is a tangible expression of our love. Facts in the physical realm harmonize with the spiritual. Many farmers know that they will have a poor yield of crops if they sow their seeds sparingly. Many believers have inward poverty because of their outward stinginess (lack of liberality). They are not rich to God or His work. They say, I am under grace, I am not under the law, so I don't need to tithe. This is true, no one is required to pay a tithe in the dispensation of grace. Still, God loves a generous son or daughter. God wants us to give without fanfare (Rom. 12:8).] **7 Every man according as he purposeth in his heart, *so let him give*; not grudgingly, or of necessity: for God**

loveth a cheerful giver. [God loves a cheerful giver, but few are. It is human nature to be selfish, to hoard, and to only care about ourselves and not others. But God wants us to care about what He is doing, and for one another in the dispensation of grace. He wants us to promote His agenda and help those who are putting it forth. What is God's agenda today? It is to build the body of Christ and to help believers know that Christ has a ministry from heaven to us through Paul (1 Tim. 2:4). God wants people to have sound doctrine built up in their inner man which is the result of studying the Bible rightly divided (2 Tim. 2:15). God does not want our gift if we are going to give grudgingly (Deut. 15:7-10). God doesn't want our gifts if we are giving out of obligation, or so that we can look good to others. God does not want us to give at all if we can't give willingly and cheerfully. Giving is a grace, a decision of the mind. We give the amount we purpose in our heart with the motive to bless others without expecting anything in return.]

8 And God is able to make all grace abound toward you; that ye, always having all sufficiency in all *things*, may abound to every good work: [Notice the use of the word "all" (all grace; always; all sufficiency; all things; every good work). Notice also that Paul does not say that God is obligated to bless us physically, but that He is able to make all grace abound to us. His grace is sufficient to make us "abound to every good work." In chapter 12, we will find out that God did not heal Paul physically, but said that His grace was sufficient. Christ's strength is made perfect in our weakness as we rely on Him and His word to help us in our lives. God is not intervening physically, but He is intervening spiritually by reprogramming our minds (the way we think) with His word. How is God gracious? He provides everything His creatures need to live. Being gracious is part of His character. He says, "If thou at all take thy neighbour's raiment to pledge, thou shalt deliver it unto him by that the sun goeth down: For that is his covering only, it is his raiment for his skin: wherein shall he sleep? and it shall come to pass, when he crieth unto me, that I will hear; for I am GRACIOUS" (Ex. 22:26, 27). God is kind, loving, considerate, thoughtful, generous, and compassionate. That is how God is. He "will be GRACIOUS to whom I will be GRACIOUS, and will shew mercy on whom I will shew mercy" (Ex. 33:19b). Grace is "the kindness and love of God our Saviour toward man . . . not by works of righteousness which we have done . . . being justified by his grace" (Titus 3:4-7). God had regard for mankind's helpless condition. We were slaves to sin, self, and Satan. We had inherited the sin nature from Adam and Eve, and added our own sins too. God's nation of Israel, even with all their privileges and favored nation status, were no better than the rest of mankind. Grace is the free and unmerited favor of God shown towards man. Salvation is a free gift. "Being justified <u>freely</u> by his grace through the redemption that is in Christ Jesus" (Rom. 3:24). His grace to us is by Jesus Christ. "In whom we have redemption through his blood, the forgiveness of sins, according to the riches of his GRACE" (Eph. 1:7).] **9 (As it is written, He hath dispersed abroad; he hath given to the poor: his righteousness remaineth for ever. 10 Now he that ministereth seed to the sower both minister bread for your food, and multiply your seed sown, and increase the fruits of your righteousness;)** [Paul quotes Psa. 112:9 which is about the blessing of a God fearing. "He hath disperse, he hath given to the poor; his righteousness endureth for ever." The "He" is capitalized since it begins the quote. There are no quotation marks at all in the King James Bible. The words in italics were added by the King James Bible translators to give the true meaning of the translation; the italics are also inspired by God. It is important, to notice the parenthesis that encloses these two verses. Because he has believed God he will enter God's kingdom. Giving materially to the poor is a righteous thing to do. The Holy Spirit through Paul adds "abroad" and changes "endureth" to "remaineth." Then in verse 10, Paul prays to God who gave the "seed" (faith in God's word) that He would bless the giver with food and multiply the money and "increase the fruits of your righteousness." The context is graciously giving a physical gift. <u>God does not perform signs, miracles, and wonders today as He did in prophecy</u>. He is not parting the Red Sea, raining manna from heaven, or stilling the storm. But, let me ask some questions: Did God put it into the hearts of the Macedonians to give to the little flock during this dispensation? Did other churches and individuals support Paul and his ministry financially? Does God put it in our hearts to help others today? The answer to all these questions is YES! God lives His life through the believer – this is the mystery of godliness (1 Tim. 3:16). It is Christ's Spirit in our hearts that enables us to have righteous fruit (1:22, 4:11, 6:16; Gal. 5:22, 23). It is righteous to give materially to those who are in need. God has said all that He is going to say in His word. He is not intervening physically today as He did for the nation of Israel with signs, miracles, and wonders. However, <u>Christ intervenes in us spiritually, and uses others to correct and bless us</u>. I believe He is more intimately involved in our lives than we can imagine. He puts love for others into our hearts. "Our sins" (1 Cor. 15:3, 4) in mystery were forgiven and we received His righteousness imputed to us. The instant we trusted in Christ's finished work on the cross, He gave us everything up front. We received "all spiritual blessings in heavenly places in Christ" (Eph. 1:3). We are "complete in Christ" (Col. 2:10); we are "sons of God" (Phil. 2:15); we are "joint-heirs with Christ" (Rom. 8:17); we are "sealed with that holy Spirit of promise" (Eph. 1:13). <u>God is the One who increases the fruit of righteousness</u>. "So then neither is he that planteth any thing, neither he that watereth; but God that giveth the increase" (1 Cor. 3:7). A righteous man works to feed himself and his family, he saves seeds for the next season, and then he shares with others. We are to take care of our family first, then after that we can be generous to the Lord and others (1 Tim. 5:8). A righteous man spreads his wealth far and wide. In prophecy, he does not harvest the corners of his field so the poor can glean from his abundance (Lev. 23:22). This man's <u>righteousness remains with him forever</u>. We will have rewards at the Judgment Seat of Christ for our good works (2 Cor. 5:10; Eph. 2:10). It is righteous to care about the needs of the less fortunate. Job was this kind of a man (Job 29:12-17). I have heard that J. C. Penny gave 90% of his income. He was a smart business owner who sold plain classic clothes (without holes) and functional things at a good price. Money kept pouring in, and he kept pouring it out. He probably lived comfortably on 10%. He was not a hoarder, but generous to God and others. <u>Paul wants the Corinthians to give material money generously because God has blessed them spiritually.</u>] **11 Being enriched in every thing to all bountifulness, which causeth through us thanksgiving to God.** [God enriches us, we enrich others, and God receives the glory. We have His all sufficient grace in all things for every good work which causes thanksgiving to be given to God for what He does through us.] **12 For the administration of this service not only supplieth the want of the saints, but is abundant also by many thanksgivings unto God;** [The administration of the monetary gift not only takes care of the needs of the poor saints in Judea, but it causes many to have thanksgiving to God.]

13 Whiles by the <u>experiment of this ministration</u> they glorify God for your professed <u>subjection unto the gospel of Christ</u>, and for your <u>liberal distribution</u> unto them, and unto <u>all men</u>; 14 And by their prayer for you, which long after you for the exceeding <u>grace of God</u> in you. 15 Thanks be unto God for his unspeakable gift. [Paul said since we have received spiritual things (salvation, access to God by faith in His Son) it is our duty to bless the poor in Jerusalem (Rom. 15:27). They in turn will bless God "for your professed subjection [obedience]." The "experiment [the opportunity to donate] of this ministration" is proof to the recipients that you yielded themselves to the "gospel of Christ" (not the "gospel of the kingdom" mentioned in Matt. 9:35 and Mark 1:14. (Matthew 10:23 was contingent on them accepting Jesus as their King, it has not happened because Israel's program has been put on hold and the "mystery" has been inserted). "Liberal distribution" is generous giving to the saints. They will glorify God when they see the gospel of Christ working in you to make you generous givers. The Corinthians have the exceeding grace of God (9:8). "Unto all men" we should be willing to give to "all men." God expands giving to <u>all men</u>. They will pray to God in gratitude for you and will want to be with you because God's grace is in you. Christ lives in us (Gal. 2:20) and we are in Him (1 Thess. 1:1). Thanks will be given to God because of the "grace of God" in you. The grace of God in us is His Spirit in us. It is like a magnet. It is Christ in us. People say there is something about that Christian that I want. So His grace in us produces the life mentioned in Titus 2:12. It was because God gave us His Son, who loved us and gave Himself for us that made grace possible. "Unspeakable gift" words cannot express God's love and grace to us. Christ died for us out of love for us (8:9) and the Father gave His only Son (John 3:16; Rom. 8:32) for us – no one can outgive God. We received His Son's imputed righteousness (5:21), are "accepted in the beloved" (Eph. 1:6), have eternal life (Titus 3:7), and His life in us. The unspeakable gift is His Son (salvation), His life and Spirit in us. Remember, God wanted the people of Israel to offer the first of their flock, a perfect unblemished lamb (Lev. 1:3)? That offering was a picture of God's perfect Son (1 Peter 2:22; Heb. 7:26). Some gave their worst, the sickly, and blemished, but the Father gave us His best. God has been so rich to us, so we should be rich to God. God sees everything we do and knows the thoughts and intents of our hearts (Heb. 4:12; Psa. 33:13, 14). Paul told the Ephesians "it is more blessed to give than to receive" (Acts 20:35). We "labour, working with his hands the thing which is good, that he may have to give to him that needeth" (Eph. 4:28). Not only that, but we have the "unspeakable gift" of His Son's life in us (2 Cor. 4:11). His life and Spirit will be in the kingdom on earth believers at His Second Coming. There is a parallel for us with the believers in Israel's prophetic program, Jesus is both the Resurrection and the Life (John 11:25).

The Lord Jesus Christ asked, "For what shall it profit a man, if he shall gain the whole world, and lose his own soul?" (Mark 8:36). That losing of the soul has to do with the soul degenerating into a worm in the Lake of Fire.

To what extent did Christ save us? Christ kept the law perfectly. Then He fulfilled every prophecy concerning His death for man's sins on the cross. Jesus Christ bore our sins in His own body on the cross (1 Peter 2:24). "For he hath made him to be sin for us, who knew no sin; that we might be made the righteousness of God in him" (2 Cor. 5:21). But He also sacrificed His soul "being made a curse for us" (Gal. 3:13). He made "his soul an offering for sin . . . and shall be satisfied: by his knowledge shall my righteous servant justify many; for he shall bear their iniquities . . . he hath poured out his soul unto death" (Isa. 53:10-12). While on earth the Lord warned His people about the Second death: "Where the worm dieth not, and the fire is not quenched" (Mark 9:43-48). In the dark hours, while Jesus was nailed to the cross, the Father poured out His wrath on His Son's soul for our sins. He became a worm in our place. "But I am a worm, and no man; a reproach of men, and despised of the people" (Psa. 22:6).

191

He experienced death in the Lake of Fire on our behalf. He became a "worm" in our stead. In the garden Jesus prayed to the Father, "let not the pit shut her mouth upon me" (Psa. 69:15). Satisfied, the Father raised Him. The sign of Jonah is about the Son's three days in the heart of the earth (Matt. 12:40). "The waters compassed me about, even to the soul . . . I went down to the bottoms of the mountains; the earth with her bars was about me for ever: yet hast thou brought up my life from corruption, O LORD my God . . . Salvation is of the LORD" (Jonah 2:5-9). Peter said that the pit could not hold Him (Acts 2:24). Christ went to the extreme measure of tasting death for all mankind, "that he . . . should taste death for every man" (Heb. 2:9). He experienced the degeneration of His soul into a "worm" in the Lake of Fire, "the second death" (Rev. 20:14, 15) so we will never have to. Thank You, LORD! After He knew that everything was accomplished He dismissed His Spirit and died physically. Our Savior did not take any shortcuts in saving us, but He went to the extreme. Why? Because we are extremely sinful, and yet, His love for us is beyond degree. At the cross, He purchased us from Satan, sin, and the second death with His own blood. He saved us to the "uttermost" (Heb. 7:25). That is the kind of Savior we need and have. Our Lord Jesus is the "unspeakable gift." He is the Redeemer for both those who will live in heaven and on earth. Here is the clincher: both groups will have the "unspeakable gift" (His life and Spirit) in them!

Four reasons why the contributions by the Gentile churches to the poor "little flock" of the believing remnant of Israel will bless God.
1) The giver was obedient to the gospel of Christ.
2) The liberal offering helped the poor in their need.
3) The recipients prayed for the giver and to God with thankful hearts.
4) They would be more appreciative and less likely to hinder Paul's ministry.

As a Post Script – Paul and several saints delivered the money to the little flock in Jerusalem. In the process, Paul almost lost his life and was arrested there (Acts 21:17, 31). Sadly, there is no record in scripture that any member of the little flock visited or helped Paul during his two-year incarceration in Caesarea. But, Paul gave without expecting anything in return and so should we. We receive a new appreciation for giving after studying chapters 8 and 9 in Second Corinthians. God wants our giving to have a ripple effect. We give to others, then they give to others. We do not just want to feed the poor physically (so they can go to hell with full stomachs), but we want to feed them spiritually also. Then they may be saved and equipped body of Christ members ready to serve Christ as adult sons in the heavenly places. Believers are an extension of Him; as sons, we are part of the family business.]

Chapter 10 The measure of apostolic authority given to Paul by Christ
10:1-18 Paul's apostolic authority was given by the Lord.

10:1 Now I Paul myself beseech you by the meekness and gentleness of Christ, who in presence am base among you, but being absent am bold toward you:
[Paul is begging the Corinthians on behalf of the meekness and gentleness of Christ to listen to what Jesus says to them through Paul. Meekness means power under control, obedience, yielding, submission to the word of God. Paul has been defending his apostleship throughout this letter, but now until the end of the letter Paul defends his apostolic authority with greater earnest. He and the holy Spirit know what is best for the believer. Many at Corinth respected Paul's authority. But false preachers had crept in and were trying to steal them away from following what Christ had appointed Paul to do. The enemy was trying to discredit Paul in the eyes of his followers and pervert their thinking from the truth (2:17). To not follow Paul today, is to not believe Christ. Paul says his outward appearance is poor in their estimation, but "Don't let looks fool you! I will be just as bold in person next time that I am with you as I am in my letters (10:10)." Paul's physical appearance may have been affected by all the things he endured for them.

Why did Paul have to defend his apostleship? Paul defended his apostleship because it was different from that of the 12. Paul received his office and message by direct revelation of Jesus Christ, not from the 12 apostles at Jerusalem (Gal. 1:11, 12; Rom. 11:13). Paul eventually went to Jerusalem when the Lord told him to and shared with them "that gospel" which Christ had given him (Gal. 2:2). They "saw" and "perceived" that Christ had given Paul a different gospel to preach (Gal. 2:7-9). *Notice that two different gospels are mentioned one to the "circumcision" and one to the "uncircumcision." Peter and Paul had different messages to different groups of people. Peter taught the gospel of the kingdom, and Paul taught the gospel of Christ (Rom. 1:16). Israel fell in Acts 7. Prophecy was temporarily postponed so more could be saved in the dispensation of grace (both lost Jews and Gentiles who trust Paul's gospel). The little flock apostles at Jerusalem finally understood why Christ had delayed the Tribulation and His return to earth (2 Peter 3:4, 9). Christ had begun a new ministry from heaven through Paul, a mystery (which God had to hide from Satan). God is only visiting the Gentiles (Acts 15:14-16). They agreed to let Paul preach to the heathen (all lost people), while they returned to care for the circumcision (the believing remnant) in Jerusalem. The believing remnant died out in the first century AD.

The nation of Israel must be born again (John 3:7; Ex. 4:22), but we are new creatures. Our eternal life began with our spiritual baptism into Christ's death. It began with the crucifixion of our "old man", the sin nature (Rom. 6:3-6; Gal. 2:20), **not** a second birth. When does the nation of Israel receive God's grace? Find the answer in in 1 Peter 1:13. We have His divine nature in us now. We are **not** going to look back to who we were. We want to continue to grow spiritually (Phil. 3:10-14). We study His word of grace which is able to build us up (Acts 20:32). We listen and follow teachers who rightly divide the word of truth (Phil. 3:17).]

2 But I beseech you, that I may not be bold when I am present with that confidence, wherewith I think to be bold against some, which think of us as if we walked according to the flesh. [Now Paul is imploring them himself, so that he will not have to castigate some of them when he arrives. Paul's confidence came from having seen the risen Lord and being commissioned by Him to be His apostle (Acts 26:14-18; 1 Cor. 9:17; Rom. 15:15, 16). Paul is the masterbuilder of the body of Christ in the dispensation of grace and his foundation is Jesus Christ "according to the revelation of the mystery" (1 Cor. 3:10, 11; Rom. 16:25; Eph. 3:1-9). Paul says, some seem to think that we walk according to the flesh, according to our own selves. Some did not believe that Christ was speaking through Paul (13:3).] **3 For though we walk in the flesh, we do not war after the flesh: 4 (For the weapons of our warfare are not carnal, but mighty through God to the pulling down of strong holds;) 5 Casting down imaginations, and every high thing that exalteth itself against the knowledge of God, and bringing into captivity every thought to the obedience of Christ; 6 And having in a readiness to revenge all disobedience, when your obedience is fulfilled.** [For though we are in these bodies of flesh, we do not war after the flesh. Paul's weapons are not carnal, but mighty through God for the pulling down of strongholds (Satan's strongholds, wrong thinking, wrong teaching, false doctrine). His mighty power is God's word rightly divided and spiritually understood and believed. Our three offensive weapons for spiritual warfare are 1) the Spirit of the Lord and His might in us 2) the word of God rightly divided 3) and prayer (Eph. 6:10, 17, 18). Some strong holds of Satan were being set up at Corinth and they needed to be cast down. Satan was making the false ministers imagine that what they were teaching and doing was right. Just like Satan, they were exalting themselves against what Christ in His ministry from heaven was doing for the Church, the body of Christ, through Paul. The Corinthian's and our every thought needs to line up with what God says in His word rightly divided. When we bring our own thoughts into obedience to what Christ says in His word, then every thought or word that is contrary to that can be "revenged" or punished, thrown out and destroyed. To not believe that Paul is our apostle today, and that Romans to Philemon is written for our edification, is to not believe Jesus Christ. When we believe Paul is the one apostle appointed by Christ and that Christ from heaven is forming the "one new man" (Eph. 2:15) then we take every thought captive to what Christ is saying in His word. His Spirit in us using His word rightly divided, can cast down man's imaginations and every high thing that exalts itself against the knowledge of God. Man's wisdom is replaced with divine wisdom, the truth of scripture. The largest denomination today, is that of the "ignorant brethren" (and we used to be one of them). They teach Christ according to His earthly ministry. But, obedience is believing what Christ's apostle says, while disobedience is not believing in Paul's sound doctrine.] **7 Do ye look on things after the outward appearance? If any man trust to himself that he is Christ's, let him of himself think this again, that, as he is Christ's, even so are we Christ's.** [Paul asked the Corinthians, are you looking at the outward appearances (5:12)? Are you judging according to what things look like on the outside? The eloquent, attractive Hebrew ministers who spoke impeccable Greek had come into the assembly at Corinth. They were false apostles. If any man thinks he is Christ's let him understand that we are also Christ's. Those who trust the false ministers are "in Christ." The false ministers may even have been "in Christ." The false apostles, were "enemies of the cross" (Phil. 3:18) and were not teaching Paul's "my gospel." If a person does not rightly divide the word of truth, they may not know that they are being used by Satan to spread a Biblical, yet false gospel. We need to be both Biblical and dispensational. Someone who is teaching that the earthly ministry of Jesus Christ pertains to the body of Christ is a false minister!!! The words "in Christ" appears 77 times in the Bible: once in Acts 24:24 referring to Paul, twice in Peter, and the rest in Paul's letters Romans to Philemon. Peter and the believing remnant were "in Christ" according to prophecy. Some examples of when Paul said "in Christ" are in Rom. 3:24, 8:1, 2, 39; 1 Cor. 1:2. A person is either "in Adam" or "in Christ" (1 Cor. 15:22; 2 Cor. 5:17).] **8 For though I should boast somewhat more of our authority, which the Lord hath given us for edification, and not for your destruction, I should not be ashamed:** [Paul could boast. He knows Christ gave him the apostleship. The Lord had given him and his coworkers their apostolic authority (but only Paul is "the apostle of the Gentiles"). Paul generously says that there were other apostles besides him that were sent to the body of Christ (Acts 14:14; 1 Thess. 2:6). They are appointed for edification, the building up or maturing of the Church, not for their destruction. Paul would not be ashamed. Christ gave him the authority to nurture the believers and build the foundation of the Church. We also need to be careful that we speak for the purpose of edification and not destruction. We need to carefully choose when we speak, what we say, and how we say it.] **9 That I may not seem as if I would terrify you by letters.** [It is not just hot air, Paul will back up his letter of reproof, with action when he visits.] **10 For his letters, say they, are weighty and powerful; but his bodily presence is weak, and his speech contemptible.** [Paul lets them know that he is aware of what some people said about him. They said, his letters are forceful and convincing but, in person he is not very impressive, and the way he speaks is contemptible (11:6; 1 Cor. 2:1, 4). Perhaps Paul's Greek was not refined. Paul met their attacks of slander straight on.] **11 Let such an one think this, that, such as we are in word by letters when we are absent, such will we be also in deed when we are present.** [Paul warns those who think these things about them. The bold way Paul is when absent is the way he will be in person when he is with them.] **12 For we dare not make ourselves of the number, or compare ourselves with some that commend themselves: but they measuring themselves by themselves, and comparing themselves among themselves, are not wise.** [Paul says with a little mocking we do not dare to be counted among you, or to compare ourselves with those who recommend themselves. They were comparing themselves among themselves (with each other), which is not wise. God's word is our final authority, not men. The Bible is our authority, our perfect standard, the measure by which everything else must be measured. The King James Bible is our perfect measuring stick. Whenever I find that I have not understood something correctly, I align my understanding with God's word.] **13 But we will not boast of things without our measure, but according to the measure of the rule which God hath distributed to us, a measure to reach even unto you.** [But we will not boast ourselves beyond what Christ has given us to do, but only what God has distributed for us to do. But ministering to you Corinthians is part of our assignment, the measure God distributed to us.] **14 For we stretch not ourselves beyond our measure, as though we reached not unto you: for we are come as far as to you also in preaching the gospel of Christ:** [We are not going to stretch ourselves beyond our power of authority which God has given us, nor say that you are not our responsibility. You are our responsibility because our preaching extended to giving you the <u>gospel of Christ</u>. Paul was the first to preach the gospel at Corinth and he has been concerned about their spiritual growth ever since. The Corinthian letters are so valuable because they help believers know <u>who we are in Christ</u>. Our sanctification described in Romans chapters 6-8 is how to have power over the presence of sin in our flesh. Sin will be present in our flesh until we die or are raptured, but we need to "walk not after the flesh, but after the Spirit" (Rom. 8:1).] **15 Not boasting of things without our measure, that is, of other men's labours; but having hope, when your faith is increased, that we shall be enlarged by you according to our rule abundantly, 16 To preach the gospel in the regions beyond you, and not to boast in another man's line of things made ready to our hand.** [[Paul repeats that they are not boasting outside of what Christ has given for them to do, "without our measure." Measure in the context of this letter means what God has given Paul and his coworkers to do; their assignment, or portion. We are not going to boast of things outside of what God has given us to do. Those Hebrew ministers at Corinth were out of bounds – they were preaching Christ's earthly ministry when that was not what Christ was doing then (or now). We are not going to claim that someone else's labor is ours. The false ministers had encroached on Paul's territory and were trying to teach the Corinthians their gospel. It was true at one time but, did not pertain then, which made it false. We have this hope that when your faith is increased and you understand more of what Christ is saying to you in my letters; that your love for us will be enlarged and that you will esteem what Christ is ministering abundantly through us to you. That you will be compelled to preach that gospel in areas beyond you. Paul wants them to partner with him in the work of spreading the gospel. <u>We follow what Christ told us through Paul</u>. We are to follow our apostle Paul and "<u>not to boast in another man's line of things made ready to our hand</u>." (This is what the false apostles were trying to do.) The Judaizers' (those preaching Christ's Messianic ministry to the men of Israel in Judah) had invaded Paul's territory and were trying to take over the church he had founded. Do you know of anyone who is preaching Christ's earthly ministry instead of His heavenly ministry? Then mark and avoid them (Rom. 16:17, 18).] **17 <u>But he that glorieth, let him glory in the Lord. 18 For not he that commendeth himself is approved, but whom the Lord commendeth</u>.** [If anyone is going to glory, let him glory in the Lord. It is as if Paul is asking, "Did the Lord really give this to them to do at this time?" At the Judgment Seat for service we will find out the truth! It is not the person that recommends himself that is approved, but the one that the Lord recommends. The thing that matters will be what Christ has done through us according to His purpose.]

197

Chapter 11 Godly jealousy, warning of false teachers, boasting in the Lord
11:1, 2 Godly jealousy over the Church.
11:3-15 Warning against false ministers in the Church.
11:16-33 Paul suffered for Christ and for His Church.

11:1 Would to God ye could bear with me a little in my folly: and indeed bear with me. [Paul's desire before God is that the Corinthians would put up with him and ignore what they consider to be his shortcomings; their superficial criticism of his weak bodily presence and contemptible Greek. It may have been that Paul spoke in the common not fancy Greek, he spoke plainly so he would easily be understood. He begged them to listen to him while he boasted for a little while.] **2 For I am jealous over you with godly jealousy: for I have espoused you to one husband, that I may present you as a <u>chaste virgin</u> to Christ**. [Paul wants to present the Church like a pure <u>virgin</u> to Christ according to mystery (Rom. 16:25). A virgin is a woman who has not known another man. He does not want them fornicatin with false ministers. Paul was jealous over the Corinthians with a godly jealousy (Ex. 20:5; Deut. 4:24). <u>Envy is wanting what belongs to someone else.</u> <u>Jealousy is wanting to hold on to what is rightfully yours out of love.</u> Like God, Paul did not want them to worship another Jesus than the one he presented to them, the glorified Lord in heaven, our Head (Eph. 1:22, 23; Col. 1:18). That "one husband" is Christ in His heavenly ministry to us, not His earthly ministry to Israel. Paul uses the marriage analogy. This does not in any way mean that the Church is the "bride of Christ," that is the new Jerusalem for Israel (Rev. 21:2, 9). Israel's Jerusalem is a "her" (Ezek. 13:16). While the body of Christ is a "he," the "one new man" (Eph. 2:15). So we cannot be the bride. <u>Paul says he espoused or engaged us to one husband</u>. "That he might present it to himself a glorious church, not having spot, or wrinkle, or any such thing; but that it should be holy and without blemish . . . For no man ever yet hated his own flesh; but nourisheth and cherisheth it, even as the Lord the church: For we are members of his body, of his flesh, and of his bones. For this cause shall a man leave his father and mother, and shall be joined unto his wife, and they two shall be one flesh. This is a great mystery: but I speak concerning Christ and the church" (Eph. 5:27-32). We are part of Christ, just like Eve was made of Adam's bone (Gen. 2:23). But Israel was God's wife that He divorced because of her spiritual adultery and Judah was even worse (Jer. 3:1, 2, 8-11). Paul does not want the believers at Corinth to commit spiritual adultery. <u>The only defense against spiritual adultery today is studying the word of God rightly divided</u> (2 Tim. 2:15).] **3 But I fear, lest by any means, as the serpent beguiled Eve through his subtilty, so your minds should be corrupted from the simplicity that is in Christ**. [Paul warns them. He is worried that just like the Serpent tricked Eve through his smooth, sneaky tactics so that

198

likewise their minds should be corrupted from "the simplicity that is in Christ." (The "Serpent" refers to Satan's nature, he probably appeared to her as an angel of light, in the form of a man.) The simplicity of Christ is lost if another gospel is followed that doesn't apply today. For example: if we put ourselves under the Law, or mix Law and grace (Peter and Paul). Either way we put ourselves under the Law; this is why it is essential to rightly divide. Because if we believe that the body of Christ began in Acts 2, and not Acts 9, then we apply all the things that belong to Israel to ourselves. Paul said that the Law actually energized his sinful flesh, and made him "exceedingly sinful" to the point that he was in despair and defeat. "For I was alive without the law once [Paul was alive in grace]: but when the commandment came, sin revived, and I died. And the commandment, which was ordained to life, I found to be unto death. For sin, taking occasion by the commandment, deceived me, and by it slew me. Wherefore the law is holy, and the commandment holy, and just, and good. Was then that which is good made death unto me? God forbid. But sin, that it might appear sin, working death in me by that which is good; that sin by the commandment might become <u>exceeding sinful</u>. . . O wretched man that I am! who shall deliver me from the body of this death?" (Rom. 7:9-13, 24). There was nothing wrong with the law (it was good). The problem was that the law showed him that his sin was extremely sinful and deserving of death. When he tried to do good in his flesh and tried to keep the law again, he suffered self-condemnation. The solution for us who are <u>in Christ Jesus</u> is to live "not after the flesh, but after the Spirit" (Rom. 8:1). Under the law people obeyed out of fear; under grace we obey out of love. THE SIMPLICITY THAT IS IN CHRIST: IS THAT HE DID EVERYTHING TO SAVE US. SALVATION IS BY FAITH IN CHRIST ALONE PLUS NOTHING. SALVATION IS 100% GOD, AND 0% MAN. We only put our faith in what He has already done. To add any of our work to that is to insult God and to nullify our salvation, to make it void "of none effect" (Rom. 4:4, 5, 14; Eph. 2:8, 9). We cannot add our "water baptism," "sinner's prayer," "public confession," "good works," or anything else to what Christ has done; because then our salvation is disqualified. Once we believe, it is as if we are put into an ENVELOPE, which is "in Christ," sealed, and addressed to heaven.] **4 For if he that cometh preacheth <u>another Jesus, whom we have not preached,</u> or if ye receive <u>another spirit, which ye have not received, or another gospel, which ye have not accepted,</u> ye might well bear with him**. [Paul says, if someone comes to you and preaches another Jesus, which <u>we have not preached</u> (such as Christ in His earthly ministry to Israel, not Jesus from heaven); or if you receive another spirit <u>than the one that you received</u> (such as in Eph. 2:2, worldliness, or legalism, not grace); or another gospel <u>which you have not accepted</u> (such as the gospel of the kingdom, not the gospel of Christ) you may put up with him. How do we know for sure that Peter and his group preached the gospel of the kingdom? What did the Lord Jesus Christ teach them during the 40 days between His resurrection and ascension? The answer is in Acts 1:1-3. What question did Christ's disciples ask Him just before He ascended? The answer is in Acts 1:6. They preached the same gospel as John the Baptist and Jesus preached (Matt. 3:2, 9:35). The disciples had signs following them (Mark 16:15-18). During the tribulation they will be able to drink poison and not die. But don't try that now. Their kingdom will be like heaven on earth (Deut. 11:21). The new Jerusalem when it comes down will be the Father's house in which there are many mansions (John 14:2).] **5 For I suppose I was not a whit behind the very chiefest apostles**. [The "chiefest apostles" refers to the 12, and Paul is not behind them in any way. Twelve is the number for Israel, so what is the number for the body of Christ? One is the number for the Church, the body of Christ. We have one apostle, Paul (Rom. 11:13). We are the "one new man" (Eph. 2:15). We have "one baptism" (Eph. 4:5).] **6 But though I be rude in speech, yet not in knowledge; but we have been throughly made manifest among you in all things**. [My speech may seem rude, but not my knowledge. Paul had made it clear to them many times that He was Christ's appointed apostle and his knowledge was from Christ. Other evidence was that he had the signs of an apostle (12:12).] **7 Have I committed an offence in abasing myself that ye might be exalted, because I have preached to you the gospel of God freely?** [Have I done wrong in abasing (lowering) myself so that you may be exalted, and in preaching the gospel to you for free? Paul is saying, have I committed a sin for not taking your money? Some were saying, <u>Paul is not a legitimate apostle or he would have accepted money for his services</u>. He had supported himself, so the gospel of Christ would not be hindered (1 Cor. 9:12) and still his critics found fault.] **8 I robbed other churches, taking wages of them, to do you service. 9 And when I was present with you, and wanted, I was chargeable to no man: for that which was lacking to me the brethren which came from Macedonia supplied: and in all things I have kept myself from being burdensome unto you, and so will I keep myself.** [Paul refused to accept any contribution to his support at all from the Corinthians. He took the money supplied by the Macedonian churches to supplement his tent making income so he could serve them. When he was with them and in need of provisions, he said, I did notask or demand any of you to help me. I have kept myself from being a burden to you, and plan to stay that way.] **10 As the truth of Christ is in me, no man shall stop me of this boasting in the regions of Achaia. 11 Wherefore? because I love you not? God knoweth**. [We have plainly revealed my apostolic authority from Christ in heaven to you. No one can stop Paul from boasting that he served the regions of Achaia without charge. Why was I not a burden to you? Was it because I don't love you? God knows that I love you.] **12 But what I do, that I will do, that I may cut off occasion from them which desire occasion; that**

wherein they glory, they may be found <u>even as we</u>. [The reason I did what I did was to cut off any reason of some saying I did it for the money. If others brag they can "be found even as we" serving for free, working to provide for themselves, teaching what we teach, and suffering what I suffered.] **13 For such are <u>false apostles, deceitful workers, transforming themselves into the apostles of Christ</u>**. [Those who glory in themselves and presume to have Christ's authority are "false apostles, deceitful workers, transforming themselves into the apostles of Christ." They are fake counterfeits. Perhaps Satan was able to approach Eve because the serpent appeared as an angel of light (Like God Adam and Eve were clothed in light Psa. 104:2). <u>Satan uses many false ministers</u> that corrupt and twist the word of God (2:17). Today many pastors and teachers will tell entertaining charming stories with a grain of truth without being able to compare and contrast prophecy and mystery. They preach and teach things that belong to Israel NOT to the body of Christ, or MIX Peter's and Paul's messages. But Paul and his coworkers had renounced the hidden things of dishonesty, not handling the word of God deceitfully, revealing the truth of the mystery sincerely to every man's conscience before God. Paul alone is our true apostle. True ministers are those who teach his ways (1 Cor. 4:16, 17).] **14 <u>And no marvel; for Satan himself is transformed into an angel of light</u>**. [Do not be surprised or caught off guard because these ministers are servants of Satan. Paul openly accuses the ministers of being servants of Satan. Someone besides Christ sent them. <u>Satan himself is transformed into an angel of light</u>. He did this when he made Eve question (doubt) God and His word in the Garden of Eden (Gen. 3:1). <u>Like God, Adam and Eve were clothed in light (Psa. 104:2)</u>. Satan was called "Lucifer" (Isa. 14:12), or light bearer. The NKJV calls him "Lucifer" but has a foot note to "day star" which is a name for Christ (2 Peter 1:19). The NIV omits "Lucifer" and calls him "morning star" which is another reference to Christ (Rev. 22:16). What does your Bible say? Isn't it interesting that Satan who wants to be like "the most High" (Isa. 14:12-14) would make the counterfeit Bibles say he is? Satan was created perfect, wise, and beautiful (with brightness) until iniquity was found in him (Ezek. 28:7, 11-19). Satan who was "the anointed cherub that covereth" convinced a third of the angels to follow him, promising them positions of power. In Galatians, Paul said that if anyone preaches another gospel than the one he and his co-workers taught they should be accursed (Gal. 1:8).] **15 Therefore it is no great thing if his ministers also be transformed as the <u>ministers of righteousness; whose end shall be according to their works</u>**. [Therefore do not be surprised if Satan's ministers are transformed into ministers of righteousness. They seem to preach and teach righteousness. Satan doesn't need to make people sin. We do that very well on our own since we are born with a sin nature. Satan took care of that nearly 6,000 years ago in the Garden of Eden. Today Satan is in churches preaching and teaching false doctrine, and also in the business of counterfeit Bibles. God will judge them according to their works. Many ministers will be surprised to learn that they were actually used of Satan to teach false doctrine and were "enemies of the cross" (Phil. 3:18).]

16 ¶ I say again, Let no man think me a fool; if otherwise, yet as a fool receive me, that I may boast myself a little. [Paul repeats that he does not want anyone to think of him as a fool but if they must, then receive him that way and allow him to boast a little (10:13). A fool applauds himself, but we will find out that Paul's wounds are his badges of authentication as the true apostle. Paul did all things so they could believe the truth of the gospel of Christ which was committed to his trust (1 Tim. 1:11).] **17 That which I speak, I speak it not after the Lord, but as it were foolishly, in this confidence of boasting.** [What I am about to say I am not speaking by the command of Jesus, but I am boasting foolishly in the confidence of the office He has permitted me.] **18 Seeing that many glory after the flesh, I will glory also.** [Since they have gloried in what they had done in their flesh (themselves), I will also. Glorying in oneself is foolish, when it is Christ who has done it all.] **19 For ye suffer fools gladly, seeing ye yourselves are wise.** [Sarcasm, you tolerate fools gladly, and consider yourselves wise. (That made them the fools.)] **20 For ye suffer, if a man bring you into bondage, if a man devour you, if a man take of you, if a man exalt himself, if a man smite you on the face.** [Someone can come into your assembly and do five things to draw them away from following Paul to follow Christ: (1) put you under bondage – the Law (Gal. 4:9); (2) devour you – to bite, fight, and devour is the fruit of legalism (Gal. 5:15); (3) takes of you – takes your money; (4) exalts himself – claims divine authority; (5) smite you on the cheek – physically punishes you or slaps you with the Law. They will take that kind of abuse from false ministers.] **21 I speak as concerning reproach, as though we had been weak. Howbeit whereinsoever any is bold, (I speak foolishly,) I am bold also.** [Paul says, he is reluctantly compelled to speak boldly about himself because the false apostles are bold in usurping his authority. Paul proves that he was not weak, only a true apostle would go through what he had.] **22 Are they Hebrews? so am I. Are they Israelites? so am I. Are they the seed of Abraham? so am I.** [Paul targets the false apostles, takes aim, and fires with both barrels: they were Hebrews like Paul. They were "little flock" (Luke 12:32) believers who refused to recognize Paul's distinctive ministry from Christ or to believe that their ministry had been put on hold. They taught a gospel (of the kingdom on earth) that was no longer valid.] **23 Are they ministers of Christ? (I speak as a fool) I am more; in labours more abundant, in stripes above measure, in prisons more frequent, in deaths oft.** [Paul is speaking as a fool because those other ministers are false. The false ministers claimed to be <u>ministers of Christ</u>, but they were ministering another gospel. The false apostles were <u>not</u> teaching what Christ is doing in the dispensation of grace and were <u>not</u> appointed by Him. Even the Lord said that unlike the hireling, the true shepherd will lay down his life for his sheep (John 10:10, 11). Paul list's his apostolic badges of courage and suffering (11:23-33; Gal. 6:17). Christ had said that he would suffer for Him (Acts 9:15, 16).] **24 Of the Jews five times received I forty stripes save one.** [195 stripes] **25 Thrice was I beaten with rods, once was I stoned, thrice I suffered shipwreck, a night and a day I have been in the deep; 26 In journeyings often, in perils of waters, in perils of robbers, in perils by mine own countrymen, in perils by the heathen, in perils in the city, in perils in the wilderness, in perils in the sea, in perils among false brethren; 27 In weariness and painfulness, in watchings often, in hunger and thirst, in fastings often** [he had to go without food], **in cold and nakedness. 28 Beside those things that are without, that which cometh upon me daily, the care of all the churches.** [Paul endured 195 lashes! None of the false ministers could say they endured as much as Paul out of love for Christ and the Church. Besides physical sufferings, he had the internal care of all the churches. He wants them to thrive. Paul prayed for them, wrote letters, sent ministers, encouraged them to appoint leaders, and visited when he could. His method was to enter a city, preach the gospel, and set up churches (often in homes), and teach them His word.] **29 Who is weak, and I am not weak? who is offended, and I burn not?** [No wonder that Paul was bodily a little weak after suffering so many things. Paul burned with anger and was offended that some of the Corinthians continued listening to false apostles rather than to him. He was not jealous for their affection for himself, but for their affection for Christ. Our great apostle would not have mentioned his sufferings at all if he wasn't defending the Gospel. Paul boasts of the sufferings he endured. We will also suffer persecution (2 Tim. 3:12). It hurts Christ who loves us if we follow false ministers today. <u>Ministers can only teach the truth of God's word if they are both biblical and dispensational.</u>] **30 If I must needs glory, I will glory of the things which concern mine infirmities.** [Paul said that if he is going to glory, that he will glory in his sufferings. <u>None of the false apostles could match what he had endured.</u>] **31 The God and Father of our Lord Jesus Christ, which is blessed for evermore, knoweth that <u>I lie not</u>.** [Paul brings their attention back on God the Father and the Lord Jesus Christ. God knows that Paul does not lie. He is the true apostle. It comforts Paul and Christ if believers follow His minister, Paul.] **32 In Damascus the governor under Aretas the king kept the city of the Damascenes with a garrison, desirous to apprehend me: 33 And through a window in a basket was I let down by the wall, and escaped his hands.** [Paul even suffered as a hunted man in Damascus. He escaped the soldiers in a basket. King Aretas died in AD 40, which helps us date events.]

Chapter 12 Further proof of Paul's apostolic authority
12:1-6 Paul's visions and revelations from Christ.
12:7-10 His "thorn in the flesh" and Christ's sufficient grace.
12:11-18 His signs of an apostle.
12:19-21 His love and courage to deal with the problems in the church.

12:1 It is not expedient for me doubtless to glory. I will come to visions and revelations of the Lord. 2 I knew a man in Christ above fourteen years ago, (whether in the body, I cannot tell; or whether out of the body, I cannot tell: God knoweth;) such an one <u>caught up</u> to the third heaven. 3 And I knew such a man, (whether in the body, or out of the body, I cannot tell: God knoweth;) 4 How that he was <u>caught up into paradise, and heard unspeakable words, which it is not lawful for a man to utter</u>. 5 Of such an one will I glory: yet of myself I will not glory, but in mine infirmities. 6 For though I would desire to glory, I shall not be a fool; for I will say the truth: but now I forbear, lest any man should think of me above that which he seeth me to be, or that he heareth of me. [Paul says that it is not advantageous for him to continue to recount what he endured for the sake of the believers in the body of Christ. He wants them to realize that Christ is working through him. He states he is continuing to come to visions and revelations. The Lord Jesus told him that He would appear to him (Acts 26:16, 22:21; 1 Cor. 14:37) and He did often and in abundance (12:7). Paul wants to share that Christ gave him a glimpse into the third heaven. But he doesn't want to be foolish and take glory for himself when it is Christ who has done everything. Paul usually shared everything he has learned from Christ, but he was hesitant to share the truth about being "caught up" to Paradise in the third heaven because he doesn't want anyone to think of him above what he is. Paul carefully shared what Christ allowed him to experience more than 14 years earlier. This event most likely refers to the time that Paul was stoned, thought to be dead and dragged out of the city of Lystra (Acts 14:19, 20). I believe Paul was stoned to death (like Stephen) not merely knocked unconscious. Paul is just a man, but he is a man who God raised from the dead, and who went to the third heaven and back. It is remarkable that Paul waited for 14 years to share this story in his writings! Most people would have mentioned an extraordinary event like this to many people, many times. "Paradise" is mentioned three times in the Bible (Luke 23:43; 12:4; Rev. 2:7). Paul says twice that he could not tell if he was in the body or out of the body. It seems that he was not conscious of his physical body at that time. Paul heard unspeakable words that were <u>not lawful</u> to utter because they were not part of what we need to know here on earth right now. God has told all believers what they need to know in His word. Paul is to speaks these truths. Paul does not want people to think more highly of him than what they see or hear.] **7 And lest I**

should be exalted above measure through the abundance of the revelations, there was given to me a thorn in the flesh, the messenger of Satan to buffet me, lest I should be exalted above measure.** [So that Paul would not exalt himself above his office as the apostle to the body of Christ, there was given him a "thorn in the flesh" the "messenger of Satan," to prevent him from being prideful because of the abundance of revelations that he received. The "thorn" was a painful reminder **not** to exalt himself above the position he had received (Acts 26:16; Rom. 11:13, 15:16).] **8 For this thing I besought the Lord thrice, that it might depart from me.** [Paul asked the Lord to remove the "thorn" three times. We do <u>not</u> know what the thorn was, but the best educated guess would be a possible eye ailment. Paul was blind for three days after he saw the light (which was brighter than the sun) and the Lord Jesus, on the road to Damascus (Acts 9:9, 17). Paul's eyes may have been affected when he was stoned at Lystra in Acts 14. We notice in Galatians, which was the only epistle that he wrote with his own hand, was written with big letters and that the Galatians were sympathetic about his eye problem (Gal. 4:15, 6:11). Perhaps the reason we do not know what Paul's thorn was, is because people have different thorns in the flesh.] **9 And he said unto me, My grace is sufficient for thee: for my strength is made perfect in weakness. Most gladly therefore will I rather glory in my infirmities, that the power of Christ may rest upon me.** [The Lord Jesus did not remove his "thorn in the flesh," but said that His grace is sufficient, because His strength is made perfect in weakness. Paul immediately cheerfully obeyed saying "most gladly" therefore would he glory in his sufferings so <u>Christ's power</u> will rest on him. Our power supply is <u>Christ in us</u> and His word/ mind (1 Cor. 2:16). The Lord stood with Paul in his darkest hours, and he will be with us, too (2 Tim. 4:17).] **10 Therefore I take pleasure in infirmities, in reproaches, in necessities, in persecutions, in distresses for Christ's sake: for when I am weak, then am I strong.** [Paul bravely says he takes pleasure in being reproached, having need, being persecuted, or in distresses for Christ's sake, because when he is weak, then Christ is strong in him. The life of Christ and His word can work in a believer who yields and depends on His wisdom and grace (1 Cor. 1:30; Phil. 1:6). Paul is weak in himself, but strong in Christ (Phil. 4:13).]

11 ¶ I am become a fool in glorying; ye have compelled me: for I ought to have been commended of you: for in nothing am I behind the very chiefest apostles, though I be nothing. [Paul says, that they forced him to carry on and glory in his infirmities. He should not have had to tell them how much he was willing to suffer for their sake. They should have commended him instead. They should have honored his apostolic authority, leadership, love in sharing the gospel, and all revelations that Christ gave him with them. He as one apostle, is not less in any way than Israel's twelve apostles, even though he is nothing. Paul knows that Christ is everything.] **12 Truly the signs of an apostle were wrought among you in all patience, in signs, and wonders, and mighty deeds.** [They had seen Paul, in all patience, do signs and wonders and mighty deeds. Notice how patience is first. We also need to be patient, which is something that is very difficult for many of us. All the things that Peter did Paul did also to show that God was now working with Paul, instead of Peter: raising the dead, casting out devils, healing, and so on. Paul had all the spiritual gifts, and spoke in tongues more than all of them (1 Cor. 14:18). When he traveled through Galatia he needed to speak several languages in that area to share the gospel. Paul gave testimony of the Lord's grace and did signs and wonders in Iconium (Acts 14:3). He healed a man crippled from birth in the region of Lyconia (Acts 14:8-10). At the Jerusalem council, Barnabas and Paul declared the miracles and wonders God had worked by them among the Gentiles (Acts 15:12). Paul cast the spirit of divination out of the young woman in Philippi (Acts 16:16-18). Diseases and evil spirits departed from people who were touched by the handkerchiefs that had touched Paul's body (Acts 19:11, 12). In Troas, Paul raised a young man named Eutychus from the dead after he fell asleep and fell out of the third story window (Acts 20:6-12). On the island of Melita, Paul was not hurt by the poisonous snake bite, he healed Publious' father of the bloody flux, and many others with diseases (Acts 28:1-10). All these sign gifts ended after Paul, through the Spirit, gave the Jews as a group up in Rome. The Jews failed three times in three different places so Paul ended his provoking ministry to them and went to the Gentiles (Acts 18:6; 13:46; 28:28; Rom. 11:11). There were no more sign gifts after that. They ended when Paul arrived in Rome, about AD 61 (1 Cor. 13:8-10). God speaks to us through His word. God is not adding to His word. The Bible is complete. Inspiration is finished, but illumination (or enlightenment) of what His word says continues. The church is "the pillar and ground of the truth" (1 Tim. 3:15). Copies of His true word are being printed. God has promised to preserve His word (Psalm 12:6, 7). I believe God helped the King James translators with His preserved word.] **13 For what is it wherein ye were inferior to other churches, except it be that I myself was not burdensome to you? forgive me this wrong.** [Sarcasm "forgive me." The Corinthian church had more sign gifts than any other church since they were next door to the synagogue (Acts 18:7; 1 Cor. 1:22). So that the Jews there would believe that God was now working through them and Paul. But Paul never asked that church for money, he graciously served them for free.]

14 Behold, the third time I am ready to come to you; and I will not be burdensome to you: for I seek not yours, but you: for the children ought not to lay up for the parents, but the parents for the children. [Paul plans to visit them for the third time. His second visit was not recorded. He probably briefly left his ministry in Ephesus and came to them in heaviness, and wants to avoid repeating that (2:1). He lovingly says he doesn't want anything from them but for them to follow him for their own sake. He wants to bless them spiritually, with more revelation. He wants to provide for their growth since he is their apostle and spiritual father, and they are his spiritual children. He shared the gospel that saved their souls and gave them new life. Parents should provide for their children, not the other way around.] **15 And I will very gladly spend and be spent for you; though the more abundantly I love you, the less I be loved.** [Paul would gladly spend his energy on them, and let his energy be spent for them just like parents do for their children. But the more he loves them it seems, the less they love him in return.] **16 But be it so, I did not burden you: nevertheless, being crafty, I caught you with guile.** [Let it be that way, but I never burdened you by asking for your money. Paul said some may argue without logic, saying "he did not burden us but somehow he used guile (cunning) to make us trust in his apostleship."] **17 Did I make a gain of you by any of them whom I sent unto you? 18 I desired Titus, and with him I sent a brother. Did Titus make a gain of you? walked we not in the same spirit? walked we not in the same steps?** [Paul says, look at the evidence, did any of the men I sent you ask for payment? I requested that Titus and a brother would go and help you. Did we not walk in the same spirit lovingly serving you for free with pure motives? Did he not also promote Christ according the revelation of the mystery given to me? Titus and I walked in the same spirit, the same steps, and said the same things (1 Cor. 1:10; Phil. 3:16). The "same steps" is sound doctrine.] **19 Again, think ye that we excuse ourselves unto you? we speak before God in Christ: but we do all things, dearly beloved, for your edifying.** [Don't think that we are excusing ourselves for not asking you for money. We are speaking truth before God in Christ, our motive in everything we do is your spiritual welfare and growth. Following Paul is what is best for them. Paul calls them dearly beloved.] **20 For I fear, lest, when I come, I shall not find you such as I would, and that I shall be found unto you such as ye would not: lest there be debates, envyings, wraths, strifes, backbitings, whisperings, swellings, tumults: 21 And lest, when I come again, my God will humble me among you, and that I shall bewail many which have sinned already, and have not repented of the uncleanness and fornication and lasciviousness which they have committed.** [Paul admits his fears that when he comes that he will not find them the way he would like, and that they will not find him the way they would like. He does not want to have to discipline the Corinthians in anger again (1 Cor. 4:21). Paul does not want those who follow the other apostles to debate, envy, have strife, talk bad and whisper behind his back because of conceit and for there to be tumults (loud commotion). He fears that when he comes to them again that God will require him to bewail many (to express sorrow and grief) for their sin of following the false ministers instead of him. That they will not have changed their mind about the uncleanness of what they were doing: listening to the false ministers and committing spiritual adultery by lusting after the false ministers. Their "fornication" in this context is spiritual, not physical. Paul warned the Philippians about three types of people: "dogs" (unsaved Gentiles), "evil workers" (the enemies of Christ, ministers of Satan), and the "concision" (the cutters, Jews who wanted them to cut off their foreskin and put them under the law of Moses, in Phil. 3:2). Paul warned those who had committed this type of spiritual fornication, because he knew the joy, freedom, and clarity they would have if they followed him. Sound doctrine leads to sound thinking, and right living, while false doctrine leads to wrong thinking and wrong behavior. We should not follow doctrine that does not pertain to us now. We can warn people to repent and change their mind, but many will persist in listening to false preachers and teachers. There are so many great grace pastors and teachers on Facebook and YouTube that there is no reason to listen to those who teach Christ's earthly ministry instead of His heavenly ministry to us through Paul. Paul had the love and courage to deal with the problems in the Church.] Notice the "**power of Christ**" in the picture below.

2 Corinthians 12:9 King James Version (KJV)

9 And he said unto me, MY GRACE IS SUFFICIENT for thee: for my strength is made perfect in weakness. Most gladly therefore will I rather glory in my infirmities, that the power of Christ may rest upon me. zeza

Chapter 13 Exhortation for self-examination: are you in "the faith"?
13:1-4 Be ready for my visit.
13:5-7 Be sure you are in "the faith."
13:8-10 Be obedient to God's Word.
13:11-14 Be mature in your faith, concluding remarks, and salutation.

13:1 This is the third time I am coming to you. In the mouth of two or three witnesses shall every word be established. [Paul repeats the admonition that he wants them to be ready when he visits them (12:14). In this context, "in the mouth of two or three witness" (Deut. 19:15) refers to the "spiritual fornicators" in 12:21. Two or three witnesses will identify (point out) those who persist in following the "false apostles of Christ" (11:13). The "false apostles" are transformed by Satan to appear to be "ministers of righteousness" (11:15), but are the fake "ministers of Christ" (11:23).] **2 I told you before, and foretell you, as if I were present, the second time; and being absent now I write to them which heretofore have sinned, and to all other, that, if I come again, I will not spare:** [Paul says that if he has to he is willing to reprove (castigate) them again, like he did on his second visit to them (2:1). He had wanted to present them as a chaste virgin who had not known another man (11:2). But, he is writing to those who have sinned (committed spiritual fornication) by following the false ministers (11:13-15) and all others that, if he comes again he will not spare.] **3 Since ye seek a proof of Christ speaking in me, which to you-ward is not weak, but is mighty in you**. [Paul says, you look for proof that Christ is speaking in me. He is the mighty power in me to you, but He is mighty in you (6:7).] **4 For though he was crucified through weakness, yet he liveth by the power of God. For we also are weak in him, but we shall live with him by the power of God toward you**. [Paul draws a parallel between Christ and him. For though He was crucified in the weak form of human flesh, still He lives by the power of God. Paul says he and his coworkers are also physically weak humans, but they have the resurrection power of God in them to deal with the Corinthians.] **5 Examine yourselves, whether ye be in the faith; prove your own selves. Know ye not your own selves, how that Jesus Christ is in you, except ye be reprobates?** [In 1 Cor. 9:3 the Corinthians were examining Paul. Now he exhorts them with all gravity to examine themselves if they are in "the faith." When Paul says "the faith" he does not mean just any faith. "The faith" is believing the revelation of the mystery Christ gave to Paul (Rom. 16:25), the sound doctrine in Romans to Philemon. Are they following Christ's ministry from heaven to the body of Christ through Paul, or Christ's earthly ministry to Israel? Our faith does not just depend on Bible doctrine, but on the "sound doctrine" given to Paul. Paul uses the phrase "sound doctrine" four times in his writings (1 Tim. 1:10; 2 Tim. 4:3; Titus 1:9, 2:1). Paul told Timothy, "Hold fast the form of sound words,

209

which thou hast heard of me, in faith and love which is in Christ Jesus" (2 Tim. 1:13). We should understand Christ's earthly ministry through a Pauline perspective (Rom. 15:8: 2 Tim. 2:7). One of the mysteries given to Paul is the life of Jesus in them (4:7, 10, 11; Col. 1:27). His life is the "power of God" in 13:4. Someone who has the life of Jesus in them is NOT reprobate. Paul asks, "Know ye not your own selves, how that Jesus Christ is in you, except ye be reprobates?" The plural word "reprobates" only appears three times in the Bible, and all in 2 Cor. 13:5-7. The Bible has its own built in dictionary. The singular word "reprobate" is in the Bible four times which helps us define the word (Jer. 6:30; Rom. 1:28; 2 Tim. 3:8; Titus 1:16). From these verses we gather that it is very important not to be a reprobate. The verse in Jeremiah makes it clear that it means to be a "reject." The dictionary defines it as not passing the test, destined to eternal destruction, not allowed. Someone who denies God's plan of salvation is reprobate because they do not have the life of Jesus in them. If they are reprobate, without Christ's life or His righteousness in them, they will not be allowed to enter heaven. If we do not have the life of Jesus in our mortal body, we are reprobates (4:11). However, Paul's gospel of Christ is the only gospel by which we are saved today. Paul gives the gospel many times in many ways in his letters, but the clearest and most concise verses are 1 Cor. 15:3, 4. It is possible for someone to put their faith in the wrong gospel (and not be saved) if they have never heard any of Paul's letters. Faith comes by hearing. "So then faith cometh by hearing, and hearing by the word of God" (Rom. 10:17). We need to hear our sound doctrine.] **6 But I trust that ye shall know that we are not reprobates.** [Paul trusts that they know that they have Christ's life in them.] **7 Now I pray to God that ye do no evil; not that we should appear approved, but that ye should do that which is honest, though we be as reprobates.** [Doing something "evil" in this context is not believing the message Christ gave to them through their apostle Paul. They should follow that honest truth (and not false ministers and their message), even if he and his co-workers are reprobates.] **8 For <u>we can do nothing against the truth, but for the truth.</u>** [Paul wants them to be obedient to God's word through him. The truth is the message Christ has given to us through Paul. The truth is that pure sound doctrine. The truth is that God is forming the body of Christ in this dispensation of the grace of God (1 Cor. 3:10; Eph. 2:13-18, 3:2). It is also true that Paul is "the apostle of the Gentiles" (Rom. 11:13). Right division is not optional; it is the only way to have our eyes open to the truth of the Scriptures. The Lord Jesus from heaven sent Paul, "To open their eyes, and to turn them from darkness to light, and from the power of Satan unto God, that they may receive forgiveness of sins, and inheritance among them which are sanctified by faith that is in me" (Acts 26:18). Sound doctrine is not only the way we are saved, but how we grow spiritually. The "knowledge of the truth" (1 Tim. 2:4) is that Christ has a ministry from heaven to us through Paul's distinctive ministry to the Gentiles. God wants "to make all men see what is the fellowship of the mystery" (Eph. 3:9). If someone does not see the mystery in the Bible, it may be because they are not using a <u>King James Bible.</u> <u>The dispensation of grace in which we live was FIRST and ONLY revealed to Paul</u> (1 Tim. 1:16; Eph. 3:1-9; Col. 1:23-29). <u>The body of Christ is not found outside his epistles.</u>] **9 For we are glad, when we are weak, and ye are strong: and this also we wish, even your perfection.** ["Perfection" is like a chaste virgin untainted by men teaching false doctrine. Like a loving father Paul is joyful, that when he and his workers are weak, that their children (the Corinthians) are strong in the truth, and grow and prosper. They will have "perfection" if they believe the glorious gospel of Christ given to Paul (that <u>Satan wants to conceal,</u> 4:1-4; 2 Tim. 2:26).] **10 Therefore I write these things being absent, lest being present I should use sharpness, according to the power which the Lord hath given me to edification, and not to destruction.** [Paul is writing this letter while he is away from them so that they will unite behind Christ's ministry through him. But also so he will not have to use sharp words according to the apostolic authority the Lord gave him (10:2, 1 Cor. 4:21). But, Paul would make the next visit another demonstration of his power and apostolic authority if he has to (Rom. 16:17, 18). But if they repent (change their minds) and stop following the false ministers, he would not have to prove his apostleship by coming to discipline them. Again Paul says that the Lord Jesus Christ gave Paul this authority for their edification, not for their destruction (10:8). Christ made Paul the "masterbuilder" of the body of Christ. "According to the grace of God which is given unto me, as a wise MASTERBUILDER, I have laid the foundation, and another buildeth thereon . . ." (1 Cor. 3:10). He is building up the body of Christ, not tearing it down.]

11 ¶ Finally, <u>brethren, farewell</u>. <u>Be perfect</u>, be of <u>good comfort</u>, <u>be of one mind</u>, <u>live in peace</u>; and the <u>God of love and peace</u> shall be <u>with you</u>. [Paul closes the letter swiftly. Notice the love that flows from these final words. Paul says, "brethren, farewell" (brothers take care). He makes no distinction between those who attacked him and those who support him. His aim is for them to "be perfect," to have spiritual maturity which comes from understanding the sound doctrine Christ gave him. He wants the believers to have "good comfort." <u>Comfort means</u> to strengthen the mind when depressed or enfeebled; to console; to give new vigor to the spirits; to cheer, or relieve from depression, or trouble. <u>Paul began the letter talking about "the God of all comfort" (1:3) and now he closes with comfort. God can comfort us through the word of God rightly divided and ministered by His Holy Spirit.</u> We can have comfort knowing who our apostle is. This way we can know that the 13 letters that all begin with his name are the instructions Christ wants the body of Christ to follow. He also signed each of his letters (2 Thess. 3:17). We are also comforted because we are saved from having to go through "Jacob's trouble" (Jer. 30:7; 1 Thess. 4:13-18). The rapture is exclusively found in Paul's letters. He wants them to be of "one mind" (Phil. 1:27, 2:2) which is another result of following Paul and the sound doctrine in his epistles using the King James Bible (1 Cor. 1:10; Phil. 3:16). Believers can "live in peace" because we have the blessed assurance that we will be raptured before the Tribulation (1 Thess. 1:10; Titus 2:13). We know we are secure and "complete in him" (Col. 2:10). We have the gracious life of Christ in us. When we follow our apostle and the doctrine of God's grace given to him, then we not only have joy and clarity, but also love and peace. Paul just said, that God is a God of love and peace (Gal. 2:20). We can have love and peace because it is a result of the life of Jesus in us, and having our minds reprogrammed by studying His word daily, to think like Him. This is how we have "the mind of Christ" (1 Cor. 2:16). We live our Christian lives by believing sound doctrine and copying Paul. "Those things, which ye have both learned, and received, and heard, and seen in me, <u>do</u>: and the God of peace shall be with you" (Phil. 4:9).] **12 Greet one another with an holy kiss.** [Members of the body of Christ, can have mutual faith, joy, and peace which helps us to be loving to one another as demonstrated by an affectionate greeting, a handshake, a hug, or kiss on the cheek.]

13 ¶ All the saints salute you. [Hello from the saints with Paul in Macedonia.]**14 The <u>grace of the Lord Jesus Christ</u>, and the <u>love of God</u>, and the <u>communion of the Holy Ghost</u>, <u>be with you all</u>. Amen.** [This verse contains the trinity. Paul graciously says "you all." His closing benediction is for the body of Christ believers. Who do you suppose the benediction in Numbers 6:22-27 is to? (Please look it up.) Paul wants all three members of the Godhead to be with them. The "grace of our Lord Jesus Christ" is His willingness to die in our place so He could dispense grace to us (SEE 8:9). The "love of God" is that God the Father gave His Son (Rom. 8:32). Because of the "communion of the Holy Ghost" we can commune with God, and one another. Paul wants believers to unite behind what Christ is doing through him. Paul through Christ was not weak to the Corinthians, but mighty.

Summary: Second Corinthians is a letter of reproof and rebuke of the believers in Corinth for not esteeming Paul as their one true apostle. Paul was comforted by God when Titus came and told him that many believers in Corinth did believe Christ's heavenly ministry to them through him (7:7). Comfort means to strengthen the mind when depressed or enfeebled; to console; to give new vigor to the spirits; to cheer, or relieve from depression, or trouble. <u>The answer to depression is not a pill, but sound doctrine.</u> Paul wants to give those who trust him ammunition to defend his true apostleship (5:12). For the sake of those who do not believe the glorious gospel of Christ which he and his coworkers preach, he vehemently defends his apostleship again (3:1-13:10). Paul has to do so because Satan wants to conceal this gospel (4:1-4). Satan had already infiltrated the church at Corinth and set up "false apostles" who masquerade as "ministers of righteousness" and "ministers of Christ" and teach false doctrine (11:13-15, 23). Paul wants to cast down those strong holds of Satan (10:5). Paul begs the Corinthians not to receive the grace of God in vain (6:1). He does not want them to yoke themselves to false preachers because then they will commit spiritual fornication (6:14-16). He pleads with them to separate from the false ministers (6:17 to 7:1). He begs them to receive him and his assistants (7:2). Paul's power is from God and Christ (4:7, 6:7, 12:9, 13:3, 4) who is speaking in him and not himself. Our treasure is the life of Christ in us (4:11). Paul wrote this strong, yet loving letter to correct them so they would not continue doing wrong (7:9, 10). His letter is not just about one person who committed physical fornication (Paul even wants him comforted, 2:7), but a warning to avoid spiritual fornication by following Christ's apostle (7:12, 12:21). Paul wants the Church to be like a chaste virgin (11:2) which he can present to Christ, not someone who has been with other men (false apostles). Paul should have been esteemed by them (12:11). He suffered many things for the sake of the ministry, did the signs of an apostle, and never took any money from them (12:11, 12). Some have "sinned already" by listening to the false apostles (12:21). Paul hopes that as their faith grows, that their hearts will be enlarged to trust his true apostleship from Christ to them (6:11, 13, 10:15). Paul knows that the best thing for the Corinthians is to believe the truth that Christ made him the "masterbuilder" (1 Cor. 3:10), to build the body of Christ in the dispensation of the grace. We should love this truth (2 Thess. 2:10). It comforts Paul, Titus, and Christ, when believers believe what the Lord Jesus has done for the body of Christ through Paul (7:7, 13).

Conclusion: Some believers were listening to the wrong authorities at Corinth. Paul wrote this letter because he wants the Corinthians to decide to follow him and the sound doctrine Christ has given him, not the false apostles and ministers before he arrives. Believers make decisions (1 Thess. 3:1, 4:3; Titus 3:12). We decide, judge, and determine what is more excellent, or the superior choice (Phil. 1:9, 10). What happens once we commit to obeying Christ's heavenly ministry to us through Paul? All our disobedience is punished and God gives us clarity (10:7). Now we can walk in wisdom redeeming the time. Before we were saved, we were not able to choose to do what was right, or to obey His word to us. We need to have spiritual godly edification from Paul's sound doctrine in order to live right. Wrong doctrine produces wrong thinking (confusion), resulting in wrong living and instability. We should not expose our minds to wrong doctrine, but avoid it. We need to renew our minds and walk in wisdom. Paul wants us to say the same thing, and have the same mind (1 Cor. 1:10; Phil. 3:16). We do this by putting sound doctrine in our minds, Romans to Philemon. It is not Bible doctrine, but sound doctrine that we need. It helps us to know what God is doing today, how we can be all that God has made us to be in Christ, and it strengthens and reprograms our minds. Sound doctrine not only gives us clarity, joy, and the comfort of the scriptures, but also makes us wiser. I believe this is the best medicine for Alzheimer's. We cannot live our Christian lives based on ignorance (Phil. 3:17; Rom. 16:17, 18). We can warn people to leave false religion, but we cannot force them to do it. They will find out later that it was a waste of time. We need to follow the apostle Christ from heaven gave us, Paul. God can comfort us through the word of God rightly divided and ministered by His Holy Spirit. This is how we can function correctly: by excellency of the power in us, the life of Jesus Christ living in and through us. "But we have this treasure in earthen vessels, that the excellency of the power may be of God, and not of us" (2 Cor. 4:7).]

Do You Know
Satan has
counterfeit apostles,
counterfeit bibles,
and
counterfeit churches
To preach a counterfeit gospel.

Galatians Commentary
Chapter 1 Paul marvels at the Galatians' quick fall for another gospel
1:1-5 Paul clearly states the gospel of Christ.
1:6-10 The reason for his letter is their soon removal from that gospel.
1:11-24 Paul defends his separate, distinct apostolic ministry from Christ.

Galatians 1:1 Paul, an apostle, (not of men, neither by man, but by Jesus Christ, and God the Father, who raised him from the dead;) [Paul is the one apostle "of the Gentiles" (Rom. 11:13) because Jesus Christ and the Father made him that. Paul begins all of his letters with his name. He vehemently denies being an apostle by men "not of men, neither by man" (see the other use of "neither" in 1:12, 17). God the Father raised Christ from the dead. Notice how Paul immediately begins by clearly declaring the gospel of Christ. He states the good news of Christ's resurrection. The Galatians needed the gospel spelled out because they did not fully appreciate the value of the power of the cross. The twelve knew Christ in His earthly ministry. Paul knew Him as Lord only in His resurrected, risen, glorified ministry from heaven. Paul had a distinct, divinely appointed apostleship, as the one apostle of the Gentiles (Rom. 11:13).] **2 And all the brethren which are <u>with me</u>, unto the churches of Galatia:** [Paul declares that others are with him who believe him so he is not alone in his doctrine. Of course Paul wants the Galatians to be "with him," too. He writes to "the churches of Galatia." The Galatians were Gaul's from France who had settled there. Galatia is a territory or province in central Asia minor which includes many of the cities Paul visited on his first apostolic journey (Iconium, Lystra, and Derbe). I believe that Paul wrote this letter shortly after his return to Antioch from the Jerusalem Council (where he received the "right hands of fellowship" (Gal. 2:9) in Acts 15:35. The date for the letter is probably around 52 AD.] **3 Grace be to you and peace from God the Father, and from our Lord Jesus Christ,** [God the Father and the Lord Jesus Christ are offering grace and peace in the dispensation of the grace of God (Eph. 3:2). In this dispensation God will save any sinner from eternal destruction if they simply believe what His Son has done. The gospel of our salvation is stated clearly and concisely: "how that Christ died for our sins according to the scriptures; And that he was buried, and that he rose again the third day according to the scriptures" (1 Cor. 15:3, 4). Christ came to save the guilty sinner. As long as a person thinks they have never done anything wrong they will not recognize their need for a Saviour. <u>We have to be bad enough to want to be saved.</u> This offer will not be available after the Rapture of the true believers, who are known as the Church, the body of Christ. After the Rapture, God will send "strong delusion" so that they will believe the lie (that Antichrist is Christ, 2 Thess. 2:11). God will resume His dealings with Israel, that He had postponed in Acts 7. (Acts 8 is part of the transition of the book of Acts). "Jacob's trouble" (Jer. 30:7) is also called Daniel's 70th Week and the Tribulation. It will begin after Antichrist signs a peace treaty with Israel that includes their offering of animal sacrifices at the temple in Jerusalem (Daniel 9:24-27).] **4 Who gave himself for our sins, that he might deliver us from this present evil world, according to the will of God and our Father:** [Paul immediately continues to give the rest of the gospel of Christ: how that Christ gave himself for our sins, so that we would be delivered from bondage to Satan and sin, in this present evil world (Eph. 2:1-3). Only Paul said Christ died for the sins of the Gentiles apart from having to go through Israel to be saved. Christ's blood completely paid for all our sins (Col. 1:14, 2:13). Paul honors Christ. But to have forgiveness we must believe what Christ did. Christ willingly gave Himself up for a sin-offering in order to deliver us from this present evil world. Christ did it according to the will of the Father's plan to redeem mankind. The phrase "gave himself," occurs five times in the Bible (Gal. 1:4, 2:20; Eph. 5:25; 1 Tim. 2:6; Titus 2:14). Jesus Christ had the faith to obey the Father's plan of salvation. We and all creation are suffering during this present time. Christ has not raptured us or renovated the heaven and the earth yet, but He will (Rom. 8:18-25). We are already delivered and seated with Christ in the heavenly places (Eph. 2:6). Christ's death for our sins was according to the will of God and our Father.] **5 To whom be glory for ever and ever. Amen.** [Paul praises God for His glorious plan to rescue believers and creation. He solved our sin problem. The Father's plan of redemption was that His Son would die in our place, so that sinners who believe what He did could be saved and receive His imputed righteousness (2 Cor. 5:21; Rom. 4:3, 22-25). This is how the Father can remain just while declaring the sinner justified (Rom. 3:21-28).]

6 ¶ I marvel that ye are so soon removed from <u>him</u> that called you into the grace of Christ unto <u>another gospel</u>: [Paul states the reason for the letter. He begins the letter abruptly with his amazement that the Galatians had so quickly done two things: (1) REMOVED THEMSELVES FROM BELIEVING CHRIST'S DISTINCTIVE MINISTRY TO THEM THROUGH PAUL, and (2) WELCOMING FALSE PREACHERS FROM JERUSALEM WHO ENTICED THEM TO FOLLOW THE LAW. Paul was astounded that the Galatians had so quickly left the truth that he had taught them. The "him" in this verse is Christ's heavenly ministry through Paul in the gospel (1 Thess. 2:4). It was Christ working through Paul that called them into the grace of being saved by faith in (2 Thess. 2:14). The Galatians had removed themselves from Christ working through Paul. He is shocked that his converts could so quickly allow themselves to be beguiled by false teachers of a perverted gospel (3:1-3). The Galatians had warmly welcomed Paul (4:15), but now they welcomed the false teachers. The Galatians had noticed that they were still sinning after they trusted Christ and thought that if they kept the law with its rules and regulations that they could live a life pleasing to God. The Judaizers did not recognize God's dispensational shift or His new apostle. The Judaizers taught that obeying the Law could control the flesh. The Law is God's perfect high standard that no mere human can keep. It is like a mirror that shows us the dirt on our face, but is powerless to clean it up. What happens when we see a sign that says "wet paint"? We touch it to see if the paint is wet. Our flesh wants to do what it is told not to do.] **7 Which is not another; but there be some that trouble you, and would pervert the <u>gospel of Christ</u>**. [The grace of Christ (v6) is synonymous with the gospel of Christ (v7; Rom. 5:19, 1 Cor. 9:18), the mystery Christ gave to Paul. Some false teachers from Jerusalem had come and deceived the believers in Galatia by preaching the gospel of the kingdom. It was "not another gospel" this gospel had been valid in a previous dispensation. But after the Jerusalem Council only Paul's gospel was valid. The false teachers agreed that salvation was of Christ, but they said that works of the law were also necessary (Acts 15:1). These false teachers <u>perverted</u> the gospel because they added the keeping of the Law to Christ's finished work of the cross. They mixed the law with the grace of Christ. Some "little flock" Jews who did not recognize Paul's ministry had enticed Gentiles to add the keeping of the Jewish Mosaic system to their faith in Christ are called "Judaisers." Satan's tactic was not to deny the gospel, but to add <u>the keeping of the Law to Christ's finished work</u>. What exactly did the other gospel include? The Galatians had been idol-worshippers, now they tried to be right in God's eyes by keeping the law. Switching to the Law now that they had been set free from it by God's grace, was to return to idolatry. The Law was a weak and beggarly way to try to be saved because no one could keep it, except Christ. (There was nothing wrong with God's perfect Law, but with the people's flesh or sin nature that was unable to keep it.) The Law could not save anyone, only Christ can save sinners. <u>They had begun to keep the Jewish Sabbath days, the priesthood, dietary laws, and holy day (4:8-11, 21). They were even getting circumcised! How foolish! They had fallen from grace by putting themselves back under the law (5:2-4). To be circumcised in this dispensation is a sign of unbelief</u> (6:12, 13). They were saved by faith and had Christ's imputed righteousness and should live by faith. People want to do something in their flesh, but they had His Spirit in them that operates through His word rightly divided. Christ doesn't want our old lives, who we were in Adam before salvation. God is not asking us to live the Christian life. In fact, we can't live it. God is asking that He might live His life through us. We are to help others to be reconciled to God through the gospel and trust in what Christ alone has done for them (1 Cor. 15:3, 4; 2 Cor. 5:18-21). We are to work with God to do His will. God's will is for "all men to be saved, and to come unto the knowledge of the truth" (1 Tim. 2:4). All saints are to follow Paul to follow Christ (1 Cor. 11:1).] **8 But though we, or an angel from heaven, preach any other gospel unto you than that which <u>we have preached unto you</u>, let him be accursed**. [Paul is angry; he is hot under the collar. He is also worried about his convert's spiritual welfare. Only the gospel Paul preached is valid today. Paul says that if anyone, even he and his co-workers, preach ANY OTHER GOSPEL than the one that you have already received from us, let him be <u>accursed</u> (anathema), damned, "cut off" or "put out" from his people or don't listen to him (Gen. 17:14; 1 Cor. 16:22; 5:10). Under the law, those who tried to tell others to worship another God were stoned to death (Deut. 13:6-11). The Galatians were not living according to the truth that Christ gave to Paul. The Judaizers were not teaching the truth; <u>so stop listening to them!</u> <u>Paul's "my gospel" is imputed righteousness of Christ by faith</u>. We are saved by faith (justification), and we live by faith (sanctification).] **9 As we said before, so say I now again, If any man preach <u>any other gospel unto you than that ye have received</u>, let him be accursed**. [For emphasis and to make sure they heard him, Paul repeats his warning (or curse) of doomed to destruction, or expulsion from the assembly. His vehement language and abruptness reveal his anger and fear over their spiritual welfare. The gospel of Christ that Paul gave to them was not only how to be saved, but included all Paul's doctrine on how to live for God (their sanctification). However, many believers are surprised when they discover that after they are saved the sin nature still resides in their mortal bodies. There is a war inside every believer between the flesh and the Spirit. This war forces us to mature and to decide moment by moment to do what is right. Our flesh did not get saved when we did. Our sin nature resides in our body, and we need our body to be a vehicle for our inner man (our soul and Spirit) until we get our immortal, glorified bodies (1 Cor. 15:51-54; Phil. 3:21).]

10 ¶ For do I now persuade men, or God? or do I seek to please men? for if I yet pleased men, I should not be the servant of Christ. [God knows what the truth is, Paul is seeking to persuade men of the truth, but not to win favor with them. His motive is not to be a man-pleaser, but a Christ-server.] **11 But I certify you, brethren, that the gospel which was preached of me is not after man**. [Paul formally confirms or attests to the fact that the gospel (the imputed righteousness of Christ, justification by faith) that he preaches was directly from Christ, and was not invented by a man. The gospel that saved them was not after man, "that gospel" was by direct revelation from Jesus Christ (2:2).] **12 For I neither received it of man, neither was I taught it, but by the revelation of Jesus Christ**. [Paul received "that gospel" independently, personally, and directly from the Lord Jesus Christ, not from the Twelve or from any other man.] **13 For ye have heard of my conversation in time past in the Jews' religion, how that**

beyond measure I persecuted the church of God, and wasted it: [I will mention three and you can guess which one is mentioned in verse 13: (1) "the church in the wilderness" (Acts 7:38), (2) "upon this rock I will build my church" (Matt. 18:16), and (3) "he is the head of the body, the church" (Col. 1:18). Which one is that church? It was (2). Paul in time past (before the body of Christ began in Acts 9), hated and persecuted the church of God (Peter and his group) who believed Christ would reign in His earthly kingdom (Acts 8:1-4; 9:1-2, 26:9-11; 1 Cor. 15:8, 9).]

14 And profited in the Jews' religion above many my equals in mine own nation, being more exceedingly zealous of the traditions of my fathers. [Paul profited (financially and in status) in the Jews' religion more than other Pharisees. Paul participated in the stoning of Stephen because he thought he was serving God (John 16:2; Deut. 13:6-11; Acts 7:58). Paul admits that he was following a religion, that God had begun, but that had deteriorated to the corrupt traditions of men.] **15 But when it pleased God, who separated me from my mother's womb, and called me by his grace,** [Without being prophesied in the Bible, God separated Paul from his mother's womb. The "mother's womb" is the nation of Israel (Gen. 12:1-3; Isa. 44:24, 49:1-5). Jesus of Nazareth dramatically saved Paul on the road to Damascus in Acts 9 (Acts 9:3-20, 22:1-16, 26:9-18). Paul was NOT saved by the gospel by the kingdom. Paul was uniquely saved, unlike anyone else while the gospel of the kingdom was still being preached. Many did not know that God had already temporarily set Israel aside in Acts 7 (for nearly 2,000 years so far). But "when it pleased God," the glorified risen Christ surprised everyone when He appeared to Paul on that road (including Satan since Paul's salvation was a completely un-prophesied mystery, 1 Cor. 2:6-8). Christ interrupted prophecy and inserted the mystery. Paul was the first into the body of Christ (1 Tim. 1:16). Paul was born out of due time, a premature birth from his Mother Israel (1 Cor. 15:8). Paul is the "due time testifier" of all that Christ accomplished by the cross (Acts 20:21; Titus 1:3; Rom. 3:26). Paul (Saul of Tarsus) was a leader during the stoning of Stephen (Acts 7:58). The stoning of the Holy Ghost filled Stephen was the unforgivable blasphemy of the Holy Ghost that Christ spoke about (Matt. 12:31, 32). God saved Paul by His grace and began a new dispensation of grace in which that blasphemy could be forgiven (1 Tim. 1:13). Paul was radically changed and forsook Judaism for the excellency of knowing Christ (Phil. 3:7-8).] **16 To reveal his Son in me, that I might preach him among the heathen; immediately I conferred not with flesh and blood**: [Paul knew that Christ indwelt him and all believers. (Gal. 2:20; 2 Cor. 4:7, 11). Having Christ's life in us means we have His imputed righteousness. Having His imputed righteousness is how we are "complete in him" (Col. 2:10). We are able to come before the Father because of His Son's imputed righteousness. This is how we are "accepted in the beloved" (Eph. 1:6). For us to say, "I need to also cut off a little piece of my foreskin, get wet, confess my sins, or keep the Sabbath" is to not understand the power of the cross. To say that we need to add anything to His cross-work is to insult God and to make our salvation void, of none effect (Rom. 4:5, 14). Christ sent Paul to preach to all unsaved heathen, both Jews and Gentiles (3:28; Eph. 3:6). Paul did not consult with a human upon his salvation.] **17 Neither went I up to Jerusalem to them which were apostles before me; but I went into Arabia, and returned again unto Damascus**. [God did everything possible to keep Paul separate from the Twelve (1 Cor. 15:5). Paul went to Arabia, most likely to mount Sinai there (4:25), to be alone with God, and learn about the mysteries of Christ. Paul is the one apostle to the one body of Christ. While the twelve will judge the twelve tribes of Israel (Matt. 19:28).] **18 Then after three years I went up to Jerusalem to see Peter, and abode with him fifteen days**. [Paul was in Damascus and Arabia for a total of about three years, before he visited Peter in Jerusalem for fifteen days. He preached Christ as the Son of God in Damascus, but had to escape the city by being let down by the wall in a basket (Acts 9:20-25). He went to Jerusalem and thanks to Barnabas he was able to visit Peter and met James. Paul had to get out of Jerusalem because the Jews wanted to kill him (Acts 9:26-30).] **19 But other of the apostles saw I none, save James the Lord's brother**. [Paul did not see any of the other apostles at that time, but he did see James the Lord's half-brother. They had the same mother but different fathers. Christ's Father was the Holy Ghost (Luke 1:35).] **20 Now the things which I write unto you, behold, before God, I lie not**. [Paul affirms that all the things that he is writing to them is the truth, before God, he is not lying.] **21 Afterwards I came into the regions of Syria and Cilicia**; [After that visit he went to Syria, and his home town Tarsus in Cilicia where he probably preached the gospel and gave his testimony to family and friends.] **22 And was unknown by face unto the churches of Judaea which were in Christ**: [But to the Messianic Judaism churches in Judaea who were "in Christ" as a result of trusting Him to be the Son of God to sit on David's throne, the gospel of the kingdom (John 17:23, Luke 9:2; Acts 2:38) didn't know what Paul looked like.] **23 But they had heard only, That <u>he which persecuted us in times past now preacheth the faith which once he destroyed</u>**. [They only heard that he who had persecuted the church in the past now preached the faith which he once destroyed. This does not mean that He preached the gospel of the kingdom because Christ gave Paul a different gospel. The gospel of the kingdom says that the kingdom of God was at hand, repent and believe that Jesus Christ is the Messiah, and prove your faith by being water baptized and anointed with oil (Mark 1:14, 15; Acts 2:38). Paul preached the "gospel of God" which had things in common with Peter's group of believers because Christ is the Redeemer for both Israel and the body of Christ and the Son of God of the seed of David for both (Gen. 3:15; Acts 9:20, 18:4, 5; Rom. 1:1-4; 2 Tim. 2:8). It is certain that Paul recognized that Jesus of Nazareth was the Nation of Israel's true Messiah. Paul preached justification by faith in Antioch of Pisidia (Acts 13:39).] **24 And they glorified God in me**. [The Jewish believing remnant (Peter's group), glorified God because he had saved His and their worst enemy. Paul calls Peter's group the "Israel of God" since they will inherit the kingdom on earth (Gal. 6:16, Luke 12:32; Matt. 19:28, 21:43). We can call Peter's group the kingdom on earth church. We learn that our destiny is in the heavens (2 Cor. 5:1). In chapter 2, we will learn that Christ gave Paul a different ministry, message, and audience than Peter.]

Gal. 1:12 'For I neither received it (gospel of grace) from man, neither was I taught it, but by the revelation of Jesus Christ.' And Him from heaven ascended to glory.

Chapter 2 Paul communicates his gospel at the Jerusalem Council.
2:1-10 Paul's gospel was approved by the apostles in Jerusalem.
2:11-21 The truth of Paul's gospel was defended before Peter.

2:1 Then fourteen years after I went up again to Jerusalem with Barnabas, and took Titus with me also. [Paul went up to the Jerusalem Council fourteen years after that fifteen-day visit with Peter (three years after his conversion) which adds up to seventeen years. I believe Christ died in AD 33 or 34, and that Paul was saved one year later shortly after the stoning of Stephen (in AD 35). God gave Israel a one-year extension of mercy to receive the prophesied kingdom because Christ pleaded on the cross for the Father to forgive them and before that (Luke 23:34, 13:6-9). The Father did forgive them. Sam Gerhardt has an outstanding timeline of Paul's ministry which is printed by permission in *Romans: A Concise Commentary* by Marianne Manley (available on Amazon). This timeline shows the five times Paul went to Jerusalem after his conversion. (Paul doesn't mention his visit to Jerusalem in Acts 18:22) So if we add 17 to 35 we get 52. In other words, it was then AD 52. Furthermore, it is interesting to note that the apostles in Jerusalem expected Christ's Second coming before that (2 Peter 3:4). Of course the reason they sold all their property after Pentecost was because they expected to go through the Jacob's trouble, the Tribulation (Jer. 30:7; Luke 12:33; Acts 2:45, 4:35). So, for seventeen years Paul had very little contact with the twelve apostles.] **2 And I went up by revelation, and communicated unto them that gospel which I preach among the Gentiles, but privately to them which were of reputation, lest by any means I should run, or had run, in vain**. [Paul went to Jerusalem by direct revelation from Christ. He was not asked to come there by the Jerusalem apostles. Paul's mission from Christ was to successfully communicate information with the leaders in Jerusalem that they did not know. He met privately so that the "false brethren" could not argue against him. Paul didn't want the false brethren to hinder his communication and foil his mission, making his trip useless (vain). Paul was preaching "that gospel" which is the imputed righteousness of Christ or justification by faith in what Christ alone had done on Calvary (1 Cor. 15:3, 4). In other words, works such as physical circumcision was not necessary for salvation in this dispensation (Eph. 2:8, 9). He wants those apostles to understand the gospel Christ gave him and that God had begun something new. Paul communicated: that means he made the leaders in Jerusalem understand Christ's new message to the Gentiles through him. Circle "communicated" in verse 2, "saw" in verse 7, and "perceived" in verse 9. He went to inform them of all that God was doing at this current time, namely: His great dispensational shift, His new apostle, and Christ's new ministry through him! What was the information Paul shared? Christ from heaven had a new and different message to a new group of believers that would live in heaven. Many in Jerusalem were asking the little flock Where is the promise of his coming?" (2 Peter 3:4). The leaders in Jerusalem did not know what the delay in Christ's Second Coming was.] **3 But neither Titus, who was with me, being a Greek, was compelled to be circumcised**: [Paul brought along a young <u>uncircumcised</u> Greek preacher Titus, as "exhibit A" and he was not forced to be circumcised. <u>If the apostles in Jerusalem did not compel Titus to be circumcised, that meant that Gentiles in the new dispensation do not need to be circumcised.</u>] **4 And that because of false brethren unawares brought in, who came in privily to spy out our liberty which we have in Christ Jesus, that they might bring us into bondage**: ["False brethren" had come in privately to secretly spy out the liberty that they had in Christ. They had most likely seen that Titus was not circumcised in the public bath houses. Our liberty in Christ is not having to do the works of the law (such as circumcision). The body of Christ believers are blessed "up front" (Eph. 1:3, 6; Col. 2:10). The law says do and be blessed; grace says you are blessed now do. The law functions by <u>fear of punishment</u>, and the <u>if-then principle</u> (Ex. 19:5, 6). Love is the biggest motivator in grace as we live by faith (2 Cor. 5:7, 14). Under the law, proselytes to Judaism, did get circumcised when they converted to Judaism (Gen. 17:10-14). Proselytes believed that Israel's God was the true God and demonstrated their faith by doing the same things as the Jews. In Esther 8:17 we read that many Gentiles became Jews. But in this new dispensation, it is a sign of unbelief to get circumcised because that is saying that what Christ did for us was not enough.] **5 To whom we gave place by subjection, no, not for an hour; that the truth of the gospel might continue with you.** [Paul and his companions stood their ground against the false brethren. Not for an hour did they agree that circumcision was necessary for salvation, or sanctification. Works of the law do not save a person, nor make a person righteous (Titus 3:5). In fact, Paul proved in Romans 7:8 that our sinful flesh is <u>energized</u> by trying to keep the law. The Law shows us how exceedingly sinful we are which leads to self-condemnation and despair. Paul wants their glorious liberty to continue. That glorious liberty is that Christ has done everything to save us and we cannot add to that.] **6 But of these who seemed to be somewhat, (whatsoever they were, it maketh no matter to me: God accepteth no man's person:) for they who seemed to be somewhat in conference added nothing to me**: [Paul says that the men of reputation (James, Peter, and John) added nothing to the information Paul shared with them. God is not impressed with humans He is impressed by what His Son has done. No man is anything because Christ did it all. Paul knew every man inherited the sin nature, and that only Christ was perfect.] **7 But <u>contrariwise</u>, when they <u>saw</u> that the <u>gospel of the uncircumcision</u> was committed unto <u>me</u>, as the <u>gospel of the circumcision</u> was unto <u>Peter</u>;** [On the contrary, Paul added to their knowledge, because he told them about the mystery. How many gospels are

223

in this verse? Before you answer that, let me ask you another question: Is circumcision and uncircumcision two different things? Your answer should be: "yes, they are different, and there are two different gospels in verse 7, one committed to Paul and one committed to Peter. The gospel of the uncircumcision is what Paul preached to the Gentiles (Christ crucified for their sins, and risen again. No works or circumcision required). The gospel of the circumcision is what Peter preached to Israel on Pentecost. Repent, (believe that the name of your Messiah is Jesus of Nazareth. Circumcision is required.) be baptized; and you will receive remission of sins and the Holy Ghost to empower you to be part of His royal priesthood in the earthly kingdom (Acts 2:38, 4:10-12; 1 Peter 2:6-10). God gave Abraham and his descendants the covenants and the token of circumcision (Gen. 17:10). Notice that the leaders in Jerusalem "saw" the truth of God's dispensational change. God had let Peter know that He had decided to change His dealings with mankind and the dietary law (Acts 10:15, 28 10, 11:8, 9). When God does something twice He establishes it, when He does something three times it is very important. The sheet full of clean and unclean animals descended three times. Peter told Cornelius, "Ye know how that it is an unlawful thing for a man that is a Jew to keep company, or come unto one of another nation; but God hath shewed me that I should not call any man common or unclean" (Acts 10:28). Peter remembered this at the Jerusalem Council saying that there is no difference between Jews and Gentiles and that both are saved by faith (Acts 15:7-11). God made the nation of Israel a vessel of honor (Deut. 7:6) during prophecy. He was not unrighteous to temporarily make the nation (of the same lump) a vessel of dishonor during the mystery (Rom. 9:14, 21). God will make the nation a vessel of honor again after the fullness of the Gentiles. We are living during the nation of Israel's spiritual blindness. However, God is not finished with Israel and will resume prophecy, once He is finished with the mystery (Rom. 11:25, 26). During the dispensation of grace, the nation of Israel is in apostasy and do not recognize Jesus of Nazareth as their King. Paul and Barnabas also declared the "miracles and wonders God had wrought among the Gentiles by them" (Acts 15:12). We know that the Jews require a sign (1 Cor. 1:22). At the end of the Jerusalem Council (Acts 15:1-35) it was determined that: (1) God is visiting the Gentiles to take out of them "a people for his name" (Acts 15:14). (2) Gentiles are not under the law and do not need to be circumcised (Acts 15:1, 24). (3) Paul was the apostle of the Gentiles (Gal. 2:9). (4) The prophetic program will resume after God is done forming that Gentile group (Acts 15:16; See also, Rom. 11:25, 26).] **8 (For he that wrought effectually in Peter to the apostleship of the circumcision, the same was mighty in me toward the Gentiles:)** [Christ, in His earthly ministry, gave Peter his authority and the holy Spirit allowed many to be saved by his preaching. Christ, in His ministry from heaven, gave Paul his authority and the holy Spirit saved many by his preaching. <u>The holy Spirit validated Paul's apostleship by having him repeat the signs Peter did during the Acts period</u>. Paul water baptized converts just like Peter had. Peter spoke in tongues and so did Paul. Peter went to the Jews first and so did Paul. Peter healed the sick and raised Dorcas from the dead, Paul also healed the sick and raised Eutychus from the dead.] **9 And when James, Cephas, and John, who seemed to be pillars,_perceived the grace that was given unto me, they gave to me and Barnabas the right hands of fellowship; that we should go unto the heathen, and they unto the circumcision**. [James, Peter, and John seemed to be pillars in Jerusalem but their authority did not impress Paul, nor was he subject to them. But when they "perceived" that God had delayed his coming (interrupted or paused prophecy, Acts 15:14-16) and had begun a new dispensation, with a new apostle, and a new message, to a new audience (Gentiles), using a new operating system (grace, not the law), then they gave their approval by shaking hands on it. Paul told the apostles at the council that God had shown grace to him, a blasphemer and made him His apostle to the Gentiles. God gave the mystery of the "dispensation of grace" to Paul. God did not make His hidden wisdom known before that (Eph. 3:2, 5, 7). Because if God had let the mystery be known Satan would not have allowed Christ to be crucified (1 Cor. 2:6-8). Satan did not know that Christ reclaimed not only the earth, but heaven also until Paul. <u>Satan lost both realms. The apostles in Jerusalem "loosed" themselves from carrying out their commission and concentrated on caring for the existing believing remnant until they died out in the first century. Paul went to the "heathen" all lost Jews and Gentiles. Perhaps Peter had realized during Paul's fifteen-day visit that he would not lead the little flock into the kingdom</u>, so he let James take over. Gal. 2:6-9 is a great section of scripture to see the mystery and so is Eph. 3:1-9 and Col. 1:24-27.] **10 Only they would that we should remember the poor; the same which I also was forward to do**. [<u>Paul was eager to remember the poor in Jerusalem and he brought them financial contributions on several occasions</u>. Peter was in prison during Paul's second visit to Jerusalem to deliver money with Barnabas (Acts 11:30, 12:25; Rom. 15:25, 26). Paul made a total of five visits to Jerusalem after his conversion. <u>The believing remnant of Israel in Jerusalem were poor because they believed that the kingdom and, therefore God's wrath (Jacob's trouble, the Tribulation) were at hand</u>. So they would not be able to buy and sell since they would not take the "mark of the Beast" (Luke 12:33, Acts 2:44, 4:32; Rev. 13:18).] **11 But when Peter was come to Antioch, I withstood him to the face, because he was to be blamed. 12 For before that certain came from James, he did eat with the Gentiles: but when they were come, he withdrew and separated himself, fearing them which were of the circumcision**. [Paul recounts an incident during Peter's visit to Antioch. <u>It is significant that Peter left Jerusalem and traveled to Antioch after the Jerusalem Council. Peter had</u>

225

understood through Paul that his gospel of the kingdom was postponed. In Antioch, Peter was sitting and eating with the Gentiles just like Paul, because he "saw" and "perceived" that the middle wall of partition was no longer up. God had a middle wall of partition between Israel and all other nations. Israel was above the other nations (Deut. 7:6, 26:19, 28:13). They had the token of circumcision (Gen. 17:10) and then the Law was added through Moses to further the distinction, by dietary and other laws. God had showed Peter, in Acts 10, with the sheet full of clean and unclean animals let down from heaven three times that the Jewish dietary laws were no longer in effect because God had changed how He was doing things. In Acts 15:7-11, Peter said that God decided that he (Peter) should preach to the Gentiles, and he did to the household of Cornelius. God showed Peter that He had changed His dealings with mankind. God was not enforcing the dietary laws that separated Israel from other nations now so Peter should not call any man "common or unclean" (Acts 10:28). Those Gentiles believed Peter's gospel and received the Holy Ghost. God did not put a difference between Jews and Gentiles. At the council Peter said, "why should we demand the Gentiles to follow the law that we cannot follow?" We believe that "through the grace of the Lord Jesus Christ we shall be saved, even as they" (Acts 15:10, 11). All people (regardless of dispensation) are saved by God's grace through faith, and not by works (Rom. 3:29-31; Rom. 11:6; Heb. 11:6). But the nation of Israel is required to have their faith accompanied by works, such as water baptism and circumcision (Mark 16:16; James 2:24). The kingdom on earth church had to believe that the name of their Messiah and King was Jesus of Nazareth. The body of Christ must believe the simple message: that Christ died for our sins, was buried, and rose again the third day (1 Cor. 15:3, 4). Gentiles are saved differently in mystery. Gentiles today do not need to go through Israel to be saved, but are saved apart from Israel and the law, by direct faith in what Christ alone has done. Paul never said that the body of Christ would enter the kingdom on earth, but that we would live "eternal in the heavens" (2 Cor. 5:1).] **13 And the other Jews dissembled likewise with him; insomuch that Barnabas also was carried away with their dissimulation**. [Dissimulation means hiding under a false appearance; false pretension; hypocrisy; to conceal the real opinion or purpose. Peter, the other Jews, and even Barnabas saw the men of James come and decided to eat apart from the Gentiles at their own table. James, who probably had a very strong personality, seemed to have understood the dispensational change (Acts 15:14-16), but then he seemed to have lost sight of that fact and had Paul do many Jewish things in Acts 21. (Law keeping is consistent with the gospel of the kingdom, but not the gospel of Christ).] **14 But when I saw that they walked not uprightly according to the truth of the gospel, I said unto Peter before them all, If thou, being a Jew, livest after the manner of Gentiles, and not as do the Jews, why compellest thou the Gentiles**

to live as do the Jews? [Peter had admitted that he could not keep the law (Acts 15:10). When Paul saw that Peter and the others were not walking according to the truth that God had (1) changed dispensations; (2) broken down the middle wall of partition; (3) made no difference between Jew and Gentile; (4) and no longer enforced Israel's favored nation status, . . . then, Paul rebuked Peter. Paul basically said something like this to Peter, "God has showed you several times by your vision and by me that He has begun a new dispensation as evidenced by Him not enforcing the dietary laws now, because the nation of Israel fell (Rom. 11:11-13). You know that no human can keep the law (Acts 15:10) so why are you forcing the Gentiles to keep the law when it is no longer in effect? Do you think you will be commended by God (1 Cor. 8:8) if you avoid eating pork chops and sit apart from the Gentiles? Are you going to make the Gentiles avoid the Pepperoni on their Pizzas? If you say that the dietary laws are in effect when God has said they are not, then you are going against what God says He is doing now. That is not walking upright according to the truth." Please notice that Peter does not say that he is the one in authority. Paul mentions the middle wall of partition in Eph. 2:14 (See Eph. 2:11-18). This does NOT mean that the Twelve are in the body of Christ. I have repeatedly said that they will judge the nation of Israel in the earthly kingdom (Matt. 19:28). It is the individual Jews and Gentiles in this dispensation that form the one body (Gal. 3:28).] **15 We who are Jews by nature, and not sinners of the Gentiles**, [Paul says that Peter and he are Jews by birth and are not sinners like the Gentiles (idol-worshippers).] **16 Knowing that a man is not justified by the works of the law, but by the <u>faith of Jesus Christ</u>, even we have <u>believed in Jesus Christ</u>, that we might be <u>justified by the faith of Christ</u>, and not by the works of the law: for by the works of the law shall no flesh be justified**. [Paul tells Peter we know that a man is not justified by the works of the law, but <u>we are justified by our faith in the faith of Jesus, the only One who kept the law perfectly. We receive Christ's imputed righteousness by faith in what Christ has done (1 Cor. 15:3, 4). Keeping the law could never justify anyone (Rom. 3:19, 20, 21, 25, 26). The modern bibles leave out the word "of" and replace it with "in" putting the emphasis of faith on the believer, instead of on Christ. The King James Bible exalts the Lord Jesus Christ more than any other English Bible. Remember, Jesus is the Redeemer for both heaven and earth believers.</u> No one knew that the household of God was a duplex before Paul. We have the same foundation which is Christ, but one side is "prophecy" (Christ ministry on earth), and the other side is "mystery" (Christ ministry from heaven). Believers in both groups put their faith in Christ's faith. It cost God a lot to redeem us by His blood. In *God's Secret* there is an excellent picture of the duplex by Paul Sadler on page 71. When Paul says "but now" that often indicates the great dispensational shift; here are a few examples (Rom. 3:21; Eph. 2:13; Gal. 4:9; Col. 1:26).] **17 But if,**

while we seek to be justified by Christ, we ourselves also are found sinners, is therefore Christ the minister of sin? God forbid. [If while we seek to be justified by Christ, we sin by not upholding the truth of what God says, is Christ the minister of sin? God forbid it. (We cannot please God in our flesh.)]**18 For if I build again the things which I destroyed, I make myself a transgressor.** [Notice Paul's use of "I" statements. If I think I can be justified by keeping the Law, I make myself a transgressor. If my actions say that the middle wall of partition is still up (that His dietary laws are still in effect) and that His nation Israel is separate and favored above other people in this present dispensation, then I deny the truth of what God says is doing now. That is sinful pretending.] **19 For I through the law am <u>dead to the law, that I might live unto God</u>**. [The law no longer has any influence over Paul so he can live unto God. <u>Paul is not trying to keep the law to be right with God. Paul has faith in Christ's faith</u>. Christ redeemed us through the sacrificial system. He also kept the law perfectly. He never sinned in thought, word, or deed. We identified with His death on the cross. We died to the law that condemned us and were crucified with Christ, so now we are able to live unto God (Rom. 8:10). We identified with Christ's crucifixion and resurrection and were spiritually baptized (identification) into Christ at salvation. We didn't feel this happening but we know it is true because God says so in His word. Our sin nature was crucified with Christ when we believed. The "old man" or "flesh" the "sin nature" cannot be made over or improved. <u>The "old man" is who we were in Adam before we were saved</u>. It must be killed and reckoned dead. We have a new divine nature; Christ lives in us. The "new man" is Christ "formed" in the believer (4:19; Col. 1:27). We are dead to the law, so that we might live unto Christ.] **20 I** [old man] **<u>am crucified with Christ: nevertheless I</u>** [new man] **<u>live; yet not I, but Christ liveth in me: and the life</u>** [new life] **<u>which I now live in the flesh I live by the faith of the Son of God, who loved me, and gave himself for me</u>**. [When I believed my <u>old man</u> was crucified with Christ who bore my sin and I received the life of Christ, the Son of God, in me (Rom. 6:3-10). We are justified by our faith in His faith, and live by His faith having received His imputed righteousness. We have been bought with a price, we are not our own, so we can let Him live His life through us.] **21 <u>I do not frustrate the grace of God: for if righteousness come by the law, then Christ is dead in vain</u>**. [We frustrate the grace of God if we believe keeping the law can save us or sanctify us. Christ saved us through the sacrificial system, not the law. We received the life of Christ in us (2:20) so we have His righteousness. Christ is "the resurrection and the life" (John 11:25) and we have Him in us; His "divine nature." <u>We frustrate the grace of God if we build the middle wall of partition again (make a difference between Jews and the Gentiles)</u>. Paul clearly said the wall is down now. "For he is our peace, who hath made both one, and hath <u>broken down the middle wall of partition between</u>

us; Having abolished in his flesh the enmity, even the law of commandments contained in ordinances; for to make in himself of twain one new man, so making peace; And that he might reconcile both unto God in one body by the cross, having slain the enmity thereby: And came and preached peace to you which were afar off [the Gentiles], and to them that were nigh [the Jews]. For through him we both have access by one Spirit unto the Father" (Eph. 2:14-18). There is no middle wall of partition today. God is not dealing with nations today, but with individuals. Individual Jews and Gentiles who believe the gospel of Christ (1 Cor. 15:3, 4) become members of the body of Christ (Gal. 3:28) and receive eternal life. If we think we can be justified by keeping the law, then we frustrate the grace of God because we build the middle wall of partition again (5:4; Titus 3:5; Phil. 3:9). Because if we could have received righteousness by keeping the law, Christ would have died for no reason. Peter, the Jews, and Barnabas were pretending by their actions that they didn't know about the great dispensational shift (the mystery) that God had ushered in with Paul. But they did! Peter and the other Jews were putting up a fake front for the men who came from James. They denied the truth that God is forming the body of Christ in the dispensation of grace. So now Paul says "O foolish Galatians" meaning that they are displaying the same "dissimulation" and denying the truth of the new Gentile opportunity to be saved apart from going through Israel. Please note that Paul does not begin a new paragraph until 3:7, so he is continuing in this thought. We can trust the punctuation in the King James Bible.]

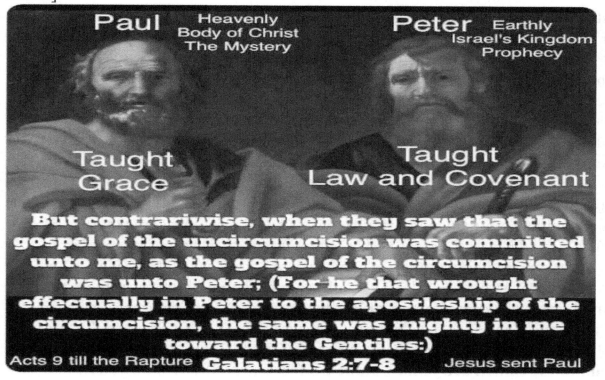

229

Chapter 3 After salvation the Schoolmaster is no longer needed
3:1-5 The Spirit's ministry of Christ's gospel to Paul in Galatia.
3:6-9 The illustration of Abraham's imputed righteousness.
3:10-16 Christ bore the curse of the law so believers could receive His Spirit.
3:17-22 The Law was added to Promise until the Seed came who kept the Law
3:23-29 After faith is come the schoolmaster is not needed, we live by faith.

3:1 O foolish Galatians, who hath bewitched you, that ye should not obey the truth, before whose eyes Jesus Christ hath been evidently set forth, crucified among you? [Paul exclaims with anguish in his voice, "O foolish Galatians, who has bewitched you, that ye should not obey the truth." They were dissembling just like Peter (2:13), there is no middle wall of partition today. Paul was worried. Not only was the purity of their conduct in jeopardy, but also the purity of doctrine he preached by the Spirit. Paul preached Christ crucified (1 Cor. 1:17, 18), not obedience to the Law, and he painted a vivid word picture of Christ's labor on the cross and resurrection. Who was persuading them to leave the truth that Paul taught them and put them under the law? The Galatians believed and were saved. Their changed lives were evidence of the Spirit of Christ living in them. "But ye are not in the flesh, but in the Spirit, if so be that the Spirit of God dwell in you. Now if any man have not the Spirit of Christ, he is none of his" (Rom. 8:9). The Galatians received salvation by the hearing of faith. "So then faith cometh by hearing, and hearing by the word of God" (Rom. 10:17). They were saved by trusting the word of God, not by obeying the Law. "In whom ye also trusted, after that ye heard the word of truth, the gospel of your salvation: in whom also after that ye believed, ye were sealed with that holy Spirit of promise" (Eph. 1:13). Although all scripture is for our learning, in the dispensation of grace people are saved by hearing the word of God that is "to us" and "about us," Romans to Philemon. It is possible for a person not to be saved because they have never heard Paul's letters. For example, the Catholics (and other denominations) concentrate on Peter and Christ's earthly ministry in the four gospels, not Paul. In Romans 16:25, 26 we learn that Paul received the revelation of the mystery that had been kept secret since the world began, but now is made known. In 2 Tim. 3:16 we learn that "all scripture is profitable." Every chapter in Galatians points to the cross (1:1, 4, 2:16, 20, 3:1, 22, 4:5, 5:11, 6:14). This life is all about where we spend eternity. The most important thing in life is to make sure we are saved. God, who is love, is also just and must judge sin.] **2 This only would I learn of you, Received ye the Spirit by the works of the law, or by the hearing of faith?** [What is the answer to Paul's question? Yes, they had trusted what Christ did and received the Spirit (Eph. 1:13); they were saved by the hearing of faith.] **3 Are ye so foolish? having begun in the Spirit, are ye now made perfect by the flesh?** [Are you so foolish to think that once you are saved by faith, you need to go back to the law for your sanctification (their spiritual growth, conduct, daily living for God)? They were saved because Paul by the Spirit, preached the truth to them. For them to go back to the law after all the Spirit had done for them was to act like fools.] **4 Have ye suffered so many things in vain? if it be yet in vain.** [They had suffered for their faith and were persecuted by those who believed differently, mainly unbelieving Jews. Paul does not want them to have suffered in vain, and is concerned that they have compromised themselves by giving into and following the Judaizers. (Those who insist that Gentiles, who believe Christ, <u>also</u> need to obey the Mosaic Laws.)] **5 <u>He therefore that ministereth to you the Spirit, and worketh miracles among you, doeth he it by the works of the law, or by the hearing of faith</u>?** [The "He" was the Spirit of God ministered by Paul and the other believing elders at Galatia. Paul and the believers had "sign gifts" by the Spirit during the Acts period, before Christ's complete revelation of the mystery was fully given to Paul (1 Cor. 13:8-13). In its infancy, God temporarily gave the Church ministers spiritual gifts (Eph. 4:11-16). Were the spiritual gifts for their edification done by the works of the law, or the hearing of faith? It was by faith. The "law of the Spirit of life in Christ Jesus" (Rom. 8:2) was working in and among them. These sign gifts died out during Paul's life time after he set the provoking ministry to the Jews aside for the third and final time (Acts 13:46, 18:6, 28:28). Paul says, "If the Holy Spirit is the One who converted you by faith in Christ, and you are indwelt by the Spirit of God, are you going to turn back to the Law to try to control your flesh?"] **6 <u>Even as Abraham believed God, and it was accounted to him for righteousness.</u>** [The Judaizers pointed to Abraham as an example to be circumcised, but Paul points to Abraham as an example <u>not</u> to be circumcised. The Judaizers infiltrated many of Paul's churches including the congregation in Antioch (Acts 15:1, 24). Paul uses the illustration of <u>Abraham receiving imputed righteousness by faith before he was circumcised when he believed God</u> (Rom. 4:1-8, 11, 12). Abraham believed that although he was "dead" reproductively, God would give him as many descendants as the stars of heaven (Rom. 4:16-22). "And <u>he believed in the LORD</u>; and <u>he counted it to him for righteousness</u>" (Gen. 15:6).]

7 ¶ Know ye therefore that they which are of faith, the same are the children of Abraham. [Abraham was justified before he was circumcised and is the "father of all them that believe . . . and walk in the steps of that faith of our father Abraham" (Rom. 4:11, 12). The blessings are by grace. <u>God did not have to impute righteousness to the believer but chose to do so.</u>] **8 And the scripture, foreseeing that God would justify the heathen through faith, preached before the <u>gospel</u> <u>unto Abraham</u>, saying, In thee shall all nations be blessed. 9 So then they which be of faith are blessed with faithful Abraham.** [God's "good news" to

Abraham was "in thee shall all families of the earth be blessed" (Gen. 12:1-3). Notice that Abraham did not believe the gospel that Paul preached, and neither did the twelve apostles who did not understand the meaning of the cross until <u>after</u> Christ rose from the dead and explained it to them (Luke 18:31-34, 24:45-48). Peter preached the death of Christ as a murder indictment, (<u>bad news</u>) in Acts 2:23. The kingdom saints must wait for their sins to be blotted out (Acts 3:19). Paul preached the cross as <u>good news</u> of Gentile salvation apart from Israel (1 Cor. 15:1-4). God's plan is to save Gentiles in both prophecy and mystery. In fact, during this dispensation of grace both individual Jews (not the nation) and Gentiles have an opportunity to be saved (Rom. 11:30-33). And during the first millennium of the kingdom, the Gentiles will have a thousand-year opportunity to be saved. They will be saved in large numbers then.] **10 For as many as are of the works of the law are under the curse: for it is written, <u>Cursed is every one that continueth not in all</u> things which are written in the book of the law to do them.** [Those who try to keep the law by works are under the <u>curse</u>, which is that they must keep <u>all of the law perfectly</u> (Deut. 27:26, Rom. 2:7; James 2:10). The people of Israel had the written law (Rom. 3:2), but the Gentiles had the law written in their hearts and everyone has a conscience (Rom. 2:15).] **11 But that no man is justified by the law in the sight of God, it is evident: for, The just shall live by faith.** [So both had the Law. No human has ever been saved by keeping the Law. Paul quotes Hab. 2:4 to demonstrate that the just live by faith. The Galatians were justified by faith, but trying to live by keeping the Law. The law is not of faith but works are required to keep the law.] **12 And the law is not of faith: but, The man that doeth them shall live in them.** [Paul quotes Leviticus 18:5, a person must live by keeping <u>all</u> the Law perfectly. The Mosaic law given to Israel is in three parts: (1) the Ten Commandments expressing the righteous will of God (2) the rules governing the social life of Israel (3) and the ordinances governing the religious life of Israel.] **13 <u>Christ hath redeemed us from the curse of the law, being made a curse for us: for it is written, Cursed is every one that hangeth on a tree: 14 That the blessing of Abraham might come on the Gentiles through Jesus Christ</u>; that we might receive the promise of the Spirit through faith.** [Paul quotes Deut. 21:23. Christ bore the curse of the law for us, as our substitute (2 Cor. 5:21). <u>The blessings of Abraham is the imputed righteousness of Jesus Christ (Gen. 15:6; Rom. 4:3, 23-25) by faith in the gospel (1 Cor. 15:3, 4) resulting in eternal life.</u> This salvation opportunity has come on the Gentiles. God put on human flesh and became a man so that He could shed His blood in man's place and redeem him (John 1:14; Phil. 2:5-8; Rom. 3:21-26). While on earth, the Lord Jesus Christ was 100% God and 100% Man. Man had sinned so it was man's blood that was required to be shed, but the blood had to be perfect so it had to be God's blood, too. Jesus Christ did not inherit the sin nature since He was born of a virgin by the Holy Ghost (Luke 1:35). God the Son had perfect faith, and obeyed His Father perfectly. The instant we trust the gospel of what He has done for us (1 Cor. 15:3, 4) we receive eternal life and His Spirit in us (imputed righteousness by faith). We identified with His crucifixion and He lives in us (Gal. 2:20). Christ is the "Seed" of Abraham and all who believe are blessed to have His imputed righteousness/His Spirit in them. The body of Christ believers have the indwelling Holy Spirit now, and will receive their glorified bodies at the Rapture while Abraham and the other earthly kingdom believers will receive their glorified bodies after Christ's Second Coming and have the indwelling holy Spirit as part of the New Covenant (Jer. 31:31-36; Ezek. 36:22-28). Pentecost was a foretaste of that Spirit (Heb. 6:4).]**15 Brethren, I speak after the manner of men; Though it be but a man's covenant, yet if it be confirmed, no man disannulleth, or addeth thereto.** [Paul uses another illustration, he says even in the case of a man's covenant the contract is binding and a third party cannot come in and add to it or cancel it. <u>The law of Moses could not cancel God's promise to Abraham.</u>] **16 Now to Abraham and his seed were the promises made. He saith not, And to seeds, as of many; but as of one, And <u>to thy seed, which is Christ</u>.** [What was God's promise to Abraham? It was natural descendants, a nation to be made from him, blessings, and a land for ever. The promise was to Abraham and his Seed (Gen. 13:15). Notice that God tells Abraham that He will receive the land "for ever" which means Abraham would be resurrected to eternal life to receive it (Matt. 8:11). Many will come and sit down with Abraham in the kingdom (Matt. 8:11). Paul identified Christ as the Seed. All nations are blessed because Christ (the Redeemer for both Israel and the body of Christ) is a descendant of Abraham (3:8); His royal lineage is through David (Matt. 1:1; John 4:22).] **17 And this I say, that the covenant, that was confirmed before of God in Christ, the law, which was <u>four hundred and thirty years after</u>, cannot disannul, that it should make the promise of none effect. 18 For if the inheritance be of the law, it is no more of promise: but God gave it to Abraham by promise. 19 Wherefore then serveth the law? <u>It was added because of transgressions, till the seed should come to whom the promise was made; and it was ordained by angels in the hand of a mediator</u>. 20 Now a mediator is not a mediator of one, but God is one. 21 Is the law then against the promises of God? God forbid: for if there had been a law given which could have given life, verily righteousness should have been by the law. 22 But the scripture hath concluded all under sin, that the promise by <u>faith of Jesus Christ</u> might be given to them that believe.** [If the inheritance was of the law it would be by works, not faith. <u>God gave Abraham the inheritance of eternal life because Abraham believed what God said. God promised Abraham His imputed righteousness by faith 430 years before the giving of the Mosaic law</u> (Gen. 15:6; Rom. 4:3). Abraham was justified by faith before he received the

233

covenant of circumcision. God gave Abraham the promise of eternal life, which is the result of imputed righteousness. God made the covenant to Abraham concerning his "seed" by promise. The promise was by God's grace. Grace and works are mutually exclusive (Rom. 11:6). See God's five "I wills" to Abraham (Gen. 17:4-8). God gave the promise to Abraham by One party, Himself alone (a one-sided covenant or contract, all on the part of God). What is the purpose of the Law then? The purpose of the law is "the knowledge of sin" (Rom. 3:19, 20). It is to make mankind conscious of the evil that dwells in our nature. We need to be awakened to the fact the we are helpless to uphold the Law. The Law also showed the power of evil in us to want to disobey God's law. It exposed our true moral condition. (This is another reason we know that the Bible is God's word, because mankind would not write such unfavorable things about ourselves.) The Law was added to the promise until the Seed would come. Sin reigned before the law came, even if it was not imputed, it still existed in the people (Rom. 5:12-14). The purpose of the Law was to make the Jews aware of their unrighteousness. Israel was a mirror for all the nations to see their sin. The Law shows all people (not only Jews) that no one can keep God's high standard. The Law condemned everyone so that all can be saved by the faith of Jesus (His perfect keeping of the law). God gave the Law to Israel, and Moses was the mediator between two parties (God and Israel), and the angels ordained it (3:19). Is the Law against the promises of God? God forbid. Paul anticipates questions and answers them before they are asked. The law was holy, just, good, and spiritual. If there had been a Law that could have given life, then righteousness should have been obtained that way. The scriptures have concluded that all are under sin, so God can show mercy to all (Rom. 3:9-18; 11:32). "That the promise by faith of Jesus Christ might be given to them that believe." Jesus had the faith to live a perfect life and die a perfect death on the cross and those who have faith in Him receive His righteousness.]

23 ¶ But before faith came, we were kept under the law, shut up unto the faith which should afterwards be revealed. [The law was in place for the interim until faith of Christ should come. The Law was Israel's "tutor" (a disciplinarian of a minor child), until the cross. Today, Gentiles are saved "by" the cross (Eph. 2:16), not "at" the cross. Our opportunity for salvation began a year after the cross when Paul was saved. Before the "faith of Jesus" came, all were kept under the Law. Everyone was shut up unto the "faith of Jesus" that would later be revealed by Christ who kept the Law perfectly and had the faith to go through with the Father's plan of the cross. "For therein is the righteousness of God revealed from faith to faith: as it is written the just shall live by faith" (Rom. 1:17). "From faith to faith" means from the faith of Christ to our faith in Him. The Son of God accomplished man's salvation on His own and did not require anything from man. Salvation is

100% God, and 0% man. It is all by grace, a gift that must be believed to be received.] **24 Wherefore the law was our schoolmaster to bring us unto Christ, that we might be justified by faith.** [We are justified by our faith in Christ's faith (2:16). The purpose of the law is to show people their failure of being able to keep it (Rom. 3:19, 20). The law is like a schoolmaster or tutor. The schoolmaster (law) says, "Sorry, you failed again, you don't measure up to God's perfect standard, you fall short, you will never measure up, your own righteousness is not really righteous, you fail to keep the Law." We cannot keep the law because we have inherited the sin nature from Adam (Rom. 5:12). We inherited the "knowledge of good and evil" from him. Even our "good" is bad (Rom. 7:18). We had no hope of eternal life because God will not accept our evil or our human good. The law energizes our sinful flesh and makes it worse (Rom. 7:9). The law showed us our need for a Redeemer (Saviour) to fulfill the Law and be the perfect sacrifice in our place; and we need His Spirit (His imputed righteousness or divine nature). The schoolmaster (the law) brought us to trust in the faith of Jesus, His redemptive work at Calvary.] **25 But after that faith is come, we are no longer under a schoolmaster.** [But once we trust Christ by faith (3:26) we don't need the Law anymore and are not under the schoolmaster. This is the point that Paul wants the Galatians to understand. The Law doesn't save us or sanctify us. A just man does not need the law, he lives righteously by walking in the Spirit and through love for others (5:13, 14, 16). Believers are not under the law, but under grace (Rom. 6:14). Paul said, the law of Moses is done away and abolished in Christ, and the holy Spirit exceeds in glory (2 Cor. 3:7-18). After salvation we are no longer under the schoolmaster we are no longer treated as children but become sons (4:6). A son voluntarily does what he had to be taught by discipline when he was a child. If the son disobeys it is no longer an issue between the child and the tutor, but between the child and his father.] **26 For ye are all the children of God by faith in Christ Jesus.** [Paul clearly says that the body of Christ believers are all children of God by faith.] **27 For as many of you as have been baptized into Christ have put on Christ. 28 There is neither Jew nor Greek, there is neither bond nor free, there is neither male nor female: for ye are all one in Christ Jesus.** [We are baptized into Christ when we believe, and we "put on Christ." We are in Him, and He clothes us with His righteousness. Baptized into Christ is identification with His death, burial, and resurrection (Rom. 6:3, 4). To "put on Christ" is to receive Christ's imputed righteousness (2 Cor. 5:21; Rom. 4:24, 25). We are baptized into the body of Christ by the Spirit (1 Cor. 12:13) and join with other believers. It is a dry spiritual baptism or identification (Eph. 4:5). Paul reminds the Galatians, that in the dispensation of grace, the middle wall of partition is down and that we are all one in the body of Christ. There is no ethnic distinction, no social status distinction, and no gender distinction. There are no distinctions of any kind. No one is above anyone else. We all have equal completeness and perfection in our position Christ. If we have Christ's indwelling Spirit, we have His imputed righteousness, and inherit eternal life (Rom. 6:23; Phil 3:9). We are heirs with Him (Rom. 8:17).] **29 And if ye be Christ's, then are ye Abraham's seed, and heirs according to the promise**. [If we have Christ's indwelling Spirit, we have His imputed righteousness, and inherit eternal life (Rom. 6:23; Phil. 3:9). We are heirs with Him (Rom. 8:17).]

Chapter 4 Don't invite the bondwoman and her son back into the family
4:1-7 Believers are adopted sons of God, not servants to the law.
4:8-14 Legalism is a form of idolatry.
4:15-20 Legalism causes loss of blessedness.
4:21-31 "Cast out the bondwoman and her son" (legalism).

4:1 Now I say, That the heir, as long as he is a child, differeth nothing from a servant, though he be lord of all; 2 But is under tutors and governors until the time appointed of the father. [Paul continues his illustration of a child under a schoolmaster. During his learning phase, the heir does not differ from a servant, even if he will eventually inherit a fortune (the riches of Christ, Eph. 3:8). Tutors teach a child what they should do, while governors tell the child what not to do. Therefore, tutors and governors were the law. But once the father determines that the child is capable of making decisions on his own, then the father places that child into the position of a fully grown son in the family. At that time, he is not under the schoolmaster's authority (the law), but the father's.] **3 Even so we, when we were children, were in bondage under the elements of the world:** [Before the dispensation of grace, the unsaved Jews were in bondage to the law and the Gentiles to idols.] **4 But when the fulness of the time was come,** [Daniel's timeline to Israel] **God sent forth his Son, made of a woman, made under the law, 5 To redeem them that were under the law, that we might receive the adoption of sons.** [Daniel's timeline was the Father's appointed time for His Son to be born. He existed before He was born under the law. He came to redeem Israel so they could evangelize the Gentiles (Rom. 15:8, 9). The Jews in the body of Christ were under the bondage of the law. The elements of the world are manmade rituals, rules, idolatry, and traditions, which have Satan and our flesh behind them. During Israel's childhood the law was their tutors (teachers) and governors (rulers). But when the fullness of time was come, God sent forth His Son to be born of a virgin woman under the law to redeem Israel (Matt. 1:21) so that they might receive the adoption of sons. Christ preached to Israel (Rom. 15:8). Christ was a ransom for the "many" of Israel (Matt. 20:28). Through Paul we learn that Christ is the ransom for "all" (1 Tim. 2:6). We are saved in spite of Israel, through her fall. "I say then, Have they stumbled that they should fall? God forbid: but rather through their fall salvation is come unto the Gentiles, for to provoke them to jealousy. Now if the fall of them be the riches of the world, and the diminishing of them the riches of the Gentiles; how much more their fulness?" (Rom. 11:11-13). The Gentile opportunity for salvation, the dispensation of grace was grafted into the olive tree (Rom. 11:17, the blessings of Abraham access by faith). Notice that the body of Christ was not grafted in, but anyone saved by faith today joins that group. We are living during the time of the nation of Israel's temporary national blindness (Rom. 11:25). The nation of Israel is in apostasy and do not recognize Jesus Christ as their Messiah. When Christ arrived on the scene, the scribes and the Pharisees had polluted the law by valuing their traditions more than the law. The First Coming of Jesus Christ was at the "fulness of time" prophesied by Daniel. Daniel was given two timelines by God. One, in a "night vision" (Dan. 2:19) to the Gentile king Nebuchadnezzar concerning the "times of the Gentiles" (Luke 21:24). The other one via the angel Gabriel to the nation of Israel (Dan. 9:21). Christ came riding into Jerusalem on a donkey declaring Himself to be the Messiah, the King of the Jews, exactly 483 years after the command was given to rebuild Jerusalem and wall (Neh. 2:1-8) on Palm Sunday. The temple took 46 years to rebuild (John 2:20) and the wall 52 days (Neh. 6:15). But Christ was "cut off" (killed) four days later on Passover. Therefore, 69 weeks (483 years) are complete, and one week (the 70th) remains to make the entire series of sevens (7x70) or 490 years (Dan. 9:24-27). The Gentiles received their salvation opportunity between the 69th and 70th week when God inserted the mystery after Paul's salvation and commissioning in Acts 9. God postponed the prophesied kingdom on earth and inserted the dispensation of grace to save a people to live in heaven. The Gentiles were also under the law which was written in their hearts. The law was bondage; no one can keep it. It reveals our sins. The "rudiments of the world" are man's pagan rituals, traditions, philosophy, imaginations, and worldly ideas (Col. 2:8-23). Pagans believe and practice a religion other than true faith in the one true God.] **6 And because ye are sons, God hath sent forth the Spirit of his Son into your hearts, crying, Abba, Father.** [Paul now includes Gentile body of Christ believers. He had said that the Galatians are adopted sons of God by faith in Christ Jesus and not under the schoolmaster, the law (3:26). We are God's sons because we have the Spirit of His Son in us (1:16). Eternal life is now promised to all who believe the one and only gospel that is valid today, Paul's (1 Cor. 15:3, 4; Eph. 1:13). The words "Abba, Father" occur three times in the KJV. We have the great privilege of calling the Father "Daddy" like Jesus did (Mark 14:36). Because of Christ, believers have that kind of a tender, intimate, love relationship with the Father as His adopted sons (Rom. 8:15). Notice that Paul says "the Spirit of his Son." The words "Holy Ghost" appear in the King James Bible 90 times and in Paul's writings 14 times. The word "Spirit" with a capital "S" appears in the Bible 172 times and in Paul's writings 80 times. In the letter to the Romans, it appears 21 times, 19 of those times are in Romans 8. This tells us that Romans 8 has a lot to do with the Spirit. The word "Spirit" does not always refer to the Holy Ghost. Jesus (who was the only Person of the Godhead to put on human flesh) said, "God is a Spirit: and they that worship him must worship him in spirit and in truth" (John 4:24). The Holy Father is Spirit, the Son is Spirit, and the Holy Ghost is Spirit. When the King James Bible says the Holy Ghost it is referring specifically to the

Holy Ghost, but when the Bible says "Spirit" then it could be referring to any one of the three Persons of the Godhead, and the context must help us decide which one. *Please note that all modern Bibles eliminate the name "Holy Ghost" and replace it with the "Holy Spirit" and therefore the distinction between them is lost. In summary, we find that the "Spirit" in Romans 8 and in Galatians is often the Spirit of Jesus Christ in the believer (Rom. 8:2). Therefore, sometimes the Spirit in us is Christ's, sometimes the Holy Ghost's, and sometimes the Father's because all three live in us.] **7 Wherefore thou art no more a servant, but a son; and if a son, then an heir of God through Christ.** [We are no longer servants to the law. Once we believed we were placed into the family as adult sons and heirs of God through Christ. The parallel passage is found in Rom. 8:11-17.]

8 ¶ Howbeit then, when ye knew not God, ye did service unto them which by nature are no gods. [They were slaves to the idols they worshipped. Before we were saved we were impressed by men and their worldly ideas. We gave attention to things that had no eternal value. This attention to man's wisdom, philosophy, and rituals is a form of idolatry.] **9 But now, after that ye have known God, or rather are known of God, how turn ye again to the weak and beggarly elements, whereunto ye desire again to be in bondage?** [Paul asks why are you going back to living under the Law which couldn't save you? Notice the words "But now" allude to the time period that we currently live in. The dispensation of grace is the Gentile's opportunity for salvation. The rapture was a mystery exclusively revealed to our apostle Paul (1 Thess. 1:10, 5:9). He said "Behold, I shew you a mystery; We shall not all sleep, but we shall all be changed . . . this mortal must put on immortality" (1 Cor. 15:51-53). At the rapture, the "shout" of the Lord and be resurrected or changed. At that same time "the voice of the archangel [Michael]" will signal to Israel that their prophetic program has begun (1 Thess. 4:16; Dan. 12:1). Another group of Gentiles will be saved as Israel rises and shines (Isa. 60:1-3). By reading the Bible we learn that the antichrist is an Assyrian Jew (Isa. 10:5; Dan. 11:37). The Galatians were saved and "known of God" because He had accepted them in Christ (Eph. 1:6). The believer is "complete in him" (Col. 2:10). Religion doesn't want us to know that. There is a big difference between living to be accepted, and living out of already being accepted. We can't get any more accepted than we already are. Our job now is to get our practice to line up with our standing. The Galatians were turning back to the Mosaic Law, which is like going back into the idolatry they had come out of. The "elements" (ABC's) is the law for Israel with its do's and don'ts, and were a shadow of things to come (Col. 2:16, 17). Paul wonders why they would desire to go back to that? Once salvation has come believers are not to go back to the "weak" (no power) "and beggarly" (bankrupt, no assets) "elements" of the law (4:9). Like a mirror, the law shows us the dirt on our face, but it cannot clean it up. There was nothing wrong with the law, it was "holy, and just, and good" (Rom. 7:12). The problem is not with the law, but with people who fail to keep it (Rom. 8:3, 4). We cannot be righteous by trying to keep the law. We cannot live righteously by trying to keep the law. Have you ever tried to keep your New Year's resolutions? Gym memberships go up, but soon gym attendance goes down. What was Israel's problem? They were too proud to say that they could not keep the law. "For they being ignorant of God's righteousness, and going about to establish their own righteousness, have not submitted themselves unto the righteousness of God. For Christ is the end of the law of righteousness to every one that believeth" (Rom. 10:3, 4). The law which was intended to show man he was a sinner in need of righteousness, was instead used by man to establish his own righteousness through carnal observances of outward requirements (Matt. 23:23). The idolater similarly debased his conscience and became the willing slave to gods who only existed in his imagination. If the Galatians went back to Judaism under the guidance of their false teachers (4:17), it would in effect be as if they went back to pagan idolatry. Why would anyone want to go back to living under something that could never save them nor make them righteous?] **10 Ye observe days, and months, and times, and years.** [The Galatians were observing the Sabbath days, the new moons, the times of the Jewish feast days, and the Sabbath years. They had gone back to practices that did not pertain to them. Even pagans revered certain days. The Druids, for example, observed and idolized the spring equinox. Stonehenge is like a big calendar marking the sun on that day. Why should they observe Israel's feast days when they already had the imputed righteousness of Christ? For a grace believer every day is important.] **11 I am afraid of you, lest I have bestowed upon you labour in vain.** [Paul was deeply concerned for their spiritual welfare and was worried that he had wasted his time on them.]

12 ¶ Brethren, I beseech you, be as I am; for I am as ye are: ye have not injured me at all. [Paul begs them to be free from the law and walk by faith dependent on the Spirit of Christ in them, like he does. He is an imperfect human with the infirmity of the flesh just like them. You are not hurting me; you are hurting yourselves.] **13 Ye know how through infirmity of the flesh I preached the gospel unto you at the first. 14 And my temptation which was in my flesh ye despised not, nor rejected; but received me as an angel of God, even as Christ Jesus. 15 Where is then the blessedness ye spake of? for I bear you record, that, if it had been possible, ye would have plucked out your own eyes, and have given them to me. 16 Am I therefore become your enemy, because I tell you the truth?** [Paul reminds them of their gracious love for him when he first preached the gospel of their salvation to them on his first apostolic journey. They should follow apostle Paul to follow Christ (1 Cor. 11:1). The truth is only Paul's gospel (1:6-9) and what Christ said through him should be followed. Although he had some kind of eye trouble (probably from all the beatings or the stoning inflicted on him when he preached Christ crucified, 6:17), they ignored it and treated him like an angel and even as Christ. They were even willing to pluck out their eyes and give them to him if they could. Has your legalism caused you to lose your blessedness? Paul mentions some of the fruit of legalism in 5:15. Paul asked them a very pointed question: he loved them enough to correct them. He reminded them that Christ spoke to them exclusively through him. Did that make him their enemy?] **17 They zealously affect you, but not well; yea, they would exclude you, that ye might affect them. 18 But it is good to be zealously affected always in a good thing, and not only when I am present with you.** [The zeal of the Judaizers was affecting the Galatians in the wrong way. They wanted to count the number of foreskins they could add to their belts (6:13). They wanted to exclude the Galatians from having rewards at the Judgment Seat of Christ. Being zealous is fine if it is in a good thing, and not only when Paul was there.] **19 My little children, of whom I travail in birth again until Christ be formed in you, 20 I desire to be present with you now, and to change my voice; for I stand in doubt of you.** [Paul calls them his "little children" because they are not behaving like adult sons. He is having to labor for the right Christ he preached to them to be formed in them. The two operating systems law and grace cannot co-exist. We are to be conformed to His image (Rom. 8:29). They have left Christ according to the revelation of the mystery (Rom. 16:25). They were mixing themselves up with Christ according to prophecy, when He was on earth under the law (as recorded in Matthew, Mark, Luke, and John). Paul wants to change his tone to a loving one, but has to be stern with them because he had serious doubts about their spiritual condition. Of course, our hearts are also very concerned for the dear, ignorant brethren who follow Christ's earthly ministry or Peter, instead of Paul, and they fail to apply 2 Tim. 2:15. Many mix Peter and Paul. We are especially concerned for those who join Messianic Synagogues. Still it could be worse, they could be unsaved, and some are. The only thing we can really trust is the King James Bible rightly divided. We must be both Biblical and dispensational.]

21 ¶ Tell me, ye that desire to be under the law, do ye not hear the law? [The law brought fear of punishment. Paul is going to let them hear the law.] **22 For it is written, that Abraham had two sons, the one by a bondmaid, the other by a freewoman. 23 But he who was of the bondwoman was born after the flesh; but he of the freewoman was by promise.** [The Galatians were foolish because they wanted to go back under the law which is bondage (slavery). Trying to be righteous by keeping the law just makes the flesh worse. Notice how Paul alludes to the warfare between the flesh and the Spirit.] **24 Which things are an allegory: for these are the two covenants; the one from the mount Sinai, which gendereth to bondage, which is Agar. 25 For this Agar is mount Sinai in Arabia, and answereth to Jerusalem which now is, and is in bondage with her children. 26 But Jerusalem which is above is free, which is the mother of us all. 27 For it is written, Rejoice, thou barren that bearest not; break forth and cry, thou that travailest not: for the desolate hath many more children** [by faith] **than she which hath an husband** [by the flesh]. **28 Now we, brethren, as Isaac was, are the children of promise. 29 But as then he that was born after the flesh persecuted him that was born after the Spirit, even so it is now.** [Paul uses an allegory of the bondwoman and the freewoman to help them to understand the difference between the bondage of the law and their liberty in Christ. An allegory is an event or story that has a hidden meaning. Agar (Greek for Hagar) the bondwoman (slave) symbolized the law, the Old Covenant made at Sinai. Her son Ishmael, was the result of Abraham trying to have a son by his own flesh. Trying to keep the law in the flesh leads to bondage. The Jews in Jerusalem today do not know that Jesus of Nazareth is their Messiah and try to be righteous by keeping the law. The free woman, Sarah, represents the "promise" of the "Spirit" under the New Covenant in the kingdom on earth in the land (Ezek. 36:27). The New Covenant is for Israel (Heb. 8:8; Rom. 9:4), but the body of Christ believers receive the Spirit of Christ by faith. The New Jerusalem in Mount Sion (Greek for Zion) in heaven above is free, and is the mother of us all (Heb. 12:22). Paul quotes Isa. 54:1 (which comes right after Isa. 53 about the Redeemer of Israel) and talks about the rejoicing in the kingdom. But Paul applies this verse to us since Sarah is the mother of the believing and will have more children by faith, than Hagar by the flesh. Sarah is also in the Hall of Faith chapter (Heb. 11:10-19). We, like Isaac was, are the children of promise (faith in God). Just like Ishmael persecuted Isaac who was born miraculously by the Spirit, the Judaizers were really persecuting the Galatians by putting them in bondage.] **30 Nevertheless what saith the scripture? Cast out the bondwoman and her son: for the son of the bondwoman shall not be heir with the son of the freewoman.** [The Scriptures said, "Cast out the bond woman and her son." But, the Galatians were trying to invite the bondwoman and her son back into the family. Law and grace, they never mix. They needed to cast out the Judaizers. The focus of the law is on what we do, while the focus of grace is on what Christ did.] **31 So then, brethren, we are not children of the bondwoman, but of the free.** [Paul says we are not children of the bondwoman (slaves), but of the free. Salvation is by grace alone, through faith alone, in Christ alone. God did not have to give anyone imputed righteousness, but He did it purely by grace (Isa. 54:17; 2 Cor. 5:21).] **5:1 Stand fast therefore in the liberty wherewith Christ hath made us free, and be not entangled again with the yoke**

of bondage. [Paul said this before a new paragraph begins. He said that Christ has set us free from the law, so stay free. Free from being entangled with the yoke of bondage to the law. Remember, that Paul marveled that the Galatians were "so soon removed from him that called you into the grace of Christ unto another gospel" (Gal. 1:6). Now Paul says, stay where you are, stand fast in the liberty wherewith Christ has made us free from the law, do not be removed from your position of freedom in Christ. Stand fast in Paul's gospel/sound doctrine.]

Chapter 5 Grace living is by faith with His Spirit living through us
5:1-12 Whosoever tries to live by keeping the law has fallen from grace.
5:13-26 Walk in the Spirit, and ye shall not fulfill the lust of the flesh.

**5:1 <u>Stand fast therefore in the liberty wherewith Christ hath made us free,</u>
<u>and be not entangled again with the yoke of bondage</u>.** [Paul told them to "cast
out" the result of <u>"works of the law" by the work of your flesh</u> (your law-keeping).
Stand fast in the result of the freewoman and her son, the promise of the Spirit of
His Son given to you by faith. Abraham found out that what he did by his self-
effort was not acceptable to God. God had already promised him a seed long
before he tried to have a child by the work of his flesh (Gen. 15:4). God gave
Abraham Isaac (a miraculous birth) by promise (Gen. 21). He blessed Abraham
purely by His grace. <u>God has power over the curse to give life where there was no</u>
<u>life</u>. The Galatians had been "so soon removed from him that called you into <u>the</u>
<u>grace of Christ</u> unto another gospel" (1:6). The other gospel to try to live by
obeying the law. Law and grace do not mix. After the Galatians were saved they
noticed that they still sinned. So they thought that they could overcome their sin
and be righteous by going back to trying to obey the law. Peter and Paul both said
that the law was a yoke of bondage that no one could keep (Acts 15:10; 3:10,
6:13). (Christ was the only one who kept all the law perfectly, so with Him in us
we can keep it.) Paul explained that Christ has redeemed us from the law (4:5), and
bore the curse of the law (3:13) for us. There is no reason to be <u>entangled again</u>
<u>with trying to keep all of God's perfect law using our sinful flesh again</u>. Christ set
us free from the bondage of the law, so stay free. As the hymn *Once for All*, by
Philip P. Bliss (1838-1876) goes: "Free from the law . . . O happy condition! Jesus
hath bled, and there is remission." We are dead to the law because our flesh was
crucified with Christ the instant we were saved. Believers need to stand firm in our
position in Christ, and live by following the instructions He gave us through Paul.
We need to stand fast in Paul's sound doctrine (Romans to Philemon).]

**2 ¶ Behold, I Paul say unto you, that if ye be circumcised, Christ shall profit
you nothing. 3 For I testify again to every man that is circumcised, that he is a
debtor to do the whole law.** [Our apostle Paul says that if you think you can live
righteously by keeping the Mosaic law, Christ will profit you nothing. You may be
saved, but His life (Spirit) will not function in you. Being circumcised is an
example of trying to be righteous by the works of the law, self-effort. Circumcision
represents the entire Mosaic system. Paul had said in 3:10 that the Mosaic law was
an all-or-nothing arrangement. If they failed to keep one law, they were guilty of
all (James 2:10). Paul's Gentile converts had forgotten what he had taught them
and had been persuaded by the false teachers (the Judaizers) to be circumcised like

to proselytes under Israel's prophetic program. But Paul tells them that keeping the Law, self-effort, will not make you acceptable to God. Christ has done everything to save us, and now we need Him to live through us. Life is all about the Lord Jesus Christ, His performance through us, not our performance. Paul demonstrated in Romans 7 that a believer who determines to please God in his own flesh is destined to fail. Paul moved on to living in victory by the Spirit in Romans chapter 8, and so should we. If the Gentiles in Galatia wanted to be physically circumcised they were in debt to keep the entire Mosaic system of laws. The Galatians had no idea of the great spiritual danger that they were placing themselves in.] **4 Christ is become of <u>no effect</u> unto you, whosoever of you are justified by the law; ye are fallen from grace.** [Justified here is not about salvation, but living a life justified before God, sanctification. Paul is not saying that a person can lose his salvation, but that they can lose the power of the Spirit of Christ in them and become ineffective to Him and themselves (5:17). Whoever believes he can live a life that justifies him before God by works of the law has <u>fallen from grace. If they put themselves back under the law, then Christ's life in them</u> (Paul says again) has become of no effect to them. <u>If they believe that their fleshly performance of the law will justify them, or make them pleasing to God, they are wrong.</u> They were called into the "grace of Christ" (1:6). This life is all about what Christ has accomplished on Calvary, and what Christ accomplishes through His Spirit in the believer. It is not about us, what we have done or what we do in our flesh, our performance, but His performance.] **5 For we through the Spirit wait for the hope of righteousness by faith.** [<u>The hope of righteousness by faith is eternal life as a result of having God's imputed righteousness</u> (6:15). <u>God did not have to give anyone imputed righteousness, but He did purely by His grace.</u> Our blessed hope will culminate at the rapture (Titus 2:13). That is when it will become evident who really are His (Rom. 8:19). I believe in once saved always saved, but make sure that you are saved and don't be left behind at the rapture.] **6 For in Jesus Christ neither circumcision availeth any thing, nor uncircumcision; but faith which worketh by love.** [We are all one in Christ (3:28). There is no physical distinction based on circumcision for those who are "in Christ." There are no distinctions of any kind in the spiritual body of Christ. Circumcision or uncircumcision do not matter, only faith in Christ which works by love. The faith of Christ and our faith in Him are what matter (3:22, 24). Love is the motivator. Christ's love for us constrains us to want to love Him and His people in return (2 Cor. 5:14). The only legitimate use of the law (the schoolmaster) in the dispensation of grace is to show us our need for the Redeemer, the Lord Jesus Christ. The "faith of Jesus Christ" in us then produces works of love. We can't do good works that please God by our self-effort; it must be His Spirit functioning in and through us that does the work.] **7 Ye did run well; who did hinder you that ye should not obey the truth?** [The

Galatians started off running well when saved by Paul's preaching (Acts 13, 14). Who has hindered them from obeying the truth? Paul's message of grace is the truth of what God is doing in the dispensation of grace (Eph. 3:1, 2).] **8 This persuasion cometh not of him that calleth you.** [This persuasion is not from the Spirit of Christ in His heavenly ministry; it is a lie from the pit of hell.] **9 <u>A little leaven leaveneth the whole lump.</u>** [A little <u>leaven</u> (the false doctrine, the law, Christ's earthly ministry) <u>can spread to the whole assembly</u>. The Judaizers taught that they had received spiritual life by faith, but could only secure holiness by works of the law. This was a great legalistic error that never brings victory. The law could not give life it was the ministration of condemnation, while the Spirit was the ministration of righteousness (2 Cor. 3:8, 9). The grace life, faith in Christ's doctrine to us from heaven through Paul works.] **10 I have confidence in you through the Lord, that ye will be none otherwise minded: but <u>he that troubleth you shall bear his judgment, whosoever he be</u>.** [Paul was uneasy when he thought of them as feeble men being seduced by false teachers, but confident when he thought of them having the Spirit of the Lord. But Paul is confident in them through the Lord that they will not continue is this legalistic error, but cast it out. But that the Judaizer will bear his punishment (1 Cor. 3:17), whoever he is. Sadly, there are so many false preachers and teachers that put people under the law by preaching that the body of Christ began in Acts 2. Because if we believe that the body of Christ began on Pentecost then we apply law-keeping, water baptism, and spiritual gifts, and other things that belong to Israel, to us. It was not until Paul was saved that we learn that Christ not only died for Israel's sins, but also for OUR SINS (the Gentiles).] **11 And I, brethren, if I yet preach circumcision, why do I yet suffer persecution? then is the offence of the cross ceased.** [To preach Christ and good works does not result in persecution, but to preach the true Gospel does. Paul had preached that circumcision was not necessary for justification because Christ's perfect work of salvation needed not to be added to. Paul's preaching did not go over well, especially among the Jews who had received the covenant of circumcision through Abraham (Gen. 17:10; Acts 7:8). The circumcision that was given to Abraham was incorporated into the law of Moses (Lev. 12:3). The offense of the cross is that Christ has done it all, everything that is needed for salvation. Believers contribute nothing. We only believe what He did and receive the gift of eternal life. Then once we are saved we live by faith. But the flesh loves to perform and be praised. The flesh wants to add self to Christ's perfect work. The flesh loves to follow a performance-based acceptance system with outward ceremonies. The flesh wants to impose its performance on top of what Christ has done for us on Calvary. It does not want to hear: Jesus paid it all; all to Him I owe, He alone is worthy of all glory, and all our praise forever. It is not about us, us, us, but about Him, Him, Him! Paul had preached in Antioch of Pisidia near Galatia, ". . . through this man [Jesus Christ] is preached unto you the forgiveness of sins. And by him all that believe are justified from all things, from which ye <u>could not be justified by the law of Moses</u>" (Acts 13:38, 39).] **12 I would they were even cut off which trouble you.** [Paul uses a play on words wishing the Judaizers would "cut off" a little more than just their foreskins, or that they were "cut off" from His people (Gen. 17:14), or "cut off" from troubling them, or "cut off" as from living (Gen. 9:11).]

13 ¶ For, brethren, ye have been called unto liberty; only use not liberty for an occasion to the flesh, but by love serve one another. [We are called to liberty. Paul reminds them that grace is not license to sin or to live any way we want to (1 Cor. 6:12). We have liberty in Christ but don't use it to serve your flesh, but by love serve each other. Grace living is not living as we please, but living to please God. A Spiritual interaction occurs when His Spirit in us uses His living word to transform us into the image of the Spirit of the Lord (2 Cor. 3:17, 18). Christ did not save us from sin to have us continue to sin, but to live like grace teaches us (Titus 2:11, 12). Grace gives us the ability to overcome sin, but it doesn't force us to overcome sin. God loves freedom and allows us the freedom to choose to follow what He says in His word. We are not robots.] **14 For all the law is fulfilled in one word, even in this; Thou shalt love thy neighbour as thyself.** [Paul says that the entire law is fulfilled in one word, "love." Then Paul quotes Lev. 19:18. This rule is also found in Mark 12:31; Rom. 13:9; and James 2:8. Our motivation is love.] **15 But if ye bite and devour one another, take heed that ye be not consumed one of another.** [The law energizes the flesh resulting in the fruit of being judgmental, unloving, critical, condemning, self-righteous, prideful, and destructive (Rom. 7:8, 11). Self-effort cannot achieve holiness through keeping the law, nor win the struggle against indwelling sin (Rom. 7:15-18).] **16 This I say then, Walk in the Spirit, and ye shall not fulfil the lust of the flesh.** [First Paul said stand fast in Christ's doctrine through him (5:1). Now he says walk in the Spirit. Those who live under the law depend on the energy of the flesh; those who live by grace through faith depend on the power of the Spirit. Paul tells the believers how to have fruits unto righteousness (Phil. 1:11). They must walk by faith in the Spirit (2 Cor. 5:7), so they will not fulfill the lust of the flesh. The Spirit of Christ, His life in us (2:20) by faith, allows us to walk (live) in victory over the sinful flesh that still resides in our mortal flesh (body). <u>Upon salvation our soul and sprit were saved, but not our bodies. The sinful flesh still exists in the body even if it has been inactivated. God makes a sinner good by giving him a new divine nature (the Spirit of His Son in us), not by cleaning up the sin nature (the flesh, the old nature we inherited from Adam). We have the Prince of Peace in us. The old sin nature is like a frog that will never become a prince no matter how many times</u>

we kiss him. We should not try to put lipstick on the frog (the flesh), or dress it up. The only way to deal with the sin nature is to believe what God says and reckon it dead, crucified (2:20; Rom. 6:6). We are dead to sin, but alive unto God because of the "faith of Christ" in us (Rom. 6:11). Because of all that Christ has done for us, it is reasonable for us to offer our bodies a living sacrifice for Him to live through us (Rom. 12:1, 2). We are baptized into Christ (identification with His death, burial, and resurrection) and have put on Christ. His imputed righteousness in us, His Spirit, His life, the faith of Jesus, are all synonymous.] **17 For the flesh lusteth against the Spirit, and the Spirit against the flesh: and these are contrary the one to the other: so that ye cannot do the things that ye would.** [This is how a person is of no effect (5:4). Paul identifies the war inside the believer's two natures, the flesh and the Spirit. The flesh and the Spirit are opposites and fight against each other so we cannot do what we want. The "flesh" is the sin nature that is dead; it still resides in the believer's mortal body. The law makes the flesh revive, and resuscitate. The believer that is operating in their flesh is rendered ineffective because the flesh cancels out the Spirit. Therefore, they are not able to have the power of the Spirit working in their life.] **18 But if ye be led of the Spirit, ye are not under the law.** [But if we are led by the Spirit then we are under the control of the indwelling Spirit of the Son and not under the influence of the law. If we are led by the Spirit then we are the sons of God (Rom. 8:14). Our only law now is the life of Christ in us; the "law of the Spirit of life in Christ Jesus hath made me free from the law of sin and death" (Rom. 8:2). Notice again that the result of the law is sin and death. When we are led by the Spirit, His life in us (2:20), then we are not under the law and we are not controlled by the lust of the flesh (5:16). "For sin shall not have dominion over you: for ye are not under the law, but under grace" (Rom. 6:14).] **19 Now the works of the flesh are manifest,** [revealed] **which are these; Adultery, fornication, uncleanness,** [impurity] **lasciviousness,** [lusts] **20 Idolatry, witchcraft,** [sorcery, drugs] **hatred, variance,** [contentions, disagreements] **emulations,** [jealousy] **wrath,** [hot temper, anger] **strife,** [quarreling] **seditions,** [divisions] **heresies,** [false teaching] **21 Envyings, murders,** [premeditated killing] **drunkenness, revellings,** [wild party] **and such like** [more similar things]**: of the which I tell you before, as I have also told you in time past, that they which do such things shall not inherit the kingdom of God.** [Paul lists seventeen "works of the flesh" and says "and such like" meaning other similar things. Paul had told them previously (time past) that people who do these things will not have eternal life with God in His kingdom. The Kingdom of God is made up of two realms: Heaven (the body of Christ believers) and Earth (the kingdom of earth believers). This life is all about making sure that we will have eternal life in His kingdom. Our faith must be a real heartfelt trust in the true gospel of what the Son of God has done (1 Cor. 15:3, 4) and not merely a mental acknowledgment of historical facts. Paul gives similar lists in other epistles (Eph. 5:1-6; 1 Cor. 6:9-11). The flesh will never produce fruit that pleases God because it has a sinful nature. It will always produce sin. However, the Spirit in us will produce fruit that pleases God because of the divine nature of the Son of God in us.] **22 But the fruit of the Spirit is love, joy, peace, longsuffering,** [patient, bearing provocations for a long time] **gentleness, goodness, faith, 23 Meekness,** [gentle, willing to obey] **temperance:** [moderation] **against such there is no law.** [These nine characteristics are a portrait of the Lord Jesus Christ. Notice that love is first on the list. It is the fruit (singular) of the Spirit of Christ. I was a Christian for 25 years before I came to understand the Bible rightly divided. It wasn't until then that I really began to feel like I finally started to produce the fruit of the Spirit. Please understand it is essential to our spiritual welfare to understand the difference between Christ's ministry from heaven to Paul (the mystery) and Christ's ministry on earth to the nation of Israel (prophesy). Remember that Paul wants the Christ he preached to be formed in them again (4:19). When we believe the doctrine in Paul's epistles the result is that the Spirit of Christ produces fruit in us effortlessly. We have love, joy, peace, and so on and show grace to others. It is an overflow of the word of God rightly divided working effectually in us who believe (1 Thess. 2:13).] **24 And they that are Christ's have crucified the flesh with the affections and lusts.** [Those who belong to Christ have crucified the flesh, our "old man," our sin nature which we inherited from Adam with its affections and lusts. Our flesh has lost its' power over us because we died with Christ. The flesh has no power over a dead man. "[6] Knowing this, that our old man is crucified with him, that the body of sin might be destroyed, that henceforth we should not serve sin. [7] For he that is dead is freed from sin. [8] Now if we be dead with Christ, we believe that we shall also live with him: [9] Knowing that Christ being raised from the dead dieth no more; death hath no more dominion over him. [10] For in that he died, he died unto sin once: but in that he liveth, he liveth unto God. [11] Likewise reckon ye also yourselves to be dead indeed unto sin, but alive unto God through Jesus Christ our Lord. [12] Let not sin therefore reign in your mortal body, that ye should obey it in the lusts thereof. [13] Neither yield ye your members as instruments of unrighteousness unto sin: but yield yourselves unto God, as those that are alive from the dead, and your members as instruments of righteousness unto God. [14] For sin shall not have dominion over you: for ye are not under the law, but under grace" (Rom 6:6-14). Our eternal lives began the moment we were saved. We did not feel that our old sin nature was crucified with Christ upon our salvation. We just have to reckon or count on that to be true, since God says so in His word. Notice these verses again that we died with Christ (2 Cor. 5:14, 15). God has always been more interested in a spiritual circumcision of the heart than a physical one in the flesh (Rom. 2:25-29). Upon salvation God circumcised us spiritually (Col. 2:11). God severed or dissected or cut off the sinful flesh in our body from our soul and spirit, freeing them from it's control. We can now make decisions moment by moment in our lives to do right not wrong without being slaves to sin, self, and Satan. Our confidence is in Christ in us, not human wisdom or actions.] **25 If we live in the Spirit, let us also walk in the Spirit.** [By faith we must understand God's word rightly divided and follow the instruction Christ gives us through our apostle Paul. We are saved by faith and we are to live the same way (by faith). "If we live in the Spirit [our position is in Christ by faith], let us also walk in the Spirit [our practice is by His Spirit in us by faith]. Paul repeats this instruction in Colossians: "As ye have therefore received Christ Jesus the Lord, so walk ye in him: Rooted [firm and solid] and built up in him, and stablished in the faith, as ye have been taught, abounding therein with thanksgiving" (Col. 2:6, 7). What God accepts today is what His Son does through us. What exactly does it mean to live in the Spirit? Compare these parallel verses to find the answer: Eph. 5:18, 19, and Col. 3:16. Did you notice that to "be filled with the Spirit" is to "let the word of Christ dwell in you richly in all wisdom"? Cornelius Stam said, "You can only believe as much as you have understood." That is why we want to understand as much of the Bible as possible, especially Paul's letters to the body of Christ. The works of the flesh and the works of the Spirit can easily be distinguished. The Spirit does not come by law-keeping, but by a walk of faith in sound doctrine. "To walk in the Spirit" means live by the control of the Spirit (being directed by the word of God rightly divided). Therefore, since good works are by His Spirit, Christ gets all the glory. We have to walk by faith in the word of God rightly divided (2 Cor. 5:17; 2 Tim. 2:15). Paul said, "Consider what I say; and the Lord give thee understanding in all things" (2 Tim. 2:7).] **26 Let us not be desirous of vain glory, provoking one another, envying one another.** [Pretending to keep the law produces boasting, pride, provocation, and envy. Let us not want to glory in our law-keeping and things we accomplish in our flesh. They are vain (empty, useless). Let us not provoke one another. Saying look what I have done. Let us not compete with one another saying, "Anything you can do I can do better. I can do anything better than you." This is not how we should live. Comparing ourselves among ourselves is not wise (2 Cor. 10:12). Christ will judge us at His Judgment Seat. If we do anything right, let us give glory to the Lord by whose Spirit, we were able to do it (1 Cor. 1:31; 2 Cor. 10:17). Envy is the result of being in the flesh. We are in the Spirit. We give a person the benefit of the doubt. We bless them and their service to the Lord and His people. We are not called to selfish living, but to godly living. To allow sin access into our lives is inconsistent with who we are in Christ. The Christian life is to let Christ live through us. We fight Satan with Christ's sound doctrine through Paul. It is His performance through us (not ours) which helps us to have victory over sins, self, and Satan, and to live a life pleasing to God. Edgar J. Haskins wrote the hymn **Since the Savior Found Me** in 1906: "Since the Savior found me I have perfect rest, Living in the realms of joy and happiness . . . Saved, saved, saved – I'm happy on the way, Saved, saved, saved, I love him more each day; Saved, saved, saved – I know He's mine each hour. He saves and keeps and sanctifies me by His Pow'r." The hymn writer knows that we are saved and sanctified by faith, but needed to add <u>as we follow Paul to follow Christ</u> (1 Cor. 11:1). Christ's imputed righteousness is synonymous with His Spirit, His life, the faith of Jesus Christ in us. It is the "power of Christ" (2 Cor. 12:9). Only by rightly dividing God's truth can we live and function the way God intends us to.]

251

Chapter 6 God is not mocked, we reap what we sow
6:1-10 Let the spiritual help those in the flesh (legalism).
6:11-18 Walk according to your new identity in our Lord Jesus Christ.

6:1 Brethren, if a man be overtaken in a fault, ye which are spiritual, restore such an one in the spirit of meekness; considering thyself, lest thou also be tempted. [The "fault" in this context is being entangled or snared into doing the works of the flesh, which is energized by trying to keep the laws by self-effort. The "spiritual" are to restore those in the flesh (characterized by being prideful, boasting, selfish people mentioned in 5:26). Those who are "spiritual" walk in the Spirit by faith in what Christ says to them through Paul, the preaching of Christ according to the revelation of the mystery (Rom. 16:25). We should do our best to correct those law-keeping people who don't follow Paul with meekness just like Paul (our pattern) has shown us when he corrected the believers in Galatia. We have to be careful not to be in the flesh when helping others. Here is an example:

Legalistic Christian: "I am going to get water baptized for the third time to show God how devoted I am."
Condemning Grace believer: "You are only getting wet! Don't you know that our baptism is spiritual? That is so WRONNNNNNNG! Don't you know anything about Paul?"
Spiritual Grace believer: "Would you please give me a few minutes of your time, I want to show you what God says about that in His word? Do you know that Paul is the apostle of the Gentiles (Rom. 11:13) and that he received his information by direct revelation of Jesus Christ (Gal. 1:11, 12)? Peter and Paul preached different gospels, to two different people (Gal. 2:7-9). Peter told the men of Israel to repent and be water baptized (Acts 2:38), but Paul told the body of Christ that we are spiritually baptized into Christ (Gal. 5:27; 1 Cor. 12:13). Did you know that God had a secret mystery that has now been revealed, but Satan wants to conceal (Rom. 16:25; Eph. 3:1-9)." (But sometimes no matter how loving we are when sharing Christ, others think we are stuffing religion down their throats.)
One of these grace believers is in the Spirit and the other is in the flesh.

In the process of trying to correct someone else, we need to be very careful that we don't fall into legalism ourselves. We need to be gentle (meek), not harsh. We do not want to be tempted to give into our flesh. We are only one step or one bad decision away from living in the flesh. If we come to a person condemning them, we have gone into legalism ourselves (5:15). We need to remember that we used to be in that error ourselves before we learned better. We want to help others to come out of the doctrinal error of legalism, into grace. We want to be gracious and kind.

"Being reviled, we bless" (1 Cor. 4:12). Grace believers who attack others have fallen from grace themselves. They are not walking in the Spirit, but in the lust of the flesh. They become self-righteous, unmerciful, and self-important. I have even seen this ugly behavior raise itself even among grace believers. We constantly have to check our actions and motives. Are we serving the Lord Jesus Christ and His people or self? Do we care about the edification of the body of Christ promoting other people's beneficial ministries or just about ourselves?]

6:2 Bear ye one another's burdens, and so fulfil the law of Christ. [We should be willing to help each other out when we recognize that someone is at "fault" or in the flesh because they are living under the law. Those at "fault" think they can somehow keep the law. They have been moved away from Christ's sound doctrine to us through Paul, or never knew it. We should bear or share each other's burdens. We are to be each other's keeper. Cain was supposed to be his brother's keeper; that is what a good, kind, loving, brother does. We should help others to walk in "newness of life" (Rom. 6:4). The problem is not with the law, but with our weak flesh (our inability to keep it all). God sent forth His Son in our likeness and judged sin. He lived the perfect life and then shed His own blood as the perfect sacrifice. Christ fulfilled the righteousness of the law. Now we who have His Spirit in us can keep the law. The "law of Christ" in this context is "love" (5:6, 13, 14). Read Rom. 8:2-4 and then notice how Romans 8 ends with "the love of God, which is in Christ Jesus our Lord" (8:39). Our flesh is circumcised and we have His perfect life in us (Col. 2:11). We can fulfill the "law of Christ," and allow the Spirit of life in Christ Jesus to control us by love. We can be loving to others when we have His life in us. But learning to "walk in the Spirit" (5:16) and to "be led of the Spirit" (5:18) is learning to live by faith in Christ's word to us through Paul. Under grace we are free to fail. Failure is one of the best teachers. We have to trust the Bible rightly divided and not be moved away from following Christ's word to us from heaven. Satan wants us to be moved away. But by studying the Bible rightly divided the sound doctrine in us helps us to make mature decisions. Some people may be tempted to not try to help the legalist, but we should try to do what we can in a kind, delicate, gracious, and gentle way. Sometimes it is difficult especially if the legalist is stubborn, and refuses to listen when we try to help them with rightly divided Bible verses. They need to be guided to come to see "the fellowship of the mystery" (Eph. 3:9), to live by faith in God's word, and to trust in Christ's ministry to us through Paul (Eph. 3:2). For many it is so new and different from what they have been taught and they refuse to listen or to use the right Bible. We want them to have the joy, clarity, and peace we have.] **3 For if a man think himself to be something, when he is nothing, he deceiveth himself.** [No one should think that they can keep the law, only Christ could. We owe Him

253

everything. We can easily fall into the lust of the sinful flesh that is lurking in our mortal bodies. (All I have to do is watch a few minutes of leftist propaganda constantly being perpetuated by the liberal media to awaken my anger.) Anger makes us aware of injustice. But, emotions should not rule us. We can be angry and not sin (Eph. 4:29). We must be ruled by the word of Christ to us through Paul. The sound doctrine in us helps us to make right decisions. God is no respecter of persons (2:6, Acts 10:34). God respects His Son's life lived out in us, as we consider what is good, better, best (or most excellent) and do that (Phil. 1:10).] **4 But let every man prove his own work, and then shall he have rejoicing in himself alone, and not in another.** [We have a personal responsibility to live our lives dependent on Christ to live through us, to produce fruit with value (Rom. 7:4). A child has to learn to walk by trial and error, they fall down and get up again. Likewise, learning to walk in the Spirit is a process. We have to unlearn many things. We, "Let the word of Christ dwell in you richly in all wisdom teaching and admonishing one another . . . with grace in your hearts to the Lord" (Col. 3:16). The word works in us and our walk becomes more steady. This doesn't just happen. We have to plan and discipline ourselves to be in the word and to apply it to our lives. Determine to read God's word attentively daily (perhaps by following a reading schedule such as three chapters per day). I usually read the Bible after a short time of prayer first thing in the morning. Also, singing "psalms and hymns and spiritual songs" (Col. 3:16) which are rich in sound doctrine and can put our minds and priorities right. "Not I, but Christ." When we exalt and glorify the Lord Jesus Christ above ourselves everything else falls into place.] **5 For every man shall bear his own burden.** [Each believer will be judged at the Judgment Seat of Christ based on what we allowed Christ to do through us in this life. That is why God says, "Study to shew thyself approved unto God, a workman that needeth not to be ashamed, [at the judgment seat of Christ] rightly dividing the word of truth" (2 Tim. 2:15).] **6 Let him that is taught in the word communicate unto him that teacheth in all good things**. [Ultimately our teacher is Christ from heaven through Paul, but also those who are "spiritual (6:1). We are to support our spiritual Bible teachers who teach Christ's word to us through Paul, financially, by prayer, by encouraging words, and in other ways. I am grateful that many of you pray for this ministry, and support it by direct donation or by buying our books on Amazon and giving them out to family and friends. This way we can have enough money for paper, ink, copiers, website, cameras, travel, tripods, and so on. Sharing the Facebook videos and YouTube lessons with others is also very helpful. We welcome your comments. I just share what God has shown me in His word and what I have learned from others. We are not perfect, only His word is perfect. Please check everything that is said with the King James Bible.] **7 Be not deceived; God is not mocked: for whatsoever a man soweth, that shall he also**

reap. [Don't be fooled into thinking that God doesn't know everything because He does. He knows who is in the flesh trying to keep the law, and who is in the Spirit (Rom. 8:5, 6).] **8 For he that soweth to his flesh shall of the flesh reap corruption; but he that soweth to the Spirit shall of the Spirit reap life everlasting**. [Those who do the works of the law by the self-effort of their flesh reap corruption (works of no eternal value). In contrast, those who walk in the Spirit by faith in the word of God rightly divided, produce fruit with everlasting value. We cannot mix "the grace of Christ" (1:6) with the law as a means of justification or sanctification.] **9 And let us not be weary in well doing: for in due season we shall reap, if we faint not.** [Let us not grow weary of reconciling others to Christ and standing for Pauline truth for we will have rewards at the Judgment Seat of Christ which last for all eternity if we don't give up (2 Cor. 5:18-21; 1 Tim. 2:4).] **10 As we have therefore opportunity, let us do good unto all men, especially unto them who are of the household of faith.** [We should be ready to seize every opportunity Christ gives us. For years I taught small grace Bible classes. I used to tell Patty that more people should hear and know this information. After some requests, we began posting the studies on Facebook and our audience increased immediately. I am happy to say that other Bible studies are popping up everywhere. Many are teaching family and friends. They say if she can do it, so can I. Many have asked me how to order the large timeline from Grace School of the Bible. Simply call, Deb Keable at Shorewood (630) 529-0520. The Timelines are about $80 each. Be sure to order some timeline brochures and "The Key to Understanding the Bible" by Pastor Richard Jordan. Let's spread the word. Let's help one another. God's will is for "all men to be saved, and to come unto the knowledge of the truth" (1 Tim. 2:4). As we have opportunity, let us do good to all men, especially to those who believe in Christ. The household of God is a duplex that includes the kingdom of heaven believers on one side, and the kingdom on earth believers on the other side. In Paul's day, the Israel of God existed but was phasing out. Today the body of Christ is the only functioning part of the household.]

11 ¶ Ye see how large a letter I have written unto you with mine own hand. [The letter was not large, but the size of each individual letter was, most likely due to some eye trouble Paul had. He may have written it urgently without waiting to dictate to an amanuensis (secretary) due to the spiritual danger the Galatians were in.] **12 As many as desire to make a fair shew in the flesh, they constrain you to be circumcised; only lest they should suffer persecution for the cross of Christ.** [Those who glory in an outward cut in men's bodies want you to be circumcised. People who preach "faith plus works" are not persecuted. Satan wants believers to be in legalistic error. Satan attacked the Galatians by spreading false doctrine, saying that law must be added to their walk. Satan attacked the Corinthians with adding the law, but he also attacked them with human wisdom, division (following various leaders), and doubt in Paul's divinely appointed apostleship. Paul needed to defend his apostleship in many of his letters. Satan wants believers to be ineffective (not functioning the way God intends them to). Only those who preach that Christ lived a perfect life, and accomplished a perfect salvation without the need for added works, are persecuted.] **13 For neither they themselves who are circumcised keep the law; but desire to have you circumcised, that they may glory in your flesh.** [Even the Judaizers cannot keep the law, but they want you to be circumcised, so they can boast about adding another notch on their belt.] **14 But God forbid that I should glory, save in the cross of our Lord Jesus Christ, by whom the world is crucified unto me, and I unto the world.** [Paul wants to glory only in the cross of the Lord Jesus Christ because it has set him free from the influence of the "present evil world" (1:4). The world is crucified to Paul and no longer has any effect on him. Paul was crucified with Christ, and Christ lives in him (Gal. 2:20; Col. 2:20). Paul is "the servant of Christ" (1:10). Through Paul we learn the full scope of all that the Lord Jesus Christ accomplished by His perfect, complete, and finished work of salvation. In one gigantic heroic act He paid the sin debt for all mankind with His own precious blood. On the cross Jesus Christ said, "It is finished" (John 19:30). He not only died in our place, but He also died our death. The Father accepted His payment in full and raised Him from the dead. He paid for the sins of all mankind nearly 2,000 years ago. When we sin we can say, Christ already paid for that. Thank You, LORD! We have His Spirit in us now as a guarantee of our eternal life and we can't lose it (Eph. 4:30). All the believers in the kingdom on earth will have His Spirit in them. But during prophecy, David did not want to lose the Holy Spirit like Saul (1 Samuel 16:14; Psa. 51:11).] **15 For in Christ Jesus neither circumcision availeth any thing, nor uncircumcision, but a new creature.** [Peter preached the gospel of the circumcision because God required the men of Israel to be both physically and spiritually circumcised. Paul preached the gospel of the uncircumcision because no physical circumcision is necessary for the members of the body of Christ. What matters is being a new creature in Christ with His Spirit in us, and not being reprobate (2 Cor. 13:5; Rom. 8:9). We didn't feel the Spirit come in because it didn't happen in the body, but in the inner man. Believers have been translated out of Adam into Christ (Col. 1:13; 1 Cor. 15:22, 45). As new creatures we have a new identity and that identity generates good works (Eph. 2:10; Titus 3:1, 8; Phil. 1:6). We should be who we are in Christ, and not look back to who we were before. We cannot move forward by looking in the rearview mirror. Five things happen at salvation. To remember these, we can use the acrostic **CRIBS**: Circumcised spiritually (Col. 2:11, 12), **R**egenerated (Titus 3:5),

Indwelt by God (Col. 1:27), Baptized into Christ (1 Cor. 12:13), and Sealed with the holy Spirit (Eph. 1:13). (Borrowed from Pastor Richard Jordan's New Creature YouTube video.) The Christian reformer Martin Luther advocated that men not be circumcised. Therefore, the Lutherans of northern Europe (Germany, Scandinavia among some of the countries) do not circumcise their sons. After all, Adam was perfectly made by God and he had foreskin.] **16 And as many as walk according to this rule, peace be on them, and mercy, and upon the Israel of God.** [Paul is not saluting everyone in Galatia, but only those who walk according to "this rule." What is "this rule"? The rule is the crucified life. It is having our flesh crucified and living in "newness life" (Rom. 6:4). It is "being crucified with Christ" and still being alive but "not I, but Christ" because "Christ liveth in me" (2:20). Paul wants peace to those who walk according to the rule of being controlled by the Spirit of His Son and only glorying in the cross of the Lord Jesus Christ. Paul wants God to show mercy to the Israel of God (Rom. 11:32). In the future, God will make the nation of Israel from this believing remnant (Luke 12:31, 32; Matt. 19:28, 21:43). This letter helped and when Paul had a chance he returned to Galatia, "strengthening all the disciples" (Acts 18:23). Sadly, many turned away from Paul even in his day (2 Tim. 1:15). Most of Christendom is ignorant of Paul's distinctive apostleship to the heaven-bound believers, the body of Christ. Satan has "hid" Christ's gospel to us through Paul (2 Cor. 4:3, 4). Satan has convinced some grace believers (like the Galatians) to move away from Paul's sound doctrine (1:8, 9). We need to "stand fast" in Christ's gospel to us through Paul and not be entangled with the law, or mix law and grace. We must understand that God's words to us are in Romans to Philemon and do them. This is how we have peace. "Those things, which ye have both learned, and received, and heard, and seen in me, do: and the God of peace shall be with you" (Phil. 4:9). Paul's doctrine to us, is God's truth to us. "Wherefore take unto you the whole armour of God, that ye may be able to withstand in the evil day, and having done all, to stand. Stand therefore, having your loins girt about with truth, and having on the breastplate of righteousness; And your feet shod with the preparation of the gospel of peace; Above all, taking the shield of faith, wherewith ye shall be able to quench all the fiery darts of the wicked" (Eph. 6:13-16). Christ gave His life for us, in order to give His life to us, so He could live His life through us.]

17 ¶ From henceforth let no man trouble me: for I bear in my body the marks of the Lord Jesus. [Paul preached the "offence of the cross" and was brutally persecuted for it and suffered to build the body of Christ (2 Cor. 11:23-33). As a servant of Christ (1:10), he calls his scars the marks of the Lord Jesus. Are we willing to take a stand for grace alone, by faith alone, in Christ alone according to the revelation of the mystery?]

18 ¶ Brethren, the grace of our Lord Jesus Christ be with your spirit. Amen.
[Paul closes the letter simply wanting the grace of the Lord to be with their spirit.]

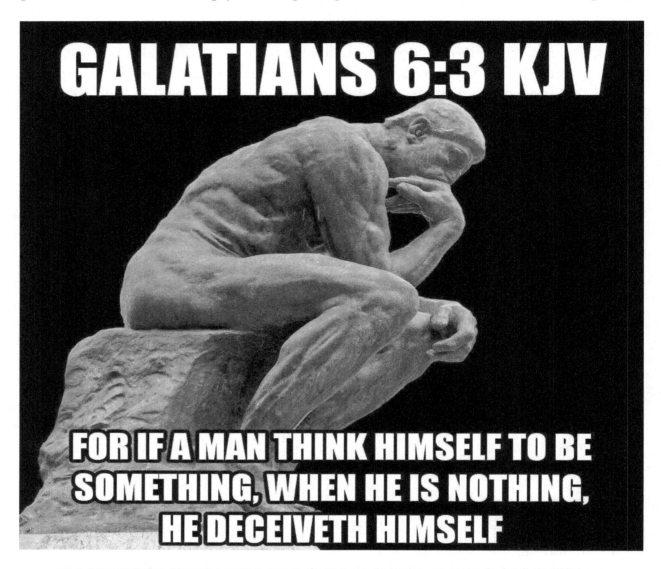

GALATIANS 6:3 KJV

FOR IF A MAN THINK HIMSELF TO BE SOMETHING, WHEN HE IS NOTHING, HE DECEIVETH HIMSELF

"But God forbid that I should glory, save in the cross of our Lord Jesus Christ, by whom the world is crucified unto me, and I unto the world."
GALATIANS 6:14 KJB

God's Timeline
(Notice the order of the books of the Bible)

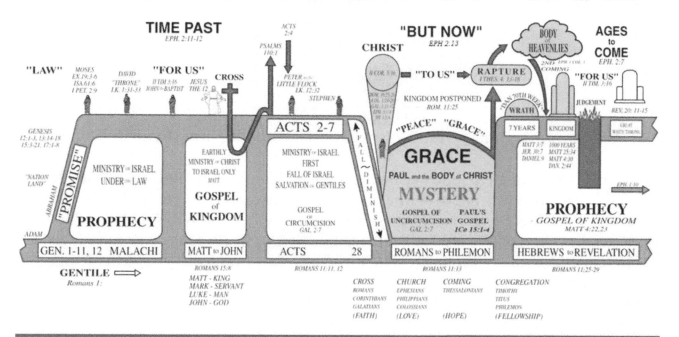

About the Author

Marianne Manley teaching the Bible Rightly Divided

She was saved in 1990. She became, not only a King James Bible user, but a King James Bible believer in 2014. She has more than twenty-five years of experience teaching the Bible, eighteen of those years were with the AWANA clubs where she earned her Citation Award for Bible memorization. In 2015, she was introduced to Pauline dispensational truth by watching Les Feldick on YouTube. After learning the basics of "rightly dividing the word of truth" (2 Timothy 2:15), she learned more from the Bible and Richard Jordan and his Grace School of the Bible. A retired nurse midwife, she has devoted the rest of her life "to make all men see what is the fellowship of the mystery" (Eph. 3:9). She teaches a Bible study in her home which is available on Facebook and YouTube (mariannemanley.com).

Her joy after understanding the Bible better led her to edify the body of Christ by writing *God's Secret* in 2017. Then *Romans: A Concise Commentary* and *First Corinthians: A Commentary* in 2018. *Second Corinthians: A Commentary* and *Galatians: A Commentary*, *Ephesians A Commentary,* and *Philippians, Colossians, Philemon Commentary*, and *Treasure Hunt Volume II* (Paul's Prison Epistles) **Why was the Earth without Form, Void, and Dark?** and *Just as God Said* for children, *The Certainty of the Pre-Tribulation Rapture* (First and Second Thessalonians Commentary), all in 2019. *Paul's Pastoral Epistles* (First and Second Timothy, Titus, and Philemon Commentary), *Treasure Hunt Volume III* (Paul's T Books) and *Acts of the Apostles Commentary Part 1, 2, 3* all in 2020. *Missed the Rapture? Read this Commentary on Hebrew!* and *How to be Saved Made Simple* and the *Rightly Dividing Study Guides* in 2021.

Other Books by Marianne Manley

God's Secret A Primer with Pictures for How to Rightly Divide the Word of Truth (on Amazon.com in **Black and White Edition**, and in Spanish *El Secreto de Dios*).

Rightly Dividing SECOND CORINTHIANS Study Guide
Rightly Dividing FIRST CORINTHIANS Study Guide
Rightly Dividing ROMANS Study Guide
Romans: A Concise Commentary (also in a Black and White Edition)
First Corinthians: A Commentary
Second Corinthians: A Commentary
Galatians: A Commentary
Ephesians A Commentary
Philippians, Colossians, Philemon Commentary
The Certainty of the Pre-Tribulation Rapture (First and Second Thessalonians)
Paul's Pastoral Epistles (Timothy Letters, Titus, and Philemon Commentary)

Treasure Hunt Volume I (Commentary only Romans to Galatians)
Treasure Hunt Volume II (Commentary only on Paul's Prison Epistles)
Treasure Hunt Volume III (Commentary on Paul's T Books)

Why was the Earth without Form, Void, and Dark?
Just as God Said
Acts of the Apostles Commentary Part One, Two, Three
Missed the Rapture? Read this Commentary on Hebrews!
How to be Saved Made Simple (This booklet is perfect for our lost loved ones.)

Could God Have a 7,000 Year Plan for Mankind? (also in Black and White and *AD 34 The Year Jesus Died for All* (same content as Could God, in 9x6 size)

The author may be contacted by e-mail at mariannemanley@sbcglobal.net

Please visit her website: www.mariannemanley.com (free .pdf files)

Follow her on Facebook at facebook.com/marianne.manley.7 and God's Secret Facebook Page at facebook.com/GodsSecretAPrimerwithPictures

Find her on YouTube (Just type in her name and find her teaching the Bible, a-chapter-at-a-time) on Truth Be Told YouTube channel or (858) 273-2049